D0848395

STUDIES IN
GERMAN LITERATURE

UNIVERSITY OF NORTH CAROLINA
STUDIES IN THE GERMANIC LANGUAGES
AND LITERATURES

Initiated by RICHARD JENTE (1949-1952), *established by* F. E. COENEN (1952-1968)

Publication Committee

SIEGFRIED MEWS, EDITOR

| WERNER P. FRIEDERICH | JOHN G. KUNSTMANN | GEORGE S. LANE |
| HERBERT W. REICHERT | RIA STAMBAUGH | PETRUS W. TAX |

For other volumes in the "Studies" see page 251.

Send orders to: (U.S. and Canada) The University of North Carolina Press, P.O. Box 510, Chapel Hill, N. C. 27514
(All other countries) Feffer and Simons, Inc., 31 Union Square, New York, N.Y. 10003
Reprints may be ordered from: AMS Press, Inc.,
56 East 13th Street, New York, N.Y. 10003

NUMBER SIXTY-SEVEN

UNIVERSITY
OF NORTH CAROLINA
STUDIES IN
THE GERMANIC LANGUAGES
AND LITERATURES

STUDIES IN GERMAN LITERATURE OF THE NINETEENTH AND TWENTIETH CENTURIES

FESTSCHRIFT FOR FREDERIC E. COENEN

FOREWORD
WERNER P. FRIEDERICH

EDITED BY SIEGFRIED MEWS

CHAPEL HILL
THE UNIVERSITY OF NORTH CAROLINA PRESS
1970

Printed in the Netherlands by Royal VanGorcum Ltd., Assen

Contents

ARTICLES

Foreword

Anyone in the United States or abroad familiar with the achievements of German Departments in the Universities of this country will be aware that the German Department at *U.N.C.*, the oldest State University in the nation, is best known for its *Studies in The Germanic Languages and Literatures*. That this should be so is almost exclusively due to the indefatigable efforts, the editorial skill and the financial acumen of the colleague and friend whom all the contributors of articles and those listed in the *Tabula gratulatoria* wish to honor with this *Festschrift*: Professor Frederic Edward Coenen.

He became editor of a Series that, uncertain of its high purpose, had progressed haltingly, and with his outstanding editorial and administrative talents put all his enthusiasm into the task. During the fifteen years of his devotion to this work, he increased the number of monographs from five in 1952 to sixty in 1968. Facing the manifold opportunities for Germanic scholarship in this country, Professor Coenen realized that the *Studies* should fulfil two purposes: first to publish scholarly investigations of distinctly literary problems; and second, to make accessible in English translation to potential readers in this country certain important works of German literature.

A perusal of the rich list of publications available in his life's work will convince the reader that he has succeeded very well indeed and that, for publishing scholars writing works that would appeal only to specialists in our field, he created an outlet for which we are all most grateful. Operating on a shoestring and never subsidized by his home institution, he achieved veritable miracles in seeing to it that deserving manuscripts should be published with a sometimes amazing profit to their authors.

Now that he has retired from our midst and that his many friends and well-wishers have assembled to congratulate him and to thank him for his friendship and loyalty, we can well applaud Professor Coenen's *University of North Carolina Studies in the Germanic Languages and Literatures* as a shining example of American self-help and initiative. Where others, even professional publishers, would have failed and might, indeed, not even have accepted the challenge, Professor Coenen, aware of the great need for this kind of undertaking in America, proved that sheer devotion could overcome any obstacle. In honoring him in this *Festschrift*, we know that we speak in the name of scores of others when we say that we all, not least among us his own home University, stand deeply in his debt.

WERNER P. FRIEDERICH

Tabula Gratulatoria

Theodor W. Alexander
Texas Technological University
Lubbock

Richard Harry Allen
The University of Nebraska
Lincoln

Arthur Tilo Alt
Duke University
Durham, North Carolina

Leonhard E. Baak
Morningside College
Sioux City, Iowa

Frederick J. Beharriell
State University of New York
Albany

Clifford A. Bernd
University of California at Davis

Werner Betz
Universität München
Germany

Baerbel B. Cantarino
The University of Texas at Austin

Allen Harris Chappel
Louisiana State University
in New Orleans

Alan P. Cottrell
The University of Michigan
Ann Arbor

Murray A. and Marian L. Cowie
Tucson, Arizona

Walter Devereux and Simone Creech
Chapel Hill, North Carolina

George B. Daniel
University of North Carolina
at Chapel Hill

Ingeborg M. B. Dent
Methodist College
Fayetteville, North Carolina

William J. DeSua
University of North Carolina
at Chapel Hill

David B. Dickens
Washington and Lee University
Lexington, Virginia

R. Sheldon Dunham, Jr.
University of Richmond
Richmond, Virginia

Martin Dyck
Massachusetts Institute of
Technology, Cambridge

Waldemar Eger
University of North Carolina
at Chapel Hill

James E. Engel
Vanderbilt University
Nashville, Tennessee

Alfred Garvin and
Mary Claire Randolph Engstrom
Hillsborough, North Carolina

Vallin Dayton Estes, Jr.
Pfeiffer College
Misenheimer, North Carolina

Joerg and *Renate Fichte*
University of North Carolina
at Chapel Hill

Horst Frenz
Indiana University
Bloomington

Werner P. Friederich
University of North Carolina
at Chapel Hill

Harold Philip Fry
University of North Carolina
at Greensboro

Christian and *Janis Gellinek*
Yale University and
Connecticut College
New Haven and New London

Henry J. Groen
Syracuse University
Syracuse, New York

Carl Hammer, Jr.
Texas Technological University
Lubbock

James N. Hardin
University of South Carolina
Columbia

Gustave A. Harrer
University of Florida Libraries
Gainesville

Virginia Redfern Heath
Monroe, North Carolina

Robert R. Heitner
University of Illinois
at Chicago Circle

Robert Eugene Helbling
University of Utah
Salt Lake City

John Lawrence Hodges
Stetson University
Deland, Florida

Almonte C. Howell
University of North Carolina
at Chapel Hill

Anton M. Huffert
Adelphi University
Garden City, New York

Klaus W. Jonas
University of Pittsburgh
Pittsburgh, Pennsylvania

George Fenwick Jones
University of Maryland
College Park

Günter F. Klabes
Duke University
Durham, North Carolina

Randolph J. Klawiter
University of Notre Dame
Notre Dame, Indiana

John T. Krumpelmann
Louisiana State University
at Baton Rouge

John G. Kunstmann
University of North Carolina
at Chapel Hill

Albert L. Lancaster
Virginia Military Institute
Lexington

George S. Lane
University of North Carolina
at Chapel Hill

Richard H. Lawson
San Diego State College
San Diego, California

Henry J. Lemmens
Duquesne University
Pittsburgh, Pennsylvania

Ralph J. Ley
Rutgers University
New Brunswick, New Jersey

Donald J. Lineback
University of North Carolina
at Chapel Hill

J. Beattie Maclean
University of Victoria
Victoria, British Columbia, Canada

Fritz Martini
Universität Stuttgart
Germany

Bertha M. Masche
Hunter College
City University of New York

Percy Matenko
Brooklyn College
Brooklyn, New York

William Harold McClain
The Johns Hopkins University
Baltimore, Maryland

Robert W. McClenahan, Jr.
Hamden, Connecticut

E. Allen McCormick
Graduate Center
City University of New York

Siegfried Mews
University of North Carolina
at Chapel Hill

Joseph Mileck
University of California
in Berkeley

Robert Mollenauer
The University of Texas
at Austin

G. H. S. Mueller
University of North Carolina
at Chapel Hill

Edward J. Newby
Louisiana State University
at Baton Rouge

Richey Novak
Duke University
Durham, North Carolina

James C. O'Flaherty
Wake Forest University
Winston-Salem, North Carolina

J. Alan Pfeffer
University of Pittsburgh
Pittsburgh, Pennsylvania

Thomas O. Pinkerton
Davidson College
Davidson, North Carolina

Mary Gray Porter
University of Alabama
University

Morgan H. Pritchett
The Johns Hopkins University
Baltimore, Maryland

Paul Frank Proskauer
Herbert H. Lehman College
Bronx, New York

William W. Pusey III
Washington and Lee University
Lexington, Virginia

Herbert W. Reichert
University of North Carolina
at Chapel Hill

Phillip H. Rhein
Vanderbilt University
Nashville, Tennessee

Victor Anthony Rudowski
University of Cincinnati
Cincinnati, Ohio

Herman Salinger
Duke University
Durham, North Carolina

Adolf E. Schroeder
University of Missouri
Columbia

George C. Schoolfield
Yale University
New Haven, Connecticut

Christoph E. Schweitzer
University of North Carolina
at Chapel Hill

Barbara Garvey Seagrave
University of Arkansas
Fayetteville

Lawrence A. Sharpe
University of North Carolina
at Chapel Hill

Edith Floyd Shewell
Chapel Hill, North Carolina

Sam M. Shiver
Emory University
Atlanta, Georgia

Walter Silz
Columbia University
New York

Jane Stuart Smith
Carson-Newman College
Jefferson City, Tennessee

Sidney Rufus Smith
University of North Carolina
at Chapel Hill

Ria Stambaugh
University of North Carolina
at Chapel Hill

Alfred G. Steer
University of Georgia
Athens

Henri Stegemeier
University of Illinois
Urbana-Champaign

Petrus W. Tax
University of North Carolina
at Chapel Hill

Ransom Theodore Taylor
University of Nebraska
Lincoln

J. W. Thomas
University of Kentucky
Lexington

Lawrence S. Thompson
University of Kentucky
Lexington

Gordon L. Tracy
University of Western Ontario
London, Ontario, Canada

Erwin Tramer
Plainfield, New Jersey

Hermann J. Weigand
Yale University
New Haven, Connecticut

Ralph A. West
University of North Carolina
at Chapel Hill

Paul K. Whitaker
University of Kentucky
Lexington

Joseph N. White
Northwestern University
Evanston, Illinois

W. L. Wiley
University of North Carolina
at Chapel Hill

Wayne Wonderley
University of Kentucky
Lexington

Ottilie Yoksimovich
Raleigh, North Carolina

Edwin H. Zeydel
University of Cincinnati
Cincinnati, Ohio

Theodore and *Yetta Ziolkowski*
Princeton, New Jersey

A. E. Zucker
University Park, Maryland

Adelphi University Library
Garden City, Long Island
New York

Austrian Institute
New York

Brooklyn College Library
City University of New York

Brown University
Providence, Rhode Island

Bryn Mawr College
Bryn Mawr, Pennsylvania

German Department
Clark University
Worcester, Massachusetts

Max Kade German Center
Department of German
Colgate University
Hamilton, New York

The Andrews Library
The College of Wooster
Wooster, Ohio

Duke University Library
Durham, North Carolina

Germanisches Seminar
Freie Universität Berlin

Department of Germanic Languages
Indiana University
Bloomington

German Department
Kalamazoo College
Kalamazoo, Michigan

David Bishop Skillman Library
Lafayette College
Easton, Pennsylvania

Department of German
La Salle College
Philadelphia, Pennsylvania

XVI

German Department
McGill University
Montreal, Quebec, Canada

Department of Germanic
Languages & Literatures
New York University

Oberlin College Library
Oberlin, Ohio

Fondren Library
Rice University
Houston, Texas

Germanistisches Institut
Ruhr-Universität Bochum

Department of German Language
& Literature
Rutgers University
New Brunswick, New Jersey

St. Lawrence University
Canton, New York

St. Olaf College
Northfield, Minnesota

DuPont-Ball Library
Stetson University
Deland, Florida

Tulane University Library
New Orleans, Louisiana

Library
University of California
Santa Barbara

Department of Germanic & Slavic Languages
University of Connecticut
Storrs

University of Illinois Library
at Urbana-Champaign

McKelvin Library
University of Maryland
College Park

XVII

Department of Germanic Languages & Literatures
The University of Michigan
Ann Arbor

Seminar für Deutsche Philologie I
Universität München

Louis R. Wilson Library
University of North Carolina
at Chapel Hill

University of Pennsylvania
Philadelphia

Department of Foreign Languages & Literatures
University of South Carolina
Columbia

Lehrstuhl für Neuere Deutsche Philologie
Institut für Literatur- und Sprachwissenschaft
Universität Stuttgart

Department of Germanic Languages
The University of Texas
at Austin

McPherson Library
University of Victoria
Victoria, British Columbia, Canada

Department of Germanic & Slavic Languages
University of Virginia
Charlottesville

University of Wisconsin Library
at Milwaukee

Department of German
Victoria College
University of Toronto

Wake Forest University
Winston-Salem, North Carolina

Yale University Library
New Haven, Connecticut

Youngstown State University Library
Youngstown, Ohio

Editor's Note

The suggestion to have a *Festschrift* in honor of Frederic E. Coenen published met with an overwhelmingly positive response among the authors of the University of North Carolina Germanic Series. As the economics of publishing demanded a limitation of the number of contributions to be published, the members of the Publication Committee deemed it necessary to give preference to articles dealing predominantly with German literature of the nineteenth and twentieth centuries — Professor Coenen's main field of interest.

Nevertheless, the more than twenty contributions with their great variety of both approaches and topics amply demonstrate the desire of those authors whom Frederic E. Coenen helped in many ways to pay tribute to the former editor of the "Studies."

As far as possible, the articles have been arranged in chronological order — dates of publication of works discussed and/or a writer's main period of creativity providing the main criteria. The task of assembling the contributions for the *Festschrift* and of editing this volume afforded me, the present editor of the Germanic Studies, the opportunity gratefully to reciprocate in some small measure the kindness and understanding I received from the former editor during my year of editorial "apprenticeship."

SIEGFRIED MEWS

Nineteenth-Century and Early Twentieth-Century Interpretations of the *Vogelhochzeit*

JOHN G. KUNSTMANN

In his justly famous *Abhandlung über die deutschen Volkslieder* Ludwig Uhland discusses what he calls "den ansehnlichen Liederstamm der Tierhochzeiten."[1] To the animal wedding songs belong the songs describing bird weddings. Uhland publishes the texts of two German bird wedding songs in his *Liedersammlung, Erstes Buch:* "Vogelhochzeit." 10A and 10B,[2] and he refers to these two texts in his notes.[3]

To be sure, Uhland did not coin the term "Vogelhochzeit." "Vogelhochzeit" (from now on abbreviated as VH) in the modern sense of "bird wedding" is used already in the 17th-century versions of the VH songs.[4] And Uhland was perhaps not the first scholar or collector to call attention to folksongs called VH or telling the story of a VH. Clemens Brentano, it seems to me, may have considered the inclusion of a VH in his and Achim von Arnim's *Des Knaben Wunderhorn.*[5] After all, shortly after the publication of the *Wunderhorn*, in ca. 1811, he wrote for "Haus Staarenberg" a poem which begins

1 Der Adelar der führte mich zum Traualtar;
2 Der Dompfaff traute uns als Schlosspfaff;
3 Der Emmerling gab mir und ihm den Fingerring;

and ends

18 Der Wiedehopf brachte uns den Nachttopf;
19 Die Schnepfe brach vor der Tür die Töpfe;
20 Und nach ihr sang Frau Nachtigall die ganze Nacht mit süssem Schall.[6]

Neither Clemens Brentano nor Ludwig Erk, who was responsible for the fourth volume of the *Wunderhorn* and who had made use of an early 17th-century version of the VH, appears to have stirred up interest in the VH. And the same is true of K. Aue. He listed in Franz Joseph Mone's *Anzeiger für Kunde der Teutschen Vorzeit*, 8. Jahrgang (1839), p. 375 as no. 144 of a collection of broadsheets "Hübscher lieder zwey, das Erst, Es wolt ein Rayger fischen etc. Das ander, Von dem Häller, fast kürtzweylig zů singen. Auf dem Holzschnitt stehn zwei Jungfrauen; die eine mit fliegenden Haaren, einem Sonnenhute und Handkorbe, die andere mit aufgebundenen Haaren, einen Reiher an der Seite. 8 Seiten." Aue prints the first and the last strophe of "Es wolt ein Rayger fischen" and the first and the last strophe of "Von dem Häller." His broadsheet is "Getruckt zů Nürnberg durch Kunegund Hergotin." The information furnished by Aue makes it very clear that he had obtained a copy of what is today known as "Die älteste deutsche Vogelhochzeit."[7] But Aue's note did not cause students of folksong to go out and collect versions of the VH and it did not inspire them to interpret the VH from the points of view of meter, rhyme, melody, poetic qualities, cultural-historical significance, etc.

It remained for Ludwig Uhland to become the first German scholar successfully to call attention to the German VH and to become the first German scholar to interpret the VH. A. Goetze is, therefore, quite right when he speaks of Uhland's "Entdeckung des wichtigen Liederstamms, den er glücklich Tierhochzeiten genannt hat."[8] Uhland's priority and prestige may very well be responsible for the fact that his, Uhland's, interpretation was, for a while, the "accepted" interpretation of the VH.

Today we know that Uhland and his followers were mistaken in their interpretation of the VH. We have known for some time that the VH was, from the year ca. 1527 on, when it was first printed, to its latest appearance on the vaudeville stage or out of the loudspeaker of the juke box, a *cantus obscoenus*, a *Schamperlied*.

It is interesting, and instructive, to look back and to find out what is responsible for the romantic interpretation that was inaugurated by Uhland. The passage in which he interprets, not so much the letter of the VH, but its spirit, reads as follows:

Vögel und Waldtiere waren in ihrer Winternot zunächst den armen Leuten gestellt, die Armen der Wildnis. Es kommt aber eine Zeit, wo es hoch bei ihnen hergeht; im grünen, dichten Walde, sicher und wohlgenährt, halten sie lustige Wirtschaft, die nach dem Bild eines menschlichen Hochzeitfestes dargestellt wird und wobei den einzelnen Tieren, teils nach ihrer Gestalt und Eigenschaft oder in scherzhaftem Widerspruche mit diesen, teils auch in spielender Willkür oder nach Laune des Reimes, die Rollen zugeteilt sind...
Die zwei deutschen Stücke dieser Gattung sind luftig und frühlingsheiter, ganz im Reiche der Vögel gehalten. Weniger feste Gestalten und Gruppen, keine so gründliche Festordnung und Bestellung des Schmauses, mehr Geflatter, spielender Scherz und Reimklang; dabei aber stets noch Handlung und persönliches Leben, weit hinaus über die allgemeinen Züge der sommerlichen Vogelwonne in den Minneliedern, wo nur etwa vom stolzen Waldgesinde gesprochen wird, oder, am

nächsten herankommend, Wolfram von Eschenbach die Vögel zur Maienzeit ihre Kinder mit Gesange wiegen lässt…

Es gehört zum Verständnis eines solchen Scherzliedes, hinauszugehen in den frischergrünten Wald, zu sehen und zu hören, was da für ein Leben ist, für ein Flattern und Gaupeln, Rauschen und Jagen im lichten Gezweig und durch die unsteten Schatten, welch vielstimmiges Singen, Zwitschern, Girren und dazwischen ein seltsamer Lachruf, ein wilder Schrei aus dem tiefen Walde…[9]

Would you not say, Fred, that this is excellent German, worthy to be placed side by side with some of the best prose written by Martin Luther and Jacob Grimm? But as an evaluation of the 16th-century VH, and all the later VHH, Uhland's statement is naive, romantic, unscholarly. And this I say with all due respect for its author, while humbly and gratefully acknowledging lasting indebtedness to the genius and the labor of the jurist-poet-parliamentarian-scholar of Tübingen. Uhland, in my opinion, has misinterpreted both spirit and letter of the VH. This may be due to any one of the following three reasons or, perhaps, to a combination of all three of them.

In the first place, Uhland, *nolens volens*, reads out of the 16th-century VH what he, previously, has read into it. Uhland is Uhland, not Heine. He looks at the VH with the eyes of the man who wrote "Des Knaben Berglied" and "Frühlingsglaube," and not with the eyes of the man who wrote

> Die Blumen spriessen, die Glöcklein schallen,
> Die Vögel sprechen wie in der Fabel;
> Mir aber will das Gespräch nicht gefallen,
> Ich finde Alles miserabel.[10]

Uhland's interpretation of the VH springs from his character. He was a "teutscher Jüngling." To such a one the VH would be or could be a "luftiges, frühlingsheiteres Scherzlied."

In the second place, Uhland's interpretation, especially that part of it where he speaks of "die lustige Wirtschaft, die nach dem Bild eines menschlichen Hochzeitfestes dargestellt wird," is not as far fetched as my summary dismissal of it seems to imply. Uhland's interpretation is by no means an impossible one, i.e., an *a priori* impossible one. There certainly exists the well-known tradition which combines into a "Frühlingssymphonie" spring and flowers and birds and nesting and love and mating, and there is evidence, German and European, earlier, contemporary (16th century), and later, of the treatment in poetry and prose of birds and bird assemblies in terms of human activities.[11] Even today the tradition referred to is fully alive. It has given birth to such a poem as G. C. Dieffenbach's "Waldkonzert" which was very popular when you were a bit younger:

Konzert ist heute angesagt im frischen, grünen Wald;
Die Musikanten stimmen schon; hör wie es lustig schallt!
Das jubiliert und musiziert, das schmettert und das schallt!
Das geigt und singt und pfeift und klingt im frischen, grünen Wald!

Der Distelfink spielt keck vom Blatt die erste Violin,
Sein Vetter Buchfink nebenan begleitet lustig ihn.
Das jubiliert usw.

Frau Nachtigall, die Sängerin, die singt so hell und zart;
Und Monsieur Hänfling bläst dazu die Flöt' nach bester Art.
Das jubiliert usw.

Die Drossel spielt die Klarinett, der Rab', der alte Mann,
Streicht den verstimmten Brummelbass, so gut er streichen kann.

Der Kuckuck schlägt die Trommel gut, die Lerche steigt empor
Und schmettert mit Trompetenklang voll Jubel in den Chor.

Musikdirektor ist der Specht, er hat nicht Rast noch Ruh',
Schlägt mit dem Schnabel, spitz und lang, gar fein den Takt dazu.

Verwundert hören Has und Reh das Fiedeln und das Schrei'n.
Und Biene, Mück' und Käferlein, die stimmen surrend ein.
Das jubiliert und musiziert, das schmettert und das schallt,
Das geigt und singt und pfeift und klingt im frischen, grünen Wald!

This tradition, then, known to Uhland, may well be responsible for his interpretation of the VH as a "lustige Wirtschaft nach dem Bild eines menschlichen Hochzeitfestes." One likes to argue *a posse ad esse*. And it seems that, in this case, Uhland was so well satisfied with the "possibility" that he neglected to look at his texts critically or, rather, having looked at them, decided to change them, not in order to suppress evidence, but in order to make the texts conform to a tradition in which they "evidently" had been written: by omitting certain passages which obviously were "obscene" and by printing an "expurgated" text Uhland, undoubtedly, believed he had "restored" the VH to its original innocuous estate.[12]

In the third place, Uhland discusses only two German VHH, printed versions of the 16th and early 17th centuries. Apparently he was not aware of the existence of other printed German versions, and he seems to have been wholly ignorant of the existence at his time of the VH as a living German folksong. He knew more Scandinavian and Baltic than German versions.[13] The relative scantiness of material at his disposal—and scanty it must be called when compared with the wealth of new German and European versions collected since the (posthumous) appearance of Uhland's essay on "Fabellieder"—in my opinion explains fully, when taken together with the other two reasons offered, why Uhland failed in his effort to interpret the VH.

His interpretation or misinterpretation had far-reaching results. It became, and in some parts it remains almost to this day, the *orthodox* interpretation of the 16th-century VH and its modern descendants. The passage quoted before, or parts of it, were referred to or cited with approval again and again down to World War I and later, e.g., by von Flugi, by Julius Sahr, Friedrich Arnold, and by Alfred Goetze, who calls it "Worte von klassischer Geltung und poetischer Feinheit."[14] Pommer characterizes a Silesian version of the VH as "reizend, unschuldig naiv."[15] Norrenberg publishes an 18th century VH-fragment and discourses in that connection on "phantasievolle Kinderseele, Verständnis der Natur, ein an dunklen Ahnungen und geheimnisvoller Poesie reiches Leben."[16] Decurtins, in commenting on an Engadine VH, mentions "Tierfabeln, die uns in den dichten Wald zurückführen, wo der Mensch noch in inniger Beziehung zu den Tieren stand."[17] And, last but not least, Otto Böckel, having quoted a few animal wedding songs, adds: "Gewiss liegt diesen Gedichten tiefes Verständnis für das Treiben der Vögel im frisch ergrünten Walde zugrunde, das Uhland so schön schildert."[18]

It is true, Böckel does not entirely approve of Uhland's interpretation. He discovers in animal wedding songs "auch scherzhafte oder spöttische Anspielungen und Parodien auf armselige menschliche Hochzeiten."[19] And there are others who disagree with Uhland. Thus Heinrich Weber calls the VH "ein im ganzen leider anzügliches Lied."[20] In this he is seconded by J. W. Bruinier who, without mincing his words, refers to "das heutzutage wieder aus dem Schalltrichter ertönende zotige Lied von der VH" which, he thinks, was conceived in a spirit of moist hilariousness.[21] Similarly, A. H. Krappe detects traces of obscenity in the VH, and although he mentions the VH only in passing, yet he indicates clearly enough why he arrives at such a verdict: the expression "ein lockerer (loser) Vogel," he thinks, is "hardly due to the myth of Loki and Geirröd but to a good observation of nature. Certain birds had the same reputation of sexual license among the Greeks. Cf. also the old folksong *Die* VH."[22] Krappe has a *reason* for seeing in the VH something different from Uhland and Uhland's interpretation. Weber and Bruinier, on the other hand, disagree with Uhland without giving an account of their reasons for disagreeing. It seems, both are or were guided by an impression, a hunch. And so their implied doubt of the accepted interpretation of the VH and their outspoken denial of the moral integrity of the VH amount to nothing but an unsupported statement. Evidently the person who, in 1915, complained to the "Strafkammer" of the "Landgericht Detmold" about the questionable character of the VH, shared the opinions of Weber and Bruinier. The court, however, found that the song, although not a suitable one for the entertainment of the public, was not immoral ("das Lied sei allerdings kein passendes, unsittlich sei es jedoch nicht").[23] One can not very well speak of "unsupported statement" in the case of Wolfgang Schultz. He discusses at length the so-called "Verwunderungslied" and the "Tierhochzeit" and the VH. They belong together, he thinks, and they must be explained mythologically. According to him the VH belongs with Germanic riddles concerning fire-making by means of a fire-drill and with such as have to do with the wedding ceremony. Originally, however, in his opinion these riddles are not riddles at all. They are symbolical descriptions, some of them in dialogue form, of the rituals of fire-making and the manufacture of the sacred intoxicating drink (the "Rauschtrank").[24]

The interpretations of Schultz, Weber, Bruinier, and Krappe have this in common that they call attention to sexual, phallic implications in the VH. In this their interpretations differ diametrically from that offered by Uhland and his followers.

There are others, to be sure, who refer to and comment on animal wedding songs. They do so, however, without specifically mentioning Uhland or the VH. They are usually satisfied with pointing out the "universality" of animal wedding songs[25] and with making a few general remarks about "satirizing tendencies" or "childlike simplicity" revealed in these folksongs. In this connection it is only fair to mention that the VH has been considered, for the moment only, a "somewhat smutty," "ambiguous," "dubious" song among people who are or were, for the time being, interested in German folksong or in the more informal side of things academic. Such opinions seem to be based on intuition or on an assumption of general depravity of human nature!

More than four decades ago—and at that time I had collected and studied over seventy German VH versions from the 16th, the 17th, the 18th, the 19th and the 20th centuries, plus many extra-German European and non-European VHH, beetle wedding songs ("Käferhochzeiten"), wonderment songs ("Verwunderungslieder"), etc.[26]—I was roundly censored after reading a brief paper on the VH before a MLA group and I was taken to task publicly for having offered proof, lexicographical, historical and folkloristic proof, that the VH from the beginning was a *cantus obscoenus*, and for doing so in the presence of decent people. Among those apologizing to the MLA group for my unseemly behavior were some who, at that time, were considered pillar saints of Germanics in the United States of America. These gentlemen, since then, have all shuffled off this mortal coil. Having been, like Uhland, "teutsche Jünglinge," they are now living it up, I am sure, in some sex-less and non-alcoholic Walhalla. I was rejected by my colleagues, but I was pleased to find myself, as far as the interpretation of the VH is concerned, on the side of the person who included a modern German VH in the collection called *Frisch gesungen! 3939 neueste und beliebteste Liederreime* (no year), and who added to the VH ("based on folksong") the critical (?) note: "Nach Walter von der Vogelweide von Danny Gürtler." I have it from eyewitnesses

6

that he who sang this "Schlager" at the beginning of the present century appeared on the *Überbrettel*-stage attired in the costume of a Minnesinger and that his audiences understood fully what was meant by the reference to Vogelweid the Minnesinger. The text of this version of the VH is exactly the same as the text of Odeon record no. 10148-A (Die Vogelhochzeit. Gustav Schönwald mit Orchester Begleitung. Recorded in Germany. General Phonograph Corporation, New York). And Walter von der Vogelweide — believe it or not! — was credited with the authorship of "The Wedding of the Birds" in a "Heidelberg Program" conducted by Marx and Anne Oberndorfer of the "Musical Pilgrimages" over Radio Station WMAQ (The Chicago Daily News Station, Chicago, Illinois) on Sunday, 6 September 1931. Tandaradei! In the meantime, I have added to my collectanea of VHH and related material and may yet put together my findings for the edification of such as you, Fred, "die auf höherer Warte stehen." I know you will recognize the quotation and will accept, I trust, in the spirit in which it is offered the second quotation which expresses my best wishes to you, the man honored by this "Festschrift":

> Hiddigeigei spricht, der Alte:
> Pflück die Früchte, eh' sie platzen;
> Wenn die magern Jahre kommen,
> Saug an der Erinn'rung Tatzen!

NOTES

[1] *Uhlands Schriften zur Geschichte der Dichtung und Sage*, ed. A. von Keller, W. L. Holland & F. Pfeiffer (Stuttgart, 1865-73), 8 vols. Vol. III: *Alte hoch- und niederdeutsche Volkslieder mit Abhandlung und Anmerkungen*, ed. Franz Pfeiffer (1866), contains *Abhandlung über die deutschen Volkslieder*. The passage in question is from the second chapter ("Fabellieder"), pp. 75-81. Perhaps more easily consulted is *Uhlands Alte hoch- und niederdeutsche Volkslieder mit Abhandlung und Anmerkungen*, 3rd ed., eingeleitet von Hermann Fischer, 4 vols. (Stuttgart & Berlin, n.y.). Vol. III contains the *Abhandlung*, and the passage in question is found on pp. 65-69. — On the significance of the *Schriften* in general and of the *Abhandlung* in particular see, e.g., *Materialien zur Geschichte des deutschen Volkslieds. Aus Universitäts-Vorlesungen von Rudolf Hildebrand*. I. Teil: *Das ältere Volkslied*. Ed. G. Berlit (Leipzig, 1900), pp. 70-71. — The passage referred to was published in 1866, after Uhland's death. It was certainly in existence a quarter of a century before; see Pfeiffer's introduction to the *Abhandlung*, passim.

[2] *Liedersammlung*, mit Einleitung von Hermann Fischer, I, pp. 38-43: Vogelhochzeit. 10 A.B.

[3] *Liedersammlung*, mit Einleitung von Hermann Fischer, II, p. 279.

[4] The term appears in the 1603, 1605, 1612, 1662 versions of the VH.

[5] Franz M. Böhme in *Altdeutsches Liederbuch* (Leipzig, 1877), p. 329, having enumerated his expurgations of certain "obscene" and "indelicate" strophes of an early 17th-century VH, states, "Der Abdruck desselben Textes im Whorn 4, 260 hat in seiner 29. Strophe die zotige Stelle abgeändert." He repeats this information in *Deutscher Liederhort*, I (Leipzig, 1893), p. 512: "Hainhofer, Lautenb. II. Bl. 131 (Handschr. v. 1603 zu Wolfenbüttel). Hier mit Auslassung von 4 obscönen Strophen. Auch so Wdh. 4, 200 (!)." It seems to me that Böhme's reference to the publication of a VH text in the *Wunderhorn* has led

7

some people to claim that Arnim and Brentano are responsible for the publication. But Böhme's reference is to vol. IV of the *Wunderhorn*, and this volume was edited by Ludwig Erk. It is a part of the third edition of the *Wunderhorn* (Berlin, 1845-46).

[6] *Clemens Brentanos Sämtliche Werke*, ed. Carl Schüddekopf, XI, p. 209. For the date see XI, Introduction, p. xxiv.

[7] *Zwickauer Facsimiledrucke No. 11: Die älteste deutsche Vogelhochzeit. Jörg Graff, Das Lied vom Heller. Nürnberg, Kunegund Hergotin, o. J.* Ed. A. Goetze (Zwickau, 1912).

[8] *Zwickauer Facsimiledrucke No. 11*, p. 3.

[9] See note 1.

[10] Heine, *Lyrisches Intermezzo*, 28. — Perhaps I should have quoted "Neuer Frühling":

> Es erklingen alle Bäume,
> Und es singen alle Nester —
> Wer ist der Kapellenmeister
> In dem grünen Waldorchester?
>
> Ist es dort der graue Kiebitz,
> Der beständig nickt so wichtig?
> Oder der Pedant, der dorten
> Immer kuckuckt, zeitmassrichtig?
>
> Ist es jener Storch, der ernsthaft,
> Und als ob er dirigieret',
> Mit dem langen Streckbein klappert,
> Während alles musizieret?
>
> Nein, in meinem eignen Herzen
> Sitzt des Walds Kapellenmeister,
> Und ich fühl', wie er den Takt schlägt,
> Und ich glaube, Amor heisst er.

[11] E.g., Hoffmann von Fallersleben, Ernst Richter, eds., *Schlesische Volkslieder mit Melodien, aus dem Munde des Volks gesammelt* (Leipzig, 1842), p. 76:
"Im Jahre 1531 schrieb Hans Sachs (im 4. Teile des 1. Buches, Nürnberg 1590, Bl. 319b-320b) ein langes Gedicht, 'das Regiment der anderthalbhundert Vögel', worin er erzählt, wie die Vögel alle hundert Jahr einen König wählen und was sie alles bei dieser Gelegenheit treiben, wie sie nach menschlicher Weise sprechen, essen und trinken und Kurzweil machen. Der König zieht mit seinem Hofgesinde ins Zelt und er nun zu Tisch sitzt:

> Der Trapp war Truchsess, trug zu Tisch
> Gar köstlich Tracht, Wildpret und Fisch,
> Schenk war Sittich, trug Trinken für
> . . . .
> . . . .
> Als nun das Mal vollendet was,
> Bett das Mönchlein das Gratias,

es wird Karten gespielt, mancherlei Turnier begonnen, dann folgt der Abendtanz, wobei es mancherlei Streit und Händel setzt, so auch bei dem Schlaftrunk. Unterdessen ist es Mitternacht geworden, der Wächter (ein Hahn) schreit: auf, es ist Zeit, macht euch davon! und jeder Vogel schwingt sich auf und seinem Neste zu." The poem is reprinted by Hugo Suolahti, *Die deutschen Vogelnamen* (Strassburg, 1909), pp. 466-72, from *Bibliothek des Literarischen Vereins*, CV, pp. 278-84. Emil Weller, *Dichtungen des sechzehnten Jahrhunderts. Bibliothek des Literarischen Vereins*, CXIX, p. 31, furnishes an example of the spring-birds-nesting-love tradition:

> Wie die vogel im glentz sind tün,
> Die ain ander locken gar schon,

Im wald sind sy vast wol singen,
Das eß herwider ist klingen.
Der bufinck schlecht den reytter zu,
Kain vogel im glentz hat kein rü;
Er locket und schechert so lang
Mit seinem senfften süssen gsang,
Piß das sy sich allsam paren
Darnach yedes par ist faren
Zu nest, nestet nach seiner art
Legt ayr, brüt die auß, sich nit spart.
Also ir, mein junges folcklein,
Tund auch wie die wald-vögelein
Im schönem (!) glentz, küelen mayen!
Syngen, tantzen, springen, rayen!

This is a part of "Ain schöne hystori, wie ain junger gsell weyben sol, deßgleichen ain junckfrau mannen. Welches alles stat auff dem sprichwort

> Wie du? wie sy? Hüt dich!
> Mein roß schlecht dich."

O. O. u. J. [Nürnberg: Jobst Gutknecht, c. 1515]. — For "den reytter zu" see Suolahti, *op. cit.*, pp. 112, 459. — One thinks in this connection of Luther's letter to his servant Wolfgang Sieberger, written in Wittenberg in 1534, commonly called "Klagschrift," in which "Wir Drosseln, Amseln, Finken, Hänfling, Stiglitzen samt andren fromen, erbaren Vögeln..." lodge a complaint against the fowling-floor established by Sieberger. With this letter one might compare the one Luther wrote to his Wittenberg "table-companions," April 1530, in which he describes whimsically the imperial diet of the jackdaws and crows seen from his window in the Koburg. — The *locus classicus* for bird assemblies-bird parliaments is Seelmann, "Die Vogelsprachen (Vogelparlamente) der mittelalterlichen Litteratur," *Jahrbuch des Vereins für niederdeutsche Sprachforschung*, XIV (1888), 101-47. Important are also W. Stammler, "Die Bedeutung der mittel-niederdeutschen Literatur," *Germanisch-Romanische Monatsschrift*, XIII (1925), 440 with note; Mone, *Übersicht der niederländischen Volksliteratur älterer Zeit* (Tübingen, 1838), p. 351 [seems to be no. 7 of Seelmann's list]; Lassberg, "Deutsche Sprachdenkmäler in der kgl. öffentlichen Bibliothek zu Stuttgart," *Graff's Diutiska* II (1827), 76-77; *Bibliothek des Literarischen Vereins*, XXX, 1375; "Wahlversammlung" in Leopold-Leopold, *Van de Schelde... Tweede Deel*, pp. 74-5 (this is, at the same time, a sort of VH); Erich Schmidt, *Charakteristiken, Zweite Reihe²*, p. 90, mentions a "Vogelsprache" in Cyrano de Bergerac's travels; Jean de Condé's *La messe des oisiaus* was not accessible to me; Bujeaud, I, 40: "Le bal des souris"; and, of course, "Owl and Nightingale," Chaucer's "Parlement of Foules", "The Book of Cupid or the Cuckoo and the Nightingale," "The Harmony of Birds" (Percy Society, VII), "The Phoenix and the Turtle," ascribed to Shakespeare. On plant, bird, animal parliaments see Voigt, "Odo de Ciringtonia und seine Quellen," *Zeitschrift für deutsches Altertum*, XXIII (1879), 283. On "Gelage zechender Tiere" see Dähnhardt, *Natursagen*, II, pp. 298 ff. and Riegler in *Wörter und Sachen*, VI (1914-15), 194 ff.

12 See Hildebrand, *Materialien* (note 1), p. 71: "Die Kritik [speaking of Uhland's *Alte hoch- und niederdeutsche Volkslieder*] lässt freilich doch hie und da zu vermissen übrig; eine streng philologische Nacharbeit wird sich einmal nötig machen." Hildebrand's statement may well be applied to Uhland's treatment of the VH since Uhland omitted important parts in the two German VHH he printed.

13 Uhland knew hardly any Slavic and Italian versions: see Landau, "Tierhochzeiten," *Zeitschrift für vergleichende Literaturgeschichte*, N.F., I (1887), 372-3.

14 Alfons von Flugi, *Die Volkslieder des Engadin* (Strassburg, 1873), pp. 19-20: "Über diese Art der Dichtung berichtet unübertrefflich Uhland im dritten Bande seiner Schriften."

Julius Sahr, *Das deutsche Volkslied*, II (1908), p. 106 [this is "Sammlung Göschen," 132 (the fourth edition, by Sartori, 1924. agrees, pp. 105 f.]). Friedrich Arnold, *Das deutsche Volkslied*, 3rd ed. (Prenzlau, 1912), pp. 127 and 128. Alfred Goetze, *Die älteste deutsche Vogelhochzeit* (see note 7 above), p. 3.

[15] *Das deutsche Volkslied*, X (1908), 131, n. 1.

[16] Norrenberg, *Beiträge zur Lokalgeschichte des Niederrheins*, IV: *Geschichte der Herrlichkeit Grefrath*, Chapter 15, p. 102.

[17] *Rätoromanische Chrestomathie*, IX, in *Romanische Forschungen*, XXVII (1910), Introduction, p. ix.

[18] "Das Volkslied der polnischen Oberschlesier verglichen mit der deutschen Volkspoesie," *Mitteilungen der schlesischen Gesellschaft für Volkskunde*, XI (1904), 48-50.

[19] *loc. cit.*

[20] "Die Storndorfer Volkslieder," *Hessische Blätter für Volkskunde*, IX (1910), 116.

[21] *Das deutsche Volkslied*, 5th ed. (1913/14), p. 124.

[22] In his review of Lessmann, *Der deutsche Volksmund im Lichte der Sage*, in *Modern Language Notes*, XXXVIII (1923), 239.

[23] Wehrhan, *Zeitschrift des Vereins für rheinische und westfälische Volkskunde*, XII (1915), 259.

[24] Wolfgang Schultz, *Rätsel aus dem hellenischen Kulturkreise*. Zweiter (Schluss-)Teil, p. 105: "Diese VH [referring to VHH in Richard Wossidlo, *Mecklenburgische Volksüberlieferungen*, I (1897), II, 1 (1899)] bewegt sich also ganz im Rahmen der bisher betrachteten Rätsel" [referring to "Kwirn und Schmiede im hellenischen Rätsel"]; p. 117: "Die germanischen Rätsel von Feuerbohren und Hochzeit, also die überwiegende Menge obscoener Rätsel, sind ursprünglich keine Rätsel, sondern symbolische, zum Teil sogar dialogisch gestaltete Schilderungen der rituellen Vorgänge der Feuererzeugung und Rauschtrankgewinnung..." Against such mythological interpretations ("vermeintliche mythologische Beziehungen") see, e.g., Vogt, *Mitteilungen der schlesischen Gesellschaft für Volkskunde*, XI (1904), 123 f.

[25] E.g., Schuller, *Romänische Volkslieder* (1859), p. 103: "Tierhochzeiten kommen in Volksliedern häufig vor" [*Romänische Volkslieder* was published before 1866. Schuller, naturally, did not think of Uhland's German VHH]. "Volkswitz und Volkshumor finden in der Zusammenstellung der Getrauten und in der Schilderung der Festlichkeiten ein reiches Feld für ihr neckisches Spiel und für parodierende Satyre." — Morf, *Die Kultur der Gegenwart*, I, XI, 1, p. 153: "Tiermärchen [according to the context this includes animal wedding songs] sind unter den Menschen überall entstanden"; he speaks also of "vermenschlichende Deutung" of animal wedding songs. — Morf, *Aus Dichtung und Sprache der Romanen*. Zweite Reihe, p. 83: "Das Thema der Tierhochzeit ist ein universelles... Die Tierlieder [including animal wedding songs] dienen der Satire, oder sie sind harmlose Kinderlieder geworden." - Gagnon, *Chansons populaires du Canada*, p. 279: "Cette chanson (c'est Pinson avec Cendrouille) n'est pas tant une chanson comique qu'une chanson d'enfants, où la chatte, le gros rat avec son violon, etc., ne figurent que pour tenir en éveil l'esprit d'un petit tapageur, en attendant que le sommeil vienne fermer ses paupières. 'Il ne faut pas, dit avec justesse M. Champfleury, demander aux nourrices qui composent ces chansons, autre chose que ce qu'elles peuvent donner; ... dans l'amour qu'elles portent aux enfants, elles trouvent de singulières associations de mots... qui frappent le nouveau-né et savent endormir ses souffrances.'"

[26] I should append here the list of animal wedding songs, VHH, beetle weddings, fish weddings, vegetable weddings and the list of the many related items, such as bird assemblies, animal testaments, battles between animal hosts, "Als die Tiere noch sprachen", etc., etc., and the use of these and similar matters and motifs in "Kunstliteratur" from Homer and Aristophanes to Goethe—to mention only these three. But there are limits to the number of words and pages as you, Fred, know only too well, and, alas, you have trained your successor only too well!

10

The Wound and the Physician in Goethe's *Wilhelm Meister*

A. G. STEER

It is the intention of this paper to deal with an element present in both great parts of the novel, an element which the critical literature[1] has, strange to say, largely ignored, the role of the wound and the physician. Since, however, there is evidence that the concepts grew in Goethe's mind as the work progressed,[2] the final portion, the *Wanderjahre*, will be treated first, for here the author's final conclusions are clearest.

Wounds are of significance, because almost all in the novel are related to love and passion.[3] That love is a central theme in the work is clear: Trunz has expressed the philosophic background of the matter: "Hier [in der Liebe] erfaßt er [Goethe] im Endlichen das Unendliche. Unsere Welt ist Zweiheit, Polarität und jeder Liebesvollzug Gleichnis einer letzten Einheit, von der alles ausgeht und in die alles wiederkehrt. So steht Goethes Liebesauffassung im Rahmen seines neuplatonischen Weltbildes der Emanation, im unmittelbaren Gefüge seiner religiösen Anschauungen und Ahnungen."[4]

Anna Hellersberg-Wendriner makes a necessary addition to the field and effect of this love: "Die Liebe ist in den *Wanderjahren* wie in den *Lehrjahren* das bindende Element der Gesellschaft. Das Individuum ist zuerst in Liebe dem kleinen Kreis der Familie verpflichtet, ehe es in größere Kreise hineinwachsen kann. Ihre Aufgabe ist es, die Wärmequelle zu sein, die die Gemeinschaft erhält. Der Dienst in der Nähe bildet die Möglichkeiten des Wirkens in weiteren Räumen gesellschaftlichen Lebens. Alles schließt sich in den *Wanderjahren* erst familienhaft zusammen, um der Gemeinschaft würdig zu werden."[5] That the family does indeed play a vital role here is confirmed by the text of the *Wanderjahre*. At the beginning of the work from the top of the mountains before entering the main flow of the novel, Wilhelm wrote Natalie words that betray an unclear and rather negative awareness of this aspect of his character and fate: "Ein Fehler, ein Unglück, ein Schicksal ist mir's nun einmal, daß sich, ehe ich mich's versehe, die Gesellschaft um mich vermehrt, daß ich mir eine neue Bürde auflade, an der ich nachher zu tragen and zu schleppen habe."[6] (VIII, 29) A little later on the mountain tops Jarno's keen analytical mind, inclined to satiric and even sarcastic language, penetrates to the core of Wilhelm's being. "Wenn du nicht kuppeln und Schulden bezahlen kannst, so bist du unter ihnen nichts nütze." (VIII, 33) The *kuppeln* refers to falling in love, which may lead to the founding of a family, as for instance Wilhelm and Mariane, or the Melinas, and the reference to debts recalls Wilhelm's payment of what the theatrical troupe owed, thus his support of a larger group or metamorphosis of the family, and that Wilhelm's main mission in life was to serve the family became clear to him in the vicinity of and under the inspiring and clarifying influence of Makarie. In his night soliloquy under the stars he comes to the insight: "… meine Absicht ist, einen edlen Familienkreis in allen seinen Gliedern erwünscht verbunden herzustellen; der Weg ist bezeichnet. Ich soll erforschen, was edle Seelen auseinanderhält, soll Hindernisse wegräumen, von welcher Art sie auch seien." (VIII, 119) The concept of the family as *Urform* and *Metamorphose* is really contained in the phrase "… einen edlen Familienkreis in allen seinen Gliedern…," but it is much more clearly expressed later as, in connection with the story of the five drowned boys, the reader hears that Wilhelm had learned this way of looking on the family and on human society from his father. In connection with overcoming the resistance to inoculation against smallpox, he said: "Mein Vater war jener Zeit einer der ersten, der seine Betrachtung, seine Sorge über die Familie, über die Stadt hinaus zu erstrecken durch einen allgemeinen, wohlwollenden Geist getrieben ward." (VIII, 278) Wilhelm's sense of responsibility then began with the family (*Urform*) and expanded to the larger metamorphoses, the city and the circles beyond. And the fact that one is justified in using the concepts of *Urform* and *Metamorphose* is corroborated in the following language: "Er [der Vater] sah die bürgerliche Gesellschaft, welcher Staatsform sie auch untergeordnet wäre, als einen Naturzustand an, der sein Gutes und sein Böses habe, seine gewöhnlichen Lebensläufe, abwechselnd reiche und kümmerliche Jahre…." (VIII, 278 f.) For these reasons then, any element which, like wounds, shows a connection to love and the family must be carefully examined.

Wounds appear in several different patterns in the novel, although one seems to be dominant. Someone, usually a man, falls in love, at which point passion either carries him to excess or else makes him so unsure of himself that he incurs an injury or wound. Felix suffered this way on no less than three occasions, all on account of Hersilie: first while peeling an apple he cut himself (VIII, 51), then he fell off a horse (VIII, 72), and finally he fell into a river (VIII, 459). In similar fashion the hero of *Die neue Melusine* is driven by jealousy into a duel in which he is severely wounded (VIII, 359). The effect of passion can also lead to a wound that is psychological. Of this Flavio in *Der Mann von fünfzig Jahren* is an excellent example. After the beautiful widow had refused his suit, he appeared in shockingly dishevelled condition, fleeing the light, dirty and in despair, like Orestes pursued by the furies. This interest in psychological wounds should not be surprising: to the 1821 version the author had prefixed lines which announced an intro-spective tendency. The wanderer, he said, did not always sing and pray:

Doch wendet er, sobald der Pfad verfänglich,
Den ernsten Blick, wo Nebel ihn umtrüben,
Ins eigne Herz und in das Herz der Lieben.[7]

One effect of a wound is of course obvious: the injured man's world shrinks until it contains little beside the suffering subject and his pain. The isolating effect is ironic; at the very moment that the individual withdraws, he is badly in need of assistance from the outer world he is rejecting. The hero of *Die neue Melusine* was alone, for he had turned his environment hostile to him (VIII, 359), and so at the end of the novel was Felix when he fell into the river.

More interesting than the isolation accompanying the physical wounds, however, is that which is associated with mental or emotional injuries, which Goethe described as befogging vision (cf. the fog in the introduction to the 1821 version noted above.) In *Wer ist der Verräter?* Lucidor's pain at hearing announced his engagement to the wrong girl is signalled by a withdrawal: "Lucidorn war's auf einmal zumute, als wenn er in tiefe Nebel hineinsähe...." (VIII, 105)

Similarly, the effects of such emotional wounds are described also as a flight from the light. Flavio, in *Der Mann von funfzig Jahren*, arrived home in such a state that he sought the isolating darkness (VIII, 203). In *Wer ist der Verräter?* Lucidor, overwhelmed with pain and despair ("wounded") fled: "*Scheu vor dem Tageslichte*... die Blicke begegnender Menschen vermeidend...." (VIII, 106, italics added) Most drastic is the isolation of each of the various individuals that obtains at the end of *Nicht zu weit*.[8]

The novel concentrates on wounds that flow from passion, but they are also an unavoidable result of maturation. In the *Lehrjahre*, in discussing education and the activities of the *Turmgesellschaft*, Wilhelm asked the Abbé: "'Aber... wird das Genie sich nicht selbst retten, die Wunden, die es sich geschlagen, selbst heilen'? 'Mitnichten', versetzte der andere, 'oder wenigstens nur notdürftig'." (VII, 120-121) The latter then went on to discuss fate and chance in such a way as to show that one of the aims of the *Turmgesellschaft* was to watch over and protect the genius from the "wounds" of fate. It is to be noted how also in the *Pädagogische Provinz* injuries of this sort are treated as an unavoidable feature of human life: "Wenn einer sich körperlich beschädigte, verschuldend oder unschuldig, wenn ihn andere vorsätzlich oder zufällig verletzten, wenn das irdisch Willenlose ihm ein Leid zufügte, das bedenk' er wohl: denn solche Gefahr begleitet ihn sein Leben lang." (VIII, 155)

At the end of *Wer ist der Verräter?* Lucidor's emotional wounds were healed by his declaration of love for and acceptance by Lucinde. "Und so zogen beide Paare zur Gesellschaft, mit Gefühlen, die der schönste Traum nicht zu geben vermöchte." (VIII, 114) The cure of the isolated wounded state results not only in a reunion of the loving couple, but also in their return to the larger group.

13

In the process of overcoming the isolated, self-centered state of emotional damage, confession is stressed,[9] a practice which immediately establishes close contact with at least one other human being, and thus a complete reversal in attitude towards the outside world. The hero of *Die neue Melusine* brings about his reconciliation with his beloved through a kind of confession (VIII, 371); Lucidor's situation, after becoming complicated through his one-sided "confessions" (soliloquies), is resolved after her confession (VIII, 107-112). Lenardo takes the first step that leads to his eventual cure by confessing to Wilhelm his emotional involvement and the reasons therefore in *Das nußbraune Mädchen*. Wilhelm resorts to confession also: at the beginning in a letter to Natalie he recalls his last confession and absolution, and the memory functions as a conscience would (VIII, 12). Then later the painter at the Lago Maggiore is taken up into the group of the *Entsagenden* by an act of confession (VIII, 241). And then in the circle of the uncle from America, confession was made into a central element of moral, almost of religious conduct. Sundays were spent quietly in awareness of man's limitations, and no-one was permitted to carry cares over into the new week. For physical troubles, one saw the doctor; for mental or emotional ones ("geistig, sittlich") the individual had to confess to a friend and ask help (VIII, 84). The uncle himself confessed to Makarie, and on Sunday evening was accustomed to ask everyone if all problems had been cleared up by confession.

In the *Lehrjahre* the attitude on wounds was similar. Laertes' wounds were brought on by passion aroused at the discovery of his bride's unfaithfulness, and the damage that resulted from the duel is called a double wound (VII, 220), i.e., both emotional and physical. A poor physician ("Feldscher") caused his wound to heal badly, both physically—black teeth and running eyes—and emotionally—he became a woman-hater.

When Lothario was wounded in a duel over a woman (VII, 429, 438, etc.), the old *Medikus* demanded that Lydie be removed from the house: "... ihre heftige und, ich darf wohl sagen, unbequeme Liebe und Leidenschaft hindert des Barons Genesung." (VII, 438) Wilhelm removed the lady, and Lothario's wound, in contrast to Laertes', healed properly.

Among wounds that are more psychological than physical, the cases of Aurelie and the *Harfner* are parallel. After her rejection by Lothario, Aurelie had attained an uncertain stability, thanks largely to her possession of a dagger. Only the constant presence of the means of ending life gave her courage to continue it (VII, 256). Similarly, the *Harfner*, in a precarious state of mental health, reported that he kept a lethal dose of morphine with him: "... die Möglichkeit, sogleich die großen Schmerzen auf ewig aufzuheben, gab mir Kraft, die Schmerzen zu ertragen...." (VII, 597) One is reminded of the youthful Goethe's attraction for the idea of suicide, and of his play with a dagger.

And Aurelie's fatal "wound" also was psychological. When she played Orsina, the parallels between Lessing's plot and her own life were too close:

she got into a state of dangerous excitement and despair and exposed herself to the cold and the wet in a way that almost amounted to suicide (VII, 354). The fatal wound of the *Harfner* was likewise psychological. When he found the manuscript that described his own past, the truth proved too much for his insecure mental balance, and on the third attempt he succeeded in taking his own life.

Mignon's wounds were all psychological. Just before the theatrical troupe is invited to the castle of the count, Wilhelm, in Mignon's presence repeated: "Ich muß fort," (VII, 142) which triggered the child's "epileptic seizure," for she feared to lose him. Then during the night after the successful *Hamlet* performance, Mignon had tried to slip into Wilhelm's room, only to find that Philine had preceded her. The resultant passionate jealousy led to a heart seizure (VII, 524), which recurred at the mere memory as she tried to tell Natalie about it. On four other occasions in the novel the memory or reminder of strong feeling had damaging physical effects similar to those of the original emotional storms; cf. Wilhelm on recalling Mariane's infidelity (VII, 78), Lydie's bad effect on the healing of Lothario's wound (VII, 438), Flavio's relapse on recalling his unhappy love (VIII, 205), and the Countess' remarkable, miniscule wound mixed with overwhelming guilty conscience (VII, 348). And in Mignon's weakened state it was the sight of Wilhelm kissing Therese that brought on her fatal attack (VII, 544).

Wilhelm's wounds are manifold and meaningful; one is reminded of the conclusion of Wilhelm and Serlo's conversation: "Der Romanheld muß leiden... sein...." (VII, 307) The first was the shock suffered on finding out about Mariane's infidelity. The language with which Goethe described the ensuing illness is explicit and emphatic (VII, 76-78). Later, when Wilhelm heard about Mariane's death: "Alle seine alten Wunden wurden wieder aufgerissen." (VII, 115)

Wilhelm had repeatedly suffered wounds due to women; at the loss of Mariane he fell into a severe illness; as a result of the attack in the woods— in which Philine, Mignon and Natalie played a role—he suffered a bullet wound near the heart and a head wound (VII, 229-30; also 231-32). Aurelie slashed his right hand, and during the wild night after the *Hamlet* performance Mignon bit him painfully on his left arm (VII, 327). There is a significant omission; in his engagement to Therese, no wound, either physical or psychological, plays any role.

Typical is the wound that Wilhelm inflicted on the countess. Wilhelm had disguised himself as the count and approached the countess (VII, 189 and 348). As Wilhelm embraces her: "... [er] drückt ihr das große mit Brillianten besetzte Porträt ihres Gemahls gewaltsam wider die Brust. Sie empfindet einen heftigen Schmerz, der nach und nach vergeht... sie hat sich fest eingebildet, es werde dieses Übel mit einem Krebsschaden sich endigen...." (VII, 348-349) Here the physical aspects shade deftly into the psychological and the weapon, the place of the wound, and the force that applied it indicate the reason for the mental effects. During the infliction of damage, whether physical or psychological, the individual may even be unconscious of what is really happening. Lenardo, in recalling his original attraction for Nachodine, stressed this element: "Ein lebhafter Eindruck ist wie eine andere Wunde; man fühlt sie nicht, indem man sie empfängt. Erst später fängt sie an zu schmerzen und zu eitern." (VIII, 133)

There are in the *Lehrjahre* 12 physical and 10 psychological wounds (only the emotional problems that are specifically termed "wounds" are so counted), in the *Wanderjahre* 9 and 8 respectively. The classification is somewhat arbitrary, as most physical wounds have a psychological aspect—of this the Countess' pricked breast is doubtless the neatest example.[10]

Goethe's treatment of the vital craft of wound-healer, of the physician, or barber-surgeon, or wound-surgeon, or chirurgeon is significant. Even in the cases in which he had merely to bind his patient's wound, the chirurgeon exerts a wider social influence. It has been noted how the wound tends to isolate the individual, and what the powers are which lead the individual out of the resultant isolation back to society. Gilg sees this same process in the act of bleeding the patient. As the chirurgeon opens Flavio's bloodvessel he releases an excess of blood: "... es wird verhindert, daß das Heftige in sich selber befangen bleibt."[11] And as Wilhelm, now himself a chirurgeon, bleeds his son Felix in the final scene of the novel, he "... eröffnet mit der verstandes-scharfen Lanzette die leidenschaftliche Ichbefangenheit, welche den Jugend-lichen der freien weiten Luft und des geistvollen Lichtes zu berauben droht und bahnt dem bedrängenden Blut einen Ausweg. So durchbricht er die Besonderung, welche dem Halbwüchsigen zum erstickenden Kerker gewor-den wäre und regt das Einschwingen in den allgemeinen Rhythmus an...."[12]

Jarno was specific about the psychological responsibilities of the physician: "Seelenleiden, in die wir durch Unglück oder eigene Fehler geraten, sie zu heilen vermag der Verstand nichts, die Vernunft wenig, die Zeit viel, ent-schlossene Tätigkeit hingegen alles. Hier wirke jeder mit und auf sich selbst, das hast du an dir, hast es an andern erfahren." (VIII, 281) This type of damage to the individual was very interesting to the author as a glance at Goethe's own life will show, for instance the Plessing episode, or the drama *Lila*.[13]

The main instance in the *Wanderjahre* of a physician acting to heal psy-chological wounds is the *Hausarzt* in *Der Mann von funfzig Jahren*. When Flavio returned home after his refusal by the beautiful widow, the physician recognized the physical symptoms of a condition brought on by emotional factors. When later the patient recalled his troubles vividly, he again became overly emotional. "Der Arzt hatte sich überzeugt, daß der Jüngling bald wieder herzustellen sei; körperlich gesund, werde er schnell sich wieder froh fühlen, *wenn die auf seinem Geist lastende Leidenschaft zu heben oder zu lindern wäre.*" (VIII, 206, italics added) When during the convalescence Flavio began

16

writing poetry, to which Hilarie replied in kind, the physician, realizing its therapeutic effect, encouraged the exchange: "... die edle Dichtkunst... heilt... alle Seelenleiden aus dem Grunde, indem sie solche gewaltig anregt, hervorruft und in auflösenden Schmerzen verflüchtigt."[14] (VIII, 206) During the years 1795-96 when he was completing the *Lehrjahre*, Goethe was also studying the writings attributed to Hippocrates.[15] Two works were the center of his attention: he owned a copy of one, the aphorisms. This work, by the way, contained a "nomos" or Hippocratic list of educational maxims, similar to Meister's *Lehrbrief*. Goethe was also at that time studying the essay *peri diaites* ("concerning the way of life"), and he made translations from it. When Goethe wrote Wilhelm's *Lehrbrief*, he did so in his own hand, in pencil *on the back of a sheet of that translation*. In addition some 14 aphorisms from "Aus Makariens Archiv" are translations of Hippocratic originals (VIII, 460-462, 5-16). In the *Wanderjahre* when Wilhelm visited Nachodine-Susanne and her fiancé in the mountains, he acted as a physician in the sense that we have been exploring. He left with them a sheet of paper to which Susanne afterwards referred (VIII, 426) and which consists of aphorisms similar to those in his own *Lehrbrief*.

A consideration of the individual physicians in the *Lehrjahre*[16] involves problems of identity. Goethe did not dignify a single one with a name; we shall resort to letter designations. The first to be mentioned (Physician *A*) appears in the *Bekenntnisse einer schönen Seele* (VII 375). The next, *B*, is the family physician of the noble family into which her sister later married, and from which the brothers and sisters of the novel (Lothario, Friedrich, Natalie, *Gräfin*) descended. She called him "...Arzt und Naturforscher, und [er] schien mehr zu den Penaten als zu den Bewohnern des Hauses zu gehören." (VII, 409) It was he who taught her the dangers of despising the body (VII, 415), and whose precept for health was: "Tätig zu sein... ist des Menschen erste Bestimmung, und alle Zwischenzeiten, in denen er auszuruhen genötigt ist, sollte er anwenden, eine deutliche Erkenntnis der äußerlichen Dinge zu erlangen, die ihm in der Folge abermals seine Tätigkeit erleichtert." (VII, 415 f.) This is almost identical with the first half of Montan's "... das Tun am Denken, das Denken am Tun zu prüfen...." (VIII, 263) The way in which this physician skillfully diverted her attention from her own introspective preoccupations to the world outside herself, and the healing effects of this shift, is reminiscent of Goethe's plan in the Plessing episode; "... da er wußte, daß... ich wirklich durch anhaltende eigene und fremde Leiden ein halber Arzt geworden war, so leitete er meine Aufmerksamkeit von der Kenntnis des menschlichen Körpers und der Spezereien auf die übrigen nachbarlichen Gegenstände der Schöpfung und führte mich wie im Paradiese umher, und nur zuletzt, wenn ich mein Gleichnis fortsetzen darf, ließ er mich den in der Abendkühle wandelnden Schöpfer aus der Entfernung ahnen." (VII, 416) She referred to this physician as "mein guter Arzt," and it was he who drew her attention to the essential character of the family in the portraits of the ancestors (VII, 417). Finally he initiated her into the educational purposes of the Abbé, in whose view introspection was dangerous for children (VII, 419).

Next chronologically is the physician who attended Wilhelm after the attack in the woods. Apparently he is not the same as the previous, and is designated Physician C. He is referred to only as *Wundarzt* and *Chirurgus:* "Seine Manieren waren mehr rauh als einnehmend, doch seine Hand leicht und seine Hülfe willkommen," (VII, 227) and so he cannot be Physician B, who is unqualifiedly skilled, particularly in psychological subtleties. There are three factors, however, that make it easy to confuse C and B. Both were associated with the noble family. C was travelling with them when called upon to assist Wilhelm. Later in the *Wanderjahre* Wilhelm in a letter to Natalie recalled the scene in the woods and referred to "... euer tüchtiger Wundarzt...." (VIII, 280) Secondly, the physician of the woods was small in stature ("untersetzt"), as was Physician B (VII, 436, 438, 520), and, thirdly, as will become evident, he was probably past middle age.

And yet Physician B and Physician C cannot be the same man, for then Wilhelm would later have failed to recognize the man who had treated him after the bandit attack. Thus, the noble family must have maintained a medical staff of two, *der kleine, alte Medikus* (B) and a chirurgeon (C) who was also small in stature, who was at least old enough to have a chirurgeon son, old enough to discontinue practice and give his instruments to his son, and who appeared only once in the two novels, in the scene after the bandit attack in the woods.[17]

The next is Physician D, who treated Wilhelm at the village inn: "...ein unwissender, aber nicht ungeschickter Mensch..." (VII, 235) for whose care of Wilhelm the family of the Amazon had paid in advance. Then finally one meets Physician E, the young chirurgeon, the son of Physician C.[18]

In any case, physician B is the most important medical figure in the *Lehrjahre*. His grasp of the family concept as he talked with *die schöne Seele* before the portraits of the family was noted (VII, 417). He also felt responsible for larger metamorphoses of the family, more as a scientist than as a strictly medical practitioner: "... so hatte er in Zeit von zwanzig Jahren sehr viel im stillen zur Kultur mancher Zweige der Landwirtschaft beigetragen und alles, was dem Felde, Tieren und Menschen ersprießlich ist, in Bewegung gebracht und so die wahrste Aufklärung befördert." (VII, 348) It was he who revealed the fate of the count and countess (VII, 349).

There are important evidences of his psychological skill: it was he who visited Aurelia in disguise (cf. Goethe's visit to Plessing), who recognized the serious damage of passion. He collaborated with the rural clergyman in curing the *Harfner* (VII, 436 f.); it was he who recognized the undesirability of Lydie's continued presence if Lothario's wound was to heal properly (VII, 438); it was he who worked with Mignon (VII, 520 f.), who deduced the main outlines of her history, and who recognized the impossibility of doing more than alleviating her suffering. It was he who, with the young chirurgeon, embalmed Mignon's body (VII, 545). He re-introduced the "cured" *Harfner* into society (VII, 595), explained his past and the precarious state of his cure. And finally it was he who explained the details of the latter's catastropic end and the seemingly miraculous salvation of Felix (VII, 603 f.).

Notable here is the high regard in which physicians are held; *die schöne Seele* even used the term as a synonym for the divinity: "... der große Arzt...." (VII, 393) In a similar light it will be recalled that in the circle of the uncle one of the almost religious duties of Sunday was to obtain help, if needed, from the physician. *Die schöne Seele* classed physician B in a supernaturally protective role with the "penates" (VII, 409) of the household, and Montan, whose words have deep importance for the novel, referring to healing as "... das göttlichste aller Geschäfte..." (VIII, 282) A comparison between the physician and the priest is appropriate, as is made clear by, among other things, the references to confession and absolution. More important even is the close connection one sees between the physician and the family. All of the important doctors of the *Lehrjahre* have such a close family connection; Physicians *A, B, C,* and *E.* Their function might be described in general terms as to repair damage, both physical and emotional, to the individual. Thus they remove the factor that isolates him and make the individual fit to return to the family or to society. To this extent then these physicians anticipate the role in life that Wilhelm will come to recognize in the *Wanderjahre* is to be his also (VIII, 119).

Although the similarities between the role of the physician in the *Lehrjahre* and the *Wanderjahre* are more important than the differences, the latter are nonetheless meaningful. In the *Lehrjahre* Goethe retained the old distinction between the *Chirurgus* and the *Medikus* and all the more important ones were of the latter type. In the *Wanderjahre*, although the two different terms are retained (VIII, 326, for example), all those described are first of all *Wundärzte.* These chirurgeons, due to study, experience, or talent, have then gone on to larger fields of medical responsibility. Gilg recognized this: "Es gilt für Wilhelm als Wundarzt die 'Seelenleiden' durch 'entschlossene Tätigkeit' zu heilen, auszugleichen, und ins Ganze einzufügen...."[19]

All doctors should begin with the skills of the wound surgeon: "Jeder Arzt, er mag mit Heilmitteln [Medikus] oder mit der Hand [Chirurgus] zu Werke gehen, ist nichts ohne die genauste Kenntnis der äußern und innern Glieder des Menschen." (VIII, 331) Goethe later expressed the same idea differently: "... was jetzo Kunst [des Medikus] ist, muß Handwerk [des Chirurgus] werden." (VIII, 332) Fortunately, it is possible to corroborate the fact that this is what Goethe really meant from a variant manuscript that twice notes the difference between the types of physician.[20]

A second distinction between the two parts of the novel is that, although the activity of the physician in the *Lehrjahre* tends to strengthen the family

19

by curing and restoring to it various of its members, nowhere is the physician's function described as aiding the founding of a family in promoting the union of loving hearts—while three important instances of this occur in the *Wanderjahre*. And finally Wilhelm's later professional ambitions in the medical field are hardly hinted at in the *Lehrjahre*.

Since the beginning of the novel it had been Wilhelm's fate to act as catalyst or magnet in the formation of families (See above, pp. 11 f.). Then it was noted how he became aware in the vicinity of Makarie that his fate involved the creating and fostering of families. It is appropriate that this family service be in the medical field for two powerful models were exerting their influence on Wilhelm. The first is referred to in connection with the story of the drowned fisherman's boys. Here the reader learns that Wilhelm's father had exerted his influence in his own time in a similar way, and as the Abbé had said: "... niemand glaube die ersten Eindrücke der Jugend überwinden zu können." (VII, 121) His father's activities had concerned medical matters: "Die großen Hindernisse, welche der Einimpfung der Blattern anfangs entgegenstanden, zu beseitigen, war er mit verständigen Ärzten und Polizeiverwaltern bemüht." (VIII, 278) This impression of parental attitudes then would have been strongly reinforced by the childhood memory that involved him directly, the tragic loss of the five boys by drowning, a loss that, as he came to believe later, could have been averted if proper medical steps had been taken in time.

Wilhelm was aware of the importance of the experience, and Goethe gave the account careful literary form. Wilhelm interrupted the tale to reflect on how, "... durch einen Umweg," influences from various sources combine to determine action. He asked Natalie: "... sollte es dem Verständigen, dem Vernünftigen nicht zustehen, auf eine seltsam scheinende Weise ringsumher nach vielen Punkten hinzuwirken, damit man sie in *einem* Brennpunkte zuletzt abgespielt und zusammengefaßt erkenne, einsehen lerne, wie die verschiedensten Einwirkungen den Menschen umringend zu einem Entschluß treiben, den er auf keine andere Weise, weder aus innerm Trieb noch äußerm Anlaß, hätte ergreifen können?" (VIII, 279 f.)

The second powerful influence on Wilhelm was the example of Physician B, for the activity of the latter had been exactly what Wilhelm in Makarie's vicinity had recognized as his task in life. And that these two examples were indeed fermenting within Wilhelm at this time is shown as Wilhelm at the beginning of the *Wanderjahre* pulled out the instrument case: "Unser Freund leugnete nicht, daß er es als eine Art von Fetisch bei sich trage, in dem Aberglauben, sein Schicksal hange gewissermaßen von dessen Besitz ab." (VIII, 40) In a later letter to Natalie Wilhelm gave a partial explanation for having the instrument case: "Es war Zeuge des Augenblicks, wo mein Glück begann, zu dem ich erst durch großen Umweg gelangen sollte." (VIII, 280) He meant primarily his love for Natalie, although the moment also played a decisive role in his choice of a profession. Jarno approved: "... aber schöner wäre es, wenn du dich durch jene Werkzeuge hättest anreizen lassen, auch ihren Gebrauch zu verstehen und dasjenige zu leisten, was sie stumm von dir fordern." (VIII, 281) Then Wilhelm told Jarno the tale of the drowned boys: "... dies [ist mir] hundertmal eingefallen... *es regte sich in mir eine innere Stimme, die mich meinen eigentlichen Beruf hieran erkennen ließ.*" (VIII, 281, italics added) Shortly after he experienced the insight at Makarie's he agreed to help Lenardo find his former love and visit her (VIII, 134). Here he is seeking out "Was edle Seelen auseinanderhält" and is attempting "Hindernisse weg[zu]-räumen." In other words, he is acting as a physician or physician's helper, in a way he has been observed to do earlier in the *Lehrjahre*, and this without medical training. Still later he assumed the authority to aid Lenardo as advisor in matters of the heart (VIII, 143), and finally, he claimed expert status: "... wer jedoch weiß, unter welchen seltsamen Formen die Neigung sich bei uns einschleicht, dem muß es bange werden, wenn er voraussieht, ein Freund könne dasjenige wünschen, was ihm in seinen Zuständen, seinen Verhältnissen notwendig Unglück und Verwirrung bringen müßte." (VIII, 144) Ironic here is of course that Wilhelm was wrong; Lenardo and Nacho-dine-Susanne presumably do later make a successful couple. Wilhelm then compounded the error by encouraging Susanne to marry her *Bräutigam* rather than Lenardo (VIII, 423), to the latter's annoyance (VIII, 425). But it was Wilhelm's fate to learn through error; that was the meaning of his theat-rical detour, and of his engagement to Therese.

The most important element of the description of Wilhelm's professional training in anatomy (VIII, 322-334) is the indication that he was being trained solely as a chirurgeon: nothing explicit is said about training for larger medical responsibilities. However, the relationship between handicraft and art (chirurgeon *and* physician) is illuminated: "... wie Kunst und Technik sich immer gleichsam die Waage halten und so nah verwandt immer eine zu der anderen sich hinneigt, so daß die Kunst nicht sinken kann, ohne in löbliches Handwerk überzugehen, das Handwerk sich nicht steigern, ohne kunstreich zu werden." (VIII, 329 f.)

Wilhelm is preparing himself to go to the new world as a physician. As he wrote to Natalie: "... bei dem großen Unternehmen, dem ihr entgegen-geht, werde ich als ein nützliches, als ein nötiges Glied der Gesellschaft erscheinen und euren Wegen, mit einer gewissen Sicherheit, mich an-schließen...." (VIII, 282 f.) When then in the final scene, Felix incurred dangerous injury, from which he is saved by his chirurgeon father, Wilhelm removed one of the "hindrances" that separated noble hearts and in this way helped to establish a potential family (Felix-Hersilie) and at the same time strengthen the larger metamorphosis thereof by adding a useful new unit to the larger group.

Thus two significant and closely related themes, the wound and the phy-sician, play key roles in both *Lehrjahre* and *Wanderjahre*, which is important evidence that the *Meister* novels, despite unevenness and loose ends, are in a sense an entity. In a letter to Schiller of 12 July, 1796, Goethe spoke of connections between the *Lehrjahre* and a later continuation (name at that time unspecified): "... man [muß] vorwärts *deuten*..., aber es müssen Verzahnungen stehen bleiben, die, so gut wie der Plan selbst, auf seine weitere Fortsetzung deuten."[21] The themes of the wound and the physician were two such *Verzahnungen*. This is all the more impressive in view of the far-reaching changes that the poet made between the 1821 version of the *Wanderjahre* and that of 1829. Included in the final form was much more about wounds (19 references to 11) and vital new material about the physician (30 references to 2), and particularly about the transforming concept of Wilhelm's medical profession. This means that Goethe, dissatisfied with the form of 1821, returned to *Lehrjahre* and further developed two of its centrally important themes in the second version of *Wanderjahre*. And yet the unity of the two works even in this restricted sense is of course far from seamless, for it is only in the *Wanderjahre* of 1829 that Wilhelm's role as physician, as the leader of individuals in service to larger social units (families and metamorphoses thereof) is clearly discernible.

NOTES

[1] Commentators disagree on whether the novel should be considered an essential unity. The negative view can be represented by Emil Staiger, *Goethe* (Zurich, 1952), III, p. 128. The positive approach is well stated by Erich Trunz in his *Hamburger Ausgabe* of *Goethes Werke* (Hamburg, 1952-60), VIII, pp. 598-602. There are a few studies that deal with a unifying theme, for instance, Christoph Schweitzer, "Wilhelm Meister und das Bild vom kranken Königssohn," *PMLA*, LXXII (1957), 419-432.

[2] See below, pp. 19-20.

[3] Exception: the count's wounded son in "Die Gefährliche Wette."

[4] Erich Trunz, "Seelische Kultur, eine Betrachtung über Freundschaft, Liebe und Familiengefühl in Schriften der Goethezeit," *Deutsche Vierteljahrsschrift*, XXIV (1950), 214-241, 226.

[5] Anna Hellersberg-Wendriner: "Soziologischer Wandel im Weltbild Goethes," *PMLA*, LVI (1941), 463.

[6] Hereafter references to *Lehrjahre* and *Wanderjahre* (*Hamburger Ausgabe*, VII and VIII) will be given in the text by volume and page. *Hamburger Ausgabe* will be subsequently referred to as H.A., *Weimarer Ausgabe* as W.A.

[7] H.A. I, 374.

[8] Cf. Ernst Friedrich von Monroy, "Zur Form der Novelle in 'Wilhelm Meisters Wanderjahre,'" *Germanisch-Romanische Monatsschrift*, XXXI (1943), 1-19, especially 13 f.

[9] Arthur Henkel, *Entsagung. Eine Studie zu Goethes Altersroman* (Tübingen, 1954), p. 49.

[10] Wounds. *Lehrjahre*-physical: 219, 224, 227, 234, 235, 236, 281, 327, 348-9, 367, 427, 602-4. Psychological: 67f., 143, 196, 226, 256, 230, 352, 412, 513-14, 527. *Wanderjahre*-physical: 25, 39, 51, 72, 155, 259, 383, 403, 459. Psychological: 51, 61, 114, 113, 203, 214, 233, 233, 241.

[11] André Gilg, *Wilhelm Meisters Wanderjahre und ihre Symbole* (Zürich, 1954), p. 89.

[12] Gilg, *op. cit.*, p. 185.

[13] Some of the more obvious examples of Goethe's psychological experiences; 1) the complex and tormenting relationship to his sister Cornelia, 2) the circumstances that attended his return from Leipzig, 3) the way in which he rid himself of his own problems by writing them out, as for instance in *Werther*, 4) the crucially important relationship to Frau von Stein.

That she in her turn acted as "moralischer Leibarzt" for Goethe is hinted at in his letter to Knebel of 3 February, 1782. This deals with other psychological relationships, and mentions Frau von Stein in these terms: "Die Stein hält mich wie ein Korckwamms über dem Wasser, dass ich mich auch mit Willen nicht ersäufen könnte." (Letter of 3 February, 1782, *Weimarer Ausgabe* [W.A.] IV, vol. 5, p. 257).

5) Plessing appealed to Goethe as a psychological advisor, and he considered acting as one, declining finally only at the last moment. The affair is described in *Campagne in Frankreich* (H.A. X, 325 f.) which includes the revealing comment "... die herrische Gewohnheit, jungen Männern meines Alters in Herzens- und Geistesnöten beizustehen, ließ mich sein doch nicht ganz vergessen."

6) In 1781 Goethe became involved with assisting the Einsiedel family with one of its older men who was insane. (Letter of 4 November, 1781, W.A. IV, vol. 5, p. 209 f.). The letter to Knebel already mentioned is interesting also from two other points of view: "Ich unterhalte dich von nichts als Lust. Inwendig siehts viel anders aus, welches niemand besser als wir andern Leib und Hofmedizi wissen können." He considered Knebel as a sort of psychological colleague: "Die Werthern gewinnt nichts durch deine Abwesenheit. Ihre Natur die Du ausgetrieben oder in die Enge getrieben hattest, kehrt in ihre alten Rechte zurück."

7) Concerning the *Singspiel Lila* Goethe wrote in 1816: "Das Sujet ist eigentlich eine psychische Cur, wo man den Wahnsinn eintreten läßt um den Wahnsinn zu heilen." (To *Graf* Brühl, 1 October, 1818, W.A. IV, vol. 29, p. 299).

8) Finally in 1785 Goethe wrote Frau von Stein about another instance in which he had taken effect as "moralischer Leibarzt": "Gestern Abend habe ich ein recht Psychologisches Kunststück gemacht. Die Herder war immer auf das hypochondrischte gespannt über alles was ihr in Carlsbad unangenehmes begegnet war. Besonders von ihrer Hausgenossin. Ich lies mir alles erzählen und beichten, fremde Unarten und eigne Fehler, mit den kleinsten Umständen und Folgen und zuletzt *absolvirte* ich sie und machte ihr scherzhafft unter dieser Formel begreifflich, daß diese Dinge nun abgethan und in die Tiefe des Meeres geworfen seyen. Sie ward selbst lustig drüber und ist würcklich kurirt. Umständlicher erzähl ich dirs und es wird dich noch mehr ergötzen." (W.A. IV, vol. 7, p. 87)

14 Not only poetic art, graphic art also can have a curative effect in such cases, see Hilarie's development at Lago Maggiore (238). In this connection cf. Arthur Henkel, *Entsagung*, pp. 169 and 122.

15 Cf. Karl Deichgräber, "Goethe und Hippocrates," *Sudhoffs Archiv*, XXXI (1937), 39–55.

16 These are more important than those of the *Wanderjahre*, as it is they who influenced Wilhelm's medical ambitions.

17 There is another possible explanation for this puzzling lack of clarity. In reply to Schiller's suggestion that there be more logical clarity in the novel, Goethe replied: "Es ist keine Frage, daß die scheinbaren, von mir ausgesprochenen Resultate viel beschränkter sind als der Inhalt des Werks, und ich komme mir vor wie einer, der, nachdem er viele und große Zahlen über einander gestellt, endlich muthwillig selbst Additionsfehler machte, um die letzte Summe aus Gott weiß was für einer Grille zu verringern." This might be one of Goethe's "mutwillige Additionsfehler" (9 July, 1796, W.A. IV, vol. 11, p. 123). In 1808 Goethe wrote Reinhard (about the *Zueignung* to *Faust*) "... ich läugne nicht, daß ... es mir von jeher Spaß gemacht hat, Versteckens zu spielen." (W.A. IV, vol. 20, p. 96)

18 For an interesting interpretation of this physician's symbolic meaning cf. Eva Alexander Meyer, *Goethes Wilhelm Meister* (München, 1947), p. 85.

19 Gilg, *op. cit.*, p. 123.

20 W.A. I, vol. 25, pt. 2, p. 138.

21 W.A. IV, vol. 11, p. 125.

23

Fear and Farce in Fehrbellin

JOHN T. KRUMPELMANN

The purpose of tragedy is to excite pity and fear. Literally it is a "goat-song," i.e., a goat is the sacrificial victim. But, if the protagonist refuses to be "the goat" (the victim) and becomes the hero, the drama might be called a "Schauspiel," as Kleist sagely entitled his *Prinz Friedrich von Homburg*. When Kleist thus named his drama, he must have intentionally selected this designation suspecting that succeeding generations would strive to place it in a more definite category. In less than a generation some distinguished authors and critics, such as Bernhard Abeken (1823), Friedrich Hebbel (1833, 1850) and Felix Bamberg (1848),[1] were calling the drama a "Tragödie." Later, especially after 1870, the appellation "Lustspiel"[2] became increasingly more common than "Tragödie," until finally Arnold Zweig categorically stated:

> Denn dieses Drama ist wie der "Kaufmann von Venedig" und "Maß für Maß" der höchste Typus der Komödie: das Leben des Menschen, voll überschaut, als Gegenstand der Rührung und des Lächelns eines Gottes, der jene Zwitter aus Geist und Leben nicht anders schaffen konnte... Es gibt als Kunstgattung im strengsten Verstande kein "Schauspiel"; was sich so nennt ist entweder ein Trauer- oder Lustspiel, dessen Dichter sich aus Wesensgründen zu voller Entschiedenheit der Weltbetrachtung nicht überzeugen konnte — eine typisch deutsche Künstlerqual; hier ist eine Shakespearische Komödie jenes letzten höchsten Typs, der durch keine menschliche Schau übertroffen werden kann.[3]

In this drama the author runs the entire gamut of human emotions, and emotes so drastically and so radically as to challenge the reader's reactions. The *fear of death* displayed by the youthful hero when he beholds the open grave intended to receive him on the morrow must excite pity on the part of his partisans and did evoke contempt and resentment on the part of the military nobility. Even in the twentieth century no less an admirer of Kleist and his master-drama than the German *Kaiser Wilhelm II.* called this work "ein Lieblingsstück von mir," to which one of his "Generaladjutanten" added: "Wenn nur die fatale Feigheitsszene nicht wäre."[4] Of course Heinrich Heine had, in condemning similar disparagements almost a century earlier, anticipated this deprecation, when he wrote:

> Mögen berlinische Gardeleutnants immerhin spötteln und es Feigheit nennen, daß der Prinz von Homburg zurückschaudert, wenn er sein offenes Grab erblickt — Heinrich Kleist hatte dennoch ebensoviel Courage wie seine hochbrüstigen, wohlgeschnürten Kollegen, und er hat es leider bewiesen.[5]

Inasmuch as so much attention has been given to the so-called "Todesfurchtszene" which, in the eyes of the military and the nobility, rendered Kleist's composition *non grata* in the controlling circles, the "Schauspiel" could not be accepted as a "comedy." In fact, it could not be accepted at all. Heinrich Heine was among the *avant-garde* when he denounced the condemnation of Kleist:

> Es ist jetzt bestimmt, daß das Kleistische Schauspiel: "Der Prinz von Homburg, oder die Schlacht bei Fehrbellin" nicht auf unserer Bühne erscheinen wird, und zwar, wie ich höre, weil eine edle Dame glaubt, daß ihr Ahnherr in einer unedeln Gestalt darin erscheine... Was mich betrifft... [hat] es mehr Wert, als all' jene Farcen und Spektakelstücke und Houwaldsche Rühreier, die man uns täglich auftischt.[6]

When the drama was first staged, by Schreyvogel in Vienna on October 3, 1821, this "gemilderte"[7] version bore the title "Die Schlacht von Fehrbellin," "da Offiziere der österreichischen Armee Prinzen von Homburg waren, und außerdem ein souveräner Fürst den Titel führte."[8] This alternate title was evidently an attempt to divert the spotlight from the compromised hero and to identify the impersonal *locus*, Fehrbellin, with the "Todesfurcht" episode. But even this version was soon interdicted by Archduke Karl and his censors, because "es auf die Armee demoralisierend wirken müsse, wenn ein Offizier so feig um sein Leben bittet."[9]

On July 25, 1828 the drama experienced its first performance in a watered-down version in Berlin. After the third performance the king decreed that the "gestern aufgeführte Stück niemals wieder gegeben werden soll."[10]

Tieck attempted to justify the Prince's paroxysm of fear by the suddenness of his plunge from fame and fortune.[11] He finds the reaction "natürlich," which evokes from Grillparzer: "Freilich! eine Natürlichkeit, aber die man anspeien muß."[12] But in Kleist there was a strong measure of naturalness and of *Errare est humanum*.

Kühn suggests that already in the Dresden text the Ludwig Tieck version of the "Todesfurchtszene" (III, 909-1053) was probably modified to furnish the version in the prompter's book of the *Münchner Hoftheaterbibliothek* used on that stage since 1857.[13] These emendations are intended to render the "Todesfurchtszene" less craven. Here it is not "Tod" but "Hinrichtung" (execution) that the Prince dreads, public ignominy, infamy. Thus would the apologists defend Kleist against the reproaches brought against his *Prinz von Homburg*. But Kleist had absorbed much from Shakespeare whose lines echo forth from most of his own dramas.[14] Every American student is taught that Shakespeare "holds the mirror up to nature";[15] young Goethe exclaimed: "Natur, Natur! nichts so Natur als Schäckespears Menschen";[16] and our Latin proverb teaches *Errare est humanum*. But when Grillparzer, romanticist and recluse, condemns Kleist's "Natürlichkeit" as something that "man anspeien muss,"[17] he pleads guilty to his inability to appreciate the *earthy* origin of the human species. Kleist was not only artistic; he was also artful. He was not only a Kantian, a metaphysician, but a physicist. He was devious enough to demonstrate that, even if an angel with a fiery sword prevented reentry to the Garden of Eden, access could be gained *via* a back portal.[18] Kleist was always a dualist.

He was well aware of the duality of all human creatures. God made man of dust and breathed into him an immortal soul. Therefore, man is a "Mittelding zwischen Gott und Kot." As a human being Kleist fears death, but later, as an immortal soul, and, as a resolved suicidist, he welcomes death and the hereafter with almost ecstatic happiness.[19] Even so, Homburg feared abject death demanded by an official (Electoral) edict, but is willing to accept death, if the decision is left up to him. So also his creator (Kleist) who, as a Prussian military officer, had no admiration for military discipline! To Christian Ernst Martini Kleist wrote:

> der Soldatenstand, dem ich nie vom Herzen zugethan gewesen bin, weil er etwas durchaus Ungleichartiges mit meinem ganzen Wesen in sich trägt... daß es mir nach und nach lästig wurde... Die größten Wunder militärischer Disciplin... wurden der Gegenstand meiner herzlichsten Verachtung; die Officiere hielt ich für so viele Exerciermeister, die Soldaten für so viele Sclaven, ... Ich war oft gezwungen zu strafen, wo ich gern verziehen hätte, oder verzieh, wo ich hätte strafen sollen, ... immer zweifelhaft war, ob ich als Mensch oder als Officier handeln mußte; denn die Pflichten beider zu vereinigen halte ich bei dem jetzigen Zustande der Armeen für unmöglich.[20]

Homburg, like Kleist, refused to remain a slave to the military dictates of the Elector, i.e., of the flesh, but as soon as the Elector, by his willingness to remit the death-sentence (Hinrichtung), makes him a free agent, the Prince voluntarily accepts death.[21] When we "Mitteldinge" transmute ourselves from the physical (dust) into the aesthetic or metaphysical state (spirit), "das wirkliche Leiden in eine erhabene Rührung auflösen"[22] in the regions of "reinen Formen,"[23] we flee the exactions of the human physical fetters.[24] To paraphrase Schiller's "Das Ideal und das Leben" (142 ff.):

Bis der Prinz, des Kriegerischen entkleidet,
Ruhig von dem Heere sich scheidet
Und sein "Gleichviel"[25] sich erfüllt,

he cannot enter the kingdom of Heaven. Another vista discloses a new approach. Kleist's creatures must reveal the machinations of their master. The Prince, representing his maker, must go *per aspera ad astra* (757). When Homburg provokes a quarrel with the Elector and is crossed by his "Vetter," the conflict assumes the semblance of a family feud. Youth must assert itself and conquer at any price or by any device.[26] Early in the play it becomes obvious that Homburg will be the victor, not the victim. Arthur, at first defiant: "Ich, ein Gefangener?" (767), is thrown off his balance ("verrückt"; 772), and, becoming officious, calls "Vetter Friedrich" "den Brutus" (777). He finally pities his errant kinsman (788) and expresses his equanimity by a triple "Gleichviel" (796, 797, 797). When he loses the next round with the actual signing of the Todesurteil, he flares up again, denouncing the action of the Elector as worse than the conduct of the "Dey von Algier," "Sardanapel" and the "Altrömische Tyrannenrei[c]he" (897-907). He concludes: "O Himmel! Meine Hoffnung!" (910). The appeal to "die Fürstin Tante," suggested by Hohenzollern, "klug angewandt" (935), fails to bring "Rettung"; however, even such an attempt to hide behind the skirts of a woman, is *a priori* "feig." Through apparent, or feigned, "Todesfurcht," or "Feigheit," the Prince does win his freedom and is victor when an insurrection of the Elector's family, military and domestic, and of all the friends of the Prince, enables the latter to accept death with equanimity and impunity at a juncture when he and the Court and the theater-audience are confident that the repudiated Elector has been outmanoeuvered by the wily dissembler,[27] who, through his capricious tantrums and sagacious tactics has achieved, instead of an ignominious execution by a firing squad, a festal garden-party with "Schloßbeleuchtung, Fackelzug, Kranz mit Kette," and he, to be his own original self, "fällt in Ohnmacht."

Our "Schauspiel" has become, by almost unanimous agreement, a "Lustspiel" which contains many farcical elements introduced intentionally by the author to counteract the tragical implications of the drama which caused many early literary critics to designate it as a tragedy and some to see in it suggestions of a sadistic nature.[28]

So, after a century of indecisiveness, the martial comedy of the *Kurfürst* and the *Prinz* joined the *Dorfkomödie* of *Dorfrichter* Adam and *Frau* Marthe, and the Divine comedy of Jupiter, Amphitryon and Sosias to complete Kleist's trilogy of eminent German comedies. In the process Kleist's tragically inclined "Schauspiel" has not been changed in form or in text. In fact the "watered" and "gemilderte" versions, produced to placate the hostile elements of society, have yielded to the pristine form. With the broadening of the point of view, both academically and geographically, of the general public, of the audience and of the readers, and with the aversion from feudal fealty to ruler, caste and social status, art, not political consideration, has decreed this great drama to be a comedy in keeping with the philosophy enunciated in the lines of Schnitzler's *Paracelsus:*

> Es war ein Spiel! Was sollt' es anders sein?
> Was ist nicht Spiel, das wir auf Erden treiben,
> Und scheint es noch so groß und tief zu sein![29]

As early as 1828 Willibald Alexis declared: "Jedes Kind weiß voraus, daß der Kurfürst den siegenden Prinzen nicht wird erschießen lassen."[30] Out of the mouths of babes and sucklings you shall hear the truth! But, since we are not so clairvoyant as "jedes Kind," the author has interlarded his tragic (?) scenes with comic, yea, even with farcical elements. The comic relief is obviously introduced to prevent the audience from becoming too concerned about the apparent tragic situation. The "way-out" comedy-elements (farce) serve to assure that, when the "Trommeln des Todtenmarsches" ceases, the outcome will be a "Gaudi," or a garden-party, not with "moonlight and roses," but with "Fackelzug," "Schloßbeleuchtung," "Kanonenschüsse," "Marsch," "Nachtviole" (1840), "Levkoyn" and "Nelken" (1841), and a "Lorbeerkranz, um welchen die goldene Kette geschlungen ist." (1845+) And, quite naturally, "der Prinz fällt in Ohnmacht." (1850+) "Ein Traum, was sonst?" (1857)[31] Verily, a "Sommernachtstraum," for does this post-Battle-of-Fehrbellin scene not occur, almost literally on Saint John's Day (June 24th)? Of course the play might as appropriately be called "A Comedy of Errors,"[32] or when the Elector reportedly betroths Natalie to the Swede, "Love's Labor Lost." Kleist, a student of Shakespeare, must have been aware of all such implications and obviously desired to keep his audience constantly conscious of the lack of seriousness of mundane existence.

Although Kleist nowhere, even facetiously, has referred to this "Schauspiel" as a comedy, as he did when he termed his "Trauerspiel" *Penthesilea* a "Hundekomödie,"[33] he was adroit enough to suggest, by innuendo, and/or by insinuation, that the Prince's situation was not so tragic as surface phenomena might seem to indicate. Both martial protagonists are *Friedrichs,* but, as most of the leaders who bear that name, they are (*lucus a non lucendo*) not men of peace. The Prince is endowed with an additional cognomen, Arthur, not to distinguish him from his antagonist, the Elector, but to mark him as of another "Schrot und Korn" from his noble (?) "Vetter." Samuel explains cryptically: "Er [der Name] deutet die gespaltene Persönlichkeit Homburgs an."[34] Arthur is not a common appellation in German political or literary annals. It may be regarded as something apart, and as unpopular, just as such male monickers as "Archibald," "Cecil," "Percival," names ordinarily discarded in America as being somewhat "sissified." There is evidence that in French and German circles of Kleist's age there was some disdain for the name.[35] All this seems to suggest that this hero, a "Nacht-wandler" who, at critical moments, falls into a swoon, who loves "Nacht-violen" ("Levkoyn") and who wishes to preserve "die Nelken... zu Hause im Wasser" (1845), shows symptoms of being effeminate and might be suspected of being a "pansy," which Webster defines as a "viola tricolor" and whose tertiary definition in the *Random House Dictionary* is: "Slang: a male homosexual, an effeminate man."

In the flower-dialogue the Prince addresses Stranz as "Lieber" (1844), a term of address otherwise reserved for Hohenzollern,[36] who seems to be Arthur's bosom friend, and who in the opening scene of the drama, mimics the effeminate antics of the Prince primping before the mirror (59-63):

> Schade, ewig Schade,
> Daß hier kein Spiegel in der Nähe ist!
> Er würd' ihm eitel, wie ein Mädchen nahn,
> Und sich den Kranz bald so, bald wieder so,
> Wie eine florne Haube aufprobieren.

These lines and the accompanying pantomime would get, not a smile, but a roar, perhaps a wolf call, out of a present-day audience and justify the blush-ing of the wreath-winding Prince (64+).

Perhaps the most ludicrous episode is the Briefing Scene (Paroleszene, I, v), which Samuel finds to be permeated with "oft ausgesprochener Komik."[37] E. L. Stahl designates "this gathering... at two o'clock in the morning," at which "the Elector's wife and Natalie are present" as "a strange circum-stance."[38] But stranger still is the fact that, while the *Feldmarschall* dictates the plan of battle to the officers, the bevy of ladies in attendance at the briefing are served "Frühstück," thus distracting the attention of the officers who should be concentrating their attention on the orders of their superiors. Instead the Prince "fixiert die Damen." (247+) Just as the Marshal repeatedly calls the "Prinz von Homburg" to receive his specific orders, the "Heyduck" intrudes to announce that the coach has arrived, and the ladies arise to take leave (266-270). A second interruption! The absence of Kottwitz causes a third (275 f.), giving the Prinz another opportunity to direct his eyes "nach den Damen." (280+) Only now does Natalie discover that she has lost one glove, which the Prince, an honorable (?) officer, had "erhascht" (70+) earlier in the night and now furtively lets fall on the stage where the Elector must be the first to espy it.

When the *Feldmarschall* mentions for the first time "die Fanfare blasen lassen" (313), the Electress, departing with her ladies and other attendants, addresses the warriors, serenely and naively:

"Auf Wiedersehen, ihr Herrn! laßt uns nicht stören." (314) The Elec-tor finds the glove, and the Prince echoes the Field Marshal:

"Dann wird er die Fanfare blasen lassen!" (322) which phrase is bantered about six more times in the next few lines. With the interruptions and the "Fanfare blasen" (eight times in forty lines) and the traumatic disturbances due to the "Rape of the Glove," how could the self-willed Arthur be other than insubordinate on the battlefield?

At the close of the scene the Elector, warning the Prince that he, a two-times loser, should not on the morrow, make "aller schlechten Dinge drei," orders his own "Schimmel" so that he may, fool-hardily, make himself a target for the enemy in the coming battle, thereby causing the rumor of his death on the battlefield to be brought back to his survivors. His heir-apparent is the successful Prince, who, flushed with victory, becomes a *miles gloriosus*, a matinee-idol, in a melodrama (566-763).[39] Thus do both the Elector, who during the briefing conducted himself like a nursemaid or an old brood hen, and the impetuous Prince cause their military establishment to appear both ridiculous and undisciplined.

Some critics object to the inordinate length of time which the Elector allows the death sentence to hang over the condemned. Howard opines: "If... we feel that the shadow of death hangs too long over the hero to permit the dispassionate detachment which belongs to true comedy, we may content ourselves... with the author's neutral designation *Schauspiel*."[40] Of course we could consider it farcical! Samuel feels: "Der Kurfürst spielt die 'Komödie' der letzten zwei Auftritte absolut konsequent—die Offiziere wissen, daß es 'Komödie' ist, Homburg dagegen nicht—."[41] Silz had previously formulated: "He thinks he is about to be executed, we know he is not."[42] Elsewhere the same critic remarks: "It is... idle to question whether it was ever the Elector's intention to execute the Prince. It seems to me one cannot doubt the intention without making a mere comedian of this noble figure, and that has in fact been done."[43] Whatever the Elector's original intention, it seems certain that his intention, or pretense, was dissipated after the severe and convincing indictments launched against him in the fifth scene of the last act by Kottwitz (1570-1608) and Hohenzollern (1633-1722).[44]

Since the tendency throughout the years has been more and more to regard *Prinz Friedrich von Homburg* as a comedy, and, since its protagonist, the Prince, is proclaimed and exalted as "Sieger in der Schlacht bei Fehrbellin" (1855) and his antagonist, the Elector, stands silently by, having uttered not a word during the last two scenes (1829) after he had been dressed down by Kottwitz and Hohenzollern, we must look to him for the comedy. Not that he is the only comic character, but because he initiated the "Scherz" in the opening scene, admitted to that fact in the second (81 ff.), and put the finishing touches to it with the "mummery" [according to Webster: "buffoonery, farcical show"] of the concluding scenes.[45]

This last scene ends, as the first began, with the Prince "halb wachend, halb schlafend"—"Ist es ein Traum?" (1856) But in the interim the Prince has become the victor both on the battlefield and in Court circles. The Elector, on the other hand, has lost control of his family circle, of his officers and of the "Scherz" which he instigated and of which he has become the victim. We must agree with one of the earliest evaluations of Kleist's creation of this character as reported by Heinrich Heine (1822) viz. a noble lady believed "ihr Ahnherr" appears here "in einer unedeln Gestalt."[46] This character was created by Kleist to be outwitted by *Der Prinz* who had to "Stoop to Conquer" and who, having been twice defeated, had learned to rise again. Like Kleist he is a "personality of rare intensity, of unhesitating loyalty to his feelings... With this impulsiveness and clear-cut decisiveness of feeling he combined a remarkable tenacity of purpose."[47] Silz tells us: "He [the Prince] finds it easy to ascribe personal motives to the Elector... He knows no others. ... feeling as he does, he has not only the right, but the duty, to save himself, by all [any?] means possible."[48] And so he acts. He may be down, but he is never out. "Ere this play is played, the Elector himself has gained a new insight into the nature and limitations of both states and human beings."[49]

If, as Passage says, Kleist "created... his Elector who has supreme self-control and his hero whose besetting sin is precisely the lack of self-control,"[50] this might indicate either that the former *never* intended to execute his kinsman, or that he lost control of the Prince and his cohorts who finally controlled the Elector and forced him to yield to the Prince's *modus operandi.* The fact is that the intention of the Prince, the *alter ego* of the author, was to survive, to be insubordinate to military regimentation, and that he, the younger man, was to become the "Sieger." So, the long-drawn-out threat of execution was only Kleist's method of lifting his *alter ego per aspera ad astra,* i.e., from impending execution to a "Johannisfeier."

This drama contains numerous elements which justify those who would consider it to be on the lighter side of the "Schauspiel." Whether we have a comedy or a farce each reader must decide for himself. There is abundance of evidence that Kleist spiced this play with a profusion of humorous episodes and devices so as to indirectly inform his auditors that they have no serious drama before them. Concerning the "Scherz" played on the Prince in the garden (I, i), Hohenzollern exposing to the Elector the somnambulant idiosyncrasies of his close friend, the Prince, Silz observes: "The humor involved here smacks more of the barracks than of the drawing room."[51] The appearance of the Elector on the stage "halbentkleidet" (V, i) may be relegated to the same category. Howard cavalierly dismisses it with the comment: "The Elector appears in undress and in full regalia."[52] To me it recalls *Dorfrichter* Adam in *Der zerbrochne Krug* (171 ff.). Levity abounds. Vulgarity is rare. "Some of the situations" Kleist "presents are so unconventional as to border on the ridiculous or the grotesque," remarks Campbell, who concludes, "and they have always been ridiculed by the conventional-minded."[53] Evidently the principle of "chacun à son goût" must prevail.

It seems reasonable to suggest that the plethora of comical and farcical material interspersed throughout this "Schauspiel" is not fortuitously scattered, but has been artistically blended by a master-chef to render the piècede-résistance piquant, the concoction appetizing, in order to lend the "Schauspiel" enough of the flavor of *Der zerbrochne Krug* or of "Sosias" to forewarn that the course of the action will not lead to the grave. Note, for example, the purposeful invention of the place-names compounded on "Hackel", e.g., "-berg," "-busch," "-höhn," "-grund," "-dorf," "-witz," which Samuel says, "erhöht den komischen Charakter der Szene."[54] Compare the fictional "Hackel-" compounds, plus "Havelberg," with "Huisum," "Holla," and "Hussahe."[55] Also "Glock zehn" and the like (13, 124, 126) reëcho the same expressions of *Der zerbrochne Krug*, (222, 289, 871, 1228, 1333, 1355). In *Der zerbrochne Krug*, *Richter* Adam must hurriedly get dressed (171); in *Prinz Friedrich von Homburg* there are two dressing scenes, the Prince's (191 ff.) and the Elector's (V, i, -1395, 1427+).

In depicting his characters, this author has used their actions, their speeches, and all other media through which they convey their thoughts, their feelings and their intentions, to flavor the "Ragout" (*Faust*, verse 100). Comparing some of the verbal antics employed in this composition with similar tropes found in Kleist's other comedies, one detects that in diction, in syntax, in idiomatic phrases and other linguistic devices, a close kinship exists among the three comedies.

Without proposing to make a rustic cavalier or a heavenly Hercules of the Prince, or a Huisum or Amphitryonic Thebes of Fehrbellin, it is suggested that all three situations have their share of "fear" and "farce," since "One touch of nature makes the whole world kin."

NOTES

1 Cf. *Heinrich von Kleists Nachruhm*, ed. Helmut Sembdner (Bremen, 1967), p. 520, pp. 535 ff., p. 539. The volume contains some sixty comments on this drama. Cited hereafter as Sembdner.

2 Sembdner, p. 552, "Eines unserer *besten* 'Lustspiele'" (Wolzogen); p. 571 ff., "*herrlichste deutsche Komödie*" (Schwiefert).

3 Heinrich von Kleist, *Sämtliche Werke*, ed. Arnold Zweig (München, 1923), I, xxxvii f. Hereafter cited as *Werke*. Cf. also Sembdner, p. 573.

4 Max Grube, *Am Hofe der Kunst* (Leipzig, 1918), pp. 158 f. See Sembdner, p. 567.

5 Sembdner, p. 526.

6 *Briefe aus Berlin*, 2. Brief, d. 16. März 1822, *Sämtliche Werke*, ed. Otto Lachmann (Leipzig: Reclam, 1887), II, 163 f.

7 Walter Kühn, *Heinrich von Kleist und das deutsche Theater* (München-Leipzig, 1912), p. 71: "Die Todesfurchtszene... war etwas gemildert."

8 Kühn, p. 71.

9 Heinrich von Kleist, *Prinz Friedrich von Homburg*, ed. Richard Samuel (Berlin, 1964), p. 10. Hereafter cited as Samuel.

10 Sembdner, p. 530.

11 Kühn, *op. cit.*, p. 74.

12 Sembdner, p. 542; Grillparzer to Folgar, 20. Nov. 1842.

13 *Op. cit.*, pp. 74 ff.

14 Cf. Meta Corssen, *Kleist und Shakespeare* (Weimar, 1930), especially pp. 37 ff.

15 *Hamlet*, III, ii, 25.

16 *Werke*, Jubiläums-Ausgabe, XXXVI, 6, 15.

17 Cf. Note 12, *supra*.

[18] "Wir müssen die Reise um die Welt machen, und sehen, ob es vielleicht von hinten irgendwo offen ist." "Über das Marionettentheater," *Werke*, IV, 72 ff.

[19] Cf. *Homburg*, V, x, especially the soliloquy (1830-1839), with Klopstock's Ode "An Fanny" and Kleist's last letters, especially "An Sophie Haza-Müller," 20. Nov. 1811; "An Marie v. Kleist," 9. u. 12. Nov. 1811; also "An Martini," 18. Mai 1799.

[20] Potsdam, d. 19. März 1799, *Werke*, IV, 193.

[21] Cf. Schiller, "Über das Erhabene," *Werke*, ed. Ludwig Bellermann (Leipzig: Bibliographisches Institut), VII, 231: "Kein Mensch muß müssen" [Lessing, "Nathan der Weise", I, iii] and ibid., p. 233: "Eine Gewalt vernichten, ... heißt nichts anderes, als sich derselben freiwillig unterwerfen." In present day parlance: "If you can't lick 'em, join 'em."

[22] *Ibid.* p. 248.

[23] "Das Ideal und das Leben," verses 122 f. N.B. The following stanza cites the experiences of ZEUS-ALKMENE-AMPHITRYON.

[24] *Ibid.*, verses 107 f. Kleist, like Schiller, studied Kant. He was a disciple of Schiller. See, e.g., the Samuel edition of *Prinz von Homburg* which cites dozens of echoes of Schiller.

[25] Cf. the Prince's "Gleichviel" in verses 132, 154, 156, 796, 797, 886, 1374. Note the grouping of occurences. Cf. Anzengruber, *Die Kreuzelschreiber* (Steinklopferhanns): "Es kann dir nix g'schehn!" III, i (six times).

[26] Cf. Walter Silz, "Heinrich von Kleist's Conception of the Tragic," *Hesperia*, Nr. 12 (1923), p. 85, "feeling as he does, he, the Prince, has not only the right, but the duty, to save himself, by all means possible, from a horrible and meaningless death."

[27] See, e.g., verses 147+, 194, 195, 209, 298+, 322+, 420, 696. Walter Silz, *Heinrich von Kleist. Studies in his Works and Literary Character* (Philadelphia, 1961), p. 233 says: "He is not a dissembler." Perhaps a strategist?

[28] E.g., E. L. Stahl, *Heinrich von Kleist's Dramas* (Oxford, 1948), p. 113 and Charles E. Passage, translator, *Heinrich von Kleist, The Prince of Homburg* (New York, 1956), p. xvi.

[29] I, xi.

[30] *Berliner Conversations-Blatt* (11. August). Cf. Sembdner, pp. 530 f. If so, the title might well have been "Viel Lärm um Nichts," which the play really is. See *Krug* (504), "Lärm um Nichts."

[31] Silz, *Studies*, p. 223 designates this scene as "a Romantic synesthesia of midsummer moonlight, music and fragrant flowers."

[32] Samuel's "Erläuterungen," *op. cit.*, pp. 175-202, note the comic elements. Cf. Notes to verses 83, 220 ff., 366, 394ff., 486-492, 1263 ff. - 1403, 1428 ff., 1479 f., 1492-1497, 1500, -1829.

[33] *Werke*, IV, 23, "Epigramme," Nr. 2.

[34] *Op. cit.*, p. 177, 87. See W. G. Howard, *PMLA*, XXXVII (1922), lxxxi: "qualities, not virile indeed, but surely none the less human for being commonly regarded as feminine."

[35] Cf. *Grande Dictionaire Universel du XIXe Siecle*, par Pierre Larousse (Paris, 1865), I, 722: "Arthur, nom mis à mode par les romanciers, que en ont singulièrement abusé pour designer ces héros de salon, aux longs cheveux, aux regards langoureux, au tient affadi, aux paroles mielleuses desquels aucune vertu ne peut résister. C'est aujourd'hui un nom presque ridicule. ... ARTHUR est donc le nom générique des Werthers, Faublas, Lovelaces et autres satellites qui gravitent dans la planisphère des lorettes." Also Sembdner, p. 530: "Arthur erscheint mir wie ein männliches Kätchen" (Karl von Holtei, 1828) and ibid., p. 552: "Unter allen Gestalten, die ich kenne, erinnert dieser Prinz zumeist an den Grafen Arthur in Herman Grimms 'Unüberwindlichen Mächten'" (Theodor Fontane, 1872).

[36] Cf. verses 94, 149, 164, 164, 206, 428, 877, 1699, 1844, 1846.

[37] *Op cit.*, p. 180, concerning verses 214 ff.

[38] *Op cit.*, p. 106.

[39] In II, vi the Prince uses in his first twenty lines thirteen pronominal or adjectival forms (first person) to extol his *"ego."*

[40] *PMLA*, XXXVII (1922), lxxxiv.

[41] *Op. cit.*, Before note on verse 1830, p. 202.

[42] *Studies*, p. 223. Kleist's deft handling of the nepotism situation tends to minimize the foreboding threat of execution. The flaunting of family ties between the Elector and the Prince should assure that *Vater, Onkel, Oheim, Vetter Friedrich* will not cause his *Töchterchen* (*Nichte*) and his wife (*Tante, Mutter*) to lose their *Vetter* (*Sohn*) and the Prince to lose his "Mutter." To affirm this Kleist piles up such epithets in the scenes after the confirmation of the Prince's sentence, thus indicating that no *Vettermord* will be exacted by the relative and ruler. About sixty per cent of the three dozen occurences of such expressions are between verses 952-1207, i.e., in III, iii and IV, i, the family intercession scenes.

[43] *Hesperia*, Nr. 12 (1923) 86.

[44] Cf. 1609 f.: "Mit Dir, Du alter wunderlicher Herr,
    Werd' ich nicht fertig!" (i.e., I can't win!)
and Hohenzollern, 1721 f. *Der Kurfürst* (1714 ff.) might as well have argued: "If Eve had note eaten the apple... etc."

[45] Cf. Howard, *op. cit.*, p. lxxxiv: "the mummery in the concluding scenes."

[46] Cf. Note 6, *supra*.

[47] Thomas Moody Campbell, ed., *German Plays of the Nineteenth Century*, (New York, 1935), p. 9.

[48] *Hesperia* (1923) p. 85. See note 26, *supra*.

[49] Walter Silz, "On the Interpretation of Kleist's *Prinz Friedrich von Homburg*," *Journal of English and Germanic Philology*, XXXV (1936), 506.

[50] Charles E. Passage, tr., *Heinrich von Kleist. The Prince of Homburg* (New York, 1956), p. xviii.

[51] *Studies*, p. 230.

[52] *PMLA*, XXXVII (1922), lxviii.

[53] *Op. cit.*, p. 9.

[54] *Op. cit.*, p. 183.

[55] "Hackel-" compounds in verses 10, 129, 225, 255, 281, 394, 395, 618, 683; "Havelberg" in verses 236, 239; "Huisum" in verses 75, 80, 81, 166, 313, 360, 446, 568, 623, 1113, 1811, 1814, 1855; "Holla" in verses 73, 81, 102, 123, 165, 329, 332; "Hussahe" in verse 169.

New Light on Rahel Varnhagen's Biography: Some Hitherto Unpublished Letters

PERCY MATENKO

Much has been written about the interesting personality of Rahel Antonie Friederike Varnhagen (1771-1833). The oldest child of a well-to-do Jewish merchant, Levin Markus, in Berlin, she married the diplomat Karl August Varnhagen von Ense in 1814. She is noted for the brilliant salon which she maintained there from 1790 to 1806 which was attended by some of the most outstanding representatives of the intellectual Berlin of that time: the Swedish ambassador Brinkman, the actors Fleck and Madame Unzelmann, the theologian Schleiermacher, the classical philologist Friedrich August Wolf, the important publicist Gentz, the brothers Humboldt, Friedrich Schlegel, Ludwig and Friedrich Tieck, to name only a few.[1] In view, therefore, of the interest that attaches to her personality and her writings I deemed it important to make public here some letters which have still not seen the light of day and are preserved in the archives of the Leo Baeck Institute, New York. These, I hope, should prove useful in filling out various aspects of her biography, for instance: Rahel's experiences in Teplitz in 1814, her dealings with Ludwig Tieck in connection with his *Aufruhr in den Cevennen*, and her appreciation of theatrical art, particularly as it refers to her admiration of the important Berlin actor, Georg Wilhelm Krüger. I shall proceed to present the letters which deal with the materials mentioned above in the order which I have indicated.[2]

* * *

The first letter which concerns us is one six pages in length addressed to Rahel's eldest brother, Markus Theodor (Levin) Robert.[3] He conducted the family business after his father's death in 1789. Previously, Rahel had visited Teplitz for a certain period from about August 22, 1811 to the middle of September. On the ninth of May, 1813, she had gone with the family of her brother Markus to Breslau to escape the disturbances of the war and had gone from there via Reinerz to Prague on May 30, 1813. After a serious illness in the winter of 1813-1814 she saw Varnhagen again in Teplitz in the summer of 1814. The date of our present letter furnishes clear evidence of their meeting there as early as July of that year. The 'friend' she refers to on page two of the letter cannot be Alexander von der Marwitz. The latter had already died in the battle of Montmirail on February 11, 1814. It must be Varnhagen von Ense, whom, as we know, she had met by July 20 in Teplitz. She married him about two months later, on September 27, 1814, although she had been secretly engaged to him since 1809. It was impossible for me to identify Zadig. Baron von Selby was Marwitz's squadron commander in the Austrian War.[4] The 'Königin' refers to Auguste Wilhelmine Amalie Luise (1776-1810), who was queen of Prussia from her marriage to Frederick Wilhelm III in 1793 to her death in 1810. The battle of Kulm and Nollendorf, located in northwestern Bohemia, occurred on August 29-30, 1813.[5] Karl Friedrich Graf von Beyme (1765-1838) was from 1808 to 1810 minister of justice with the title of a grand chancellor. During the War of Liberation he was civil governor in Pomerania. In 1791 he married the widow Charlotte Ernestine [Kammergerichtsräthin] Schlechtendal, the daughter of the mayor and sub-prefect Meyer of Colberg. München is probably the Bavarian light cavalry colonel Gottfried von München. Heinrich Theodor von Schön (1773-1856) was one of the most significant collaborators in the reforms of Stein. In 1813 he was governor general of the land between the Vistula and the Russian border. In 1816 he was the president in chief of West Prussia and from 1824 to 1842 of the whole province of Prussia. Heinrich Friedrich Theodor Kohlrausch (1780-1865) has won deserving fame for his labors in connection with the educational systems of Prussia and Hanover. He also made a name for himself by his school text on German history which by 1875 had reached the sixteenth edition. A great admirer of Napoleon in 1811, he turned against the French two years later when he witnessed the disgraceful flight of King Jerome in Barmen. Under the influence of this sentiment he wrote *Deutschlands Zukunft in 6 Reden* (Elberfeld, 1814), for which Fichte's famous *Reden an die deutsche Nation* (1807-1808) undoubtedly served as a model. In 1814 he came to Düsseldorf to assist his friend Kortüm in reestablishing the Lyceum which had been neglected by the French. Gentz had an extremely negative opinion of Kohlrausch's views on the future condition of Germany.[6] The Prussian infantry general Bogislaw Friedrich Emanuel Graf Tauentzien von Wittenberg (1760-1824) took part in the campaign of the Northern Army under the Crown Prince of Sweden (Bernadotte) in the War of Liberation. He stormed Wittenberg on January 13, 1814, and in August, 1814, became commanding general in the marches to the right of the Elbe and in Pomerania. The ruling monarch was the Prussian king, Friedrich Wilhelm III (1770-1840) who reigned from 1797 to 1840. The Crown Prince was Friedrich Wilhelm IV (1795-1861) who ascended the Prussian throne in 1840. 'Bethmann' probably refers to the important actress Friederike Auguste Konradine Bethmann (1760-1815) who in 1805 had married the Berlin actor Heinrich Eduard Bethmann after her marriage to the actor Karl Wilhelm Unzelmann was dissolved in 1803. To judge by this letter she collaborated actively with Rahel and Madame Goldstein in supporting the various arrangements in behalf of the memorial to the battle of Kulm. 'Die Staats[räthin] Jordan' refers to the wife of Johann Ludwig von Jordan (1773-1848) who was councillor of state in the Prussian Foreign Ministry from 1810 to 1814. At the beginning of the uprising of 1813 he followed the state chancellor Hardenberg from Berlin to Breslau and remained at his side during the campaigns of 1813 and 1814. On September 5, 1814, Rahel arrived in Berlin where she stayed with her brother Moritz. In October 1814 Varnhagen went as a member of the diplomatic corps to the Congress of Vienna. Rahel followed him in the same month.[7]

Some other matters pertinent to our understanding of this letter are: "Hans" is a name also given in Rahel's letters to Henriette, the wife of Rahel's brother, Markus Theodor Robert (Friedhelm Kemp, *Rahel Varnhagen und ihre Zeit* (*Briefe 1800-1833*) [München, 1968], IV, 402); 'die Schleierm[acher]' is undoubtedly Henriette Schleiermacher, née von Mühlenfels. Schleiermacher had married her in 1809 following the death in 1807 of her first husband, the young pastor Ehrenfried von Willich. 'Purren' (*cf.* 'anpurren' below) in this context is a North German expression meaning 'to tease or to plague.' The *Morgenblatt für gebildete Stände* was published from 1807 to 1865 by the Cotta publishing house in Stuttgart and Tübingen. I could not, however, find any article in Varnhagen's collected works describing the memorial to the battle of Kulm. 'Mar[ianne?] *Saling*-tochter' refers perhaps to Marianne Saaling (1786-1869), a daughter of the royal Prussian court jeweler Salomon Jakob Salomon and his wife Helene, née Meyer. With her brothers and sisters she became converted to Christianity, adopting the name of Saaling. She was an aunt of the novelist Paul Heyse. A person of great beauty, Marianne attained the height of her popularity at the Congress of Vienna and enjoyed the admiration of kings and princes.[8] Julius Eduard Hitzig (1780-1849) was a well-known Berlin jurist of criminal cases, author and publisher. He wrote biographies of Zacharias Werner, E. T. A. Hoffmann, and Chamisso. 'Arm zu seyn "die größte Plage!"' is a slightly faulty quotation from Goethe's poem, "Der Schatzgräber." This and the following line read: "Armuth ist die größte Plage, Reichthum ist das höchste Gut!"[9] Madame Magnus is probably the mother of the Berlin portrait painter Eduard Magnus (1799-1872) and his brother, the chemist and physicist Heinrich Gustav Magnus (1802-1870).

RAHEL VARNHAGEN TO MARKUS THEODOR ROBERT

Tepliz den 20 t July 1814 Mittwoch. Mit ein[em] wort wie mit 100 mit ei[nem] Brief wie mit 10000; kommt her! denn ich gönne mir das herliche Mükenlose, mit all[em] was zum Spatzier-Leb[en] nur erforderte Thal nicht!! Keine Wolke, kein[en] Baum, kein[en] Schein, keine farbe keine blume! Da ich euch im sumpfig[en] sandig[en], Mükigen Thier-gart[en] weiß. Kommt ein wenig! und bald![1] Ich leide wenn ich genieße soll; und schähme mich, es allein zu genießen, und so dünkt es mich un unterbroch[en] wenn ihr nicht da seid. Vorzüglich schrey' und jammre ich nach hans: die es so sehr *goûtirte!* Theuer ist nichts, als die *Quartiere:* und auch diese Doch nicht: da der *Louisd*[or] 18 *fl:* 30X steht oder 19. Ich leider habe schon in *Prag* gewechselt: und da ich mein[en] Aufenthalt hier nicht bereuen kann, darf ich mir d[en] jetzig[en] *cours* nicht Einmal zu Nutze mach[en]. Einmal also wie Tausend! — und auch darum weil ich platter-dings nicht schreib[en] kann./: und mir nun gar die Schleierm[acher] so geschrieb[en] hat, d[a]ß ich ihr heute noch antwort[en] muß![2] Im ganzen befinde ich mich gut; und muß die Wirkung des Bades lob[en]; weil mein Kreutz so sehr viel leichter geword[en] ist, und das bald; wie immer, nach dem 7t[3] Bade. Das wird euch gewiß sehr freuen. Mein bein aber, welches nur *partizipando* gelitt[en] hat, ist nicht so versöhnlich; das mukt und purrt, und will nicht dien[en]: boßt sich über das Wetter, und d[er] g[leichen]. Doch Gehe ich vortrefflich! und ein bergsteig[en], welches ich voriche[4] Woche unversehens exekutir[en] mußte, weil wir uns etwas verlauf[en] hatt[en], und bey welch[em] steig[en] und herabsteig[en] ich ich[5] bis dahin gerade sehr litt: hat mir plötzlich ohne alles Verhältnis geholfen. Sprech' Mal Einer mit. Aber ich leide sonst sehr vom Bade. Blutsteig[en]! hals-zuschnur, und rechte bedeutende, ja, sehr unangenehme Nervenzufälle, weil sie mich so plötzlich und ohne alle Veranlaßung überfall[en]; und ganz und gar das Schreib[en] un möglich mach[en]. Meist auch das Lesen. Obgleich mein lieber Freund schon die größte Bibliothek von d[en] neust[en] und best[en] alt[en] Sach[en] um mich hergestellt hat. Er selbst ist sehr[6] fleißig; schreibt von früh bis spät in der Nacht; und seiner Gesundheit weg[en] muß ich meine ganze Gewalt über ihn aufbieth[en], d[a]ß er nur in die Luft kömmt. Er versüßt und verschönert durch Sorgfalt und Treue aller Art, mein Leb[en]; weiß mich so zu ehr[en], daß auch alle Ander[n] es müßen; wohl oder übel; läßt mich und sich dabey ohne alle *gêne* noch irgend ein affektirtes! Ich soll euch auf[s] Freundschaftlichst[e] grüßen. Dabey hatte ich das große Vergnüg[en] ein paar Tag[e] nach meiner Ankunft unser[n] Freund Zadig mit seiner schönen Schwester hier zu find[en]. Wie der sich freute! Er behauptete nur meinetweg[en] gekomm[en] zu seyn und wird auch komm[en]. Wir war[en] beständig zusamm[en] und hatt[en] die herrlichs-t[en] innerlichst[en] Gespräche! Auch andere: wo Varnh[agen] und ich die Jud[en] und d[en] Kaufmannsstand vertheidigt[en], er diese und England

---

[1] 'bald' underscored three times.
[2] 'muß' underscored three times.
[3] 't' underscored twice.
[4] *Sic!*
[5] *Sic!*
[6] 'sehr' underscored three times.

angriff. Als er das erste Mal kam, war es nach Tische, und ich wollte mich gleich niederleg[en] lag schon: „ich stöhre Sie wohl„ "Ja!„/: es war große hitze.:/ "Da! leg[en] Sie sich auch hin!„ So zeigt' ich ihm ein Kanape[e] im Ander[n] zimmer, er mußte d[en] *Rok* abzieh[en] und sich hinleg[en]: gleich mit ein[em] gut[en] Buche: die Schwester ging wieder. jetz[t] leb[en] wir mit ihr: weil ihr das sehr *convenirt: Selby's* sind auch sehr gut mit ihr. Ihre Equipage ist angenehm aber alle partien mach[en] sie hier im Sonnenschein: und wenn wir komm[en], sind alle andern Leute schon da: ich behaupte daher, sie komm[en] d[en] Tag zuvor. Mich *fatiguirt* dies sehr. Auch will ich heute nicht nach Kulm, wo alle Mensch[en] hinfahr[en]; "weil wir Preuß[en] in unserer Königin Nahm[en] und Sinn, Gestern den Kulmern zu helfen trachtet[en]: (:Varnh[agen] wirds im Morgenblat beschreib[en].:) Prediger Grell[1] hielt uns und ander[n] eine Rede wo bey wir in Trauer war[en] (:worauf ich anhielt:) der Regier[ungs] President Hempel aus Stetin übergab's d[em] Kriegshauptmann Baron Münich: (alles in Galla.); der antwortete Schön: auch in einer Rede, und überreichte es d[em] Kulmer Prediger. Tausend *fl:* bekam[en] die Kulmer und noch 2 Dörfer; immer einer zu 80 *fl:* 60, 50 *fl:*.die Kinderreichst[en], und ärmst[en]. Das las mit d[en] Nahm[en] der Baron weinend vor. Dann sind d[ie] arme[n] Preuß[en] hier da bekam jeder 50 *fl:*. und eine Summe für andere die noch komm[en] könnt[en] ist verwahrt. Ich gab 4 Napoleon Varnh[agen] 2. *Mam*[2] Goldst[ein] 50 *fl:* das *encouragirte* die Ander[n]. Ich hatte es mir zu d[em] Behuf an mei[nem] Leib schon in Prag abgespahrt. Ich traute mir kein[e] *bout*[eille] Schampanger:[3] z: B:! das stärkte mich 1000 Mal beßer! Ich habe für nichts in der ganze[n] Welt Sinn als Gutes zu wirk[en] und finde mich gar nicht wieder; keine Angst, und keine Besorgung mehr zu hab[en]. Ich schäme mich so um her zu geh[en]. Und wirke mit Varnhag[en] d[en] ganz[en] Tag. Mit Schreib-[en], Red[en], anordn[en], ausdenk[en], anpurren. Lies also auf der Stelle, "Deutschlands Zukunft in sechs Reden von *Dr: Fr:* Kohlrausch. Professor der alt[en] Litteratur und der Geschichte am Gymnasium zu Düsseldorf. Dies ist aber nicht genug. Gieb es unsern[4] Patron dem Grafen Tauenzien in mein[em] Nahmen. Er hat uns rühmlichst den Krieg gewinnen helfen, und sich große Ehre erworben die sich auf so gründlich[e] Eigenschaft[en] stützt, das er jedes Weltbürg[er]liche und ehrenvolle Zutrauen einflößt. Er hat dabey das Glik ein Vornehmer Mann zu seyn auf welch[em] *pied destal*[5] er gleich sein Leb[en] begin[nen] konnte. Also ist's an ihm dieses Buch voller guter, echter, derber Gesinnung, und trefflicher Vorschläge unter d[ie] Aug[en] desjenig[en] Monarch[en] zu bring[en], der sie am willigst[en]

---

[1] A sign like (≠) is written after 'Grell'. At the left-hand margin there is written 'aus Berlin', i.e., 'Prediger Grell aus Berlin'; on the lower margin upside down there is written: 'mit einer hübsch[en] *Mar*[ianne?] *Saling*-tochter. Beym's sind hier; er nicht.'
[2] The 'a' of 'Mam' is underscored twice.
[3] *Sic!*
[4] *Sic!*
[5] *Sic!*

leichtesten[1] und geschwindest[en] ausführt; daß[2] ist zum Glük unser König. Kann ein fürstlicher Regent auch nur ein theil der Dinge ausführ[en] laßen, die hier zur Sprache kam[en]; so hat er dòch zu Groß[em] d[en] Anfang gemacht, und es fördern half; mehr kann der größte unter d[en] Mensch[en] nicht. Und könnte keiner dieser Vorschläge in Ausübung gebracht werd[en], so kräftig[en] sie die Seele, erhell[en] d[en] Geist, mach[en] denk[en], und beleb[en] das Menschlichste, Wohlwollendste. Einem klug[en] König muß jeder[3] Fortschritt in seiner Nazion;[4] jeder gute Wunsch für sie womöglich zu Gesichte bekomm[en]. Unser König ist jetzt in Urbanität und Redlichkeit d[en] ander[n] Fürst[en] Deutschlands ein Vorbild! und auch aus dies[em] Grunde darf der geringste seiner Unterthanen,[5] der Letzte in Deutschland beytrag[en] woll[en] ihm alles zu verschaff[en] was er nur irgend zu seinem erhaben[en] herrlichen *métier* gebrauch[en] kann. Er läßt sich ja willig — denn er erkennt es an — mit Gut, und Blut von uns helf[en]; er wird den reinst[en] Will[en], der jed[en] gut[en] Gedank[en] hergeb[en] möchte eb[en] so wenig verschmehen. Am wenigst[en] von sei[nem] ausgezeichnet[en] längst gekanndt[en] General. In dies[em] Sinne schike so gleich d[em] G[eneral] Tauenzien dies Buch — von hitzig — Er wird es dann zur liebe von Dir, der König von ihm von ihm an[ne]hm[en]. Mache, daß es der Kronprinz liest; und alle Vornehm[en]. Die Kaufleute, alle. Ander[en] Prinz[en] im ausland soll es auch schon zukomm[en]! Ich bin sonst, so deutsch nicht! aber dies ist gründlich: der Mann ohne Vorurtheil. In d[em] Sinne, damit etwas entstehe, ein Nationales Gute, hab' ich das gestrige Fest sehr unterstützt;[6] mit worte[n], Rath, That, Betrag, Ermunter[ung]. Bethman[n] und *Mam*[7] Goldst[ein] hatt[en] die meiste Mühe; aber mit d[em] herrlichst[en] Erfolg. Die Staatsr[ätin] *Jordan* beneidete *Mam*[8] G[oldstein] sehr! Sie konnte nicht so wirk[en]; und sagte es. Unsere Liste war die größte. Hat in 14 Tag[en] G[ene]r[al] T[auenzien] das Buch nicht. So schik' ich's ihm, und schreib' ihm dabey das hoffe ich aber nicht lieber Bruder. Du hilfst auch redlich gerne, und bist so gut mit ihm! Nun kann ich vor *Echauffement* nicht mehr leb[en], und soll ins Bad! Dein Brief worin du mich über unsere Vermög[ens] Umstände auf's Klare setztest hab! ich hier richtig, ei[nen] Tag nach d[em] ich Dir geschrieb[en] hatte, erhalt[en]. Du hast mich sehr beruhigt: und so gerne und freudig ich Dir und d[en] Kindern Gutes erzeug[en] möchte, so freudig dank ichs Dir, und gönne ich Dir die Freude. Bezahl[en] kön[n]en, wo man nicht geschenkt nehm[en] kann, ist eine Nothwendigkeit der[en] nichterfüllung mir die ganze Ruhe raubte. Arm zu

---

[1] 'leichtest' written, crossed out, and 'leichtesten' written above it.
[2] *Sic!*
[3] 'guter Wun' written and then crossed out.
[4] *Sic!*
[5] 'Untherthanen' was written and the first 'h' was then crossed out.
[6] Cf. note 6.
[7] The 'am' of the word '*Mam*' is underscored.
[8] The 'am' of the word '*Mam*' is underscored twice.

seyn "die größte Plage!,, Nun[1] mußt Du mir noch antwort[en], wie viel Du für die 1000 fl.: gezahlt hast. ob ich künftig alle 4 t el[2] Jahr, 200 rh:, anstatt monathl[ich] 66 rh: erhalt[en] kann; und ob ich dies nicht durch Dich erhalt[en] kann? Und ob, wenn ich in 4 oder 5 oder 6 Woch[en] nach Berlin komme, ich in Deiner Einquartierungsstube wohn[en] kann, bis ich ein *quartier* habe; oder wieder wegreise: welches von Varnh[agens] Anstellung abhangt.[3] *Mam*[4] *Magnus* both[5] mir in Prag an, wenn sie keine Einquartierung hat, unt[en] zu wohn[en], wo Du wohntest. Willst Du da einmal nach höher? hat man noch Einquart[ierung]? Ist das alles nichts, so steig' ich in der Stadt *Rom* — da ist's sehr gut — ab und miethe mir *chambre garnie* bis ich weiß wo ich bleibe. Noch weiß ich nicht Einmal ob ich komme. Kommt ihr! ich bitte! Das Leb[en] ist so elend, so un gewiß. Der Angst so viel! Kommt! *Rh.*[6]

* * *

The next letter concerns Rahel's negotiations in regard to a French translation of Ludwig Tieck's *Aufruhr in den Cevennen*. Tieck began this work in 1820 and finished it in 1826. While four sections were planned, only the first two appeared, the *Novelle* being published by Reimer in Berlin in the latter year. The addressee of this letter, Georg Andreas Reimer (1776-1842), and his son Georg Ernst Reimer (1804-1885) published a considerable number of Tieck's works, including the former's *Schriften* in twenty volumes from 1828 to 1846, and a twelve-volume edition of his *Gesammelte Novellen* from 1852 to 1854. 'Louis Robert,' who is referred to at the beginning of this letter is the second brother of Rahel, Ludwig Robert-Tornow (1778-1832). His most significant work was the self-styled "bourgeois tragedy," *Die Macht der Verhältnisse*, which appeared in 1819. The historian Friedrich von Raumer (1781-1873) met Tieck at Ziebingen in 1810. He became a close friend of Tieck's and remained so until the former's death. Tieck and Raumer shared many personal and literary interests, publishing together, for instance, the two-volume edition of *Solger's nachgelassene Schriften und Briefwechsel* in 1826.

As far as can be gathered from the evidence available, Rahel, in a letter from Berlin, dated September 8, 1824, had requested Tieck to permit a young man of her and her husband's acquaintance who was connected with the French legation, to translate the *Cevennen* into French. This suggestion had been made to her by Varnhagen after she had originally had in mind that the young man attempt to translate Kleist's *Erzählungen*. She considered him

---

[1] Inferred. An illegible word.
[2] The 'e' is underscored twice.
[3] *Sic!*
[4] The 'am' is underscored twice.
[5] *Sic!*
[6] The following addendum occurs in another handwriting at the end of the letter: 'Rahel (Frau Varnhagen von Ense geb. Robert).'

highly competent and asked that Tieck inform her of his decision. She also informed him of Reimer's consent to have the *Cevennen* translated sheet by sheet into French and to publish the translation at the same time as the original.[10] To judge by the letter we are publishing Robert had received a reply from Tieck "a week ago last Saturday", in answer to Rahel's letter. This reply evidently stated that Tieck had himself considered a translation and that Raumer had come about a week before to Berlin to bring Reimer some "necessary material." This, however, did not occur. Since Rahel already had Tieck's consent in Robert's letter, she requests here the first printed sheets of the *Cevennen* from Reimer, in order that the translator may get an idea of the work. Nothing seems to have come of these negotiations, since we do not hear any further of a French translation of Tieck's *Cevennen*.

RAHEL VARNHAGEN TO GEORG ANDREAS REIMER

Berlin den 28 t *Septbr:* 1824[1]
Bogen A-M

Dienstag
Den letz[t]en Sonnabend vor 8.
Tagen erhielt ich einen Brief
von meinem Bruder *Louis Robert*
in Antwort von ein[em] den ich *Tieck*
geschrieben hatte. d[a]ß er selbst an
eine Uebersetzung seiner *cevennen*
gedacht habe, und d[a]ß H: v: Raumer
Gestern vor 8, Tagen nach Berlin
kommen würde, und Ihn[en] verehrter
Herr, „das Nöthige„ mit bringen
würde. H: v: Raumer hat aber
nichts gebracht; und auch weiß ich
nicht genau was dieses "Nöthige„
eigentlich seyn sollte: wenn nicht
nach Bogen, oder eine Art von
Ausführlicher Genehmigung.
Da aber solche schon in meines
Bruders Brief sich befindet,
d[em] ich auch die Ehre haben kann
Ihn[en] zu zeigen, so würde
ich Sie gütigst um die ersten
Bogen der *cevennen* bitten!
Weil unser junger Uebersetzer

---

[1] As far as I can judge, the words, 'Bogen A-M' are written in another handwriting than Rahel's. They evidently refer to "die ersten Bogen" of the *Cevennen* referred to in this letter.

sie bald wünscht; und Tie[c]k mir
schreiben lies,[1] dieser möchte sich
mit dem Ganzen bekandt[2] machen,
so weit es da ist, um eine
Idee davon zu bekommen.
Ich bitte Sie nochmals so gütig zu
seyn, als Sie es bey Bewilligung
des Ganzen waren, und mir
die Bogen schiken zu woll[en]!
Hochachtungsvoll
Friedrike Varnhagen.

* * *

The third letter reveals Rahel's appreciation of theatrical art. It is addressed
to "Sr. Wohl[ge]b[ohren] dem Herrn Krüger. Mitglied des königl[ichen]
Theaters alhier." Georg Wilhelm Krüger (1791-1841) was one of the most
important actors in the Berlin Hoftheater from 1820 to 1837. "Alexander"
no doubt refers to his role in the tragedy *Alexander und Darius* by Peter
Friedrich von Uechtritz (1800-1875). This was written in the winter of 1824
to 1825, was performed in 1826 in Dresden, Berlin and Vienna, and appeared
with a preface by Tieck in Berlin in 1827. To be sure, Rahel's admiration of
Krüger's acting of this role as deriving from pure inspiration[11] must be qualified somewhat. Eisenberg considers him to have been a master of declamation rather than of character representation.[12] Anna Milder-Hauptmann
(1785-1838) was a noted contemporary operatic singer and tragic actress who
distinguished herself particularly in the parts of Gluck's classical heroines.
She performed in Vienna from 1808 to 1815, and in Berlin from 1816 to
1829. "Stael" undoubtedly refers to the famous salon-lady and novelist
Madame Germaine Necker de Staël (1766-1817), the enthusiastic French
champion and interpreter of contemporary German literature.

RAHEL VARNHAGEN TO GEORG WILHELM KRÜGER

Berlin den 11 t Merz 1826

Unzählige Male habe ich seit Gestern Abend zu bedauern gehabt keine
Stael, keine Fürstin zu seyn und von allen Tittlen[3] entblößt, um Ihnen
meinen Dank und meine Bewundrung für den Alexander in allgemein-
gültiger Ausprägung zuschiken zu können!
Ich mag mich nicht entschuldigen, d[a]ß ich hier etwas Ungewöhnliches,

[1] *Sic!*
[2] *Sic!*
[3] *Sic!*

43

und in so fern vielleicht nicht ganz Schikliches unternehme: Sie aber, der
Sie so beseelt und begeistert von einem nie gesehenen Menschen zu seyn
vermögen, werden es am beßten begreifen, wie eine ganz gelungene bis im
kleinsten Theil lebendige Kunstdarstellung von einem lebendigen vor
unsern Augen sich bewegenden,[1] wiederum uns beseelen und befeuren kann,
und muß, uns drängen muß, solchem Künstler zu sagen, d[a]ß er verstanden,
geschätzt, eingesehn, bewundert wurde!

Laßen Sie sich nicht daran stöhren, d[a]ß der Beyfall Gestern stum[m]
war: ich weiß es durch Mehrere; Sie haben nicht nur für sich allein so
ganz vortrefflich gespielt; und zur Zeit werden es wenigstens die stum-
men Blätter gewiß der sich für Kunst interessirenden Welt auseinander-
setzend mittheilen, wie Sie diese Rolle schufen, und was Sie leisteten.
Schade, daß *Robert* es nicht sah, der würde es die Theaterfreunde gebührend
und schnell haben lesen laßen!

Alle meine Freunde und Bekanndte[n] werden Sie das nächste Mal sehn.
O! Spielen Sie nur akkurat wie Gestern. Ich vermag vermag[2] nicht zu
unterscheiden, wie bey jeder äußersten Leistung, ob nach der vollständigs-
ten Ueberlegung, Sie nicht doch nur aus reiner Eingebung spielten; denn
nicht allein so vollkommen, sondern auch mit solchem Glüke gaben Sie die
ganze Rolle vom ersten Moment des Auftretens, bis zu dem meisterhaften
wahrlich tiefsinnigen Abgehn: bey welchem man eine unabsehbare Reihe
von innern Vorstellungen und Handlungen erst anheben sah! —

Alles glükte Ihnen Gestern; jeder Schritt, jede Bewegung, jede Silbe, jede
Miene. Ich gratulire Ihnen auf dieser ganz neuen Stufe, zu der eine frische
Base führte, und von der eine neue beginnt, vom Grund des Herzens! und
so auch danke ich Ihnen für den ganz herrlichen Genuß noch Einmal. *bravo!*
bravo! rief ich Ihnen mit meiner Nachbarin *Mam*[3] *Milder* hundert Mal zu,
und jetzt wieder! Sie werden es fühlen, d[a]ß es ein Bedürfniß ist Zustim-
mung und Bewundrung über solche Rolle, so gefaßt, und gezeigt, auszusprechen: von welchem Bedürfniß Anmaßung, grad am entfern[te]sten ist.
Hätte die Menge, hätten berühmte Dichter und Fürsten Ihnen zugerufen;
wäre ich schon für Freude, und theilnahme verstummt. So aber gestatten
Sie mir meinen glükwünschenden Dank!

Hochachtungsvoll ihre ergebene
Friedrike Varnhagen von Ense.

[1] The word 'sich' was written again at this point and then crossed out.
[2] The word 'vermag' is written twice.
[3] 'a' is underscored twice.

NOTES

[1] Edwin H. Zeydel, Percy Matenko, Robert Herndon Fife eds., *Letters of Ludwig Tieck
Hitherto Unpublished, 1792-1853* (New York, London, 1937), pp. 136 f.; Hannah Arendt,
Rahel Varnhagen, Lebensgeschichte einer deutschen Jüdin aus der Romantik (München, 1959),
pp. 61 f., 285 ff. The first will henceforth be referred to as 'Zeydel, Matenko, Fife',

and the second as 'Arendt'. The work by Hannah Arendt was first published under the following title: Hannah Arendt, *Rahel Varnhagen. The Life of a Jewess*. Published for the (Leo Baeck) Institute by the East and West Library (London, 1957). Translated from the German MS, by Richard and Clara Winston.

² A check of *Bibliographie der Deutschen Zeitschriften-Literatur* from 1896 through 1964 did not reveal that these letters were published in any of their listings, nor could I find any reference in any letter collections or diaries available to me.

I am indebted to the Leo Baeck Institute for their gracious permission to publish the letters contained in this article and to Dr. Max Kreutzberger and his staff for their very helpful assistance while I was working on it.

An attempt has been made to publish these letters exactly as they were written. Abbreviations in words, spelling, and punctuation are inconsistent. Occasionally the full word or the capital is written, sometimes not. There is also the peculiar use of the colon or semicolon for the comma. The endings 'em', 'en', where omitted in the manuscript, are indicated for the most part by a short curve written down from the line where the word occurs. In our transcription they have been added to all of the words where this occurs to facilitate reading. They are marked by square brackets. Except for obvious abbreviations, incomplete words, such as '*Louisd:*', 'Schleierm:' have been written out in full, i.e., '*Louisd*[or]', 'Schleierm[acher]'. Moreover, the abbreviation 'u' has been normalized to 'und', 'm̄', 'n̄', to 'mm', 'nn', respectively. It should be noted that the text of these letters is written in Gothic script. Where, however, certain words occur in the Roman script in the original text, they are indicated by italics. Underscoring in the original is indicated by spacing.

For some time now I have been working on an extensive and for the most part hitherto unpublished correspondence between Rahel Varnhagen and her brother Ludwig Robert which is also available at the Leo Baeck Institute, New York. The latter, which received this material through the kindness of Dr. F. H. Eisner of London (cf. note 3, below) has given me permission to work on this correspondence of which the letters published here are to form a supplement. I am indebted to the Leo Baeck Institute and to Dr. Eisner for their kind permission to publish this material and intend to do so in the near future.

³ The Leo Baeck Institute possesses a very competent transcription of this letter together with a considerable number of excellent comments. It could not, however, offer any information concerning the origin of this material, except to state that it comes "from Erich Loewenthal's property" ("aus Erich Loewenthals Besitz"). The writer of the above-mentioned comments actually proved to be Erich Loewenthal (cf. below). He stated on the basis of remarks on the handwriting similar to the ones noted above that this is an authentic letter by Rahel. It is further attested to by the following letter, signed by E. Lamprecht, president of the See[handlun]gs-Bankdirektorium, and dated, *Berlin*, 24 *Novbr.* 1844: "Den anliegenden Brief der Geheimen Legations Räthin *Varnhagen von Ense* geb *Robert* an ihren Bruder, den Banquier *M. Th. Robert*, meinen Schwiegervater, *de dato Teplitz* den 20t *Juli* 1814 habe ich heute Herrn Regi.ments Arzt *Dr. Puhlmann* zu *Pots.dam* für seine Autographen Samm.lung mitgetheilt."

The 'E. Lamprecht' mentioned above is very likely the Emil von Lamprecht who married Hanne Robert, a daughter of Rahel's brother, Markus Theodor Robert (*cf. Rahel Varnhagen. Ein Frauenleben in Briefen*. Ausgewählt und mit einer Einleitung versehen von Dr. Augusta Weldler-Steinberg, Zweite durchgesehene Auflage [Weimar, 1917], p. 534. This work will henceforth be referred to as 'Weldler-Steinberg').

Concerning Erich Loewenthal the following may be said: A well-known Heine scholar in Germany, he had planned to publish on the basis of the Varnhagen collection in the Berlin *Staatsarchive* the letters of Rahel which Varnhagen had not printed in full in his collection and had done preliminary work on it. Unfortunately, he perished at the hands of the Nazis in Auschwitz before he could complete his task. When he died in 1944, his library and all his manuscripts were confiscated, carried off, and presumably disappeared. Nevertheless, two notebooks of copies of notes and letters were preserved and came into the hands of Loewenthal's friend, the Heine scholar, Professor F. H. Eisner,

45

who is now in London. At the suggestion of Professor Hanns Günther Reissner, I inquired from Dr. Eisner whether Loewenthal was the commentator of the letter under discussion. He not only confirmed this but, in order that I could work on them, kindly donated the above-mentioned two notebooks to the Leo Baeck Institute. The latter very generously made photostat copies of the two notebooks available to me. The Rahel Varnhagen archives of the Berlin *Staatsarchive* were transferred to Silesia for safekeeping during World War II and subsequently disappeared. Thus the copies now in the possession of the Institute are probably all that is left of this once famous collection (cf. *LBI News* of Spring 1966, 5-6; *Rechenschaft 1925-1965. Ein Almanach* [Heidelberg: Verlag Lambert Schneider], 55-57; letter from Dr. F. H. Eisner to myself of May 7, 1965; letter from Lambert Schneider to myself of May 20, 1965).

[4] Heinrich Meisner, *Rahel und Alexander von der Marwitz in ihren Briefen. Ein Bild aus der Zeit der Romantiker.* Nach den Originalen herausgegeben (Gotha, Stuttgart, 1925), 73, 74, 88 f., 133, 290, 293, 307 (henceforth referred to as 'Heinrich Meisner'); Arendt, 285, 286; K. A. Varnhagen von Ense, *Denkwürdigkeiten des eignen Lebens*, Dritte vermehrte Auflage, Dritter Theil, "Siebenundzwanzigster Abschnitt. Töplitz 1811." (Leipzig, 1871) 188, 230; Weldler-Steinberg, 544.

[5] Cf. Heinrich von Treitschke, *Deutsche Geschichte im Neunzehnten Jahrhundert* (Leipzig, 1886), Erster Theil, 485 f.; Oskar Jäger, *Deutsche Geschichte* (München, 1919), II, 321 f.

[6] Cf. Gentz an Rahel, Baden, den 7. August 1814 in: *Galerie von Bildnissen aus Rahel's Umgang und Briefwechsel.* Herausgegeben von K. A. Varnhagen von Ense. (Leipzig, 1836), II, 222 f. Rahel's enthusiasm for Kohlrausch's *Deutschlands Zukunft in 6 Reden* adds credence to Arendt's exposition of Rahel's patriotism. According to Arendt, Rahel's patriotism arose from her belief that the War of Liberation was in the spirit of what Fichte's *Reden an die deutsche Nation* had prophesied for a much later generation: the abolition of all classes in a general advance of the people as a whole (Arendt, 180). In a later letter to her brother Markus, dated, "Töplitz, den 13. August 1814", Rahel thanks her brother for delivering a copy of the book to Dr. von Tauentzien. She asks Markus to recommend it to A. Mendelssohn, who in turn is to give or recommend it to his brother-in-law Bartholdy and he in turn to the state chancellor, i.e., Hardenberg ([Karl August Varnhagen von Ense, ed.], *Rahel. Ein Buch des Andenkens für ihre Freunde*, Berlin, 1834, II, 234 f.).

[7] Arendt, 286-87.

[8] Percy Matenko, "The Goethe, Schiller and Byron Translations of the Saaling Album," *Modern Language Quarterly*, VI (March, 1945), 55; Maximilian Stein, "Paul Heyse und die Berliner Salons," *Vorträge und Ansprachen* (Frankfurt am Main, 1932), 23; Heinz Friedländer-Danzig, "Julie Heyse," *Jüdisch-liberale Zeitung* (Berlin, 5. Nov. 1926), p. 2; S. Wininger, *Große Jüdische National-Biographie*, V [1930-31], 320.

[9] *Goethes Werke.* Herausgegeben im Auftrage der Großherzogin Sophie von Sachsen, I. Abtheilung (Weimar, 1887), I, 181.

[10] Karl von Holtei, *Briefe an Ludwig Tieck* (Breslau, 1864), IV, 147 f., Friedrike Varnhagen an Ludwig Tieck, Berlin, den 8t Septbr. 1824. Helmut Sembdner published in *Heinrich von Kleists Nachruhm. Eine Wirkungsgeschichte in Dokumenten* (Bremen, 1967), p. 637, cf. pp. 679, 684, a part of this letter, as well as a fragment of the letter to Reimer I am publishing in full in this article.

[11] For further confirmation of Rahel's high opinion of Krüger's interpretation of this role, cf. her letter to Tieck, dated, Berlin, Sonntag, den 18t. März 1827 in Holtei, *op. cit.*, IV, 152 f. Cf. also, Friedhelm Kemp, *Rahel Varnhagen und ihre Zeit (Briefe 1800-1833)* (München, 1968), IV, 301 f.

[12] Ludwig Eisenberg, *Großes Biographisches Lexikon der Deutschen Bühne im XIX. Jahrhundert* (Leipzig, 1903), pp. 553-554.

Edgar Allan Poe's Contacts with German as Seen in His Relations with Ludwig Tieck

EDWIN H. ZEYDEL

In concentrating this investigation of Poe's experience with German on Tieck, I am fully aware that Poe's attention to German literature has been shown to center not on Tieck but on E. T. A. Hoffmann, the author of such weird tales as the *Fantasiestücke* and the subject of Offenbach's opera. Poe's occupation with Hoffmann has been treated in some detail in two older published studies, the monograph of Palmer Cobb, *The Influence of E. T. A. Hoffmann on the Tales of Edgar Allan Poe*,[1] and an article by Gustav Gruener, "Notes on the Influence of E. T. A. Hoffmann upon Edgar Allan Poe."[2] In both studies a case, at first glance seemingly strong, is made out for more or less direct dependence of Poe upon Hoffmann. However, it turns out that this dependence derives, more indirectly, from English translations of Hoffmann's tales, eleven of which were available by 1847.[3] It derives also from articles on him in British and American magazines to which Poe had access.

Neither Cobb nor Gruener presents any indisputable evidence that Poe ever read anything by Hoffmann in the original German. The "influence" that exists is chiefly to be found in Poe's use of Hoffmann's device of mingling the real and imaginary worlds, his penchant for the weird and arabesque, his overwrought fantasy, his spooky atmosphere and *diablerie*.

Henry Zylstra, in his unpublished Harvard dissertation of 1940, "E. T. A. *Hoffmann in England and America*," sums up: "Translations and criticisms of Hoffmann significantly affected Poe's most characteristic and best work... The combined effect of these influences justify [*sic*] the statement that to a considerable extent Poe's art sprang from a journalistically Hoffmannesque context."[4]

In the present study, on the other hand, I chose Tieck as the focus because I feel that Poe's interest in him is more circumscribed and more tangible, and therefore easier to identify.

It becomes obvious from the state of research on the subject published so far that, while Poe had a limited familiarity with a small sector of German literature, the question of the extent of his knowledge of, and contact with, German has never been settled to the satisfaction of everyone concerned. In his article on "Poe's Criticism of Hawthorne," now almost seventy years old,[5] Henry M. Belden stated that Poe knew no German at all. One of Poe's more recent biographers, Arthur Hobson Quinn, looking at the question from the point of view of Poe's writings as a whole, says: "The attempt to derive his work from German sources has not been very successful."[6] Others, however, besides Gruener and Cobb, among them Killis Campbell[7] and Van Wyck Brooks,[8] tend to believe that he did indeed know some German. In his article in *Modern Philology* (referred to in note 2), Gruener alludes to several bits of circumstantial evidence to substantiate this. He says that besides French and Latin, in which we know he was proficient, Poe may have taken lessons in German from the German Professor Blaettermann during the calendar year he spent as a student at the University of Virginia.[9]

In one of the most important, comprehensive, and painstaking studies to come out recently on the impact of German letters on American writers, *Ludwig Tieck and America* (referred to above in note 3), Percy Matenko also inclines to the view that "Poe must have known" at least one of Tieck's *Novellen* "in the original, or at least enough of it to understand the title and something of its richly imaginative content." (p. 72) To this important statement we will revert later.

More than one critic, then, has been led to detect direct influence of German upon Poe and to suspect that he had some first-hand acquaintance with some German writings. Indeed, we are struck by several references that Poe makes to Tieck. To be sure, one of these, in *Mystification*, identifying Tieck as the "scion" of Hungarian nobility and a devotee of *grotesquerie*, is obviously a mere spoof. Two other references, however, are of greater importance. They are found in a review of Hawthorne's *Twice-Told Tales* and *Mosses from an old Manse*, which appeared in *Godey's Magazine and Lady's Book*, XXXV (1847). Not being well disposed toward Hawthorne and in general critical of his writings, Poe charges him with lack of originality and finds him unduly dependent on Tieck. The passages in question read as follows:

> The fact is, that if Mr. Hawthorne were really original, he could not fail of making himself felt by the public. But the fact is, he is *not* original in any sense. Those who speak of him as original, mean nothing more than that he differs in his manner of tone, and in his choice of subjects, from any author of their acquaintance — their acquaintance not extending to the German Tieck, whose manner, in *some* of his works, is absolutely identical with that *habitual* to Hawthorne.... These points properly understood, it will seem that the critic (unacquainted with Tieck) who reads a single tale or essay by Hawthorne, may be justified in thinking him original; but the tone, or manner, or choice of subject, which induces in this critic the sense of the new, will, — if not in a second tale, at least in a third and all subsequent ones — not only fail of inducing it, but bring about an exactly antagonistic impression.[10]

The question arises, discussed by Belden and more recently by Matenko: How did Poe come by such intimate knowledge of Tieck as to enable him to venture utterances as categorical as these? Contradictory solutions may be offered; their nature depends upon the proponent's convictions regarding Poe's knowledge or ignorance of German.

To one familiar with German, it was easy even in Poe's day to procure copies of Tieck's writings. He enjoyed an enviable reputation in the western World from 1832 on as the inheritor of Goethe's toga. But we have no evidence whatever that Poe made any effort to procure such copies. Those not familiar with German, on the other hand, had a wide choice of translations, stemming chiefly from England. Between 1823 and 1845 four English renderings of *Der blonde Eckbert* became available, three each of *Der getreue Eckart und der Tannenhäuser, Der Runenberg, Die Elfen, Liebeszauber* and *Der Pokal*, two of *Die Gemälde*, and one each of about fifteen other works, including the play *Blaubart* (1833), the novels *Dichterleben* (1830), *Der Aufruhr in den Cevennen* and *Vittoria Accorombona* (both in 1845). Among the translators were such excellent craftsmen as Carlyle, Froude, and Hare.[11] Evidence that Poe was widely familiar with these translations is at best sparse and dubious. There are only two possible exceptions. It is likely, though not proved, that he read the translation of the *Novelle Die Freunde* in the American magazine *Democratic Review* of May, 1845, reprinted from the Hare-Froude volume *Tales from the Phantasus* (London, 1845). It is *quite* likely that he read one of the translations of *Liebeszauber*.

As for articles on Tieck appearing chiefly in British magazines, Poe probably read the one in *Blackwood's* for February, 1833, and surely one of September, 1837. Here he learned among other things that Tieck's tales contain "a vigorous moral couched under the playful cover of the marvellous." He may also have seen the article in the London *Monthly Review* of April, 1841. In the last-mentioned we may find one of the roots for his conclusion about the dependence of Hawthorne upon Tieck, which might well have become his conviction after reading *Die Freunde*. This *Novelle*, directed against the "egotism of fancy," as both Belden and Matenko point out, reminds one of Hawthorne in its programmatic trend.

Of value is Belden's statement that Poe was probably encouraged to risk his querulous contentions against Hawthorne by an article entitled "American Humor," published originally in the *Foreign and Colonial Quarterly Review* (October, 1843), and reprinted, notably in the aforementioned *Democratic Review* (April, 1845), a magazine to which Poe himself contributed. Here it is stated that: "As a recounter of mere legends, Mr. Hawthorne claims high praise. He reminds us of Tieck, in spite of the vast difference in the materials used by the two artists." The article, continued in the September issue, refers to Hawthorne as "the Tieck of this American literature of ours." We now leave the Tieck-Hawthorne-Poe triangle to return to it later.

In the light of these circumstantial but strong indications that Poe's knowledge of Tieck is largely based upon second-hand information derived from British and American sources, what are we to say concerning his interest in one of Tieck's *Novellen* never translated into English? It has the long title *Das alte Buch und die Reise ins Blaue hinein* (originally published in 1834 in the annual *Urania auf das Jahr 1835*). This is the work about which Matenko expresses the opinion, noted above, that "Poe must have known it" in the original "or at least enough of it to understand the title and something of its richly imaginative content, which Van Wyck Brooks suggests, he could apply to the fantastic atmosphere of his own tale [*The Fall of the House of Usher* (1839)]."

As for the *Novelle Das alte Buch...*, it is true Poe mentions it in his well-known "thriller," but only by the latter part of its title, *viz.*, *The Journey into the Blue Distance*, as if that were the complete title. He catalogs it together with some nine other works in a list of Usher's weird readings, among them *Heaven and Hell* of Swedenborg, the *Directorium Inquisitorum* by a Dominican monk, and the *Vigiliae Mortuorum*. But does this justify Matenko's conjecture that Poe actually read any of this work in its only available form—German? And does it justify Van Wyck's bold conjecture that the "fantastic atmosphere" of Poe's story owes something to *Das alte Buch...*?

Tieck's tale is a series of stories within more stories and long discussions, starting as an account of the discovery of an old fragmented medieval book. This tome, revised by later writers, tells of Athelstan, a dreamer and adventurer who, engaged in the "Reise ins Blaue hinein" in search of romantic bliss, has run away from home. We meet humble folk who talk like sages and turn up as poets reborn or later to be such. We are caught in mazes of wordiness but never shocked by anything gruesome or horrible. Athelstan (later also called Oberon) is wedded to and endowed by a fairy Gloriana (Titania) with the power of blessing poets like Shakespeare. The ultimate purpose of the loquacious *tour de force* is to give Tieck an opportunity, in a postscript, to ridicule writers like Hoffmann, Heine, and Victor Hugo, who are "blessed" by Athelstan's foe, the "arsenic prince."

Poe's story concerns the invalid, mentally unstable, ghastly Roderick Usher and his still ghastlier dying twin sister Lady Madeline, the last survivors of the mysterious ancient Usher family. They dwell in their gloomy, age-worn mountain castle in a region where even the vegetable life is "sentient." By mistake Madeline, seeming to have died, is buried alive by her brother but freed from her tomb only to perish with him just before their dwelling crashes down upon their corpses in the horror of a storm-swept night.

The only discernible similarity is that in each case the author is the storyteller. Tieck's has a conventional setting, relieved by a romantic fairy tale, full of caprice but devoid of fantastic horror. Poe's is a tale of studied horror, spookiness, and extreme grotesque terror.

At this point some digressive but pertinent remarks suggest themselves. The truncated title *The Journey into the Blue Distance* used by Poe has led to the embarrassment of at least three American writers. In keeping with the axiom that German literature is "off-limits" to some American editors, Thomas Wentworth Higginson, in *Margaret Fuller Ossoli*,[12] could not find the title among Tieck's works, and concluded that Poe had invented it. Henry A. Beers in *A History of English Romanticism in the Nineteenth Century*,[13] recounts Higginson's experience: "à propos of Poe's sham learning and his habit of mystifying the reader by imaginary citations, [Higginson] hunted in vain for this fascinatingly entitled 'Journey into the Blue Distance,'" and was "laughed at for his pains by a friend who assured him that Poe could scarcely read a word of German." Margaret Alterton and Hardin Craig in the notes to *Edgar Allan Poe. Representative Selections*,[14] note: "The work referred to has not been located." For a careful investigator with some knowledge of German this should not be an insoluble problem—if indeed it is worth solving at all.

One is reminded of similar unfamiliarity with German sources on the part of American writers. Tieck becomes its victim in the Trent-Hellman edition of *The Journals of Washington Irving*.[15] The editors, unable to decipher the hand of the very man whose writings they were editing, not conversant with the German literary scene after 1832, and inhospitable to expert help, garbled the name of Irving's Dresden host and read "Treck."

To return to our subject, we have found that there is no relationship between the plot of Tieck's *Novelle* and that of Poe's tale. Therefore it is folly for Van Wyck to suggest that the "fantastic atmosphere" of *The Fall of the House of Usher* came from Tieck. As for *Das alte Buch...*, it was again a magazine article on Tieck—the one in *Blackwood's* of September, 1837—that supplied Poe with *all the necessary information* concerning Tieck's *Novelle*. But he misinterpreted what he read, as we shall see. The partial title, "The Journey into the Blue Distance," by which Poe knew Tieck's work, is taken over just as it appears in *Blackwood's*. If Poe had been familiar with the original work, it would seem unlikely for him to happen upon the identical wording. Granting that the prosaic first part of Tieck's title did not fit into Poe's scheme, he could have rendered 'Die Reise ins Blaue hinein' in several different ways: 'The Journey (or Voyage, or Trip, or Excursion) into the Blue (or into the Cerulean).' It was the eerie title in *Blackwood's*—hardly understood fully by Poe[16]—that attracted him. In addition, he was attracted, and misled, by certain remarks he discovered in the article. The work is described as "an extraordinary caprice," an extravaganza with "revolting situations," which resembles a dream in its abruptness and is psychologically unsound. Poe misinterpreted this to mean that Tieck's work was frighteningly eerie, weird, and weighted with horror, when in reality it was a playfully fantastic extravaganza which the British critic deemed to be in bad taste.[17]

It has been noted that besides *Die Freunde* Poe may have read Tieck's *Novelle Liebeszauber*. The basis for this belief—circumstantial, to be sure—

is that Poe's protagonist in *The Fall of the House of Usher* bears the name of Tieck's protagonist in *Liebeszauber*, namely Roderick.

From what has been said it should be clear that at no point where he is concerned with German literature does Poe reveal the slightest knowledge of German, or any acquaintance with a German literary work based directly upon that work itself. He may have read some of Hoffmann's tales in English translation, and two of Tieck's, but most of what he knew, or thought he knew, about these authors was derived at second or third hand. Nowhere in his writings have I found a single statement about a German author or work which cannot be traced to an available secondary source.

We return to the Tieck-Hawthorne-Poe relationship. In the light of what has been said, and in spite of Hawthorne's occasional dependence upon Tieck, it seems like sheer effrontery for Poe to attack Hawthorne as severely as he did for what would amount to plagiarism of Tieck.[18] Certainly one must be surer of his ground than Poe was to justify such a charge. The accusation in the form in which Poe makes it is both untrue and unfair. Nor can I agree with Belden in his article in *Anglia*, p. 404, that Poe "might in all honesty and with very little exaggeration say that 'Tieck's manner, in some of his works, is absolutely identical with that *habitual* to Hawthorne.'" As Matenko says (p. 88):

"Thus Hawthorne's narrative writing resembles Tieck's in motivation, though not in style. The resemblance in motivation is general, such as one is likely to find 'in the air' during a period when the influence of English and German romanticism was dominant."

Moreover, by injecting a foreign writer like Tieck with whom Americans, including Poe, were not conversant (Hawthorne being an exception), Poe displays "sham learning," to use a phrase of Higginson. Poe is notorious, not only for his glee in outguessing his readers; he also delights in impressing them with knowledge and accusations that at times rest upon shaky foundations.

However, if Poe was unfamiliar with German or gave misleading impressions of his knowledge of it, writers in Germany, for their part, were guilty of spreading unfounded rumors about him. One reported that Poe was found wandering about in Russia as a beggar, and deported home to America.[19] Another lists him as an "eclectic of poetry," who "has gathered much honey from German poetry."[20] Such exaggeration was not uncommon among German writers of the nineteenth century when expatiating on German "influence" on American literature.[21]

In the following remarks Poe denies his own dependence upon what he calls "Germanism":

I am led to think that it is the prevalence of the arabesque in my serious tales which has induced one or two of my critics to tax me, in all friendliness, with what they have pleased to call Germanism and gloom...

The charge is in bad taste and the grounds of the accusation have not been sufficiently considered. Let me admit for the moment that the "phantasy pieces" now given are Germanic or what not. But the truth is that with a single exception there is no one of the stories in which the scholar should recognize the distinctive features of that species of pseudo-horror which we are taught to call Germanic for no better reason than that some of the secondary names of German literature have become identified with its folly. If in many of my productions terror has been my thesis, I maintain that terror is not of Germany, but of the soul.[22]

While these words surely contain an understatement of his relationship to Hoffmann, yet, on the whole, Poe warns the reader fairly and reasonably enough not to overestimate his indebtedness to German writers.

NOTES

[1] Chapel Hill, 1908.
[2] *PMLA*, XIX, New Series XII (1904), 1-25. Also important in this connection is Gruener's article, "Poe's Knowledge of German," *Modern Philology*, II (1904), 125-139.
[3] These eleven, with the dates of their translation into English, are: *Die Elixiere des Teufels* (1824); *Das Majorat, Das Fräulein von Scuderi*, and *Meister Floh* (all in 1826); *Der goldene Topf* (1827); *Datura Fastuosa* (1839); *Der Elementargeist, Der Sandmann*, and *Die Jesuiter-kirche in G...* (all in 1844); *Signor Formica* (1845); and *Meister Martin der Küfner* (1847). These statistics are based on B. Q. Morgan, *A Critical Bibliography of German Literature in English Translation, 1481-1927. With Supplement Embracing the Years 1928-1935*. Second Edition; completely revised and greatly augmented (Stanford, California, 1938), pp. 237 f.; E. H. Zeydel, *Ludwig Tieck and England* (Princeton, 1932); and Percy Matenko, *Ludwig Tieck and America* (Chapel Hill, 1954).
[4] Quoted by Matenko, *Tieck and America*, p. 75.
[5] *Anglia*, XXIII (1901), 376-404.
[6] *Edgar Allan Poe. A Critical Biography* (New York and London, 1941), p. 289. In the more recent biographies by William R. Bittner (Boston, 1962) and Irwin Porges (Philadelphia and New York, 1963) the subject is not even mentioned, and Hoffmann's name does not appear.
[7] "Poe's Reading," *Studies in English*, No. 5 (*University of Texas Bulletin*, No. 2538 [October 8, 1925]), p. 188.
[8] *The World of Washington Irving* (Philadelphia, 1944), pp. 207, 341.
[9] Bittner, *Poe, a Biography*, p. 54, claims only that Blaettermann gave Poe "a smattering of Anglo-Saxon, old Germanic and Norse literature," but he does not mention modern German.
[10] Issue of November, 1847, pp. 252-256. In 1842 Poe had discussed Hawthorne's *Twice-Told Tales* in *Graham's Magazine*, XX, 298 ff., but here Tieck is not mentioned at all – an indication that he could not yet have been aware of Hawthorne's "dependence" on Tieck. This awareness probably came in 1845, as will be pointed out below.
[11] See note 3 above for the sources of these statistics.
[12] Boston and New York, 1884, p. 45.
[13] New York, 1901, pp. 162 ff.
[14] New York, Cincinnati, *etc.*, 1935, p. 515.
[15] Boston, 1919, I, p. 155. See my remarks in *PMLA*, XLVI (1931), 946-947.
[16] It simply means: A (sentimental) journey without a definite goal.

[17] Compare the remarks in my review of Matenko's book in *Modern Language Quarterly*, XVI (1955), 279-281.

[18] Such striking accusations often prompt later writers to echo them. Matenko, pp. 77-78, quotes James Russell Lowell in 1848 as calling Hawthorne "a Puritan Tieck" (an idea already found in the article in the *Democratic Review* of September, 1845). Matenko also finds minor writers like Frederick B. Perkins, Edmund C. Stedman, and George E. Woodberry linking the author of the *House of the Seven Gables* with Tieck.

[19] H. W. Hewett-Thayer, *American Literature as viewed in Germany, 1818-1861*. University of North Carolina Studies in Comparative Literature, No. 22 (Chapel Hill, 1960), p. 76, n. 58.

[20] *Ibid.*, p. 15.

[21] *Ibid.*, p. 69.

[22] From the preface to the *Tales of the Grotesque and Arabesque*. Also quoted by Matenko, p. 71.

Karl Lebrecht Immermann's Portrait of a Folk-Hero in *Münchhausen*

WILLIAM MCCLAIN

Doubtless the most important insight contributed by recent interpreters of Karl Immermann's *Münchhausen* is that the unity of the novel has been achieved by a skillful blending of two contrasting visions of reality.[1] Both of these worlds are fictitious. One, however, the world of *Schnick-Schnack-Schnurr*, seems pure artifice, while the other, the world of the *Oberhof*, seems to have been conceived in historical terms. For whereas the former appears unreal and bizarre, the latter impresses us as being firmly rooted in reality, and its inhabitants seem normal people who live together in plausible relationships.[2]

By allowing his readers alternating glimpses of these two worlds, Immermann creates a kind of modal counterpoint which, though delightful in itself, proves as well to be an effective means of accomplishing the novel's moral purpose, which is to portray both the negative forces undermining spiritual life at that time and the positive counterforces by which Immermann hoped they might be neutralized.

In spite of its ironic overtones, the second of the two appended letters seems, indeed, to suggest that Immermann's main aim in the novel may have been moral rather than satirical. For the purpose of the tale, we are told here, was to relate a love-experience "bis zu dem Punkte, wo sie [die Liebe] den Menschen für Haus und Land, für Zeit und Mitwelt reif, mündig, wirksam zu machen beginnt."[3] Such a message, the *Herausgeber* insists, is sorely needed by the present age, which, though a time of great achievements, is also a period in which "das Herz der Menschheit noch nicht wieder recht aufgewacht ist." This sleeping heart must be reawakened, he warns in conclusion, if the present generation is to discover the way that all generations must follow on earth, "denn vom Herzen ist alles größte auf Erden ausgeschritten."

If we are willing to believe our whimsical narrator here, we can consider the love-relationship between Oswald and Lisbeth in the *Oberhof*-sequences as illustrating the moral of the novel. For through their love, which triumphs over all prejudices and conventions and ends in a happy marriage, the young Swabian aristocrat and his foundling sweetheart visibly grow to a point where they become "reif, mündig und wirksam für Zeit und Mitwelt."

During his sojourn at the *Oberhof*, however, Oswald's maturation is also furthered by another individual, his host, the *Hofschulze*, whom he comes to admire not only for his own sake, as a man of unusual qualities, but also as the incarnation of certain values and attitudes which he discovers in this rural Westphalian community, and which impress him profoundy. Since the values of the heart meant for Immermann in a larger sense "die Grundbezüge der Menschheit," as Benno von Wiese has pointed out,[4] the *Hofschulze*, as the main representative of traditional "Grundbezüge" in this extended sense, becomes one of the main figures through whom the moral message of the novel is communicated, and hence a figure of major importance. Earlier studies have dealt with the kinds of values the *Hofschulze* stands for, but none has treated the equally important problem of how Immermann managed to make this simple man seem a plausible embodiment of those values. In the following pages I should like to focus on this problem, which might be described in Northrup Frye's terms as that of discovering the means by which Immermann sought to transform an ordinary man into a hero of the "high mimetic mode."[5] By addressing such a question to the novel, one is led, as I hope to show, to some rather surprising conclusions as to the kind of hero the *Hofschulze* is.

Immermann encourages us in various ways to believe that the *Hofschulze's* world is a real world. The *Hofschulze* himself is modeled in part on a farmer named Ewald who owned a prosperous *Schulzenhof* near Meckingsen;[6] and the authenticity of the *Oberhof* is even documented, as it were, by the long passage from Kindlinger's *Münsterische Beiträge* at the beginning of Chapter 3 of Book II,[7] which explains the nature of the *Oberhöfe* and their importance in the community life of rural Westphalia. In the narrator's comments on this document, which is supposed to introduce us to the locale of his story and to its hero, we sense not only his enthusiasm for the way of life which it describes, but also an elegiac note in his remark that this manner of existence has survived only because individuals such as the *Hofschulze* have emerged from time to time in the community.[8]

The opening scene of Chapter 1 of Book II, which introduces us to the world of the *Oberhof*, at once communicates an impression of purposeful and constructive activity. From the first moment the focus is on the central figure of the scene, the *Hofschulze*, who is at his forge, heating a piece of iron to repair a broken piece of the track of a rack-wagon wheel. With swift, sure blows of the hammer he rivets the piece to the wheel. His work finished, he astonishes the reader and the two men who are watching, by pulling the heavy wagon single-handed across the courtyard to test the wheel. In his conversation later with the two observers, a tax-collector new to the district and a Jewish horse-trader who has come to buy one of his horses, both the nature of his reflections and his manner of formulating them create the impression of a man who is not only physically energetic, technically competent, and a good manager, but also mature, sagacious and self-honest.

Later episodes which portray the *Hofschulze* in his relationships with his daughter, his servants, the other farmers in the community and with Oswald, reveal that he is an absolute ruler in his own household and a respected leader in the community. His promise to Lisbeth to bring pressure on any farmer in the community who defaults in paying the rent which her guardian, the Baron of Schnuck-Puckelig-Erbsenscheucher, has sent her to collect,[9] even contains a hint of extraordinary powers that he wields. From the remark of another farmer, who has overheard his promise, we receive an inkling that the special means of coercion to which he alludes is the *Femgericht*, which, as we soon learn, the old farmer has revived as an institution of justice in this region.

Immermann's first device for making his *Hofschulze* seem a heroic figure is, as implied above, that of assigning to him attributes and qualities which cause the reader to feel him superior in quality to the other characters. A second is the rhetorical device of associating him with heroic figures of history and legend. Two examples occur in Oswald's letter to an absent friend in Chapter 6 of Book II. The first association is with the patriarchs of Biblical days, when Oswald remarks that the *Hofschulze* reminds him of an "Erzvater, der dem Gotte seiner Väter von unbehauenen Steinen ein Mal aufrichtete und Trankopfer darauf gießt und Öl und seine Füllen erzieht, sein Korn schneidet und dabei über die Seinigen unumschränkt herrscht und richtet."[10] The second mental connection established is with the time of the nation's beginnings as recorded by Tacitus in his *Germania*.[11]

While Oswald admires the qualities in his host which justify such exalted comparisons, he has not allowed these to blind him to the flaws in his character, as we note in his remark in the same letter that he has never encountered "eine kompaktere Mischung von Ehrwürdigem und Verschmitztem, von Vernunft und Eigensinn," an evaluation whose accuracy is amply born out by later developments in the narrative.

Immermann's third device for surrounding the *Hofschulze* with an aura of the heroic is that of portraying him in situations in which his true eminence becomes apparent. Two striking examples are the situations which give Oswald his deepest insights into the customs and traditions of the region: the ceremony in association with the collection of the *Hofschulze*'s gifts of produce to the church and the wedding of his daughter a few days later.

During the gift-giving ritual,[12] every detail of which is dictated by custom, the *Hofschulze* plays his appointed role unfalteringly and with a dignity that seems all the more impressive in contrast to the comically rigid behavior of the *Küster*. Here he seems a kind of natural aristocrat. For our understanding of Immermann's devices for making the *Hofschulze* seem a heroic figure this episode is also illuminating as an example of how the old farmer himself contributes a dimension by consistently behaving, as he does here, in accordance with his exalted self-image.

The *Diakonus* who is introduced into the action in this episode turns out to be an old school friend of Oswald's, and after the ceremony the two renew acquaintance. Still under the spell of the ceremony, Oswald exclaims that it has impressed upon him more profoundly than any previous experience the meaning of tradition in the life of a people:

> ... Aber mich hat hier die Empfindung stärker als selbst in meiner Heimat angefaßt: Das ist der Boden, den seit mehr als tausend Jahren ein unvermischter Stamm trat! Und die Idee des unsterblichen Volkes wehte in mir im Rauschen dieser Eichen und des uns umwallenden Fruchtsegens, fast greiflich möchte ich sagen, entgegen.[13]

The *Diakonus* replies, with equal fervor, that he has also sensed here, and in the same almost mystical manner, the immortality of the "Volk." He goes on then to praise the qualities which have enabled the "Volk" ever to renew itself through the ages, carefully explaining, however, that he is using the term in a restrictive sense to mean "die besten unter den freien Bürgern und den ehrwürdigen, tätigen, arbeitsamen Mittelstand," which to him represents a kind of reservoir of the finest life-values:

> In ihm [dem Volk] gebiert sich immer neu der wahre Ruhm, die Macht und die Herrlichkeit der Nation, die es ja nur ist durch ihre Sitte, durch den Hort ihres Gedankens und ihrer Kunst, und dann durch den sprungweise hervortretenden Heldenmut, wenn die Dinge einmal wieder an den abschüssigen Rand des Verderbens getrieben sind.[14]

In his candid admission here, that the call to serve in this rural community had saved him from a serious spiritual crisis, the *Diakonus* becomes for a moment a kind of mouthpiece of the author by citing some of the disturbing trends which Immermann saw as signs of an impending crisis in the national spiritual life.[15] While working as house-tutor to a wealthy young "Vornehmen" in the city after his university years he came into contact, as he explains, with "allen den geistreichen, eleganten, schillernden und schimmernden Gestalten" of the day and became, under their influence, "ebenso geistrich, halbiert, kritisch und ironisch." During that period he became "genial in meinen Ansprüchen, wenn auch nicht in dem, was ich leistete, unbefriedigt von irgend etwas Vorkommendem, und immer in eine blaue Weite strebend; kurz, ich war dem schlimmeren Teile meines Wesens zufolge ein Neuer, hatte Weltschmerz, wünschte eine andere Bibel, ein anderes Christentum, einen andern Staat, eine andere Familie und mich selbst anders mit Haut und Haar."[16] At that critical juncture the saving call came to serve in this rural parish, where among these "wunderlichen, aber achtbaren Originalen" and "unter diesen ländlichen Wehrfestern" he has found peace and also the courage to establish "ein liebes Verhältnis,"[17] and has thus been able to strike real roots at last.

The *Diakonus*'s confession is significant, in terms of the larger moral purpose of the novel, as the account of the only character who possesses the critical intelligence, the experience, the human understanding and the power of expression necessary to assess critically, as he does here, the relative advantages and disadvantages of urban and rural life. For the same reasons he is the character who is best able to see the *Hofschulze* in critical perspective. What he says about him is thus particularly significant.

At this point the stalwart old farmer still seems the individual who best exemplifies the qualities of the "Mittelstand" which the *Diakonus* praises in his conversation with Oswald. Even though he seems comically overdressed on his daughter's wedding day in the nine splendid vests which he wears, not for comfort, as he explains, but because he can afford them, and because his father and grandfather before him always wore nine jackets to weddings and christenings, he nevertheless cuts an imposing figure. The dignified manner which he feels compelled to assume even inspires the narrator to compare him with a king. In the course of inspecting the preparations for the wedding banquet, we are told, he notices a pot boiling over which he could easily have removed from the fire, had he not feared "so die Haltung des Brautvaters, welche ihm verbot, irgend etwas an diesem Tage selbst anzufassen, zu verlieren." And so he simply watches as the pot boils over, "ruhig wie jener spanische König, welcher die glühende Kohle lieber seinen Fuß versengen ließ, als daß er sie etikettewidrig selbst weggenommen hätte."[18] To appreciate the ironic overtones of this comparison we must realize that the king to whom the narrator refers is Don Pedro IV of Aragon who, because of his exaggerated concern for appearances was nicknamed "el ceremonioso." It seems apt in a more serious sense as well, however, when we recall that Don Pedro's strict adherence to tradition also made him rigid and resistant to change, and hence also a kind of prisoner of the values by which he lived.

The wedding day ends most unhappily for the *Hofschulze*. While everyone is at table an old enemy enters the empty farm house and hides the sword which the old farmer prizes above all other possessions because he believes it, in spite of all evidence to the contrary, to have been Charlemagne's, and, far more important of course, because, as the weapon with which he has always presided at the sessions of the *Femgericht*, it is a symbol of his authority in the community. For these reasons, as the narrator explains, the loss of the sword is a tragic event for the *Hofschulze*, and he attempts to make us feel it as such by calling the chapter devoted to it (Chapter 7 of Book VII) *Ein Trauerspiel im Oberhofe*. At the beginning of the chapter he even invokes the muse of tragedy. By departing from iconographical tradition, however, he prepares us for a special kind of tragedy. His Melpomene, he tells us, has not one, but two daggers. One, shining and sharp, cuts quickly and cleanly, while the other, rusty and full of notches, tears the flesh. With the first, he continues, "tritt sie Könige und Helden an," whereas with the second she steals into the lives of peasants and burghers.[19] The nature of the tragic experience differs correspondingly, always involving for individuals of lofty status "große, unleugbare Güter" such as "Krone, Reich, Leben," but often arising out of seeming "Nichtigkeiten" in the case of those of inferior status. Since we know that the *Hofschulze*'s missing sword is not really Charlemagne's, and hence has neither the real value nor the symbolic value which he assigns to it, our natural tendency here would be to regard his tragic experience as being of the latter type. Because he values it so highly, however, its loss for him, the narrator assures us, is truly "die leidenschaftlichste Tragödie," and he attempts in his description of the old man's systematic, but futile search to prove to us that this is indeed the case. As we watch the *Hofschulze* move from room to room we cannot but admire his incredible self-control. At the same time we feel compassion and also anxiety, lest for one of his age the stress should prove too great. Only after he has thoroughly searched in the last possible place does he finally cry out:

Das brennende Licht entsank seiner Hand, er setzte sich oder fiel vielmehr auf einen dort stehenden Kasten und stieß einen furchtbaren Schrei aus, einen von den Lauten, die sich nicht beschreiben lassen, weil die Natur in ihnen ihre eigensten, nur sich selbst vorbehaltenen Rechte übt.[20]

In this moment of despair, which the narrator conveys with appropriate pathos, the *Hofschulze* becomes through the very intensity of his suffering a heroic figure. He has here something of the stature of a Job, an Oedipus or a Faustus. At no other point in the narrative does he seem more closely akin to the heroic figures of world literature than in this moment of abject misery.

While still reeling under the blow of this loss, the *Hofschulze* suffers yet another staggering blow when Oswald inadvertently becomes a witness of the secret proceedings of the *Femgericht*.[21] After Oswald has politely excused himself and departed, the farmers, indignant at this intrusion, demand death for the offender. The *Hofschulze* promises to settle the matter, assuring his colleagues that he has learned from his father a means of keeping their illicit activity from coming to light. The means to which he alludes, as we soon see, is mortal combat. In the terrible moment, in the locked upstairs room, when he suddenly makes known to Oswald the reason why he has brought him there, he seems like a man deranged. When Oswald refuses to do battle over what he calls "Possen," the old farmer's anger mounts to the point of fury, and real tragedy is averted only by the timely, if somewhat grotesque appearance of Lisbeth from behind the *Saatlaken*. The shock of her sudden appearance has the effect of immediately dissipating the old farmer's feverish excitement, and, dropping the axe which he had just raised in challenge, he leaves the room "stumm und gebeugt," like a broken man.[22]

In witnessing this outburst of primordial anger, which Oswald accurately describes as "Berserkerwut," we come to know a negative side of the *Hofschulze's* character which we have as yet not been shown, the fanaticism with which he is capable of defending the traditions to which he so stubbornly clings. In this way the episode might be said to reveal in him what *Aristotle* called *hamartia*.

The *Hofschulze's* next appearance, which is also his last in the novel, is at the court trial of *Patriotenkaspar*, the enemy who has concealed his sword as a means of getting even with him for having made him, through the ban of the *Femgericht*, a social outcast. To the *Diakonus*, who sees him here for the first time in several weeks, the old man seems worn and haggard, but he delivers his long explanation of his reasons for reviving the *Femgericht* in the region in a firm voice and eloquently, and with a dignity, too, that is reminiscent of former times. The impact of his patriotic peroration is conveyed to us through the reported reactions of the judge and the *Diakonus*, who are both visibly moved:

> Leuchtend waren die hellblauen Augen des Hofschulzen während des letzten Teils dieser Rede geworden, seine weißen Haare hatten sich wie Flammen emporgerichtet, die Gestalt stand wieder groß und gerade da. Der Richter sah vor sich nieder, der Diakonus dem Alten in das Antlitz; er gemahnte ihn wie ein Prophet des alten Bundes. Mit höflicher Verbeugung und stillem Gruß entfernte sich der alte Bauer.[23]

As he plays this last scene to its stirring close, the old farmer again seems for a brief moment larger than life size. It is thus all the more shocking to encounter, in the anteroom immediately after the hearing, the very different image, which is however the real one now, of a simple farmer who is "krank" and "angegriffen." Since this is our last image, our final impression is thus, in stark contrast to our initial one, that of a broken old man.

To give his *Hofschulze* the stature necessary for his role in *Münchhausen* as a representative of the integrated way of life which the novel offers as an ideal contrast to the anti-ideal portrayed in the Münchhausen-episodes, Immermann has endowed the old farmer, as we noted, with superior attributes and qualities; has represented him in situations in which his charismatic powers could be revealed; has added dimension by comparing him with Old Testament prophets, primitive Germanic tribal leaders and other heroic figures; and has finally even made him hero of a middle-class "Trauerspiel." While we find him admirable and impressive, in consequence of all this, we nevertheless find it difficult to think of him in truly heroic terms because he so conspicuously lacks the essential heroic quality of grandeur. Doubtless the main reason for this lack is his extreme rigidity, which we sense most strongly in his inordinate stubbornness and in his fanatic belief in tradition. Since the *Hofschulze* best exemplifies the "Erinnerungskraft," which the

Diakonus praises as one of the finest virtues of the "Volk" in his conversation with Oswald cited above, one can agree with interpreters such as von Wiese, who see the old farmer as an important representative of "die Welt des 'Positiven'" in the novel.[24] Because of his hideboundness, however, he also arouses negative feelings which make us wish to qualify our acceptance of him as a representative of the positive values of the novel. For it is apparent that his cult of tradition, though in itself admirable, also has the negative effect of making him totally unable to move forward. This is reflected in his expressed opposition to all change. The danger inherent in such a mentality becomes painfully manifest in his hour of trial. When his world of traditional values is suddenly threatened, he himself disintegrates, as though he were unable to exist in any other world.

To counterbalance the *Hofschulze*'s unyielding reactionary attitude, Immermann has introduced a more critical perspective on the past through the *Diakonus*. Thanks to his enlightened and critical attitude he is able to perceive what is most valuable in the legacy of the past. His exhortation to the *Hofschulze* in the anteroom following the hearing might actually be cited as a kind of summary of the moral values which Immermann wished his novel to express:

'Laßt den Freistuhl verfallen, das Schwert aus dem Auge des Tages geschwunden sein, laßt sie die Heimlichkeit von den Dächern schreien!' rief der Diakonus mit geröteter Wange. 'Habt Ihr nicht in Euch und mit Euren Freunden das Wort der Selbstständigkeit gefunden? Das ist die heimliche Losung, an der Ihr Euch erkennt, und die Euch nicht genommen werden kann. Gepflanzt habt Ihr den Sinn, daß der Mensch von seinen Nächsten abhange, schlicht, gerade, einfach, nicht von Fremden, die nur das Werk ihrer Künstlichkeit mit ihm herauskünsteln, zusammengesetzt, erschroben, verschroben; und dieser Sinn braucht nicht der Steine unter den alten Linden, um gutes Recht zu schöpfen. Eure Männlichkeit, Eure eisenfeste Natur, Ihr alter, großer, gewaltiger Mensch, das ist das wahre Schwert Karls des Großen, für des Diebes Hand unantastbar!'[25]

In this episode the roles are reversed. The man who had seemed so strong, so self-possessed, so self-sufficient and so heroic now seems a fallen hero. Sensing his need, the *Diakonus* tactfully offers to help, and the old farmer promises to think over his offer. A new relationship begins here in which the young man will be the leader.

To those who regard the *Oberhof*-narrative as a kind of archetype of the nineteenth-century *Dorfnovelle*, its favorable picture of the *Volk* may seem to justify thinking of it as an early example of the enthusiasm for folk-lore which was ultimately to lead to the kind of "völkisch" thinking reflected in works such as Wilhelm Heinrich Riehl's *Land und Leute*. To interpret the tale in this way, however, is to distort its meaning. For Immermann intended his image of Westphalian life only as a kind of reassurance to those who shared his fear of an impending value-crisis. As long as there are individuals such as the *Hofschulze*, Oswald, Lisbeth and the *Diakonus*, he seems to be saying, we can always be certain that the best of the past will be carried over into the future.

NOTES

[1] Benno von Wiese has provided most important insights into the inner unity of *Münchhausen* in his "Interpretation von 'Münchhausen'" in *Der deutsche Roman* (Düsseldorf, 1963), pp. 353-406 and in his chapter on the novel in *Karl Immermann. Sein Werk und sein Leben* (Bad Homburg v. d. H. — Berlin — Zürich, 1969), pp. 204-251. Most radical of the recent studies which argue the organic unity of the novel is Dimiter Statkow's essay, "Über die dialektische Struktur des Immermann-Romans 'Münchhausen,'" *Weimarer Beiträge*, XI (1965), 195-211, which attempts to demonstrate that Immermann consciously built a dialectical principle into his novel as a unifying device.

[2] Immermann's technique of contrasting real and unreal worlds is reminiscent of Cervantes' procedure in *Don Quijote*, of which we hear so many echoes in *Münchhausen*, and can actually be described in the sixteenth-century aesthetic terms used by Bruce Wardropper in his study of Cervantes' novel as a blending of history and story, "*Don Quijote:* Story or History?," *Modern Philology*, LXIII (1965-66), 1-11.

[3] *Immermanns Werke*, hrsg. von Harry Maync (Leipzig und Wien, 1906), Vol. II, p. 415. All subsequent references are to this edition, which will be indicated by the letter *M*.

[4] Benno von Wiese, *Karl Immermann. Sein Werk und sein Leben*, p. 237.

[5] Northrup Frye, *Anatomy of Criticism. Four Essays* (Princeton, N.J., 1957), pp. 33-52.

[6] As Maync points out, *M*, Vol. II, p. 451.

[7] Nikolaus Kindlinger, *Münsterische Beiträge zur Geschichte Deutschlands, hauptsächlich Westfalens* (Münster, 1790), Vol. II, p. 1 ff.

[8] *M*, Vol. I, p. 181.

[9] *M*, Vol. I, p. 168.

[10] *M*, Vol. I, p. 208.

[11] *Ibid.*

[12] In his notes (*M*, Vol. II, pp. 454-455) Maync points out that Immermann's description of the gift-giving ceremony, like his portrait of the *Hofschulze*, is in part based on reality, the main details having been taken from a clergyman's eye-witness account of a similar ceremony.

[13] *M*, Vol. I, p. 237.

[14] *Ibid.*, pp. 237-238.

[15] Immermann shared with many contemporaries this sense of impending crisis. Karl Viëtor suggests in his essay, "Die deutsche Literatur in der Krise der europäischen Literatur," in *Weltliteratur: Festschrift für Fritz Strich zum 70. Geburtstag* (Bern, 1952), pp. 137-154, how very widespread this sense of crisis was in Immermann's day.

[16] *M*, Vol. I, pp. 238-239.

[17] *Ibid.*

[18] *M*, Vol. II, p. 18.

[19] *M*, Vol. II, p. 299.

[20] *Ibid.*, p. 303.

[21] *M*, Vol. II, p. 316. Immermann's description of the *Femgericht* in this chapter is drawn, as Maync points out (*M*, Vol. II, p. 309[n]), from various historical sources, the main one of which was Paul Wigand's *Das Femgericht Westfalens* (Hamm, 1825).

[22] *M*, Vol. II, p. 325.

[23] *M*, Vol. II, p. 382.

[24] B. von Wiese, *Karl Immermann*, p. 222.   [25] *M*, Vol. II, pp. 382-383.

Clarity and Obscurity in
Annette von Droste-Hülshoff's *Judenbuche*

CLIFFORD ALBRECHT BERND

Much that is illuminating has been written on one of the most dense pieces of German narrative in the nineteenth century: *Die Judenbuche* by Annette von Droste-Hülshoff.[1] But a remarkable clue to the understanding of this elusive *Novelle* has, it seems, gone unnoticed. I am speaking of the impact that Levin Schücking's concept of narrative form had on the inception of Droste's *Novelle*. Schücking was, for a long time, Droste's closest friend. This, of course, has often been stated in the biographical studies of her. Again and again we read about the hopeless love affair, and of how some of her verse reflects the love she felt for him.[2] But true as this may be, there exists another good reason for referring to Schücking when we speak about Droste and her literary legacy, and that is that a study of his narrative prose (a real desideratum in German literary scholarship[3]) helps us to comprehend more fully her narrative intentions. The similarity of form in Schücking's *Novelle*: *Die Schwester*, first published in 1848, and *Die Judenbuche*, which appeared in 1842, is striking indeed.

The publication dates could, of course, suggest that, should there be a similarity between the two *Novellen*, then Schücking learned more from Droste than she from him. But taking into consideration the fact that he was her almost constant companion while she wrote the *Judenbuche*, the six years which separated the publication of the two works do not mean much; and who influenced whom is, after all, merely an academic question. Far more important is the existence of the conspicuous parallels, for they alert us to the fact that both works – the products of two literary minds who worked so closely together – complement each other: The discovery of certain elements of form in one work makes us more sensitive to the appearance of similar elements in the other, and the finding of similarities in the latter confirms our discoveries in the former.

It would, naturally, far exceed the limitations of space in this essay, were we to analyze in any detail Schücking's *Die Schwester*. Such an analysis would also not be too convincing because there are few readers, if any, who are acquainted with that text or who could even locate it without great difficulty;[4] consequently, the reader would hardly be able to verify the conclusions drawn. I shall content myself, therefore, with the statement that again and again in Schücking's *Novelle* the theme of alternating clarity and obscurity boldly asserts itself, and that this theme must be taken as the governing principle of form which injects meaning into all the elements which make for the composition of that narrative.

The purpose of the following statements will be to try to show that a similar tension between clarity and obscurity also reigns throughout Droste's *Judenbuche*. Above all, this becomes apparent in the viewpoint of the narrator. At times he seems to reveal everything to the reader; but, in other instances, he appears to lose this ability and can make only superficial observations. He alternates correspondingly between two perspectives: he can stand directly in the stream of events, or he can stand above the *Novelle* as a whole. Secondly, this paradoxical relationship of simultaneous clarity and obscurity manifests itself in concrete objects. For example, an object, described on the one hand with precise clarity, escapes the grasp of the narrator and becomes veiled by the darkness of the night or the forest, by the blurring effect of the moonlight or even by the limited perception of the human mind itself. All-knowing perspective and very precise description on the part of the narrator serve to give the reader a secure feeling of having a certain knowledge; but this sense of security is destroyed when the narrator no longer appears to be omniscient or when the real world seems to dissolve into a blurred world of deception. As a result, the reader remains a captive within this alternating force-field of omniscience and ignorance.

Let us turn to the text itself. At the opening of the *Novelle* the first thing which comes to our attention is the poem, which stands, as it were, distinct from the rest of the work as far as form is concerned. Since the motto is, with respect to content, an integral part of the *Novelle*, we shall consider it also as being uttered by the narrator, or at least as an element within the narrative situation. The perspective of the poem is omniscient. The narrator addresses the reader—"Du Glücklicher, geboren und gehegt / Im lichten Raum, von frommer Hand gepflegt" (882)[5]—and begs him to be understanding. The reader should not judge this "arm verkümmert Sein". As is apparent from the poem, the narrator is familiar with this poor creature, who as yet remains anonymous. The narrator hints that this creature will commit some action of which we should take a tolerant viewpoint; therefore he seems to know both what this action is and the mitigating circumstances which are behind it. Indications of the underlying causes are found in the phrases: "beschränkten Hirnes Wirren"; "eitlen Blutes Drang"; "jedes Wort, das unvergessen / In junge Brust die zähen Wurzeln trieb." (882) Consequently, the reader knows the underlying causes, yet he has no idea of what will happen nor of who is to do it; nor is it made clear whether the narrator himself possesses this knowledge, even though his perspective is one of an all-knowing, all-seeing speaker. As a result of this cloudy glimpse into the future, the tension in the *Novelle* becomes apparent. The reader's frame of mind becomes questioning, expectant.

The suspense is eased somewhat by the concrete facts in the first sentence: "Friedrich Mergel, geboren 1738...." (882) This may be the figure whom the reader should observe so objectively. Yet again he is unsure, for the narrator ignores this figure and, instead, goes on at length about the village, the area, and the people. Nevertheless, the reader retains his confidence in the narrator, for the latter seems to be omniscient as he gives his panoramic description of the land and the customs. Suddenly the narrator makes an admission: "Es ist schwer, jene Zeit unparteiisch ins Auge zu fassen; sie ist seit ihrem Verschwinden entweder hochmütig getadelt oder albern gelobt worden, da den, der sie erlebte, zuviel teure Erinnerungen blenden und der Spätergeborene sie nicht begreift." (883) Here the viewpoint is the same as in the poem; that is, the period to be described lies far in the past for the narrator, since he is familiar with both those critics who lived in a former age and those who lived later. Because of the superior viewpoint of this narrator, the reader expects a statement of the narrator's position, a proof of his own objectivity, but no such statement follows. The narrator rather avoids taking a definite stand and falls back instead on a very general phraseology: "Soviel darf man indessen behaupten...." (883) What he goes on to say—"daß die Form schwächer, der Kern fester, Vergehen häufiger, Gewissenlosigkeit seltener waren" (883)—is also extremely vague and general. The reader cannot be sure what is meant by "Form" and "Kern," whether it refers to the customs, to the individual or to the people as a whole. In any event, the expected claim and proof of objectivity does not come; on the contrary, the narrator penetrates deeply into the realm of subjectivity when he goes on to speak of "Überzeugung," "seelentötend" and "das innere Rechtsgefühl." The fact that he refuses to claim an objective viewpoint (even though he seems to in so many words), and even tends toward a subjective one, gives rise again to a tension within the reader and to the question as to whether the narrator can be trusted implicitly. If he is omniscient, then we can trust not only what he sees, but also what he thinks; if he is not, we must be on guard against any subjective conclusions made by him.

The narrator continues his description as if the whole area were spread out before his eyes. He has knowledge of the wood-poaching, as well as of the co-operation between the poachers and the river-boatmen. Even the individual inhabitants of the village are visible to him: "Die Zurückgebliebenen horchten sorglos..."; "Ein gelegentlicher Schuß, ein schwacher Schrei ließen wohl einmal eine junge Frau oder Braut auffahren; kein anderer achtete darauf." (884) But a curious limitation of the narrator's omniscience manifests itself here: his whole description of the poaching is as if it is seen from the village. He neither penetrates into the forest nor describes the actual events taking place there. This fact is important, for of all the incidents taking place in the forest—Hermann Mergel's death, the murders of Brandis and Aaron,

66

Friedrich's death[6]—the narrator does not directly observe any of them, nor does he seem to know more about them than the reader. The forest exercises its power of concealment even upon the narrator.

Now the narrator touches upon Friedrich Mergel again — "In diesen Umgebungen ward Friedrich Mergel geboren…" (884)—but, as before, he digresses into a more general description: this time of the house and Hermann Mergel. From his omniscient perspective he is able to relate the highpoints of Hermann's past life, yet suddenly he loses this ability and is forced to make a conjecture about Hermann: "Ob nun den Mergel Reue quälte oder Scham …." (885) The limitation of the narrator's perspective becomes even more pronounced as he describes Hermann's second marriage. His statements become less definite. For example, he ventures a guess about Margreth's reasons for marrying Hermann: "Wir glauben den Grund eben in dieser ihrer selbstbewußten Vollkommenheit zu finden." (886) Obviously, the narrator is not positive about this statement.[7]

Apparently he also knows very little firsthand information about the past married life of the Mergels, for he often relies on reports of others: "… sah man sie abends aus dem Hause stürzen…"; "Es hieß…"; "… denn Margreth soll sehr geweint haben…"; "… man meinte sogar …." (886) But, at the same time he knows that Friedrich was carried "unter einem Herzen voll Gram," (886) a statement which indicates complete insight into the people.

The narrator continues in this rather paradoxical manner, speaking, at times, with complete authority and all-penetrating insight as he describes the very thoughts and feelings of the characters: "… [Friedrich] lag aus Furcht ganz still" (887); "Friedrich dachte an den Teufel…" (888); "… nun begriff er… aus den Reden…" (888); "Die Mutter war ihm ganz unheimlich geworden…" (889); "… eine mit Grausen gemischte Zärtlichkeit…" (890); "… bei Friedrich wuchs dieses Gefühl…" (890); "Es war ihm äußerst empfindlich…." (890) The narrator reveals not only Friedrich's but also Margreth's inner emotions: "Der armen Margreth ward selten so wohl…" (891); "Sie war ärgerlich und ängstlich und wußte…" (895) At one point the narrator is not only omniscient, he is also omnipresent; in other words, he can observe Friedrich from a distance, while at the same time revealing Friedrich's feelings: "… und wie Friedrich so langsam seinem Führer nachtrat, die Blicke fest auf denselben geheftet, der ihn gerade durch das Seltsame seiner Erscheinung anzog…." (893) The narrator's insight is indicated here by the fact that he knows just what attracts Friedrich to Simon.

But, along with this wealth of revealing observations, the narrator also betrays a certain reservation toward his statements. Again he must rely on reports of others: "Friedrich hatte seinen Vater auf dem Stroh gesehen, wo er, wie man sagt, blau und fürchterlich ausgesehen haben soll." (890) This reservation is likewise emphasized by the use of the verb "scheinen," which indicates he no longer has the all-knowing insight into the characters he knew so thoroughly a moment ago: "… [Friedrich] schien ungern daran zu denken." (890); "Simon schien dies zu überhören." (892); "Simon schien nach-denkend, der Knabe zerstreut...." (893)

We have just cited several instances in which the narrator betrays an ambivalent viewpoint in relation to this subject; he can stand far above the story or he can be caught within it and be blinded by his very nearness to the events. The same tension between obscurity and clarity also comes into focus when we become aware of the dates in the story. The times given seem to be in themselves reasonably clear and exact—some extremely so—and they allow the reader to place all important events at least within the proper year, sometimes within the exact month. On two rare occasions even the day is given,[8] and thus the reader has the comfortable feeling that he knows when all took place; he is impressed by the chronicle-like exactness and objectivity of the narrative. Yet, on a closer examination, the dates turn out to be far less exact than they seem. Only two events can be placed to the exact day or even to the approximate time: the murder of Brandis occurred on the eleventh of July, 1756, sometime after four o'clock in the morning. (902; 909) The second such event is Friedrich's return on Christmas Eve of 1788. (926) Another series of events can be only approximately fixed according to date: the death of Hermann Mergel — January 6? ("um das Fest der heiligen drei Könige" [886]) 1746 or 1747? ("Friedrich stand in seinem neunten Jahre" — was he born before or after Jan. 6, 1738?); Friedrich insulted by Aaron, Aaron's death — October 1760 (914); Friedrich's flight — probably in October 1760 also; Friedrich's death — September 1789 (936).[9] Concerning Aaron's death, we know from the report given that it took place soon after ten o'clock on the evening of the wedding (920). Yet we cannot determine the date any closer than the month of October 1760. This fact is strange, especially when we consider that the event was probably the most important one in Friedrich's life. By way of contrast, the death of Brandis, which we can place to the year, month, day and approximate hour, has no lasting effect on Friedrich's character; the last words in connection with this event and Friedrich's guilt feelings are: "Der Eindruck, den dieser Vorfall auf Friedrich gemacht, erlosch leider nur zu bald." (913) A third series of events can be placed only within the proper year: Friedrich's birth — 1738 (882); Simon's visit — 1750 ("Er war zwölf Jahre alt..." [890]). Such is the ambiguous nature of the dates in the narrative. They are clear and at the same time obscure.

Parallel to the dates, in revealing the web of clarity and obscurity, are the names of places and persons. They are frequently indicated only by the first letter. The villages are designated as follows: "Dorf B." (882, 883, 902, 924) or simply "B." (915, 920); "M." (906); "S." (920); "L." (924); "P." (925, 930, 932). That does not mean, however, that all the village names are thus abbreviated; compare for example: "Brede" (890, 895) or "Heerse" (930). Also the forest and its various sections are designated always with the full name: "Brederholz" (890, 893, 894, 924, 935); "Telgengrund" (892); "Roder-

68

holz" (892); "Teutoburger Wald" (892, 893); "Mastergrund" (905); "Master-holz" (906). With the names of the characters the narrator is much more specific; from a rather impressive number of characters (seventeen), he abbreviates the names of only two, namely, Herr and Frau von S.

The first explanation of the abbreviated names which comes to mind is that Droste wanted to protect the people and places she used in her *Novelle*. Two passages in her letters might be cited to strengthen this claim: "Schlimmer ist es, daß die Leute hierzulande es noch gar nicht gewohnt sind, sich abkonterfeien zu lassen und den gelindesten Schatten als persönliche Beleidigung aufnehmen werden" (to Schlüter, Dec. 13, 1838);[10] "... aber ich fürchte, meine lieben Landsleute steinigen mich, wenn ich sie nicht zu lauter Engeln mache" (to her sister, Jan. 29, 1839).[11] Another argument in support of this appears in the fact that Droste, when speaking of towns farther removed from Westphalia, has no qualms about giving the full names: "... bis Freiburg im Breisgau" (930); "... nach Amsterdam ...." (931)

Doubtless, Droste was concerned with the reactions of her countrymen, but this cannot be the reason for the abbreviations. Consider the example "Herr von S.": in this case the abbreviation is useless, since the actual name was "Herr von H.," as we learn from Haxthausen's report.[12] What can be the sense of abbreviating a name which is already fictitious? As for the names of the villages, their initial letters seem to indicate geographical realities, and one is therefore tempted to find these just because the initial letter is given. In most instances, however, these attempts to determine the village fail, and this is the case, as we might now expect, for "Dorf B." This village has combined characteristics of two small towns in Westphalia, namely Bellersen and Bökendorf. In short, Droste did not adhere to geographical reality.[13] In addition, "Dorf B." and "Brede," geographically distinct and separated at first, intermingle in the course of the *Novelle*, particularly after Friedrich's return from slavery.[14] Heitmann brings out this point, citing the fact that Friedrich returns from Turkey to "Dorf B.," yet as Johannes he should go to Brede, his hometown. Nevertheless, he is recognized and welcomed as if it were his home; and it seems as if both Johannes and Friedrich had come from the same village, even though at the beginning of the narrative the towns were clearly separated by a long trek through the Brederholz.[15] This is a prime example of clarity receding into a blurred ambiguity.

The abbreviated names serve the same function as do the dates: namely, to create a tense atmosphere of ambiguity, while at the same time giving the appearance of reality. Just as the dates are fictitious, so are the names of the characters. The geographical names do not allow a precise definition of the scene, either in reality or within the *Novelle* itself. In some cases the full name of the village is given — e.g., Brede (890, 895), Heerse (930) — but these names indicate relatively unimportant places, just as the more precise dates define only prelusive events. The same is true for the forest names, none of which are abbreviated; yet they designate only broad areas of forest and thus afford no precise point of reference. Therefore, the names in general do not, under closer scrutiny, provide the link with reality which is supposedly present in a true story.

The abbreviations of these names do, however, indirectly strengthen the impression of reality, as Heitmann observes: "Die Abkürzung derselben [Ortsnamen] erweckt den Eindruck, als habe die völlige Enthüllung der Wirklichkeit Bedenken, insinuiert also dem Leser geschickt die Wirklichkeit des Erzählten."[16] Therefore, the reader accepts these abbreviations as being necessary to protect the anonymity of the real people and places appearing in the narrative. Thus he finds himself in the peculiar position of reading what is supposed to be a true recounting of events and yet not knowing exactly where or when these events took place.

The dialogue is another means which helps convey the over-all atmosphere of suspense and uncertainty. Lore Hoffmann terms them "ein Frage- und Antwortspiel," in which everyone tries to bring out the secrets of the other without giving away his own.[17] Most often the dialogues lead to no definite end or spoken conclusion; rather they end, like the two trials, abruptly and unsatisfactorily. The characters fail to convey content to each other, and indeed this is the very thing they are striving to avoid. Benno von Wiese, significantly, deems this element important: "Gespräche sind bei der Droste keine Brücken von Mensch zu Mensch, sondern fast immer... in eine Atmosphäre des Unheils getaucht."[18]

We can say that the conversations of Friedrich as a young boy with his mother are without ulterior motives, but they do end unsatisfactorily, in that the questions of both remain unanswered. For example, early in the narrative Friedrich asks why his father is not coming home; Margreth answers evasively: "Ach Gott, wenn der alles hielte, was er verspricht! Mach, mach voran, daß du fertig wirst!" (887) Later Friedrich queries: "Aber wenn nun der Vater kommt?" to which Margreth bitterly replies: "Den hält der Teufel fest genug!" (887)—an answer which, of course, leads Friedrich to ask about the devil: "Wo ist der Teufel, Mutter?" (887) His question is cut short by the impatient, threatening reply: "Wart, du Unrast! Er steht vor der Tür und will dich holen, wenn du nicht ruhig bist!" (887) The whole situation is very real; Margreth's bitter answers are typical of an impatient, almost desperate mother. She clearly wants to avoid becoming involved in an explanation of evil, and therefore she completely evades the simple, yet probing questions of her child.

Later the situation is reversed; Margreth, now the inquiring one, tries to extract a promise from Friedrich to stay out of trouble: "Fritzchen, ... willst du jetzt auch fromm sein, daß ich Freude an dir habe, oder willst du unartig sein und lügen, oder saufen und stehlen?" (889) Only the last word of the question—"stehlen"—seems to strike a chord in Friedrich, for he evades her question with the simple reply: "Mutter, Hülsmeyer stiehlt." (889) Thus the mother's question remains unanswered.

Friedrich is finally forced to his last question—"Mutter, lügen die Förster?" (889)—by Margreth's prejudiced viewpoint. The boy simply cannot understand why Hülsmeyer is not guilty of stealing, since he has seen it and Brandis claims the same. Margreth will not answer his question directly; moreover, she is well aware that Friedrich will not understand the reply she does give, in which she utters the rationalizations of those in the village who would justify their illegal acts. The main characteristic of both these encounters is that of evasiveness. Friedrich, even at this young age, shows a tendency to avoid answering questions: a tendency which shows itself much stronger in his encounter with Brandis.

With the introduction of Simon we can begin to speak of ulterior motives. During his visit with Margreth all his questions are of one purpose—to see whether Friedrich will qualify as a look-out for the wood-poachers. Consider his questions: "Du läßt ihn die Kühe hüten?"; "Aber wo hütet er?"; "... auch des Nachts und früh?" (892) Even Margreth is somewhat puzzled by his last question, for she replies: "Die ganzen Nächte durch; aber wie meinst du das?" (892) But Simon, purposely, ignores her query: "Simon schien dies zu überhören." (892) The fact that Friedrich herds cows all night in the woods makes him ideally suited for Simon's purposes, yet it is important to remember that the reader cannot know of Simon's illegal activities at this point (or at any point, for that matter; Simon is never mentioned directly in connection with the wood-poaching). The narrator allows this part of the conversation to remain a mystery.

Simon's words with Friedrich, as they enter the forest, are equally puzzling, but they have again the same goal. Simon wants to see whether Friedrich drinks or is excessively pious, both of which would make it risky to entrust him with any knowledge of secret dealings. But Friedrich is no longer the innocent child, and his reactions here show already a certain slyness. At one point he even lies when he claims that he falls asleep when his mother prays in bed (894). Since, as his mother said earlier, he herds the cows all through the night (892), he could not be present when she prays in bed in the evenings. Here Friedrich is being evasive, while Simon's questions stem from motives which are hidden both from Friedrich and the reader. The loss of Friedrich's childish directness is subtly indicated by the description of him: "Der Knabe lachte halb verlegen mit einem durchtriebenen Seitenblick." (894) This is the first time we see Friedrich acting unnaturally, but it is only the beginning of a long development, the culmination of which is seen in the complete emergence of Friedrich in another character, namely Johannes Niemand.

The encounter between Friedrich and Brandis is, perhaps, the most confusing of all in the *Novelle*. There are two reasons for this: first of all, Friedrich is desperately trying to cover up, and his behavior is therefore intended to lead astray. Secondly, the confusion stems from the fact that a great deal was purposely cut out of the original conversation, so that much of what

71

remains is actually impossible to understand correctly without knowledge of the original draft.

Among these ambiguities is Friedrich's first action—stoning and cursing his dog. Heitmann gives a logical reason for this, namely that it is only a pretext for Friedrich's loud whistling—which in turn must have been a prearranged signal.[19] The original draft corroborates Heitmann's explanation, for there Friedrich continues to complain about Fidel in a very loud voice, which would alert the poachers even more. Brandis realizes this and orders him to speak more softly.[20] But Friedrich speaks even louder, until a very stern glance from Brandis quiets him. That is, then, the origin and effect of the glance in the *Novelle*: "Ein Blick begleitete diese Worte, der schnell wirkte." (904) Also, the line—"Herr Brandis, denkt an meine Mutter!" (904)—is more understandable in the original, whereas here it is, to say the least, unexpected. The original context reads thus: "Herr Brandis, denkt an meine Mutter, ... bringt sie nicht ins Elend um einen Erlenzweig nicht...."[21] Had Heitmann known this version, he would not have given his proposed explanation, namely: "Friedrichs Worte 'Herr Brandes, denkt an meine Mutter!' sind der Ausdruck einer momentanen Angst des Achtzehnjährigen vor dem starken, rauhen Manne. Auch will die Dichterin hier eine gute Seite in Friedrichs Charakter hervorheben...."[22] Actually, Friedrich is only continuing under the guise of pretending that Brandis is angry because of the damage to the young shoots. Knowledge of the original also refutes a second claim of Heitmann's: "Die ganze Schimpfrede ist nicht recht motiviert."[23] In the original it is very well motivated, because Brandis accuses Friedrich's mother of lying to his wife, and in return Friedrich insults Brandis and his mother: "... meine Mutter ist besser als die Eurige war, die drey Wochen vor eurer Geburt Hochzeit machte."[24] The reason for Brandis' rage is evident, and also the reason for Friedrich's next comment: "Herr, ... Ihr habt gesagt, was Ihr nicht verantworten könnt, und ich vielleicht auch." (904)

Even the connection of Friedrich with the poachers is obvious in the original, for Brandis voices his suspicions directly: "... meinst du ich sehe nicht, daß du die Schildwache machst bey deinen Kumpanen...?"[25] Droste obviously intended to heighten the suspense and confusion by leaving this out.

Paralleling the intermingling of clarity and obscurity in the narrative composition, and further adding to its aesthetic portrayal in the *Novelle*, is the interplay of light and darkness. Just as the changing perspective of the narrator gives us now a clear, now a blurred picture of reality, so does the shifting of light and darkness affect the perception of reality.

Of course, the darkness—whether caused by the time of day or by the depths of the forest—serves the purpose of concealment. It incites the characters to those actions they would not attempt in sunlight — murder and wood-poaching as examples. However, in so doing, the darkness also reveals the true character of the persons involved; it acts as a catalyst to bring to the fore those emotions which normally remain buried within the individual.

Paradoxically, it is not only the darkness which hinders the perception of reality, but also that which should bring clarity—the light itself. The importance which the narrator attaches to the elements of light and darkness is attested to by the fact that the main events are set in darkness or twilight; this background alone lends an uncanny atmosphere to the *Novelle*. The one exception to this is the discovery of Friedrich's body, and that this takes place in broad daylight seems to parallel the nature of the event as a final revelation. However, that is not the case. What seems to be most clear — the identification of the murderer in broad daylight — is anything but clear. Actually, it remains veiled in darkness, as Henel has shown.[26]

The shifting of light and darkness is illustrated most clearly, doubtless, in the passage describing Simon's and Friedrich's trek through the Brederholz. As they approach the woods, the light gradually disappears, and correspondingly the number of adjectives of darkness increases: "einen sehr dunkeln Grund" (893). There is some light from the moon, but it is weak: "seine schwachen Schimmer." (894) This light does not help to reveal the objects, but rather just the opposite: "... seine schwachen Schimmer dienten nur dazu, den Gegenständen, die sie zuweilen durch eine Lücke der Zweige berührten, ein fremdartiges Ansehen zu geben." (894) This light conceals rather than reveals the nature of the objects; they lose their distinct outlines, not in the darkness but in the light itself: "Es kam ihm vor, als ob alles sich bewegte und die Bäume in den einzelnen Mondstrahlen bald zusammen, bald voneinander schwankten." (894)

A decided change of light occurs as the pair enters the clearing; all the objects emerge into clarity, and the description becomes correspondingly more precise: "Jetzt schien sich in einiger Entfernung das Dunkel zu brechen, und bald traten beide in eine ziemlich große Lichtung." (894) The very word "Lichtung" conveys the impression of light. The moonlight is now strong: "Der Mond schien klar hinein und zeigt, daß ...." (894) It no longer conceals; it now has the power to reveal ("zeigte") the work of the poachers. A felled beech tree is described in detail: "... denn eine Buche lag quer über dem Pfad, in vollem Laube, ihre Zweige hoch über sich streckend und im Nachtwinde mit den noch frischen Blättern zitternd." (895) Everything has become distinct now; even the leaves of the beech tree are seen to be still fresh. Friedrich can even see that the oak tree in the middle of the clearing is hollow. The contrast of this precise picture with the blurred, nightmarish world of the previous scene is striking, and the effect of the shift is very similar to that of the narrator's changing perspective. Both give the impression of looking through a lens system which is constantly going in and out of focus.

It is interesting to note a recurring formulation which the narrator uses when speaking of the effect of light. We have already seen the first instance: "... seine schwachen Schimmer dienten nur dazu, den Gegenständen ... ein fremdartiges Ansehen zu geben." (894) Again almost the same formulation occurs in the scene with Johannes: "Der Schein spielte auf seinen Zügen und gab ihnen ein widriges Ansehen von Magerkeit und ängstlichem Zucken." (896) The last occurrence of the formulation is in reference to Simon: "... und die vom Mondschein verursachte Blässe des Gesichts gaben ihm ein schauerlich verändertes Ansehen." (912) The light does not reveal, but rather it conceals the object, gives it an unreal aspect. Only in the case of Johannes does it reveal what is probably the true appearance of his face, yet the narrator calls it, nevertheless, "ein widriges Ansehen." Strangely enough, the first sign of recognition comes to Margreth after she approaches Johannes; at this moment he looks up to her, and therefore his face must now be enveloped in the surrounding darkness of the kitchen.

Typical, too, is the scene in which Friedrich and Simon argue about confession (not mentioned by chance in this *Novelle*, for in the confessional sins are revealed to the priest; and at the same time concealed from everyone else). When Simon first appears, he is illuminated (although not clearly revealed) by the pale moonlight (912). Yet when the light is most important and could be most revealing—namely, when Simon swears he is innocent—the sky clouds over and Simon's face remains in darkness: "Er hätte viel darum gegeben, seines Ohms Gesicht sehen zu können. Aber während sie flüsterten, hatte der Himmel sich bewölkt." (913) The answer to the question of Simon's guilt, which could have been perhaps revealed by his facial expression, is characteristically left enveloped in darkness.

Climaxing the portrayal of the tension between clarity and obscurity in Droste's *Judenbuche*, as well as in Schücking's *Die Schwester*, is the forest. The impenetrable darkness of the "Teutoburger Wald" provides, it may be said, a cover under which the more violent side of man comes to the fore. The name itself calls immediately to mind connotations of a primitive, violent past. Thus, the forest brings on the one hand an element of clarity to the *Novelle* — by encouraging, like a catalyst, inherent characteristics of the people which would normally be hidden by the veneer of society: "Seine Lage [Dorf B.] inmitten tiefer und stolzer Waldeinsamkeit mochte schon früh den angeborenen Starrsinn der Gemüter nähren." (883) It encourages not only such inherent traits, but also certain criminal tendencies—i.e., poaching and murder. Then, like a mute witness, it attests to this violent side of man by revealing the evidence—devastated strips of forest, the bodies of Brandis, Aaron and Friedrich.[27] Nevertheless, the forest guards part of its secret jealously; only the results are revealed. How and by whom these crimes are carried out remains unknown. All efforts to solve this final unknown element are of no avail, as we see from the outcome of the trials. The reader, knowing so much and yet so little, is forced to make assumptions of his own on the basis of the evidence presented.

Thus the forest, like the darkness, fulfills the same double function of revealment and concealment. The manner in which it effects this is even parallel to that of darkness, since darkness, of course, is the dominant characteristic of the forest. However, the forest differs from the darkness in that the former seems to reveal its secrets actively and according to a will of its own. In the deaths of Brandis, Aaron, Friedrich, even of Hermann Mergel, the forest is the ever-present setting, the cover under which these things take place. In each case the forest seems to guard its secret completely for a time; then at a certain point it chooses to reveal the evidence to the eye of man. All of the bodies are found, not as the result of an intensive search, but rather by accident.

The circumstances surrounding the discovery of Brandis, Aaron and Friedrich have, in addition to the element of chance, a paradoxical aspect. All the bodies are hidden by something which is very much a part of the forest— "Brombeerranken" (910); "dürres Laub" (921); "die Buche" (935)— yet the forest itself is instrumental in bringing about the discovery. Brandis is found because the bushes happen to catch on a forester's "Flaschenschnur" (910). Aaron is found because his wife, who has given up the search, takes shelter from a storm under the beech tree where her husband's walking stick lies. Friedrich is discovered only because young Brandis happens to retire from the heat and seek refreshment under the beech tree where Friedrich's body is concealed.

How well the forest fulfills its role in the interplay of revealment and concealment may be seen, too, in the way it quickly brings into full view the figure of Brandis, and just as quickly again hides him from sight: "Hier sank ein Zweig hinter ihm, dort einer; die Umrisse seiner Gestalt schwanden immer mehr. Da blitzte es noch einmal durchs Laub. Es war ein Stahlknopf seines Jagdrocks; nun war er fort." (905) Only moments before the same forest played the reverse role as it gradually revealed Brandis to Friedrich's eye: "In demselben Augenblicke wurden die Zweige eines nahen Gebüsches fast ohne Geräusch zurückgeschoben, und ein Mann trat heraus ...." (903)

No discussion of clarity and obscurity, revealment and concealment, in the *Judenbuche* would be complete without mentioning the Hebrew inscription, which is referred to twice: once with its message concealed (925) and the other time with its meaning revealed (936). At the first instance the reader of the German text is confronted with a set of Hebrew letters which he cannot understand; later, at the end of the narrative, the words are translated into the language of the story, into German. Why this linguistic change? The narrator could just as easily, the first time, have stated that the inscription was written in Hebrew and then translated it right then and there. But this he did not choose to do. Deliberately, therefore, by employing a tongue foreign to his readers, he conceals from them what the message is about. Nevertheless, it may likewise be said that it is not his intention to conceal the message either, for later on he plainly reveals it with his translation. We have at hand, therefore, but one more artistic, linguistic device for rendering visible the narrator's uncomfortable realization that the forces controlling the world in which he and we live are clear, and at the same time obscure.[28]

75

NOTES

[1] For an extraordinarily intelligent discussion of the more recent criticism see the essay by Heinrich Henel: "Annette von Droste-Hülshoff: Erzählstil und Wirklichkeit," *Festschrift für Bernhard Blume: Aufsätze zur deutschen und europäischen Literatur*, ed. Egon Schwarz, Hunter G. Hannum and Edgar Lohner (Göttingen, 1967), pp. 146-172. The cogency of Mr. Henel's argument has opened up, I believe, new vistas to Droste scholarship.

[2] See e.g., Clemens Heselhaus, *Annette und Levin*. Schriften der Droste-Gesellschaft, VIII (Münster, 1948), p. 5: "Als das tiefste und symbolischste Ereignis im Dichterleben der Droste will mir das Schücking-Erlebnis erscheinen, das sich in jenen fünf Gedichten spiegelt, welche die Dichterin direkt an Levin Schücking gerichtet hat."

[3] This becomes all the more a necessity when we take note that Friedrich Hebbel, hardly a critic of unsound judgment, once stated: "Viele ringen um den Preis der modernen Novelle; wir möchten ihn Schücking zuerkennen." See Friedrich Hebbel, *Sämtliche Werke*, ed. Richard M. Werner, XII (Berlin, 1913), 252.

[4] The first publication was in *Urania, Taschenbuch auf das Jahr 1848*. It reappeared, with a different title: *Die Wilddiebin*, in Levin Schücking, *Familiengeschichten* (Prag, 1854), and in the author's *Gesammelte Erzählungen und Novellen*, VI (Hannover, 1866). Using the title of the first publication, Paul Heyse and Hermann Kurz included the *Novelle* in their *Deutscher Novellenschatz* (München, 1871-1874), XV, 169-291.

[5] This and subsequent numerals refer to pages in Annette von Droste-Hülshoff, *Sämtliche Werke*, ed. Clemens Heselhaus (4. erw. Aufl. München, 1963).

[6] Heinrich Henel, p. 146, persuasively argues against the acceptance of previous critics' unquestioning belief that the character who is found dead at the end of the *Novelle* should be Friedrich. For our discussion here it is not important to know whether the character is Friedrich or not. We merely use the name Friedrich because the *Gutsherr* refers to him as such, and because of lack of proof that another name would be more accurate.

[7] This becomes all the more apparent when we compare the *Novelle* with its first draft. We learn that in the first draft Hermann's sudden marriage is well motivated, but that later Droste cut out many details, and unclear motivation replaced the earlier clear one. See Karl Schulte-Kemminghausen, *Die Judenbuche von Annette von Droste-Hülshoff mit sämtlichen jüngst wieder aufgefundenen Vorarbeiten der Dichterin und einer Handschriftenprobe* (Dortmund, 1925), p. 94. See, too, Heinrich Henel, pp. 161-162.

[8] The first such date must be taken from two sources in the *Novelle*: "Es war im Juli 1756 früh um drei." (902) The exact day is given later in the testimony of the foresters: "Brandis habe sie am zehnten abends zur Runde bestellt..." (909) The second such date is obvious: "Es war am Vorabende des Weihnachtsfestes, den 24. Dezember 1788." (926)

[9] See note 6.

[10] *Die Briefe der Annette von Droste-Hülshoff*, ed. Karl Schulte-Kemminghausen, I (Jena, 1944), 313.

[11] *Ibid.*, 339.

[12] Karl Schulte-Kemminghausen, pp. 61-71.

[13] Felix Heitmann, *Annette von Droste-Hülshoff als Erzählerin. Realismus und Objektivität in der 'Judenbuche'* (Münster, 1914), pp. 8-9.

[14] See note 6.

[15] Felix Heitmann, p. 9.

[16] *Ibid.*, p. 54.

[17] Lore Hoffmann, "Studie zum Erzählstil der 'Judenbuche'," *Jahrbuch der Droste Gesellschaft*, II (1948/50), 142.

[18] Benno von Wiese, *Die Deutsche Novelle von Goethe bis Kafka*, I (Düsseldorf, 1956), 166.

[19] Felix Heitmann, p. 10.

[20] Karl Schulte-Kemminghausen, p. 178.

[21] *Ibid.*, p. 179.

[22] Felix Heitmann, pp. 10-11.

[23] *Ibid.*, p. 11.

[24] Karl Schulte-Kemminghausen, p. 182.
[25] *Ibid.*
[26] See note 6.
[27] *Ibid.*
[28] The author of this essay wishes to express his gratitude to the American Philosophical Society in Philadelphia for generously supporting his research on the genesis of *Die Judenbuche.*

German Travellers in the South, 1865-1900

LAWRENCE S. THOMPSON

Almost four decades ago the present writer first met Fred Coenen in the classroom. The honoree of this essay was already a seasoned and perceptive traveller in North America. We read one classic travel book (*Die Harzreise*) and talked about many others informally and constructively. It was first here that this writer understood fully the value of travel literature as mirror of manners and customs, economic and social conditions, agriculture, geography, transportation, education, history, religion, and all the other elements that go into a national culture.

It is hoped that the present essay may be considered the second in a series, ultimately to reach back to travel books of the period of exploration and discovery as De Bry's "Grandes voyages" and "Petites voyages" (in Latin and German, despite the popular title!). The first in the series was "German Travel Books on the South, 1900-1950" in the *Thirtieth Report of the Society for the History of Germans in Maryland* (Baltimore, 1959). This second study pushes the bibliography back to the period of the final capitulation of our Southern Confederacy. It ends with the rise of the United States as a great economic power, when many of the more thoughtful German travellers were very definitely worried about this country as a competitor to Germany and England for world markets.

While the German travellers in these three decades were barely a fourth as numerous as they were to become in the twentieth century, they identified most of the salient aspects of Southern culture and described them accurately. It is rather striking, however, that few of them visited Florida (a point of attraction for travellers since 1920) and that the coastal plains between the Virginia Capes to New Orleans were largely by-passed. So too were the Southern Appalachians, not of easy access to any travellers in the late nineteenth century. Moreover, the burgeoning industry of the Piedmont failed to attract them. They seemed to be more inclined to follow, in general, the rivers of the great interior valley, to the heavily German cities of Louisville, Saint Louis, and New Orleans, and to Texas, always a magnet for the German colonist.

Our period begins when the South was still prostrate from having been the battleground of the most disastrous war of our history; and the reminiscences, effects, and visible results of the War play a major role in the observations of travellers in this period. Becker's *Die hundertjährige Republik*[1] gives attention to military campaigns in Virginia, Tennessee and Georgia. Kapp's *Aus und über Amerika* provides backgrounds of the War such as slavery and the John Brown affair. Hesse-Wartegg, one of the most intelligent of observers, has many significant comments on the free Negro and his political and economic role.

The Southern Negro has always fascinated travellers, both for his colorful personality and for the more serious aspects of his struggle for full equality. Becker's discussion of the Reconstruction and the Negro is an enduring bit of evidence, and he involves it skillfully with his review of the status of Southern agriculture of the period. Hesse-Wartegg's *Mississippi-Fahrten* contain prophetic observations on the exodus of the Negro from the agricultural regions of Mississippi and Louisiana, looking forward to the day when the race issue is largely a problem of the yankee. Lindau's *Altes und Neues aus der Neuen Welt* picks up much of the color of the Negroes he saw in Savannah and New Orleans. It must be noted at this point that the few books cited here and elsewhere in this essay are essentially a sample, that each work in the bibliography at the end must be examined for observations on various aspects of Southern culture. In the case of the Southern Negro, the works of nearly all the authors who commented on him in any language, from the beginnings to 1950, will be included in a forthcoming major bibliographical work of the present author, probably to be entitled *The Southern Black in Slavery and Freedom: a Bibliography*, with some 4,000 references to books and pamphlets.

Among the post-Civil War phenomona, the Klu Klux Klan has few commentators other than Hesse-Wartegg, a rather surprising fact in view of the nativistic and pro-Protestant dogmas of the Invisible Empire in later years. Even though a large proportion of the German immigrants in Baltimore, Louisville, and Saint Louis followed the Roman Catholic confession, German Catholicism in America comes in for little comment, except for a partially antiquarian work such as Kist's *Amerikanisches* (special attention to Catholic churches in Baltimore). In no work has the present writer found any comments on Protestant fundamentalism, a trend which made Dayton, Tennessee, a focal point of interest for Europeans after 1925.

Reidenbach's *Amerika* has the appropriate sub-title of "ein Rathgeber für Auswanderer," and several of the books were directed specifically at prospective immigrants. The *Deutsche Gesellschaft* in New Orleans commissioned John H. Deiler to write *Louisiana, ein Heim für deutsche Ansiedler*. Deiler, a prototype of the twentieth-century promotion artist, wrote for similar purposes *Die europäische Einwanderung nach den Vereinigten Staaten*

[1] For exact references see the appended BIBLIOGRAPHY.

von 1820 bis 1896, in which there is less history than appeal to restless central Europeans, eager for the economic opportunities of the New World. Deiler's account of cotton leaves out many of the realities of this monoculture. Even Kapp's rather serious work is more concerned with the history of the plant than with its meaning for the Southern economy. Meyer's *Ursachen der amerikanischen Concurrenz* also tells a detailed story of King Cotton, but with no anticipation of his decline and fall, the tragedy of many an immigrant farmer. Of other studies of German immigrants in the United States, Scherff's *Nord-Amerika*, dealing with Saint Louis and southwest Missouri, and Schütze's *Jahrbuch für Texas und Emigranten-Führer für 1883* should be noted. Pfleiderer's *Amerikanische Reisebilder* deals with German immigrants in all parts of the United States, but it is included here as a comprehensive survey and a work which cannot be ignored in any study of the German element in the South.

The Old South of crinoline and magnolia grandiflora had little appeal for German travellers, perhaps because relatively few immigrants became great planters. Hesse-Wartegg mentions the alleged grandeur of the ante-bellum South on a few occasions. More significant are the keen observations of von Versen's *Transatlantische Streifzüge* or of the *Sozialistische Briefe aus Amerika*. Zschokke's *Nach Nordamerika und Canada* has much economic and social data of a statistical character, but, like so many travel writers of the period, Zschokke thought that the repetition of statistics gleaned from standard sources was a greater contribution than his own commentary. Temcer's *Amerika* is much the same type of work.

The bibliography which follows these comments has many implications for future research. Much of it is pure trash, and yet it represents the attitude of the reasonably well educated late nineteenth-century German towards the South. Just as the tertiary influence of the dime novels of Mr. Beadle and Mr. Monroe on a writer such as Karl May formed the central European notion of the North American frontier, so too these travel accounts had their influence on the German's notion of the South. Yet there were some solid books of enduring value. All should be pulled together—at least when this bibliography is completed for the period before Appomattox—as a major corpus of material for a much-needed work on German ideas about the South. In addition, the German immigrant in the South has never been studied in meticulous detail. Many sources other than the present compilation must be used, but the works of travel writers are essential. Finally, these works have many a gem unseen for American historians. The linguistic illiteracy of most Americanists is appalling; and if an essay such as this one and others in the series of bibliographies can only call to their attention the existence of long-neglected source material, it is worth the paper and ink used to print it.

A colleague in American history who was kind enough to look over this essay commented simply, "Piscem natare doces." The compiler could only quote to him from Acts, xvii, 23, "Ignoto Deo"—to the unknown God of bibliography, worshipped by all too few scholars.

BIBLIOGRAPHY

Becker, John H. *Die hundertjährige Republik. Soziale und politische Zustände in den Vereinigten Staaten Nordamerikas...* Mit Einleitung von Friedrich von Hellwald. Augsburg: Lampart & Comp., 1870.

Bodenstedt, Friederich Martin von. *Vom Atlantischen zum Stillen Ocean.* Leipzig and New York: F. A. Brockhaus, 1882.

Deiler, John Hanno. *Die europäische Einwanderung nach den Vereinigten Staaten von 1820 bis 1896.* New Orleans: Im Selbstverlag, 1897.

Deiler, John Hanno. *Louisiana, ein Heim für deutsche Ansiedler.* New Orleans: Druck der "New Orleans Zeitung," 1895.

Hellwald, Friedrich Anton Heller von. *Amerika in Wort und Bild... Eine Schilderung der Vereinigten Staaten.* Leipzig: Heinrich Schmidt and Carl Günther, 1883-85.

Hesse-Wartegg, Ernst von. *Curiosa aus der Neuen Welt.* Leipzig: C. Reissner, 1893.

Hesse-Wartegg, Ernst von. *Mississippi-Fahrten. Reisebilder aus dem amerikanischen Süden (1879-1880)... Mit zahlreichen Abbildungen...* Leipzig: C. Reissner, 1881.

Hesse-Wartegg, Ernst von. *Nord-Amerika, seine Städte und Naturwunder, das Land und seine Bewohner in Schilderungen... mit Beiträgen von Udo Brachvogel, Bret Harte, Theodor Kirchhoff.* Leipzig: Gustav Weigel, 1886-88.

Hesse-Wartegg, Ernst von. *Tausend und ein Tag im Occident. Kulturbilder, Reisen und Erlebnisse im Nordamerikanischen Kontinent.* 2 vols. Leipzig: Carl Reissner, 1891.

Hopp, Ernst Otto. *Transatlantisches Skizzenbuch. Federzeichnungen aus dem amerikanischen Leben.* Berlin: O. Janke, 1876.

Kapp, Friedrich. *Aus und über Amerika. Thatsachen und Erlebnisse.* 2 vols. Berlin: J. Springer, 1876.

Kist, Leopold. *Amerikanisches...* Mainz: Franz Kirchheim; New York: F. Pustet, 1871.

Kriegsau, Adolph, Freiherr von ("B. Aba"). *Skizzen aus Amerika.* Wien: Druck und Verlag von Carl Gerold's Sohn, 1885.

Lauterburg, Anna. *Ein Jahr in Amerika.* Bern: R. F. Haller-Goedschach, 1885.

Liebknecht, Wilhelm. *Ein Blick in die Neue Welt.* Stuttgart: Verlag von F. H. W. Dietz, 1887.

Lindau, Paul. *Altes und Neues aus der Neuen Welt. Eine Reise durch die Vereinigten Staaten und Mexico.* Berlin: Carl Duncker, 1893.

Meyer, Rudolf Hermann, ed. *Ursachen der amerikanischen Concurrenz.* Berlin: Hermann Bahr, 1883.

Neelmeyer-Vukassowitsch, Heinrich. *Die Vereinigten Staaten von Amerika. Nach eigenen Beobachtungen geschildert.* Leipzig: Franz Duncker, 1884.

Oberländer, Karl. *Ein Ausflug nach Amerika.* Hamburg: Hof-Buchdruckerei F. W. Rademacher, 1893.

Ott, Adolf. *Der Führer nach Amerika. Ein Reisebegleiter und geographisches Handbuch, enthaltend Schilderungen über die Vereinigten Staaten von Amerika und Canada unter steter Berücksichtigung der wirthschaftlichen Verhältnisse sowie der Kolonisation.* Basel: Im Selbstverlag des Verfassers, 1882.

Paasche, Hermann. *Kultur- und Reiseskizzen aus Nord- und Mittel-Amerika.* Magdeburg: Verlag von Albert Rathke, 1894.

Pfleiderer, Joh. Gottlob. *Amerikanische Reisebilder mit besonderer Berücksichtigung der dermaligen religiösen und kirchlichen Zustände der Vereinigten Staaten.* Bonn: Verlag von Johannes Schergens, 1882.

Reidenbach, J. A. *Amerika. Eine kurze Beschreibung der Vereinigten Staaten sowie ein Rathgeber für Auswanderer.* Nördlingen: C. H. Beck, 1870.

Scherff, Julius. *Nord-Amerika. Reisebilder, sozialpolitische und wirtschaftliche Studien aus den Vereinigten Staaten.* Leipzig: Verlag von Otto Wigand, 1898.

Schütze, Albert. *Schütze's Jahrbuch für Texas und Emigranten-Führer für 1883*. Austin: Albert Schütze, 1883.

Sozialistische Briefe aus Amerika. München: Carl Merhoff Verlag, 1883.

Steiner, Heinrich. *Künstlerfahrten vom Atlantischen bis zum Stillen Ozean. Gesammelte Reiseskizzen*. Mit einer Vorrede von Marie Geistinger. New York: The International News Company, 1883.

Temcer, Armi. *Amerika. Der heutige Standpunkt der Kultur in den Vereinigten Staaten. Monographien aus der Feder hervorragender deutsch-amerikanischer Schriftsteller*. Berlin: Stuhrsche Buchhandlung, 1884.

Versen, Maximilian von. *Transatlantische Streifzüge. Erlebnisse und Erfahrungen aus Nordamerika*. Leipzig: Duncker und Humblot, 1876.

Zschokke, Hermann. *Nach Nordamerika und Canada, Schilderungen von Land und Leuten*. Würzburg: Verlag von Leon Woerl, 1881.

Eros and Creativity in Nietzsche's
Birth of Tragedy

JAMES C. O'FLAHERTY

In the present study I shall undertake to show that Nietzsche's treatment of the relation of Socratic thought to Greek tragedy in *Die Geburt der Tragödie aus dem Geiste der Musik* suffers from a fundamental inconsistency. Since Wilamowitz' opening and, for the most part, misconceived attack on the treatise, criticisms of the Nietzschean version of Socrates have by no means been lacking.[1] To what extent the author has done violence to the facts concerning the historical Socrates is a question which cannot concern us here. It is my concern, however, to discuss the puzzling hiatus which suddenly appears in Nietzsche's argument when he turns from the brilliant and convincing exposition of Greek tragedy as a fusion of Apollonian and Dionysiac elements to a consideration of the effects of "Socratism" on tragedy. In so doing I shall invoke a category which Nietzsche himself does not hesitate to employ in another connection. It is my contention that his failure to see the relevance of the idea in question to the central problem of his treatise led to the lack of consistency with which I shall be concerned in this study. The idea to which I refer is the notion of emasculation or "castration," which becomes for Nietzsche a metaphor for the effect which Christian morality has on the healthy instincts of the normal human being. Thus, in *Der Wille zur Macht* many years later he expresses this point of view quite unambiguously:

> The [Christian] logic is: the desires often produce great misfortune—consequently they are evil, reprehensible. A man must free himself from them: otherwise he cannot be a *good* man.
> This is the same logic as: "if thine eye offend thee, pluck it out." In the particular case in which that dangerous "innocent from the country," the founder of Christianity, recommended this practice to his disciples, the case of sexual excitation, the consequence is, unfortunately, not only the loss of an organ but the *emasculation* of a man's character—and the same applies to the moralist's madness that demands, instead of a restraining of the passions, their extirpation. Its conclusion is always: only the castrated man is a good man.[2]

The victory of Christianity means for Nietzsche therefore that "the victory of unnaturalness, of the castrationist ideal, the victory of the pure, good, sinless, blessed is projected into the future as conclusion, finale, great hope, as the 'coming of the kingdom of God.' "[3]

It is obvious from these and similar passages that Nietzsche considered the concept of castration or eunuchism useful only in connection with the idea of the "good"; it has no particular relevance to the idea of the "true" or even of the "beautiful." Thus, it is a concept with ethical relevance only. It was undoubtedly his contempt for the theory of knowledge which caused his failure to see the relevance of this idea to the problem of the Socratic dialectic as he conceives it in *Die Geburt der Tragödie*, with his consequent later curious twisting of the notion of *décadence* to explain Socratism. Strangely enough, if we turn to an eighteenth-century forerunner of Nietzsche, namely, Johann Georg Hamann, we find that, like Nietzsche, he employs the idea of castration or eunuchism but with the important difference that it is for him primarily an *epistemological* concept. For in Hamann's view all abstraction is the castration of knowledge.[4] Hence, philosophical eunuchism is not restricted by Hamann to the area of morality, but is a possible form of cognition in general. This concept stems from Hamann's Biblically-derived idea of *knowing* as properly involving the whole man of faith, hence his sexuality. It may seem ironical that Hamann, the arch-conservative in matters of religion, should appear here as a more radical thinker than Nietzsche, but, as far as the relation of sexuality to cognition is concerned, such is the case.[5] However, it must be borne in mind that our procedure in this study involves judging Nietzsche as far as possible in the light of Nietzschean concepts, even though it means taking certain steps which he neglected to take, but which are logically justified.

For the most part, the study will be based on the internal evidence of the work itself. There will be occasion to draw upon other pertinent writings, but this is done only where necessary, and where the relevance of the additional material is clear. The steadily increasing influence of *Die Geburt der Tragödie* —and one encounters especially increasing references to the Apollonian-Dionysiac duality in quite diverse fields today[6]—a century after it was written suggests the importance of understanding and evaluating it as objectively as possible. In the following pages I shall confine myself to only one aspect of the treatise, albeit one of prime importance for an understanding of the whole.

In developing his arguments concerning the nature of Greek tragedy, Nietzsche appeals primarily to aesthetic categories. This procedure is to be expected, for it is quite in harmony with his belief in the preeminence of art over religion and science. Repeatedly throughout *Die Geburt der Tragödie* he expresses the thought that "nur als *ästhetisches Phänomen* ist das Dasein und die Welt ewig gerechtfertigt."[7] Nevertheless, when he turns to the task of explaining the decline of the tragic art, he suddenly shifts his ground and invokes epistemological categories to account for its demise. One may therefore justifiably raise the question as to why, if it is important to have a clear idea of the kind of knowledge which destroyed Attic tragedy, it is not just as important—indeed perhaps even more so—to have a clear idea of the kind of knowledge which produced it in the first place.

In *Die Geburt der Tragödie* Nietzsche assumes two modes of knowledge which are strictly antithetical to one another; namely, the Dionysiac and the Socratic. The former is veridical, the latter spurious. The former is based on an instinctive intuition of reality, which issues in the wisdom of Dionysos and Silenus, that is, in awareness of the pain and contradiction of existence with its terrible and inevitable suffering. Such knowledge constitutes "wahre Erkenntnis, der Einblick in die grauenhafte Wahrheit." (vii, 48) Of this mode of knowledge he writes further: "In der Bewußtheit der einmal geschauten Wahrheit sieht jetzt der Mensch überall nur das Entsetzliche oder Absurde des Seins, jetzt versteht er das Symbolische im Schicksal der Ophelia, jetzt erkennt er die Weisheit des Waldgottes Silen: es ekelt ihn." (vii, 48) It is quite important to recognize that there is no purely Apollonian knowledge in the proper sense of the word. For what one perceives under the aegis of Apollo is, by definition, illusion: it is the "beautiful illusion of the dream-world" (i, 22) or, more specifically, the "illusion of illusion,"[8] for it is a reflection of the Dionysiac level of being, which is in turn a reflection of noumenal reality. In accordance with this principle *der tragische Mythus* ist nur zu verstehen als eine Verbildlichung dionysischer Weisheit durch apollinische Kunstmittel."[9] For the normal human being who is able to distinguish between reality and illusion, the Apollonian realm is not to be confused with reality: "Bei dem höchsten Leben dieser Traumwirklichkeit haben wir doch noch die durchschimmernde Empfindung ihres *Scheins*."[10] When the normally antagonistic forces of Apollo and Dionysos are reconciled, when there is a blending of Dionysiac knowledge with Apollonian illusion, the conditions for great art are present. The most notable example of such reconciliation occurred, according to Nietzsche, in Greek tragedy of the fifth century B.C. In the purely Apollonian art of a Homer, no knowledge in the proper sense is present, for such art deals in pure illusion:

Die homerische Naivetät ist nur als der vollkommene Sieg der apollinischen Illusion zu begreifen... Dies ist die Sphäre der Schönheit, in der sie ihre Spiegelbilder, die Olympischen sahen. Mit dieser Schönheitsspiegelung kämpfte der hellenische Wille gegen das dem künstlerischen korrelative Talent zum Leiden und zur Weisheit des Leidens: und als Denkmal seines Sieges steht Homer vor uns, der naive Künstler. (iii, 31-32)

The second mode of cognition, the polar opposite of the Dionysiac, is the Socratic, which arises "aus zu viel Reflexion, gleichsam aus einem Überschuß von Möglichkeiten..." (vii, 48) Its method requires above all a strict adherence to the law of causality, which Socrates found to be breached by the older tragedians, for he saw in their dramas "etwas recht Unvernünftiges, mit Ursachen, die ohne Wirkungen, und mit Wirkungen, die ohne Ursachen zu sein schienen..." (xiv, 78) Logic and, more specifically, the syllogism are the chief weapons in the arsenal of Socratism. Syllogistic thinking is further one of the major roots of the illusory optimism characteristic of rationalism: "... denn wer vermöchte das *optimistische* Element im Wesen der Dialektik zu verkennen, das in jedem Schlusse sein Jubelfest feiert und allein in kühler Helle und Bewußtheit atmen kann..." (xiv, 80) The Socratic dialectician is therefore the mortal enemy of music and myth, hence the negator of that profound pessimism which alone can produce genuine tragedy.

Nietzsche apparently considered Socratic dialectics to be a hypertrophy of the Apollonian tendency: "in dem logischen Schematismus hat sich die *apollinische* Tendenz verpuppt." (xiv, 80) Just how this can be is not at all clear, i.e., how one can proceed from the Apollonian world of illusion to the domain of pure rationalism is by no means explained. Nevertheless, the contrast between the instinctive knowledge of Dionysiac man and the rational knowledge of Socratic man is quite clear. This antithesis lies at the center of Nietzsche's thinking in *Die Geburt der Tragödie* and dominates all phases of it. Socratic dialectics disrupted the Apollonian-Dionysiac synthesis, but that mode of cognition has no affinity for either of those elements. It cannot ally with the Apollonian element, since that is mere illusion, nor can it ally with the Dionysiac, since that element is its deadly antagonist. In fact, Socratic knowledge might be functionally defined as *that mode of knowledge which is incapable of uniting with either the Apollonian or Dionysiac components in life or art.* (Cf. "Und weil du [Euripides] Dionysus verlassen, so verließ dich auch Apollo." x, 64). One becomes so accustomed to speaking of the antithesis Apollo–Dionysos that he tends to overlook the fact that it is the antithesis Socrates–Dionysos which is here of primary importance.[11] I believe it is not without significance that, after the first publisher rejected the manuscript of *Die Geburt der Tragödie*, the only part Nietzsche selected for printing at his own expense and distributed to his friends was entitled: "Sokrates und die Tragödie."[12]

The preceding discussion brings to the surface some central facts about Nietzsche's analysis which he is content to allow for the most part to remain submerged, but which shed considerable light on his study of Greek tragedy. Nietzsche is essentially an ontological thinker, dealing with epistemological questions only when forced by his own logic to do so, and then as briefly as possible. That Nietzsche was, in fact, "deeply distrustful of the dogmas of epistemology"[13] is well-known and is quite consistent with his view that the problem of values takes precedence over the problem of cognition. Further, since art is in his view what makes life liveable, he is impatient with the purely technical questions of philosophy or with metaphysical system-building. However, viewed from the standpoint of its epistemology, *Die Geburt der Tragödie* suffers from a fundamental inconsistency. Metaphorically speaking, we may say that a massive seam runs through the middle of the work, revealing the imperfect suture of the two halves.

It is obvious from the beginning that Nietzsche has cast his thought in sexual terms. Thus, the very title of the work announces that tragedy comes into existence after the manner of the human being, namely, through the womb, through the portal of birth. Hence, the provenance of a work of art is radically different from that of a mere artifact, for the latter results from mechanical manipulation or construction of one sort or another. In the case of Greek tragedy it is the Dionysiac matrix which gives birth to the Apollonian illusion, or, to be more specific, it was historically the Dionysiac chorus expressing itself in the dithyramb from which the scenic illusion of the dramatic action sprang.

In the following paragraphs the sexual imagery which Nietzsche employs in connection with the Dionysiac impulse in art will be discussed. However, it should be noted that the instinctive creativity of the artist is by no means a surrender to his subjectivity, but is rather the attuning of himself to the creative or, more specifically, the *procreative* power of nature. This principle is quite clearly stated in connection with the delineation of the satyr:

> Die Natur, an der noch keine Erkenntnis gearbeitet, in der die Riegel der Kultur noch unerbrochen sind — das sah der Grieche in seinem Satyr... es war das Urbild der Menschen, der Ausdruck seiner höchsten und stärksten Regungen, als begeisterter Schwärmer, den die Nähe des Gottes entzückt, als mitleidender Genosse, in dem sich das Leiden des Gottes wiederholt, als Weisheitsverkünder aus der tiefsten Brust der Natur heraus, als *Sinnbild der geschlechtlichen Allgewalt der Natur*, die der Grieche gewöhnt ist mit ehrfürchtigem Staunen zu betrachten.[14]

It is also quite explicitly stated that the Dionysiac Greek is to be equated with the satyr, and that he desires to perceive truth in its fulness like that creature of unspoiled nature: "der dionysische Grieche will die Wahrheit und die Natur in ihrer höchsten Kraft—er sieht sich zum Satyr verzaubert." (viii, 50) At this point Nietzsche reveals himself again to be a genuinely ontological thinker, for the really creative man, like the satyr, is essentially the instrument of a power which transcends the individual, a power which constitutes in fact the "ewigen Kern der Dinge, dem Ding an sich," that is, the ultimate reality as contrasted with the phenomenal world. (viii, 50)

It is not only the creative artist, however, who is open to the perception of Dionysiac truth. The spectator himself, if he is not spoiled by rationalism or by convention, if he is one of those, "die unmittelbar verwandt mit der Musik, in ihr gleichsam *ihren Mutterschoß* haben,"[15] may be attuned to the perception of the ultimate wisdom. For instance, in rejecting Aristotle's explanation of man's delight in tragedy, Nietzsche personifies nature as the "primordial mother" who says to the spectator: "Seid wie ich bin! Unter dem unaufhörlichen Wechsel der Erscheinungen die ewig schöpferische, ewig zum Dasein zwingende, an diesem Erscheinungswechsel sich ewig befriedigende Urmutter." (xvi, 93) Our pleasure in the destruction of the protagonist is possible because we do not identify with him but with "the one living reality behind the phenomenal world, in whose procreative delight we share" ("das

87

eine Lebendige, mit dessen Zeugungslust wir verschmolzen sind," xvii, 93). This delight in destruction is like that of the child who builds sand-castles only to knock them over once they have been completed. Thus, the cathartic function of fear and pity, which Aristotle assumed to occur as a result of the tragic action, becomes irrelevant, for authentic tragedy yields what Nietzsche calls a "metaphysical comfort" in its place:

> Der metaphysische Trost — mit welchem, wie ich schon hier andeute, uns jede wahre Tragödie entläßt — daß das Leben im Grunde der Dinge, trotz allem Wechsel der Erscheinungen unzerstörbar mächtig und lustvoll sei, dieser Trost erscheint in leibhafter Deutlichkeit als Satyrchor, als Chor von Naturwesen, die gleichsam hinter aller Zivilisation unvertilgbar leben und trotz allem Wechsel der Generationen und der Völkergeschichte ewig dieselben bleiben. Mit diesem Chore tröstet sich der tiefsinnige und zu zartesten und schwersten Leiden einzig befähigte Hellene... (vii, 47)

For the ancient Greek the metaphysical comfort in tragedy derived from his awareness of the eternal fecundity of nature as symbolized by the chorus of satyrs; for the modern spectator who is imbued with the spirit of music such a "metaphysischer Trost" is still a reality.

We have seen that, when man is under the sway of Dionysos, he is in harmony with the most elemental aspects of nature, and therefore his artistic creations are authentic. So fundamental for all human living, however, are the realms of Apollo and Dionysos that they express themselves in the individual psyche as dream ("Traum") and intoxication ("Rausch") respectively. (i, 20) In the body social these two antipathetic realms express themselves primarily as orgiastic excitement or mysticism on the one hand, and as the passion for social or political order on the other. Let us consider the power of Dionysos to rule the collective psyche, even when his votaries are unaware of the source of their frenzy:

> Auch im deutschen Mittelalter wälzten sich unter der gleichen dionysischen Gewalt immer wachsende Scharen, singend und tanzend, von Ort zu Ort: in diesen Sankt-Johann- und Sankt-Veittänzern erkennen wir die bacchischen Chöre der Griechen wieder, mit ihrer Vorgeschichte in Kleinasien, bis hin zu Babylon und den orgiastischen Sakäen. (i, 24)

The driving force of such behavior was obviously of a sexual nature: "Fast überall lag das Zentrum dieser Feste in einer überschwenglichen geschlechtlichen Zuchtlosigkeit, deren Wellen über jedes Familientum und dessen ehrwürdige Satzungen hinwegfluteten; gerade die wildesten Bestien der Natur wurden hier entfesselt, bis zu jener abscheulichen Mischung von Wollust und Grausamkeit, die mir immer als der eigentliche 'Hexentrank' erschienen ist." (ii, 26-27)

Among the Greeks, however, the orgiastic festivals never represented the unleashing of such bestiality as characterized the Dionysiac barbarians with their repellent "witches brew" of lust and cruelty. Nietzsche speaks of the "immense gulf" which separated the Greeks from the barbarians in this regard. (ii, 26) But in spite of the great difference between the Greeks and the non-Greeks, the sexual origin of the Dionysiac frenzy among the former also is strongly affirmed. Its sublimation into a higher form entails no denial of its elemental origin. Thus, Nietzsche traces the development of Indian Buddhism back directly to "Orgiasmus." (xxi, 114) He further indicates that Greece was saved from traveling a similar route only as a result of the admixture of the Apollonian element. Likewise, it was saved from the extreme of excessive Apollonianism with its attendant hypertrophy of the political instinct, whose "most magnificent but also most terrifying expression was the Roman Empire." (xxi, 114)

As we have already seen, Nietzsche makes a distinction between the two levels of illusion which are present in Dionysiac and Apollonian art. The former is the primary illusion or appearance, reflecting the pain and contradiction of existence; the latter is secondary and grows out of the former. Thus, the Dionysiac illusion is elemental; the Apollonian derivative. By way of illustration Nietzsche makes use of Raphael's masterpiece "Transfiguration" with its two levels of artistic illusion: the suffering figures of Christ's bereaved followers below, and the glorification of the same Christ above. Of this painting he writes: "Hier haben wir, in höchster Kunstsymbolik, jene apollinische Schönheitswelt und ihren Untergrund, die schreckliche Weisheit des Silen, vor unseren Blicken und begreifen, durch Intuition, ihre gegenseitige Notwendigkeit." (iv, 33) Paradoxically, the Dionysiac component, in addition to being illusion, is, as we have noted earlier, also genuine knowledge. The roots of this contradiction seem to lie in Nietzsche's tendency to regard the Dionysiac insight as illusion, whenever aesthetic questions are involved, but as truth, whenever epistemological questions are involved.

Nothing is clearer in *Die Geburt der Tragödie* than the sexual nature of the Dionysiac impulse. We have seen that it has its roots outside of man in an aspect of nature, but that it is also fundamental to human nature. Hence, it is both ontological and psychological. When Nietzsche addresses himself to the problem of artistic creativity, the principle of human sexuality becomes central. In the sequel we shall examine the striking and consistent use which he makes of such imagery in this connection. However, it should be noted from the outset that sexuality is attributed chiefly to the influence of Dionysos, not of Apollo. This is not to say that he does not occasionally impute in one way or another such an impulse to the Apollonian artist, but generally it is reserved for the Dionysiac artist.[16]

It is my own opinion that one is here confronted with a weakness in Nietzsche's argument, for it is by no means obvious how the creativity of the strictly Apollonian or "naive" artist such as Homer is related to the sexual impulse. For Apollonian art has its roots neither in the "intoxication" of the individual nor in the "Orgiasmus" of the crowd, but in the "dream-world" and in the *principium individuationis.* At one point it is even asserted that the Apollonian component of great art saves man from "orgiastic self-destruction," a statement which, if it does not show Apollo to be hostile to the Dionysiac eros, at least represents him to be neutral in that regard. (xxi, 118) In the latter case Apollonianism would constitute as it were a prismatic medium which diffuses the orgiastic elements over a wide spectrum, thereby reducing their destructive power. This view finds its corroboration in a statement made many years later:

> In the Dionysian intoxication there is sexuality and voluptuousness; they are not lacking in the Apollinian. There must also be a difference in tempo in the two conditions — The extreme calm in certain sensations of intoxication (more strictly: the retardation of the feelings of time and space) likes to be reflected in a vision of the calmest gestures and types of soul. The classical style is essentially a representation of this calm, simplification, abbreviation, concentration — *the highest feeling of power* is concentrated in the classical type. To react slowly; a great consciousness; no feeling of struggle.[17]

But let us now examine the metaphors and similes which Nietzsche feels compelled to employ when speaking of the artist who creates under the influence of the Dionysiac spirit.

As indicated previously, the true artist never creates out of his subjectivity, but becomes a vehicle or instrument of a power outside of himself. Paradoxically, this is true of that type of artist who is often considered to be the most subjective of all: the lyric poet. Thus, in speaking of the emotional outpourings of such a poet, Nietzsche says: "Das 'Ich' des Lyrikers tönt also aus dem Abgrunde des Seins: seine 'Subjektivität' im Sinne der neueren Ästhetiker ist eine Einbildung. Wenn Archilochus, der erste Lyriker der Griechen, seine rasende Liebe und zugleich seine Verachtung den Töchtern des Lykambes kundgibt, so ist es nicht seine Leidenschaft, die vor uns in orgiastischem Taumel tanzt: wir sehen Dionysus und die Mänaden..." (v, 37) The references to "orgiastic transport" as well as to Dionysos and the maenads, attest to the true nature of the lyric poet's emotion. Although he is above all attuned to the spirit of music, whence he draws his real power, such music is bound up at its source with the procreative drive. In referring to the change in the course of time from the Apollonian art of Homer to the Dionysiac art of Pindar, Nietzsche asserts:

> Man denke nur einmal tiefer über die sprachliche Differenz der Farbe, des syntaktischen Baus, des Wortmaterials bei Homer und Pindar nach, um die Bedeutung dieses Gegensatzes zu begreifen; ja, es wird einem dabei handgreiflich deutlich, daß zwischen Homer und Pindar die *orgiastischen Flötenweisen des Olympus* erklungen sein müssen, die noch im Zeitalter des Aristoteles... zu trunkner Begeisterung hinrissen... (vi, 42)

The author has emphasized the primordial, indeed divine alliance between music and eros by underscoring in his own text the phrase "orgiastic flute-melodies of Olympus." In summary, one may say that the lyric poet, because of his surrender to the spirit of music, is preeminently the one who has access to the "Mothers of Being," that is, to the "inner core of reality." (xvi, 88; cf. 20, 113)

Having considered the relationship of the lyric poet to the Dionysiac impulse, we may now turn to the Attic tragedian, whose art arose under the aegis of both Dionysos and Apollo, deities normally in opposition to one another but who were reconciled at a propitious moment in history: "Diese Versöhnung ist der wichtigste Moment in der Geschichte des griechischen Kultus... Es war die Versöhnung zweier Gegner, mit scharfer Bestimmung ihrer von jetzt ab einzuhaltenden Grenzlinien und mit periodischer Übersendung von Ehrengeschenken; im Grunde war die Kluft nicht überbrückt." (ii, 27) However, as long as the reconciliation lasted it was a highly creative "fraternal union of the two deities." (xxi, 120) We shall find that it is precisely in connection with the tragedies of Aeschylus and Sophocles, both characterized by a felicitous union of Apollonian and Dionysiac elements, that Nietzsche most frequently invokes the symbolism of procreation. Thus, reiterating the idea expressed in the title of the work, he speaks of the Dionysiac aspect of reality as "der gemeinsame Geburtsschoß der Musik und des tragischen Mythus." (xxiv, 131)[18] Similarly, the choric parts of a Greek tragedy, from which the dialogue and scenes of the drama arise, are referred to with the term "Mutterschoß." (viii, 52)

In the opening lines of his study Nietzsche lays down the principle already hinted at in the title of the work itself, namely, that tragedy is produced by the spirit of music. It is important to recognize that by the "spirit of music" he means a *musical mood* ("musikalische Stimmung," v, 37). When Nietzsche speaks of the periodic reconciliation of Apollo and Dionysos he compares such a reconciliation to the union of the male and female, a union which represents only a temporary truce in the perennial battle of the sexes: "Wir werden viel für die ästhetische Wissenschaft gewonnen haben, wenn wir... zur unmittelbaren Sicherheit gekommen sind, daß die Fortentwicklung der Kunst an die Duplizität des *Apollinischen* und des *Dionysischen* gebunden ist: in ähnlicher Weise, wie die Generation von der Zweiheit der Geschlechter, bei fortwährendem Kampfe und nur periodisch eintretender Versöhnung abhängt." (i, 21) He continues to employ sexual imagery in speaking of the mutual stimulation which the two impulses provide for one another, even when they are competitive rather than cooperative: "Beide so verschiedne Triebe gehen nebeneinander her, zumeist im offnen Zwiespalt miteinander und sich gegenseitig zu immer neuen kräftigeren Geburten reizend..." (i, 21) Having thus, from the very beginning, invoked the imagery of procreation in connection with the fusion of the two basic instincts, the author is to reiterate it again and again.

Greek tragedy at its height represents for Nietzsche the felicitous union of forces which had, on the one hand, produced the epic and, on the other, the lyric, and which he found to be represented above all in Greek culture by Homer and Archilochus, the "Urväter" of Greek literature—here again having recourse to the imagery of procreation. (v, 36) But it is not only in tragedy that such a fruitful union of the two disparate elements takes place. The same miraculous process occurs on another level, namely, in the folksong. That art form is not our concern here, but one should not fail to note that the terminology with which we have become familiar also appears in connection with the discussion of the folksong:

> Was aber ist das Volkslied im Gegensatz zu dem völlig apollinischen Epos? Was anders als das *perpetuum vestigium* einer Vereinigung des Apollinischen und des Dionysischen: seine ungeheure, über alle Völker sich erstreckende und in immer neuen *Geburten* sich steigernde Verbreitung ist uns ein Zeugnis dafür, wie stark jener künstlerische Doppeltrieb der Natur ist: der in analoger Weise seine Spuren im Volkslied hinterläßt, wie die *orgiastischen* Bewegungen eines Volkes sich in seiner Musik verewigen.[19]

Tragedy is, however, not only the most important expression of the harmony of Apollonian and Dionysiac elements, it is also the form in which those elements appear in a discrete, yet mutually dependent relationship. It is important to note that the chorus is conceived as the matrix of the scenes, i.e., of the dialogue with its attendant dramatic action. Nietzsche assumes that the dialogue and dramatic action are born of the chorus, i.e., of the spirit of music. (xxiv, 131, 133) Therefore, he speaks of "die Befähigung der Musik, *den Mythus*, d.h. das bedeutsamste Exempel zu gebären und gerade den *tragischen* Mythus: den Mythus, der von der dionysischen Erkenntnis in Gleichnissen redet."[20]

In hailing the expected re-emergence of tragedy in modern times, particularly in Germany and as a result of Wagner's music-dramas, Nietzsche repeatedly uses the words "Geburt" and "Wiedergeburt."[21] Along with the rebirth of tragedy, the Dionysiac spectator will also appear, for, like tragedy itself, he will also be born of the spirit of music. It is to such a Dionysiac audience that Nietzsche addresses himself in *Die Geburt der Tragödie:* "nur an diejenigen habe ich mich zu wenden, die unmittelbar verwandt mit der Musik, in ihr gleichsam ihren Mutterschoß haben." (xxi, 116) So constantly does Nietzsche employ terms having to do with birth and re-birth that they constitute a sort of stereotype—a fact significant in itself, since as a consummate stylist he is never at a loss for a colorful and suggestive variation on any idea he chooses to express. Therefore, one cannot escape the conclusion that for Nietzsche all veridical knowledge—from which alone great art can arise—is bound up with eros. As we have seen, even Apollonian creativity is dependent upon it, though Nietzsche by no means makes the nature of this dependency clear. It is clear, however, that the Apollonian element, united in tragedy with the Dionysiac ecstasy, acts as a kind of shield or protection against the overwhelming effect of that emotion:

> Dieser edlen Täuschung [the Apollonian myth in tragedy] vertrauend darf sie [tragedy] jetzt ihre Glieder zum dithyrambischen Tanze bewegen und sich unbedenklich einem

orgiastischen Gefühle der Freiheit hingeben, in welchem sie als Musik an sich, ohne jene Täuschung, nicht zu schwelgen wagen dürfte. Der Mythus schützt uns vor der Musik, wie er ihr andrerseits erst die höchste Freiheit gibt. (xxi, 115)

One is tempted at this point to employ a non-Nietzschean simile and to say that just as some kind of insulator is necessary in order to make use of electricity, while at the same time avoiding its destructive effects, so the Apollonian component is necessary to control and channel Dionysiac power. All this has, however, nothing to do with knowledge. *Only Dionysos can give genuine knowledge.*

The second half of *Die Geburt der Tragödie* is devoted to the thesis that Socrates, in alliance with Euripides, destroyed Attic tragedy by driving out the Dionysiac spirit, an act which could only have the most ruinous consequences, since that spirit was the real source of its greatness. As noted earlier, Socrates could only accomplish this, because his solution to the problem of knowledge is according to Nietzsche the only possible alternative to the instinctive knowledge of Dionysus or Silenus. "This is the new antithesis: the Dionysiac and the Socratic, and the art of Greek tragedy was to perish as a result of it." (xxi, 71) Apollonian illusion plays no part in the Titanic struggle between these forces. When Nietzsche says of the epistemology of Socrates: "In dem logischen Schematismus hat sich die *apollinische* Tendenz verpuppt ..." (xiv, 80) he is either carried away by his own rhetoric or simply in error. For this statement ill accords with his basic and often repeated assertion that the Apollonian realm is that of mere illusion or appearance. It is at this point that we may concede some truth in Nietzsche's statement when he complained some years later of the lack of "logical cleanliness" of *Die Geburt der Tragödie*.[22]

Before we proceed to a more systematic consideration of Nietzsche's treatment of Socrates, it is quite instructive simply to set side by side the provocative and sometimes contradictory descriptive phrases which he applies to Socrates throughout the treatise. The following periphrases are listed in the sequence in which they appear in the text. Socrates is "the second spectator [Euripides being the first] who did not understand tragedy, and therefore did not esteem it" (xi, 69; xii, 75); "a demonic power speaking through Euripides... an entirely newly-born demon named Socrates" (xii, 71); "the antagonist of Dionysos, the new Orpheus" (xii, 75); "the foremost and supreme Sophist, the mirror and quintessence of all sophistical strivings" (xiii, 75); "the most problematical figure of antiquity"; "a true monstrosity *per defectum*"; "the specific *non-mystic*... in whom the logical capacity is just as excessively developed, through a superfetation, as instinctive wisdom is in the mystic" (xiii, 77); "Socrates, the true eroticist"; "the dying Socrates... the new, never before realized ideal of the noble youth of Greece" (xiii, 78; xv, 85); "the dialectical hero of the Platonic drama" (xiv, 80); "the mystagogue of science"; "the turning-point and vortex of so-called world-history" (xv, 85); "the prototype of the theoretical optimist" (xv, 86); "the music-making Socrates" (xv, 87; xvii, 95); "the prototype and primal ancestor of theoretical man" (xviii, 99). From the mere juxtaposition of these hyperbolic phrases it becomes evident that Nietzsche's version of Socrates is an extraordinary and disturbing conception.

It is not my concern in this study, however, to dwell on the coruscations of Nietzsche's many-faceted and fascinating work, but to show that his theory of knowledge is the crucial factor in his argument, and, further, that in dealing with the Socratic-Euripidean development he abandons his earlier position that knowledge essentially involves eros, abruptly introducing a kind of cognition which is not a perversion or mutilation of man's sexuality but a simple negation of it. In other words, he finds that the "newly born demon named Socrates" was able, by employing such neutral categories as causality and such methods as purely syllogistic reasoning to rout the god Dionysos. This is not to suggest that a metaphysical dualism involving sexual and non-sexual factors interacting on the world-stage would not be a viable and self-consistent world-view, but such is not Nietzsche's basic position. He certainly accepts no dualism of the flesh and the spirit!

In comparing Socratic or theoretical man with the creative artist, Nietzsche makes use of a parable which very aptly illustrates his thinking. He contrasts the search of theoretical man and of the artist for truth to the unveiling, garment by garment, of a goddess. But once the naked goddess stands before them, theoretical man, whose chief interest was really the unveiling process itself, remains satisfied with the cast-off garments, while the artist keeps his gaze fixed enrapturedly on what is still hidden from him.[23] In this parable Nietzsche unconciously reveals through his imagery the basic assumption that eros is involved in the search for truth as far as the artist is concerned but not as far as theoretical man is concerned, for, once the goddess is unveiled, the latter retains an interest only in that which was cast off. The reason for the man of theory to turn away from the goddess of truth so conceived is obvious: she no longer represents that which can be rationally apprehended; she stands before him simply as an irreducible phenomenon, which can only *symbolize* truth. The rationalist is not interested in symbols, however, but in factual data.

According to Nietzsche the history of Greek drama in the fifth century B.C. is the record of a sad decline from the lofty heights of Aeschylean achievement to the lowlands of Euripidean drama, with the work of Sophocles representing, as it were, the middle ground between them. The dramas of Aeschylus manifest those qualities which we have seen to be essential to tragedy in Nietzsche's view, namely, scene and dialogue, which grow out of the tragic myth, on the one hand, and the dithyrambic chorus, which gives birth to the myth, on the other. If the essence of tragedy was to be destroyed it was necessary for music to be driven out of tragedy and to be replaced with something else. This is precisely what happened under the aegis of Socrates:

94

Die optimistische Dialektik treibt mit der Geißel ihrer Syllogismen die *Musik* aus der Tragödie: d.h. sie zerstört das Wesen der Tragödie, welches sich einzig als eine Manifestation und Verbildlichung dionysischer Zustände, als sichtbare Symbolisierung der Musik, als die Traumwelt eines dionysischen Rausches interpretieren läßt. (xiv, 81)

Socratic logic was put at the service of one universal principle, namely, that whatever is either good or beautiful must accord with reason, and may not rest on mere instinct. (xii, 72, 75) Euripides, who was intent upon rationalizing the drama, was therefore the natural ally of Socrates. In other words, what the philosopher was doing in the realm of ideas, the dramatist was doing in the aesthetic realm. "So ist Euripides vor allem als Dichter der Widerhall seiner bewußten Erkenntnisse; und gerade dies verleiht ihm eine so denkwürdige Stellung in der Geschichte der griechischen Kunst." (xii, 74)

What does it mean to say that Euripides made the drama an "echo of his conscious knowledge," thereby suppressing his instinctive intuitions? Specifically it means that the chorus is reduced to a mere appendage in the tragedy, instead of being the source of the dramatic action; thus, dramatic action becomes secondary, the explanatory prologue having anticipated its main features with the result that suspense is virtually eliminated (xii, 73-74); dialogue becomes all-important but primarily as pathos or lyrical effusion; character protrayal becomes more important than plot; the sequence of events must be reasonable, not as in the Aeschylean drama where a Socrates finds only "something quite unreasonable, with causes apparently without effects, and effects apparently without causes." (xiv, 78) Thus, naturalism comes into its own with Euripides. Finally, the *deus ex machina* is employed to give the denouement credence, for it is axiomatic in the Socratic-Euripidean world-view that all knowledge must be certified. One must not be left to gaze into the abyss of Dionysiac mystery with its "disaster at the very center of things... the contradiction at the heart of the universe." (ix, 59) Instead of such brokenness at the heart of reality one must somehow see wholeness and order, even if the attempt means reducing reality to such proportions as may manifest those qualities. In such a way the mythic and metaphysical dimensions of the earlier Greek tragedy were eliminated. Only in his old age did Euripides recant and acknowledge the sovereign power of Dionysos after all in the drama, the *Bacchae*. (Nietzsche accepts this work as quite seriously intended by its author and by no means as a satire.) But as far as Greek tragedy was concerned it was already too late: "... als der Dichter widerrief, hatte bereits seine Tendenz gesiegt. Dionysus war bereits von der tragischen Bühne verscheucht und zwar durch eine aus Euripides redende Macht." (xii, 71)

What Nietzsche is saying here is simply that it was Euripides' espousal of a new kind of epistemology, a new mode of knowledge, which succeeded in driving Dionysos from the stage and transforming the drama. For the "demonic power speaking through Euripides" was none other than Socrates or, more precisely, the Socratic dialectic. Every innovation in the typical

95

Euripidean drama over against the Aeschylean and Sophoclean art obviously arose from the desire to make the drama more rational, therefore more naturalistic. Thus, the Euripidean plays are prime examples of "aesthetic Socratism." (xii, 72) Nietzsche suggests a tendency in Socrates at the very end of his life to doubt his own rational principles by reference to the "music-making Socrates" (xv, 87; xvii, 95); but this insight into the limits of his logical universe prevailed only briefly before his death, and therefore had no effect on the tenor of his life as a whole.

The fundamental question, which I do not believe Nietzsche satisfactorily answers, is this: What is the essential nature of the Euripidean creativity, hence of the Socratic-Euripidean conception of knowledge? It has already been noted that Socratism is essentially rationalism with great emphasis on deductive reasoning, i.e., on the syllogism. It has also been noted that Nietzsche conceives of such cognition as involving no sexual element, although he does occasionally employ sexual terminology in connection with it.[24] Yet he stands quite ready to acknowledge the genuine artistry of Euripides.[25] Is it possible that any sort of art, however decadent—and we shall see that the idea of decadence is implicitly ascribed to Socrates in *Die Geburt der Tragödie* and explicitly in later writings—can come into being entirely apart from eros? One may argue with justice, I think, that Nietzsche would have been on more solid ground, had he seen in aesthetic Socratism either a perversion or a mutilation of the sexual instinct. As stated earlier, the Hamannian idea that abstraction is castration or "eunuchism" would have lent a consistency to Nietzsche's argument which it lacks. It will be necessary in what follows to go beyond Hamann's formulations, but that is simply a matter of deriving the corollaries from the main proposition.

First, it should be said that the eunuch can be described as the one in whom general power as a normal male human being is reduced while at the same time his specific powers may be increased, that is to say, the energies which would normally express themselves as eros, with all the manifold implications for the individual's relationship to others, may now be channeled in particular ways. We are not concerned, of course, with literal eunuchism. Nevertheless, it is helpful by way of illustration to recall that history is replete with examples of eunuchs who have been individuals of extraordinary accomplishment as thinkers, statesmen, military leaders, singers, etc. One need only think of Bagoas, Persian statesman and conqueror of Egypt; Origen of Alexandria, the famous Christian theologian; and Farinelli, the operatic singer of unparalleled ability in the eighteenth century, to be aware of their achievements. Perhaps there is something of a parallel here to the idea of sublimation in contemporary depth psychology, but one should bear in mind that purely psychological categories are irrelevant to our purpose.

There are occasions when Nietzsche seems to adopt, even if unconsciously, the point of view regarding Socratism which I have undertaken to defend in this investigation, as for instance when he speaks of the "great Cyclops-eye" of Socrates, which "never glowed with the blissful madness of artistic inspiration."[26] When one reflects on this figure of speech as descriptive of Socrates, he realizes that it is a metaphor which parallels the idea of philosophical eunuchism quite closely. For in this case also general power is replaced by specialized power. Two eyes are normal for the human being, and, although their vision is limited, they are possessed of three-dimensional vision. The man who possesses one eye, even though it be the giant eye of the Cyclops, can see in only two dimensions. Thus, the one great eye of the Cyclops is more powerful than two normal eyes, but paradoxically it sees less, because it is blind to a whole dimension. The fact that Nietzsche invokes optical rather than sexual imagery at this point is in keeping with his general tendency to view Socratic knowledge in non-sexual terms.

The idea of philosophical eunuchism is further useful in the attempt to solve a puzzle presented by Nietzsche's account of Socrates as the prototypal intellectual, for the intellectual, whom Nietzsche designates as "Alexandrian," is characterized by both great strength and great weakness at the same time. For instance, in discussing the cerebral type of individual who deplores the tendency of human beings to give themselves up periodically to Dionysiac frenzy, he writes:

> Es gibt Menschen, die aus Mangel an Erfahrung oder aus Stumpfsinn, sich von solchen Erscheinungen wie von "Volkskrankheiten," spöttisch oder bedauernd im Gefühl der eigenen Gesundheit abwenden: die Armen ahnen freilich nicht, wie leichenfarbig und gespenstisch eben diese ihre 'Gesundheit' sich ausnimmt, wenn an ihnen das glühende Leben dionysischer Schwärmer vorüberbraust. (i, 24)

When we remember that Socrates is the great prototype of these sickly individuals, it is most difficult to reconcile the kind of extreme impotence suggested here with the vast cultural power attributed to him and his followers. This fundamental contradiction is built into Nietzsche's portrait of Socrates in Die Geburt der Tragödie, for, on the one hand, he is the "divinity" or "demonic power" speaking through Socrates (xii, 71), the one whose influence on future generations is like "a shadow cast by the evening sun, growing ever larger" (xv, 83), and, on the other hand, he is the prototype of all those "corpse-like" and "ghostly"[27] individuals who deplore the advent of Dionysos, and of "Alexandrian man, who is basically a librarian and proofreader and who blinds himself miserably over dusty books and typographical errors." (xviii, 103) If Nietzsche had, however, adopted the idea that abstraction is castration, and therefore had interpreted Socrates as eunuchoid, he would have been able to explain the philosopher's vast cultural influence, while at the same time explaining why, in terms of his system, violence had to be done to that which is natural. For Nietzsche always assumes the natural priority of the Apollonian and Dionysiac instincts over the Socratic, the Apollonian arising from the dream-state, the Dionysiac from the state of intoxication. But in the normal, healthy individual there is no "Socratic" instinct. When a powerful instinct for logic occurs in an individual like Socrates, it is simply a monstrosity, hence an aberration of nature. (xiii, 77) I have reiterated throughout this study that Nietzsche should have related the idea of castration to cognition in general in order to solve the problem of Socratism. However, this may not be quite correct, for he seems to have conceived of castration as the complete elimination of eros rather than the "economizing" or redirection of that impulse into narrower channels, a process which is assumed in this study.[28]

Just what is the underlying conception of Socrates in *Die Geburt der Tragödie?* The question is an imperative one, for the surprising fact is that, in spite of the considerable amount of space devoted to the philosopher and in spite of the stimulating, if controversial, observations on his meaning for Western culture, it is difficult to bring the picture of Socrates into clear focus—a difficulty which does not arise in connection with the conception of Dionysos or even of Apollo as cultural symbols. Obviously the contradictory elements which we have seen to enter into the Nietzschean portrait of Socrates constitute a difficulty, but they are by no means the only important factor. The matter is further complicated by the obvious admiration and poetic feeling which the figure of Socrates evokes for the author at times. (Cf. xiii, 78 *et passim*) The truth is that one must go outside the present work in order to find the term which Nietzsche finally settles on as descriptive of the essence of Socrates. It is not necessary to look far, however, before one discovers that Nietzsche has settled on the term *décadent*, which he borrowed from the nineteenth-century literary movement in France which the adjective describes. In *Ecce Homo* he writes: "Meine Leser wissen vielleicht, inwiefern ich Dialektik als Décadence-Symptom betrachte, zum Beispiel im allerberühmtesten Fall: im Fall des Sokrates."[29] In the section of the work where he deals specifically with *Die Geburt der Tragödie* Nietzsche avers that the two principal innovations of his youthful work were an understanding of the Dionysiac phenomenon among the Greeks and the understanding, for the first time, of Socrates "als Werkzeug der griechischen Auflösung, als typischer *décadent...*"[30]

It is my contention that, while Nietzsche is obviously correct in calling attention to the two major emphases of *Die Geburt der Tragödie*, the former is far more successful than the latter. Nowhere does his faulty conception of Socrates become more evident than in the astonishing notion that the father of Western philosophy can be viewed under the aspect of nineteenth-century French *décadence*. To understand the genesis of this idea it is necessary to recall that, after his break with Wagner, Nietzsche saw the composer as a "typischer *décadent*."[31] The interesting fact about this point of view is that Nietzsche intuitively connected Wagner with Baudelaire as being kindred spirits long before he knew of their actual relationship. This intuition, which he found later to be so well-founded, impressed Nietzsche deeply. In a letter to Peter Gast sixteen years after the publication of *Die Geburt der Tragödie* he discusses the matter and asserts: "Baudelaire ist *libertin*, mystisch, 'satanisch', aber vor allem wagnerisch."[32] The question as to whether this equation of Baudelaire's position with that of Wagner is justified is irrelevant to our purposes. However, since Socrates is asserted to be a *décadent* (and Nietzsche repeatedly uses the French word in connection with him), it is necessary to deal forthrightly with the questions which it raises.

If we examine the generally acknowledged characteristics of nineteenth-century literary *décadence*, we find that its main aesthetic principle, which grows out of its opposition to literary naturalism, is "art for art's sake"; its main moral principle is a subversion of or a setting of oneself beyond bourgeois values ("Außerbürgerlichkeit");[33] and its main religious principle is blasphemy or travesty of Christian orthodoxy, issuing quite often in Satanism. Epistemologically, the *décadent* is an intuitive thinker, since he is essentially an artist; metaphysically, he is a dualist, in so far as he accepts the principle of evil as a positive force. Further, he is often characterized by exaggerated sensibilities and overrefined and often extravagant taste, hence his craving for the unusual and exotic experience and his dandyism. He is frequently androgynous, with the men tending toward effeminacy and the women toward masculinity.[34] His inordinate urge toward an expansion of the ego is often matched only by his coldness toward others.

Had Nietzsche created his own definition of decadence, relevant to the Greece of the fifth and following centuries, it would not be necessary to relate Socrates in any way to the literary movement which came to flower in nineteenth-century France. But since he so clearly and consistently does this in writings subsequent to *Die Geburt der Tragödie*, it is necessary to ask whether the main features of *décadence* do indeed characterize Socrates as he appears in that work. In the first place the philosopher is portrayed not as divorcing art from the life of the people, but as eliminating the Dionysiac element from it so that it becomes "reasonable" and naturalistic, hence more readily understandable to the average spectator. Socrates, far from divorcing art from the life of the people, brought the two closer together: "Der Mensch des alltäglichen Lebens drang durch ihn [Euripides under the influence of Socrates] aus den Zuschauerräumen auf die Szene." (xi, 65) In questioning the role of instinct and tradition in legitimizing moral values, Socrates was of course regarded by the majority of his contemporaries as subversive of those values, but his attack on them was quite different from the libertinism of the nineteenth-century *décadents:* his desire was simply to establish the rule of reason. In his demythologizing efforts, however, he did undermine the foundations of popular Greek religion, but here again his purpose was not the enjoyment of the perverted thrill afforded by blasphemy, but simply to test religious beliefs in the light of reason.

If the typical *décadent* is an outright egotist who rejected any sense of social responsibility, Socrates, the ideal of the noble youth of Athens, was above all a leader of men, whose death for what he conceived to be the good of the state became a powerful inspiration to his followers. (xiii, 78; xv, 85) Nietzsche, far from representing Socrates as an effete, neurasthenic dandy, actually represents him as a superhuman power, a deity. It must be conceded that Nietzsche, in representing Socrates as the "wahrer Erotiker" (xiii, 78) deviates slightly from his heroic portrayal; for though we find here a concession to the idea of an androgynous Socrates, this feature of the portrait is a very minor one.

It is true that Nietzsche gives in *Der Fall Wagner* a definition of *décadence* which is designed to express its essence:

> Womit kennzeichnet sich jede *literarische décadence*? Damit, daß das Leben nicht mehr im ganzen wohnt. Das Wort wird souverän und springt aus dem Satz heraus, der Satz greift über und verdunkelt den Sinn der Seite, die Seite gewinnt auf Unkosten des Ganzen — das Ganze ist kein Ganzes mehr. Aber das ist das Gleichnis für jeden Stil der *décadence:* jedesmal Anarchie der Atome...[35]

This formulation expresses what I take to be the fundamental fallacy in Nietzsche's thought about the subject, namely, his equation of logic and dialectics with decadence. For it is not the *décadent*, who as an artist is an intuitive thinker, but the rationalistic philosopher and the man of theory in general who atomizes knowledge. One could substitute in the above passage, for example, the word *Aufklärung* and find that as a result it make even more sense. When Goethe points out in *Dichtung und Wahrheit* that Hamann insisted on wholeness it must be borne in mind that this insistence was made over against the atomizing, fragmenting tendencies of the *Aufklärer*, those arch-rationalists in whatever they undertook, whether in the area of the arts or sciences. At any rate, Nietzsche, is much more convincing when he represents Socrates as a thoroughgoing rationalist than as a *décadent* after the fashion of Wagner and Baudelaire.

It is now time to return to the main argument of this study, namely, that the first half of *Die Geburt der Tragödie*, dealing with the Apollonian-Dionysiac creativity, accords to eros its rightful place in knowledge, but that in second half, dealing with Socratism, there is an abrupt disjunction, leaving the relation of eros to that phenomenon unresolved. If Nietzsche had not insisted on identifying *décadence* with a most rigorous form of rationalism, he would have been able to avoid this inconsistency. For the fact is that the adherents of the *décadence* and *fin de siècle* movements were most significantly related to eros: they were Dionysiac in the strictest sense of the word! It is my opinion that Nietzsche, having represented Socrates as the paragon of theoretical man, who has no relationship whatsoever to sexuality, unconsciously sought to correct this defect by invoking a concept which might somehow accomplish his purpose, but found it necessary to redefine the notion to accord with the interpretation of Socrates which was central to his argument.

We may now conclude that the idea of abstraction as the castration of knowledge furnishes us with the means of solving the dilemma posed by the Nietzschean Socrates. Let us think for the moment of the Italian *castrato*, who was made a eunuch, not for the Kingdom of Heaven's sake, but for the sake of operatic music. He starts out as a normal boy, but because of emasculation he never enters into normal manhood. All the energy of eros is now channeled, not toward the opposite sex, but toward his art. The *castrato's* general power as a man is thus transformed into the special power of his art, which is dependent upon the preservation of the voice of his boyhood. This occurs in the same way as the normally diffused rays of the sun are collected by a lens and focused upon one small area where their power is considerably intensified. No one will deny the achievements of the *castrati*, but their art is the result of a tampering with nature. This allusion is, incidentally, by no means inappropriate in our context, for Nietzsche maintains in *Die Geburt der Tragödie* that Socratic culture is above all the culture of the opera. (xix, 103) Further, he writes in *Der Wille zur Macht* in discussing Christian morality as the emasculation of natural man:

Whence comes the seductive charm of such an emasculated ideal of man? Why are we not disgusted by it as we are perhaps disgusted by the idea of the castrato? — The answer lies precisely here: the voice of the castrato does not disgust us, despite the cruel mutilation that is its condition: it has grown sweeter — Just because the "male organ" has been amputated from virtue, a feminine note has been brought to the voice of virtue that it did not have before.[36]

In such a way Nietzsche comes within a hair's breadth of breaking through to the conception that eros is involved, even if in strictly sublimated form, in the kinds of art which he reprobates as cut off from the source of Dionysiac power.

In the preceding investigation we have seen that the key to an understanding of Nietzsche's argument in *Die Geburt der Tragödie* is his distinction between two radically different modes of knowledge, the one involving eros ("Orgiasmus") and the other rigidly excluding it. We have also seen that there is another possible approach to the problem of the relation of sexuality to cognition. On this view, sexuality would be involved in both of Nietzsche's cognitive modes, i.e., in both intuitive and abstract knowledge, inasmuch as eunuchism does not mean a total negation of sexuality, but as it were an oblique reference to it. For eunuchism cannot be understood apart from a reference to normal sexuality. It is clear that such an epistemology would not only have lent a greater consistency to the argument of *Die Geburt der Tragödie*, but it would also have been more in accord with the dominant thought of Nietzsche's philosophy that, in the last resort, nothing escapes the power of Dionysos.

¹ Nietzsche's general antipathy for Socrates is well attested, not only in *Die Geburt der Tragödie*, but throughout his writings. For a survey of the conception of Socrates in other works of Nietzsche's, see Kurt Hildebrandt, *Nietzsches Wettkampf mit Sokrates und Plato* (Dresden, 1920). However, Walter Kaufmann presents a dissenting view in his article, "Nietzsche's Admiration for Socrates," *Journal of the History of Ideas*, IX, 4 (1948), 472-491 and in *Nietzsche: Philosopher, Psychologist, Antichrist* (Princeton, 1950), pp. 342-360. Ernst Bertram argues that, in hating the rationalistic Socrates, Nietzsche was in actuality hating the rationalist within himself. See *Nietzsche: Versuch einer Mythologie* (Berlin, 1929), pp. 341 ff.

² Friedrich Nietzsche, *The Will to Power*, trans. Walter Kaufmann and R. J. Hollingdale (New York, 1967), Sec. 383, p. 207. I have cited this translation because of the general excellence of the edition. For the most part, quotations from Nietzsche will be in the original German. However, I shall depart from this practice occasionally for stylistic or other reasons, where the original language is not deemed necessary. Unless otherwise noted, the translations are my own.

³ *Ibid.* Sec. 204, p. 122. Cf. also: Sec. 248, pp. 143-144; Sec. 351, p. 192.

⁴ In attacking the *Aufklärer* Hamann writes: "Ihr wollt herrschen über die Natur und bindet euch selbst Hände und Füße durch den Stoicismus, um desto rührender über des Schicksals diamantene Fesseln in euren vermischten Gedichten fistulieren [to sing in a falsetto voice like a *castrato*] zu können. Wenn die Leidenschaften Glieder der Unehre sind, hören sie deswegen auf, Waffen der Mannheit zu seyn? Versteht ihr den Buchstaben der Vernunft klüger, als jener allegorische Kämmerer der alexandrinischen Kirche [Origen] den Buchstaben der Schrift, der sich selbst zum Verschnittenen machte, um des Himmelreichs willen? Die grösten Bösewichter gegen sich selbst [i.e., those who have castrated themselves], macht der Fürst dieses Aeons zu seinen Lieblingen..." *Aesthetica in nuce.* J. G. Hamann, *Sämtliche Werke*, ed. Josef Nadler (Vienna, 1950), II, p. 208; cf. also *Wolken*, where the *Aufklärer* is equated with "der Verschnittene," *ibid.*, p. 97; cf. further *Glose Philippique*, *ibid.*, p. 293 *et passim*. I shall treat this aspect of Hamann's thought in some detail in a forthcoming book on his life and work. The idea of abstraction as castration is of course, not Hamann's alone. Thus, Schiller has Karl Moor indict his rationalistic age as "das schlappe Kastraten-Jahrhundert." *Die Räuber*, I, i.

⁵ It should be noted that the category which I have employed is not used by Hamann in the interpretation of Socrates, since his version of that philosopher is at the opposite pole from Nietzsche's. Rather it is derived from certain other works of Hamann's. I have treated the difference between his and Nietzsche's interpretation of Socrates in an article, "Socrates in Hamann's *Socratic Memorabilia* and Nietzsche's *Birth of Tragedy*: A Comparison," which is to be included in a *Festschrift* for Philip Merlan (now in press). It should also be remarked that Nietzsche, despite all differences with Hamann, expresses his admiration for the latter's *Sokratische Denkwürdigkeiten* in *Die Philosophie im Tragischen Zeitalter der Griechen*. See Friedrich Nietzsche, *Werke*, ed. Karl Schlechta (Munich, 1966), III, sec. ii, p. 359. Further, I have employed the term "eros" not in Plato's sense but simply as the equivalent of sexuality.

⁶ Consult the *International Nietzsche Bibliography*, rev. ed. by Herbert W. Reichert and Karl Schlechta (Chapel Hill, 1968) for a convenient survey of the scholarly literature devoted to this work as well as to the subjects "Apollonian" and "Dionysian."

⁷ Friedrich Nietzsche, *Werke*, ed. Schlechta, I, sec. v, p. 40. (All references to the text of *Die Geburt der Tragödie* will be to this volume; brief references will be inserted parenthetically in the text, the lower case roman numerals referring to sections and arabic numerals to pages. References to other volumes of the Schlechta edition will be identified by the editor's name and volume number only.)

⁸ "Schein des Scheins," iv, 33.

⁹ xxii, 121. Cf. also: "Jener bild- und begrifflose Widerschein des Urschmerzes in der Musik, mit seiner Erlösung im Scheine erzeugt jetzt eine zweite Spiegelung, als einzelnes

Gleichnis oder Exempel." v, 37; further, the plastic Apollonian arts are merely an "Abbild der Erscheinung," whereas Dionysiac music is an "Abbild des Willens selbst." vi, 88.

[10] i, 22. Even the Apollonian *principium individuationis* does not mean that the work of Apollo has to do with reality, since individuation is essentially unreal: it is but part of the veil of maya, hiding the "mysterious primordial unity" of all things. i, 25; cf. 23. Apollonianism is thus illusion through and through.

[11] One of the most striking features of Nietzsche's method is the extent to which he thinks in *Begriffspaare* or conceptual opposites. He remarks: "Im Gegensatz zu allen denen, welche beflissen sind, die Künste aus einem einzigen Prinzip, als dem notwendigen Lebensquell jedes Kunstwerks, abzuleiten, halte ich den Blick auf jene beiden künstlerischen Gottheiten der Griechen, Apollo und Dionysus, geheftet und erkenne in ihnen die lebendigen und anschaulichen Repräsentanten *zweier* in ihrem tiefsten Wesen und ihren höchsten Zielen verschiedenen Kunstwelten." xvi, 88. However, in addition to his principal *Begriffspaar* there are scores of others ranging from the important Dionysos-Socrates antithesis to a number of minor ones — whose relevance is sometimes quite hazy. In any case, this method is consistent with his basic metaphysical principle that there is a "Widerspruch im Herzen der Welt." ix, 59. Whereas his Socrates would seek to reconcile opposites through reason, Nietzsche delights in sharpening their antithesis.

[12] Elisabeth Förster-Nietzsche, *Nietzsche's Werke*, Taschen-Ausgabe (Leipzig, 1906), I, p. 526.

[13] *The Will to Power*, trans. Kaufmann and Hollingdale; sec. 410, p. 221. Karl Jaspers says: "Epistemology, conceived as an attempt critically to analyze man's cognitive faculty, is simply an object of Nietzsche's contempt. *Nietzsche: An Introduction to the Understanding of His Philosophical Activity*, trans. C. F. Wallraff and F. J. Schmitz. (Tucson, 1965), p. 288.

[14] viii, 49. Italics not in original. Cf. also viii, 53.

[15] xxi, 116. Italics not in original.

[16] When sexual imagery is ascribed to the Apollonian element, however, it is usually in conjunction with the Dionysiac. Thus, the two artistic impulses stimulate one another to "immer neuen aufeinanderfolgenden Geburten." iv, 35. Further, he speaks of the "geheimnisvolles Ehebündnis" of the two impulses, whose offspring is Attic tragedy. *Ibid.*

[17] *The Will to Power*, trans. Kaufmann and Hollingdale, sec. 799, p. 420.

[18] The word "Geburtsschoß" is apparently a coinage of Nietzsche's. I could not find it listed in the Grimms' *Deutsches Wörterbuch* or elsewhere. Cf. xii, 71.

[19] vi, 41. German words not italicized in original.

[20] xvi, 92. Cf. also: "Nimmt nun zwar auch die musikalische Tragödie das Wort hinzu, so kann sie doch zugleich den Untergrund und die Geburtsstätte des Wortes danebenstellen und das Werden des Wortes, von innen heraus, verdeutlichen." xxi, 118.

[21] Cf. xi, 67; xvi, 88; xix, 103; xix, 110; xx, 112; xxii, 123; xxiii, 126; xxiv, 133.

[22] "Attempt at a Self-Criticism," in *The Birth of Tragedy and The Case of Wagner*, trans. Walter Kaufmann (New York, 1967), p. 19.

[23] xv, 84. In connection with this allegory I cannot refrain from calling attention to the parallel which it manifests with a passage which appears at the end of Hamann's famous letter to Kant of July 27, 1759: "Die Wahrheit wollte sich von Straßenräubern nicht zu nahe kommen laßen, sie trug Kleid auf Kleid, daß man zweifelte ihren Leib zu finden. Wie erschracken [sie], da sie ihren Willen hatten und das schreckl. Gespenst, die Wahrheit vor sich sahen." *J. G. Hamann. Briefwechsel*, eds. W. Ziesemer and A. Henkel (Wiesbaden, 1955), I, p. 381. The letter was published in the Roth-Wiener edition of Hamann's writings (1821-43), and therefore could easily have been read by Nietzsche. The representation of truth as a veiled goddess is, of course, familiar from Schiller's and Novalis' use of the symbol. However, it is Nietzsche's and Hamann's brief formulations which are so similar.

[24] Cf. "Sokrates… in dem die logische Natur durch eine Superfötation… exzessiv entwickelt ist…" xiii, 77; "im Schoße der theoretischen Kultur." xix, 107.

[25] Nietzsche speaks of Euripides as a "Genius." xi, 67; further, he speaks of the "reichbegabten und unablässig zum Schaffen gedrängten Künstler." xi, 68; "Von ihm könnte man sagen, daß die außerordentliche Fülle seines kritischen Talentes, ähnlich wie bei

Lessing, einen produktiv künstlerischen Nebenbetrieb, wenn nicht erzeugt, so doch fort-während befruchtet habe." xi, 68.

²⁶ xiv, 78. Occasionally Nietzsche hints at the same thing in general terms: "Beide Namen [i.e., of Socrates and Euripides] wurden von den Anhängern der 'guten alten Zeit' in einem Atem genannt, wenn es galt, die Volksverführer der Gegenwart aufzu-zählen: von deren Einflusse es herrühre, daß die alte marathonische vierschrötige Tüchtig-keit an Leib und Seele immer mehr einer zweifelhaften Aufklärung, bei fortschreitender Verkümmerung der leiblichen und seelischen Kräfte, zum Opfer falle." xiii, 75.

²⁷ Rektor Kleist in Georg Kaiser's play of the same name (1905) is an example of the sickly intellectual who is the antagonist of the instinctive Dionysiac forces with which he is surrounded. Herbert W. Reichert remarks that "it is interesting to note that Socrates was in the author's mind when he created Kleist." See "Nietzsche and Georg Kaiser," Studies in Philology, LXI, 1 (January, 1964), 96.

²⁸ The effects of the Nietzschean idea of castration are indicated in the following passage dealing with the emasculation of the natural impulses by Christianity: "Instead of taking into service the great sources of strength, those impetuous torrents of the soul that are so often dangerous and overwhelming, and economizing them, this most shortsighted and pernicious mode of thought, the moral mode of thought, wants to make them dry up." The Will to Power, trans. Kaufmann and Hollingdale. sec. 383, p. 207. However, Karl Jaspers remarks: "It was Nietzsche's psychological discovery that the resentment of impotence — in other words, the will to power even in impotence — can be creative in evaluations, ideals, and reinterpretations." Nietzsche and Christianity, trans. E. B. Ashton (Chicago, 1967), p. 30. Cf. p. 42. If this is indeed the case, Nietzsche fails to relate this discovery to Socratism in Die Geburt der Tragödie.

²⁹ Schlechta, Vol. II, p. 1071. Nietzsche writes in "Das Problem des Sokrates": "Auf décadence bei Sokrates deutet nicht nur die zugestandne Wüstheit und Anarchie in den Instinkten: eben dahin deutet auch die Superfötation des Logischen und jene Rachiter-Bosheit, die ihn auszeichnet." Ibid., Vol. II, p. 952. For further references to décadence, see ibid., Index, pp. 58-59.

³⁰ Schlechta, Vol. II, p. 1109.

³¹ Schlechta, Vol. II, p. 916.

³² February 26, 1888, Ibid., Vol. III, p. 1280.

³³ Fritz Martini, "Dekadenzdichtung," Reallexikon der deutschen Literaturgeschichte. 2nd ed., eds. Werner Kohlschmidt and Wolfgang Mohr (Berlin, 1958), I, p. 225.

³⁴ The ideal of the décadents is not the spiritual or mystical androgynism of antiquity but the "hermaphrodite in whom both sexes exist anatomically and physiologically. They are not concerned with a wholeness resulting from the fusion of the sexes but with a super-abundance of erotic possibilities." Here we encounter the "degradation of the symbol." Mircea Eliade, Mephistopheles and the Androgyne: Studies in Religious Myth and Symbol, trans. J. M. Cohen (New York, 1965), p. 100.

³⁵ Schlechta, Vol. II, p. 917.

³⁶ The Will to Power, trans. Kaufmann and Hollingdale; sec. 204, p. 120.

Theodor Storm's *Über die Heide*

WALTER SILZ

ÜBER DIE HEIDE

Über die Heide hallet mein Schritt;
Dumpf aus der Erde wandert es mit.

Herbst ist gekommen, Frühling ist weit —
Gab es denn einmal selige Zeit?

Brauende Nebel geisten umher;
Schwarz ist das Kraut und der Himmel so leer.

Wär ich hier nur nicht gegangen im Mai!
Leben und Liebe, — wie flog es vorbei!

Brief though it is, the poem here reproduced reveals essential aspects of its author's lyric art and of his view of life. Its very brevity illustrates a cardinal point in Storm's criteria for lyric poetry. "Zu sagen, wie ich leide" and to say it in few and fitting words was for him the writer's supreme accomplishment. Doubtless this was one reason why he never attempted a novel, but restricted himself to "Novellen" and "kurze Gedichte." These were in his mind closely related forms. Their limited compass offered him an artistic challenge; he might have said, with Goethe, "in der Beschränkung zeigt sich erst der Meister."

It is impossible, of course, to say exactly how much of Storm's "lyric theory," embodied in letters and occasional essays and prefaces, represents an initial ideal and how much is later codification of his own practice and that of the poets he admired, including the nameless masters of the *Volkslied* in its short, well-stressed, singable forms.[1]

Thus, in a preface to an anthology of 1870, Storm states his conviction "daß die Forderung, den Gehalt in knappe und zutreffende Worte auszuprägen [valid, he implies, for all literature], hier [in the lyric] besonders scharf hervortritt, da bei dem geringen Umfange schon *ein* falscher oder pulsloser Ausdruck die Wirkung des Ganzen zerstören kann." (SW, VIII, p. 115)

This requirement is conspicuously fulfilled in the present poem. It is a masterpiece of conciseness and clear, uncomplicated communication. Its brevity approaches that of the epigram. Its compression is such, and there is such suggestive force implicit in the condensed statements, that one could conceive each of the couplets developed into an individual poem (dealing respectively with landscape, the seasons, life's duality, retrospect). As in the earlier, even shorter, poem *Juli*,[2] each line is a complete sentence, and monosyllabic words are greatly in the majority. Every word is "knapp und zutreffend"; the only small exception is the "so" in line six, one of those "taube Worte" (in this case a colloquial particle) that Storm had elsewhere censured in contemporary German poetry (in a *Vorrede* of 1859; SW, VIII, p. 106).

The poem has the basis in experience which Storm declared indispensable: "Bei einem lyrischen Gedichte... muß geradezu das *Erlebnis* das Fundament ... bilden" (in an 1854 review; SW, VIII, p. 71). It is not only laid in the familiar heath landscape that forms the background of Storm's life and writing, but it was called forth by a definite occasion. In 1875, ten years after the death of his wife Constanze, he was again in her native Segeberg, the scene of their courtship and marriage, to attend the funeral of her father, with whose passing another link to the past was broken. One can imagine how many memories were stirred up by that return, perhaps by an actual solitary walk out on the *Heide*.

Revisiting scenes of the past is a Romantic proclivity. We find it already in Goethe's *Werther* (which anticipates Romanticism in many ways), together with the notion of Man as *Wanderer*, transitory and soon forgotten. Revisiting may produce sad-sweet *Stimmung*, but it can also bring home poignantly the tragic speed of life's relentless change, the fugacity of the individual and his happiness. Years before, from this same Segeberg, Storm had written to Constanze of his haunting "leise Furcht, daß im letzten Grunde doch nichts Bestand habe, worauf unser Herz baut; die Ahnung, daß man am Ende einsam verweht und verlorengeht; die Angst vor der Nacht des Vergessenwerdens, dem nicht zu entrinnen ist."[3] Now Constanze was ten years gone in that night of oblivion. This is the last of the poems that have reference to her. Storm had remarried and readjusted his life; but he was ten years closer to his own confrontation with the unsolved riddle of death.

In the *Vorrede* of 1870 already quoted, Storm had demanded not only that the words of a poem be carefully chosen for precision and appropriateness, but that the rhythmic movement and "tone-color" of the verses they constitute should produce something like a musical composition and thus be resolved again into the emotion in which they originated: "diese Worte müssen auch durch die rhythmische Bewegung und die Klangfarbe des

Verses gleichsam in Musik gesetzt und solcherweise wieder in die Emp-findung aufgelöst sein, aus der sie entsprungen sind." (SW, VIII, p. 115)

In the poem before us, this rhythmical and musical-emotional effect is achieved with a minimum of means. The meter chosen is a dactylic-trochaic tetrameter, catalectic, riming in pairs. Terseness of expression is heightened, as in Meyer's *Huttens letzte Tage*, by the lapidary couplet form; and Storm's line is even shorter than Meyer's. The first five verses contain two dactyls each; but for the catalexis, we should have a succession of adonics ('xx 'x), two to a line, making a gentle movement suitable, perhaps, for a song of wistful love or revery. Instead, the catalexis brings us up short in a weighted, braked ending without any lightening "Ausschwingen." The monosyllabic rime adds emphasis. There is a hammering ictus on key words throughout; the meter suggests a tense striding (*Schritt*) that differs from the lovers' walk (*gegangen*) in the spring of years ago.[4]

Because of the meter chosen, with its stressed starts and cut-off closes, the beginnings and endings of the lines carry unusual weight. Even the initial preposition *Über* is stressed, balancing the stressed *mit* at the end of the couplet; *mit* is by no means a slight prefix but underlines the inescapable dogging of Man's mysterious fate. At the other end of line two, *Dumpf* gets added emphasis by being advanced from its normal adverbial position. It is characteristic of Storm's musical nature that he begins his poem with an acoustic perception and in his words differentiates the brighter, resonant sound above ground from the lower-pitched, muffled echo below. The element of contrast, indeed, is a structural factor throughout: the objective perception of line one and the subjective of line two; present and past, autumn and spring, the known and the unknown, happiness and sorrow.

In line six, chiastic arrangement brings special stress on the terminal ad-jectives *schwarz* and *leer*. Aside from first and last positions, the meter also ensures strong emphases within verses, for example on *einmal* (line 4), which is in effect a heavy, slowing spondee.

Storm shows great skill in the choice and placing of words in his limited space. "Brauende" is a most effective epithet: the swirling mists, in ghostly motion, brew evil fate like Macbeth's witches on the blasted heath or the sinister *Nebelstreif* of the Erlkönig in Goethe's ballad. "Geisten" is a rare and evocative verb.[5] The frost-blackened herbage, the vacant stare of the sky add to the picture of desolation. The omission of the article before "Herbst" and "Frühling" is in keeping with the laconism of the poem, and "Herbst ist gekommen" sounds like a sad variation of traditional phrases like "Der Lenz ist gekommen" (or "sumer is icumen in"). "Selige Zeit" too lacks an (indefi-nite) article; in sound and meaning it marks a high point of the past, in-voked in the middle of the poem before it descends into darkness and despair. Alliteration is used sparingly: the H-h of the first verse balances the L-L of the last.

Not only does each of the four couplets have a tone of finality, but each individual line has definite terminal punctuation; there are no run-overs, not even commas. Twice Storm interposes a dash, like a gasp or a catch in the stride as the mind seeks to grasp an appalling thought: was the happy past an illusion? how fast life and love have flown by! The next-to-last line is not a conditional clause with the shallow meaning "if only I had not walked here in May, or come a different way today, all would be well"; this line is an anguished outcry, and its last word, "Mai," the most poetic of month-names, bears in its simple monosyllable a tremendous charge of emotion: it is the only word that characterizes that earlier walk, and it recalls once more all life's youthful bliss that is forever lost. Its "düstres Reimwort" *Vorbei*, which sums up and ends the poem, could well have furnished its title, in place of the actual, colorless one that is simply borrowed from the first three words.

Storm has no poem with this title, but there is one among Eichendorff's, and it is possible that Storm wished to avoid repeating it. Eichendorff's *Vorbei* (1839) also confronts Man and Nature, present and past, and the poet recognizes sadly that youth and love are gone and old age has crept upon him. It is he that has changed, while Nature has remained constant. The last line, "Vorbei ist das schöne Lieben," includes two important words of Storm's close, but with less tragic depth.

Another comparable late-Romantic poem is Gustav Schwab's *Rückblick* (1835), which shares with Storm's the figure of the vigorously striding man in the prime of life who returns to a Nature-scene of long years ago and is overcome with the sense of his own passing and the dreamlikeness of life. Here, as in Eichendorff, Nature abides, Man alters and ages. But here too the recognition, while melancholy, is not frantic, because for both Eichendorff and Schwab, each secure in his creed and church, Man, though a transient on earth, had a home in heaven, an afterlife. Storm had no such faith; he stood defenseless and dismayed before the fact of death.

These two poems are notably longer than Storm's and lack its compact force. Schwab's three-stress line has a marching swing; Eichendorff's measure is a folksong-like four/three alternation; in both cases the meter is less distinguished than Storm's. Schwab's poem, like Storm's, ends in an exclamation: "O kurzer Traum des Seins!" echoes an ancient *topos* then much in vogue.

The theme of *Vergänglichkeit* was a favorite with German Romantic poets. It appealed to their historical sense, their reverence for the relics of the past. Its expression was more often longing than tragic. In no Romanticist, certainly, not even if we count Lenau as one, does the thought of human transiency have quite the gloomy, nihilistic force that it has in Storm. His oppressive sense of Man's fugacity and utter annihilation in death deepened desperately with the passing years. He felt the specter lurking in all the backgrounds of his existence: "das Gespenst der Vergänglichkeit, das für mich in allen Ecken sitzt und auf allen Treppen schleicht."[6] Writing to Mörike of Constanze's death, he had declared that "Einsamkeit und das quälende Rätsel des Todes" were the two fearful powers that he must now wrestle with incessantly.[7] But death was the ultimate enigma, the final and endless loneliness. Tormenting uncertainty became conviction that beyond death there is nothing: it brings "Vernichtung." (*Tiefe Schatten*, 5; SW, I, p. 109) Unable to accept any dogma of immortality, Storm saw in death "den Abgrund; Darin das Nichts." (*ibid.*, 3) The dying young man in *Geh nicht hinein* vanishes into an "Abgrund, bodenlos, ganz ohne Boden," and there is nothing more to say; "Weiter nichts" are the poem's last words.[8]

Storm was aghast at the incomprehensible coming and going of the individual, from dark into dark, and his final extinction. The horror he expresses with lyric measure and restraint in our poem he had uttered with drastic directness in the prose of *Der Amtschirurgus* / *Heimkehr* (1870): "Hu! Wie kommen und gehen die Menschen! Immer ein neuer Schub, und wieder: Fertig!—Rastlos kehrt und kehrt der unsichtbare Besen und kann kein Ende finden. Woher kommt all das immer wieder, und wohin geht der grause Kehrricht?" (SW, III, p. 167) Again some years later he was to use the same macabre figure for the same hopeless insight: *Zur Chronik von Grieshuus* (1883-84) ends with a "Spruch" that makes no pretension to lyric grace:

> Auf Erden stehet nichts, es muß vorüberfliegen;
> Es kommt der Tod heran, du kannst ihn nicht besiegen.
> Ein Weilchen weiß vielleicht noch wer, was du gewesen;
> Dann wird das weggekehrt, und weiter fegt der Besen.
>
> (SW, VI, p. 293)

Our only help against the oblivion of death is in the minds of those who survive and (perhaps) remember us; but such memory must die with the rememberers. The poet's "immortality" does not avail to comfort the yearning heart.

Storm's gruesome concept of the broom of time before which men are but sweepings is comparable to Raabe's symbol of the horrible dumpcart for the dead in *Der Schüdderump* (1870).[9] Unlike Raabe, Storm was no student of Schopenhauer and other professional thinkers of his time; but he could not help sharing, and contributing to, the increasingly pessimistic intellectual atmosphere of the later nineteenth century, which prepared for the still more radical "existential" questionings of the twentieth. *Über die Heide*, the brief poetic record of personal experience and feeling, is symptomatic also of a more general trend of thought; appearing at a time of military victory and rising national confidence, it nevertheless forebodes a future "age of anxiety."

NOTES

[1] See Albert Köster's remark in his edition of Storm's *Sämtliche Werke in acht Bänden* (Leipzig: Insel, 1923) — henceforth cited as SW — I, p. 19.
[2] See my discussion of *Juli* in *Germanic Review*, XLII (1967), 298 ff.

[3] Letter of July 21, 1859; Storm's *Briefe an seine Frau*, ed. Gertrud Storm (Berlin-Braunschweig-Hamburg, 1915), p. 82.

[4] The meter suggests a vigorous *Schreiten* but does not realistically imitate it; one cannot stride to Storm's poem (as one can, for example, to Meyer's *Säerspruch*) without spoiling its rhythm for the "inner" ear.

[5] Mörike had preceded Storm in the use of it (also with the factor of motion) for eerie *Stimmung*: "Es geisten die Nebel am Ufer dahin" in *Die Geister am Mummelsee* (1828). Storm used it again in *Ein Doppelgänger* (1886): "der Gedanke an den unsichtbar umher geistenden Tod" (SW, VII, pp. 142 f.).

[6] To Keller, December 1879; Storm-Keller *Briefwechsel*, ed. Köster, 3. Aufl. (Berlin 1909), p. 77.

[7] June 3, 1865; Storm-Mörike *Briefwechsel*, ed. H. W. Rath (Stuttgart [1919]), p. 111.

[8] See the interpretation of this poem by Fritz Martini in *Schriften der Theodor-Storm-Gesellschaft*, 6 (1957), pp. 9-37.

[9] See my article, "Pessimism in Raabe's Stuttgart Trilogy," *PMLA*, XXXIX (1924), especially 697 ff.

Symbolism in Gottfried Keller's *Sinngedicht*

HERBERT W. REICHERT

The resurgent interest in Keller's *Sinngedicht*, observed during the 1960's, is characterized for the most part by a rather comprehensive re-evaluation of the views which have prevailed virtually unchallenged for the preceding forty years. These views, put forth by a great pioneer in Keller research, Emil Ermatinger,[1] attributed to the *Sinngedicht* classical symmetry with the epigram at its core. The dichotomy inherent in the epigram was explained in terms of *Freiheit* and *Sitte*, which Ermatinger subsumed under the same general polarity of *sinnlich-sittlich* that he applied to Keller's other works.[2]

In the years that followed only minor modifications to this interpretation were suggested. Karl Essl[3] felt that the epigram should be considered primarily as a motif. Priscilla Kramer[4] believed that Keller was additionally seeking to depict the ideal personality. Pongs[5] and Elema[6] pondered the tragic cast of *Regine*. Max Hochdorf[7] and Edgar Neis[8] noted briefly that the work was a defense of *Geistesfreiheit*, and the present writer[9] discussed the story in terms of Keller's own particular conception of intellectual freedom.

In 1962 F. J. Stopp[10] presented a thesis hitherto given only peripheral attention: "Behind the general theme of the choice of a partner there comes into view a whole new problem: whether chance has a meaning of its own, whether there is a teleology in contingency... The topic which is really being debated most of the time is the mysterious interplay of character and chance." (280-81) In his discussion of *Regine* Stopp considers Ermatinger's analysis as "wholly unconvincing" (283) and translates the problem "into the terms of reference of the Barock theater." (284) "The touchstone of character, in this view, would be that a man should penetrate through the 'Schein-werte' thrown up by life." (285) Contingency is thus linked with illusion and deception. Referring to *Regine*, Stopp writes, "'Blendwerk' was that 'Bild verklärten deutschen Volkstums' in Erwin's mind, which Regine was to become; 'Blendwerk' no less, the net of circumstantial and deceitful evidence which destroyed her." (285) *Don Correa* parallels *Regine* in structure. The hero, like Erwin, makes an initial mistake in attempting to conceal his identity; in the later part of the story, the Jesuits assume the role held by the Fates. Don Correa "was making (in Barock terms) a mistaken distinction between 'Sein' and 'Schein'. These attributes are a part of himself not to be stripped off... without a loss of metaphysical substance." (286) "The Barock problem of 'Sein und Schein' appears, in another aspect, as the identity and distinction of 'Schale' and 'Kern'." (288) Stopp develops this idea in terms of Keller's frequent symbolic allusion to a transparent glass bowl. He concludes, "'eine lebendige Kristallglocke' is the term of Reinhart's journey and the epitome of Keller's wisdom in this work." (289) Stopp's article has generally been overlooked or disparaged,[11] but it contains the basic notions and terminology of the new critical direction.

Karl Reichert wrote two closely related articles, one in 1963[12] and one in 1964[13] which on the basis of a generic study of the *Sinngedicht* generally reaffirmed Ermatinger's thesis.

The *Sinngedicht* was a "krönender Abschluß"[14] and tightly knit: "die Binnenerzählungen sind mit innerer Notwendigkeit in die 'Rahmenfabel' eingefügt." The epigram was the direct expression of the antinomy inherent in the confrontation of the principal characters: "Das Sinngedichtmotiv des 'errötenden Lachens' deutet auf die ideale menschliche Persönlichkeit hin, in der sich die Kräfte des Gefühls und Verstands, naturhafter Bindung und vernunftklarer Selbstbestimmung, Lust und Scham oder Sinnlichkeit und Sittlichkeit in harmonischem Ausgleich befinden."[15] In the later essay, however, Reichert also spoke deprecatingly of the "ältere Keller-Forschung, die in der ersten Hälfte dieses Jahrhunderts von der Autorität Emil Ermatingers überschattet wurde, [und die sich] beim 'Sinngedicht' auf das deutende Begriffspaar, 'Sinnlichkeit-Sittlichkeit,' superlativische Werturteile und die Aufzählung fragwürdiger 'Symmetrien' in der Werkstruktur beschränkte,"[16] and added, "die Probleme von Stand und Herkunft, Besitz und Bildung... treten hinter Kellers Primärfrage nach dem Wesenskern des Menschen, der Dialektik von Schein und Sein als sekundär bedeutsam zurück."[17] Using terminology similar to that of Stopp and Preisendanz, he asserts "das zentrale Thema des 'Sinngedichts', wie aller Epik Gottfried Kellers ist das Verhältnis von Schale und Kern, Äußerem und Innerem, Erscheinung und Wesen, Schein und Sein des Menschen."[18]

In 1963 Wolfgang Preisendanz[19] argued, independently of but in close parallelism to Stopp, that at the heart of the *Sinngedicht* lay Keller's concern with the difficulty of penetrating appearances and the problem of communication. Not *sinnlich-sittlich* but *Sein-Schein* was the underlying dichotomy. In similar fashion to Stopp, Preisendanz interpreted *Regine* as the attempt of a young German-American to impose his romanticized version of German womanhood upon his wife. "Und schließlich erwächst das katastrophale Ende ganz und gar aus dem Mißverhältnis von Vorstellung und Wirklichkeit, aus dem Kontrast von Schein und Sein." (134) Referring to Ermatinger's views, Preisendanz asks pointedly, "Inwiefern ist hier das Verhältnis von Freiheit und Sitte, oder auch von Natur und Kultur, Ursprünglichkeit und Bildung zum Thema geworden?" (135) Preisendanz concludes, "Damit sind diese Erzählungen als solche selbst ein Beispiel, ein Bild oder ein Gleichnis dessen, was in ihnen immer wieder Motiv ist: Beispiel dafür, wie sich der Mensch vermummt, verhehlt, verbirgt, verschließt, wie er sich in den Anschein hüllen, wie er sich besonders im Sprechen entziehen oder vorenthalten kann." (142) Ultimately Keller had meant to tell us that no law can probe the human dimension. "Und so ist am Ende Gottfried Kellers 'Sinngedicht' selbst eine parabelhafte, fabelmäßige Darstellung der 'Reichsunmittelbarkeit der Poesie', indem es zeigen kann, über welche Dimension der 'moralischen Welt' nicht eine der mit der Signatur Darwin angedeuteten Möglichkeiten der Menschenkunde, sondern allein die Dichtung zu sprechen befugt ist." (151) Louis Wiesmann's analysis (1967)[20] reflects to a degree the new trend. Erwin, in *Regine*, "hascht nach dem Schein…" (197) and Don Correa "bedient sich des Scheins." (202) However, Wiesmann considers the epigram of primary importance and interprets it in terms of *sinnlich-sittlich* as represented by Judith and Anna in *Der grüne Heinrich*. This leads him to identify the pale laughing girl at the bridge with Judith and hence to conclude disappointedly with regard to Lucie, "[es] fehlt ihr doch allzuviel von Judith." (210)

Henrich Brockhaus[21] agrees with Stopp and Preisendanz that the interior stories overshadow the plot of the frame and terms the epigram "a rather weak link." In contradistinction to them, however, he believes that themes such as "man's necessity of penetrating through appearance to reality" [Sein-Schein] were of secondary importance. Brockhaus shares with Miss Kramer and Karl Reichert the conviction that Keller was in search of "the well-rounded person in complete, lasting and responsible touch with reality."

The most recent study, by Ernst May,[22] takes the rather extreme position that, although all the rest of Keller's prose "vom Grünen Heinrich bis zum Martin Salander" is imbued with symbolic meaning and "fordert den Interpreten heraus," the *Sinngedicht* provides a notable exception: "Einzig das 'Sinngedicht' gibt sich so unbeschwert und problemlos, daß es denjenigen erfrischt, der nicht nach Tiefen schürft." (9) The *Sinngedicht* reflects the wisdom of old age, and this wisdom restrained Keller from expressing fixed opinions: "zur Weisheit gehört aber, daß Keller im Kunstwerk immer mehr davon abrückt, feste Ansichten zu äußern." (9) May concludes that it is incorrect procedure to search "nach Meinungen und Problemen" or to look exclusively for "bestimmte Themen." (9)

Needless to say, the new direction in Keller criticism has thrown valuable new light on the *Sinngedicht*. At the same time, the increasing emphasis on the interior stories, the de-emphasis on the frame, and the recent denial of an encompassing symbolism, raise doubts, not quelled by general words of praise, as to the story's fundamental artistic merit. Is the *Sinngedicht* structurally a consummate work of art as has been so consistently maintained, or is it really after all only a delightful vehicle for Keller's *Altersweisheit*? With this question foremost in mind, we have ventured once again into the much furrowed field of *Sinngedicht* interpretation. We shall probe the presence or absence of a pervasive symbolism, adhering closely to the text, in the hope of shedding some light on the clouded issue of underlying structure. To discuss the possibility of an underlying symbolism in the *Sinngedicht*, it is obviously necessary to consider the frame or main story. This is concerned with two young people, Reinhart and Lucie, and their relationship to one another. The first pages of the story deal exclusively with Reinhart. If this is not a symbolic but rather a realistic novel, we should expect a wealth of psychological and sociological detail. We get very little. We learn that Reinhart is a young scientist working in a laboratory. We don't know where he lives, his circumstances, or his background. In fact the narration is characterized by the warm vagueness of the fairy tale, a genre of which Keller was very fond.

Yet the first pages are devoted to Reinhart. What do they tell us? That his study is that of a Faust "ins Moderne, Bequeme und Zierliche übersetzt."[23] That the study is filled with learned journals, shiny instruments, maps, minerals, and organic specimens. That his library contains an abundance of scientific books. From all this and the opening lines, "Vor etwa fünfundzwanzig Jahren, als die Naturwissenschaften eben wieder auf einem höchsten Gipfel standen," we may deduce that he is a competent researcher. Reinhart's concern is with natural law, evident from the fact that he is investigating the movement of light through a crystal, "um sein Verhalten in demselben zu zeigen und womöglich das innerste Geheimnis solcher durchsichtigen Bauwerke zu beleuchten." (2) We learn, in fact, that he has concentrated so long on the study of natural law that he felt truly happy only "wenn er bei seiner Arbeit das große Schauspiel mitgenoß, welches den unendlichen Reichtum der Erscheinungen unaufhaltsam auf eine einfachste Einheit zurückzuführen scheint, wo es heißt, im Anfang war die Kraft oder so was." (4)

As regards his youth, all we are told is that Reinhart had observed his fellow men sufficiently, "um von der Gesetzmäßigkeit und dem Zusammenhange der moralischen Welt überzeugt zu werden, und wie überall nicht ein Wort fällt, welches nicht Ursache und Wirkung zugleich wäre." (3) But now "hatte er seit Jahren das Menschenleben fast vergessen." (4) And whereas he did not deny the existence of the moral law, he paid little attention to it:

> Die moralischen Dinge, pflegte er zu sagen, flattern ohnehin gegenwärtig wie ein entfärbter und heruntergekommener Schmetterling in der Luft; aber der Faden, an dem sie flattern, ist gut angebunden, und sie werden uns nicht entwischen... (4)

Reinhart has been performing his light experiment in a darkened room, shutting the windows every morning when the sun rose "vor der schönen Welt mit allem, was draußen lebte und webte," and permitting only a single ray of light to enter. (3) Eventually his eyes had begun to ache and he realized that if he continued his labors he might damage his sight permanently. This thought caused him to sit back and reflect, whereupon he immediately began to think of the outside world of people he had so long neglected. Particularly, "die menschliche Gestalt, und zwar nicht in ihren zerlegten Bestandteilen, sondern als Ganzes," (4) came to mind. He suddenly realized how completely he had been cut off from life and "es gelüstete ihn plötzlich, auf das durchsichtige Meer des Lebens hinauszufahren." (5) But he had become so absorbed in his studies of natural law that he could find no link with the moral world: "Aber es fiel ihm nicht der geringste Anhalt, nicht das kleinste Verhältnis ein zur Übung von menschlicher Sitte; er hatte sich vereinsamt und festgerannt, es blieb still und dunkel um ihn her." (5) Then, fortunately, he discovered the Logau epigram which promised on a suitably scientific basis a reentry into the moral world.

To sum up, the first pages of the story tell us little more about Reinhart than his relation to natural and moral law. The many unmistakable allusions make it clear that his visual impairment is a humorous symbol indicating a short-sighted absorption in natural law. He realizes that he has cut himself off from the moral sphere and yearns to get out of his darkness into the light of human activity. What we learn, then, about Reinhart is that he is a representative or symbol of natural law *exclusive* of moral law.

If we turn our attention to his female counterpart, Lucie, we find again that there is a minimum of realistic description. But Keller wastes no time in making it known that she had a rather independent manner, that she is illuminated "von einem hellen inneren Lichte," (29) and that she has an excellent collection of biographies and art works. What is Keller telling us? Lucie's independent manner, as Reinhart soon realizes, does not reveal the emancipated bluestocking, but rather the keen and independent mind of a person who is accustomed "in der Freiheit über den Dingen zu leben, die Schicksale zu verstehen und jegliches bei seinem Namen zu nennen." (55) So strong is her concern for knowledge and truth, that she exerts an almost magic compulsion on Reinhart, forcing him to blurt out the truth:

Denn solange er unter den Augen seiner jetzigen Gastherrin saß oder stand, trieb es ihn wie ein Zauber zur Offenherzigkeit, und wenn er die ärgsten Teufeleien begangen, so würde ihm das Geständnis derselben über die Lippen gesprungen sein. (41)

Lucie's name—her uncle likes to call her "*Lux, mein Licht*"—and the obviously symbolic reference to her "bright inner light" enhance her status as a person whose ultimate concern is knowledge and truth. Light symbolism for Keller was virtually always related to enlightenment. In *Don Correa*, for example, there is kindled in Zambo "das Licht eines guten Verstandes." (310) And Don Correa is delighted to see "wie von Tag zu Tag das Verständnis heller aufging und die junge Frau mit dem Lichte menschlichen Bewußtseins erfüllte." (313)

Lucie's biographies indicate the direction of her search. We recall that Reinhart had only scientific books in his library: "kein einziges Buch handelt von menschlichen oder moralischen Dingen, oder wie man vor hundert Jahren gesagt haben würde, von Sachen des Herzens und des schönen Geschmacks." (2) Lucie's library, on the other hand, is concerned almost exclusively with human affairs. At its core are the biographies of such famous people in the history of western civilization as Augustine, Dante, Goethe, and Rousseau. Lucie is seeking, as she herself says, "die Sprache der Menschen zu verstehen." (343) One need not be familiar with the discovery of the moral law in history by such Keller protagonists as Heinrich Lee and Arnold Salander to recognize that Lucie's interest in these famous people reveals her search for and concern with the functioning of the moral law. As for Lucie's art collection, it served to reveal her "guten Geschmack," which Keller in his comment on Reinhart's library had directly linked with the idea of moral sensitivity. Lucie is by no means a wan allegorical figure, but what we do learn about her makes her in our eyes the exponent of moral law.

At this point it should be quite clear that Keller's initial concern in presenting his characters was to reveal to the reader their underlying symbolism. One must conclude that whatever else their ultimate relationship, one important facet will pertain to the relationship of natural law to moral law.

So far we have concerned ourselves with the frame novella. Now the important question must be posed: does the symbolism evident in the frame novella carry on through the *Erzählduell* and the concluding events of the story.

The interior stories have many layers of meaning, including the battle of the sexes and the illusory nature of appearances. But on one of the deepest, if not the most profound of these layers, the symbolic significance of the principal narrators, Reinhart and Lucie, is maintained. To be sure, they are portrayed with greater psychological realism than before, and their growing love for one another is reflected both in the tone and events of the stories. Yet each maintains his basic viewpoint, one may say his symbolic integrity, and while, occasionally, in subtle ways attempting to appease his opposite, does not essentially compromise his own position. Throughout the *Erzählduell*, Reinhart consistently remains the spokesman of natural law, defending the primacy of biological attraction and physical parity to a successful marriage. Prior to narrating *Regine*, he insists that the most important thing to marriage is "ein gründliches persönliches Wohlgefallen, nämlich daß das Gesicht des einen dem andern ausnehmend gut gefalle," (57) and a short time later he repeats, "das Gesicht muß ihm gefallen und hernach abermals gefallen." (58) *Die Baronin* has a cultured rather than a naive woman as its heroine, inasmuch as Reinhart is parrying a thrust by Lucie that educated men seem to marry only "Dienstmädchen, Bäuerinnen und dergleichen."

(144) And pity is the first emotion that motivates the hero. But essentially male superiority and physical attraction are stressed far more than moral considerations. Reinhart's last story, *Don Correa*, may well be interpreted as signifying a rapprochement with Lucie—Zambo is permitted to be the off-spring of an old culture, and in the end shows in bearing and speech that she is Don Correa's equal—but the admiral's selection of the simple native girl on the basis of her beauty and charm is essentially a reaffirmation of Reinhart's thesis.

Lucie, in her turn, continues to represent the moral law. *Von einer törichten Jungfrau* has as its theme not so much the contrast between city and country, as the fact that both young people lacked the education and intelligence to recognize their own nature and inner necessity, the freedom to act morally, which Lucie considered essential to a happy marriage. In *Der Geisterseher*, Hildeburg, when pressed to make a choice between two marriageable men, lets the outcome rest on a test which will reveal which of the two has an intelligent and open mind, free from arbitrary notions and superstitions. She wisely lets the determination rest in that factor which is most important to happiness in marriage and life in general, intellectual freedom.

Preisendanz speaks of her "verzweifelte Prüfung"[24] and May feels, "die Entscheidungsfreiheit Hildeburgs erweist sich als recht begrenzt. Sie ist vom einen, seiner Vernunft und Beherztheit wegen, viel mächtiger angezogen als vom andern und nimmt ihre Zuflucht zur fragwürdigen Auslese durch den Mitternachtsspuk."[25] It is true that Hildeburg prefers Mannelin. But her unquestioned upright character would have prevented her from taking un-fair advantage of the Marschall. That she acted unconsciously or in des-peration is again not likely for she is a very alert and intelligent girl. It is significant that on occasion she laughs and blushes almost simultaneously. And she is so keen that she sees through the Marschall's naive self-deception when he expresses the hope that Mannelin is not dead: "'Den Teufel hoffst du!' rief sie mit funkelnden Augen und lachte jählings auf, indessen mich das Gewissen Lügen strafte." (213) But whether her act is conscious or uncon-scious, the aspect of key symbolic importance is that she places the highest value on intellectual freedom. Wiesmann recognizes, "gegenromantische, aufgeklärte Ansichten bestimmen die Erzählung."[26]

Die Berlocken furnishes a kind of counterpoint to *Die Baronin*. Just as Reinhart in the latter story had countered Lucie's thrust by reversing the naivete-culture relationship while maintaining his thesis, Lucie in the former permits naivete to triumph over pseudo-culture while continuing to stress the need to act morally, from inner necessity.

When the *Erzählduell* has run its course, Keller permits the love between Reinhart and Lucie to ripen slowly and realistically in consonance with his deep belief that all things of value including matrimony should develop in a natural and organic fashion. But the final lines of the story return in tone and spirit to the initial symbolism. Reinhart views the time before he had come

117

to know Lucie as "*ante lucem*, vor Tagesanbruch." (380) These words can have only one meaning when we recall his one-sided absorption with natural law, his diligent search for a re-entry into the moral sphere and his ultimate union with Lucie, the symbol of the moral law. This meaning can only be that a belief in natural law without a concomitant belief in moral law is shortsighted and unacceptable.

There is a more or less explicit assertion in several recent *Sinngedicht* studies that when he became older Keller lost interest in metaphysical idealism and that consequently metaphysical symbolism in the *Sinngedicht* is either absent or unimportant. It is true, of course, that in later years Keller became somewhat disillusioned and pessimistic. But we must ask to what extent did this disillusionment affect his metaphysical outlook. To consider this question, let us turn to perhaps his most significant work, the autobiographical novel *Der grüne Heinrich*, which critics generally agree expresses his basic views. *Der grüne Heinrich* is particularly suited to our needs as the first edition was completed in 1855, the same year in which the first fragment, possibly the first third, of the *Sinngedicht* was written, and the second edition, a quarter of a century later, preceded by one year completion of the *Sinngedicht*. Thus both works spanned Keller's maturity and ultimately, after a long interim, were put into final form in close succession.

In the original version of *Der grüne Heinrich*, the protagonist Heinrich Lee learns at the university that man is subject to natural law. But Heinrich thinks that the anthropology professor (like Reinhart) is limited in his outlook. Heinrich is of the opinion that things are more than the sum of their parts, a coffin more than a few boards, and a rose more than a few chemicals. In everything formed there lies an idea, and the idea of the human organism, Heinrich feels, is free-will and moral discernment. He likes to link moral and natural law in the picture of a riding school. The stable and riding ring represent the world and material reality: "Der Boden derselben ist das Leben dieser Welt... und kann zugleich den derben Grund aller Materie vorstellen." The horse is "das besondere, immer noch materielle Organ, der Reiter darauf der gute menschliche Wille, welcher jenes zu beherrschen und zum freien Willen zu werden trachtet, um über jenen derben Grund wegzukommen; der Stallmeister endlich... ist das moralische Gesetz, das aber einzig und allein auf die Natur und Eigenschaften des Pferdes gegründet ist und ohne dieses gar nicht vorhanden wäre." (XIX, 51)[27] Thus, Heinrich is opposed to the notion "des bestimmten und unbeschränkten freien Willens, göttlichen Ursprungs." (XIX, 50) At the same time he believes in moral freedom and, like Lucie, sees evidence of the moral law in history where each action has the duration of its inner necessity. History points to "die Rechtsgeschichte und bestätigte deren Qualität in der Menschennatur." (XIX, 59)

Heinrich is here speaking for Keller. This is evident from the fact that other Keller spokesmen in the story such as Ferdinand Lys personify the same viewpoint. In the scene preceding the duel between Heinrich and

Ferdinand, for example, the former, still immature, embodies Keller's notion of the arbitrary orthodox believer and the latter, the enlightened atheist. Lys tells the young hothead, "du hast getan, was du nicht lassen konntest, du tust es jetzt, und du wirst es tun, solange du lebst." (XVIII, 237) And he repeats, "du wirst zu jeder Zeit... das lassen, was dir unangenehm ist." Lys is speaking with particular reference to the matter of falling in love, and it is obvious that he thinks very much like Reinhart. But he also thinks like Lucie, for shortly thereafter he says, "Ich bin frei und meines Willens Herr, gegen ein Weib sowohl wie gegen alle Welt." (XVIII, 240) Here we see the same admixture of belief in natural and moral law as expressed by the mature Heinrich and in the *Sinngedicht*. Keller takes pains to make it clear that Lys is speaking for him by having Lys conduct himself in a calm and thoughtful way prior to the duel, whereas Heinrich wanders aimlessly through the night afraid to listen to his inner voice.

But, one may still ask, did not Keller change his mind in the revised version? Does not the much publicized spider episode questioning the very existence of free-will invalidate the views expressed in the first edition?

To be sure, Keller felt differently in 1880 than he did in 1855. But a moment's reflection will bring to mind how drastically free will had actually been restricted in the first edition. Even there free will had been limited to *Einsicht*, recognition of one's inner nature. Moral action had for all practical purposes become a facet of natural law. So it is not surprising, when we look at the revised version of the novel, that we find the moral law still as evident in history as it was in the original version. Heinrich says:

> Ich sah, daß jede geschichtliche Erscheinung genau die Dauer hat, welche ihre Gründlichkeit und lebendige Innerlichkeit verdient und der Art ihres Entstehens entspricht. Ich sah, wie die Dauer jedes Erfolges nur die Abrechnung der verwendeten Mittel und die Prüfung des Verständnisses ist und wie gegen die ununterbrochene Ursachenreihe auch in der Geschichte weder Hoffen noch Fürchten, weder Jammern noch Toben, weder Übermut noch Verzagtheit etwas hilft, sondern Bewegung und Rückschlag ihren wohlgemessenen Rhythmus haben. (VI, 22)

Like most mortals, Keller in old age was beset with doubts. But again, like most mortals, it would appear that in the main he held firm to his established metaphysical position. In Keller's last and admittedly rather pessimistic work, *Martin Salander* (1885), the son Arnold is nevertheless an unequivocal advocate of intellectual freedom who also sees the moral law functioning in the course of history.

One thorny problem remains to be discussed, the epigram, the so-called core of the *Sinngedicht*. Where does it fit in?

Before undertaking this discussion, we would like briefly to say an additional word about Keller's conception of intellectual freedom. This was a key idea in Keller's thought throughout his life. Along with political and religious freedom, it was a central theme in the *Freiheitsgedichte* of the 1840's. It became virtually identical with moral action in Keller's eyes after the Feuerbach experience of 1849. It is a central topic in all his work and was most clearly revealed in symbolic tales such as the humorously allegorical fairy-tale *Spiegel, das Kätzchen*.

Spiegel recognizes and obeys the law of his own being. When starvation dulls Spiegel's wits, he loses this awareness and becomes a glutton—the loss of intellectual freedom permits him to fall into the sorcerer's clutches. But with renewed physical well-being and restoration of his mental powers, Spiegel again recognizes the law of his being and the need to obey it. The plot is humorously structured so that by leading his normal life of chasing lady cats across rooftops at night, Spiegel automatically outwits the sorcerer, who is rewarded, in turn, for his arbitrary outlook and lack of intellectual clarity with an ugly, overbearing witch as wife.

Space limitations prevent citing a host of further examples. But it cannot be overstressed that enlightenment was Keller's everpresent ideal and was for him synonymous with moral conduct and action in accord with natural law. In a word, intellectual freedom permitted recognition of *innere Notwendigkeit*.

Two symbols in particular were used by Keller to denote the intellectually and morally free individual: *Ruhe* and *Lachen*. Keller heroes such as Ferdinand Lys, Frau Regel Amrain, Pankraz, Salomon Landolt, and Arnold Salander demonstrate *Ruhe* at critical junctures. Occasionally the symbolism is further heightened with easy laughter. The best example is Jukundus in *Das verlorene Lachen* who regains his ability to laugh when he regains his intellectual freedom.

Now let us return to the epigram which reads:

Wie willst du weiße Lilien zu roten Rosen machen?
Küß eine Galathee: sie wird errötend lachen. (XI, 5)

Since Ermatinger's interpretation initiated much of the present discussion and prevailing dissension as to the epigram's importance, let us begin with his view. Ermatinger says, "Erröten, als der Ausdruck der Befangenheit, weist auf die innerlichst gefühlte Schranke der Sitte, die Scham hin... im Lachen aber spricht die Lebenslust des geistig freien Menschen sich aus."[28] Reinhart on his amorous quest first encounters a girl who when kissed laughs without blushing and a second who blushes without laughing. Ermatinger is of the opinion that the first girl reveals "Freiheit ohne Sitte" and the second "Sitte ohne Freiheit."[29]

The first girl, daughter of a bridge toll collector, does not, however, appear either immodest or immoral. She is not a brazen hussy but rather a pale, slender, attractive lass "mit einem feinen, lustigen Gesicht und kecken

Augen." (XI, 7) By no means does she give Reinhart the kiss on demand. Only after he has refrained therefrom and paid his toll, does she kiss him with a merry laugh. We learn that she has been spurned by a young suitor in favor of an ugly but wealthy girl. Time has healed the wound and the pretty lass can now laugh at her former suitor, but she makes him wait when he crosses the bridge, clear evidence that she is still chagrined. The girl's misfortune has led her to suppress her femininity. Is this immoral? Let us turn to the second girl, the minister's daughter, who blushes but fails to laugh. The exemplary relations in this family are indeed in the moral sphere, but they are as bloodless as the self-righteousness of the three combmakers, and Keller voiced his displeasure by stating that this was a world "worin nicht ein dunkles Gefühl im verborgenen stürmen könnte." (XI, 13) The daughter, just become a young lady, blushes when she first sees the handsome young scientist and again when he blackmails her into a kiss. Here, then, blushing clearly indicates femininity and at the same time is definitely related through the doer to the moral sphere; not only is the girl a part of this exemplary moral household, but she gives Reinhart a letter to Lucie and thus symbolically guides him to his proper moral goal. She is, so to say, a first step in the right direction.

Blushing, then, and femininity must here be considered as related to moral conduct. Keller with his strong belief that conduct should be in accord with inner necessity and his apparent dislike of excessively emancipated women, clearly felt that woman's primary function was to be womanly. Confirmation of this may be found in his Galathea legends such as the one concerning Eugenia. Hence unwomanly action, suppression of femininity, was regarded as immoral.

But the girl at the bridge is in every way more appealing than the awkward minister's daughter "deren längliche Nase gleich einem ernsten Zeiger andächtig zur Erde wies." (XI, 12) Furthermore, it is evident that in appearance and action Lucie is virtually the counterpart of the girl at the bridge. Reinhart, it will be recalled, was initially inclined to think Lucie a bluestocking and Fränkel, first editor of the definitive Keller edition, tells us that in an early version of the Sinngedicht Lucie had many characteristics of the emancipated female. (XI, 403) What are we to think?

Keller's emphasis on intellectual freedom supplies the answer. Conventional morality by itself was not enough. The morality of the minister's daughter was abhorrent to Keller. She was lacking in intellectual freedom and would forever remain in her limited sphere. At the same time, however, he was unwilling to condone the arbitrary freedom of the lass at the bridge who had suppressed her *innere Notwendigkeit*. But as she was obviously not *Unnatur*—like the beautiful but villainous Donna Feniza in *Don Correa* who also laughed without blushing—and had merely suppressed her normal womanliness as the result of unfavorable circumstances, her laughter reveals that she has the potential for moral action. Hence she is more favorably presented. Thus it is clear that both elements of the epigram, laughter and blushing, intellectual freedom and inner necessity, are needed to embody true morality. Ermatinger's basic explanation of the dichotomy inherent in the epigram as *Freiheit-Sitte* seems then appropriate. But if this be so, a new puzzle presents itself. As Lucie laughs but does not blush initially, how can she be considered a representative of true morality any more than the girl at the bridge? Lucie is scarcely more decorous and, in fact, only regains her femininity at the very end of the story; when she then not only laughs but also blushes, her blushing is occasioned "von einem lange entbehrten und verschmähten Gefühle." (XI, 379) On the other hand, if she is not initially the symbol of true morality, what are we to make of the early clues that link her with Keller's ideal of moral enlightenment?

Here indeed lies a critical point in the structure of the story. On the metaphysical plane of interpretation it would appear that Lucie is the ideal to whom the ailing Reinhart comes for succor. His eye ailment is only a humorous allusion to his moral infirmity. On this plane there is little initial talk of Lucie's infirmities but rather hints that she embodies the moral perfection implicit in the epigram. When Reinhart first accosts her, for example, she is dressed all in white and holding a large bouquet of roses—a definite allusion to the white *Galathee* and red roses of the epigram. Furthermore, her maids laugh and blush almost simultaneously. Most important of all she is imbued not with an arbitrary freedom but with moral enlightenment, which for Keller was always associated with an *ipso facto* recognition of natural law.

Yet it is also true that toward the end of the story Keller inserts the snake episode which reveals that she has attained a deeper sympathy for nature, that is, a deeper understanding of natural law. And, again toward the end, Keller has Lucie narrate at length about her conversion to Catholicism and her frustrated love with the obvious purpose of explaining her hitherto unfeminine restraint. These two factors would indicate that Lucie was imperfect at the outset, lacking an awareness of natural law. They also introduce a new inconsistency in the epigram, as blushing and femininity are not linked as before with the moral law but with natural law.

How is this confusion regarding Lucie and the epigram to be resolved? With Ermatinger, one may restate *Freiheit-Sitte* as *sinnlich-sittlich*, arguing that the minister's daughter acted from a natural impulse like Keller's naive heroines who lacked *Freiheit*. Blushing would then be related to *Natur*. This line of reasoning would, however, force us, again with Ermatinger, to identify Reinhart with *Freiheit* when it is quite clear that *Freiheit* is always associated with Lucie, in the frame story, in the duel, even in the final fulfillment of the epigram at which time she *blushes* for the first time. She had always laughed and laughter was the symbol of freedom. Reinhart can only be remotely considered as a symbol of freedom insofar as in the battle of the sexes he represents masculine aggressiveness and initiative.

Or one may conclude with Ernst May that Keller intended no prevailing symbolism. This would solve the dilemma certainly, but would cast a dubious light on the work's artistic merit. What would have been the purpose of the many symbolic allusions?

A third possibility seems to provide the most likely answer. The *Sinngedicht* took three decades to complete. In that time Keller changed his mind radically about Lucie. If we are indeed to believe Fränkel, she was in the first version of the manuscript an emancipated and snippy miss much like Eugenia. The story would then no doubt have been confined to the humorous taming of a shrew, with Reinhart as the hero. But then somewhere along the way, possibly not so very much later, Keller apparently decided to imbue his characters with a metaphysical symbolism. No doubt natural law and moral law were to be set off against each other rather equally. But just as Keller's feelings toward Betty Tendering mellowed, so did his early hostility toward Lucie. And when Lucie came to represent not only moral law as such, but Keller's own personal notion of intellectual freedom, she changed from a shrew to the delightful apotheosis of an ideal. Or rather, as Keller sought to retain both the original story and the later symbolism, he sought to imbue Lucie with attributes both of the snippy miss and the ideal. The resulting compromise is amazingly successful even though a trifle contradictory.

As for the epigram, Keller dispensed with its initial symbolism when he had Lucie solemnly burn the paper on which it was written. No doubt the difficulty of distinguishing between the subtle nuances of his views induced him to discard all but his basic symbolism. In the final scene of the story, Keller imbued the epigram illogically but dramatically with the basic symbolism of *sinnlich-sittlich*, enabling him in one grand picture to synthesize initial fable, epigram, and basic symbolism.

We have finished our discussion. What may we conclude? There is a basic symbolism in the frame novella linking the principal characters with the concepts of natural and moral law. This symbolism is also manifest in the interior stories and the conclusion, and thus furnishes the structural backbone of the work. The importance of the implicit metaphysical outlook to Keller is evident from the fact that the same outlook is given prominence in both versions of *Der grüne Heinrich*.

The symbolism of the epigram is initially *Freiheit-Sitte*, not to be equated with *sinnlich-sittlich* or the two principal characters. If this is done Reinhart is equated with *Freiheit* and it is clear that in the story Lucie is unequivocally linked with the concept of freedom. The final scene, however, does indeed imbue the epigram with *sittlich-sinnlich* symbolism. The logical incongruity was slight cost for an impressive picture that synthesized all elements of the story.

Lucie is a charming if slightly inconsistent heroine. She wavers initially between the freedom of an emancipated woman and a moral ideal. But rarely has a slightly vague symbolism detracted from an otherwise interesting character.

One final comment. Our findings do not vitiate the major conclusions of the recent *Sein-Schein* studies, except to the extent that these deny structural unity to the *Sinngedicht*. The notion of *Schein* contains the idea of illusion or deception against which Keller directed his appeal for intellectual freedom. Whether one stresses the desired enlightenment of the subject or the illusory nature of the object is only a matter of perspective. *Sein* is in either case true being and may be equated with *innere Notwendigkeit*.

NOTES

[1] Emil Ermatinger, *Gottfried Kellers Leben. Mit Benutzung von Jakob Baechtolds Biographie.* 4th ed. (Stuttgart and Berlin, 1920), pp. 580–609.

[2] *Ibid.*, p. 592: "Was er [Keller] aus dem Spruch des gescheiten Epigrammatikers herauslas war... das Verhältnis von Sinnlichkeit und Sitte."

[3] Karl Essl, "Über Gottfried Kellers 'Sinngedicht'," *Prager Deutsche Studien* (Reichenberg i. B., 1926).

[4] Priscilla Kramer, *The Cyclical Method of Composition in Gottfried Keller's Sinngedicht* (New York, 1939).

[5] Hermann Pongs, *Das Bild in der Dichtung.* II: *Voruntersuchungen zum Symbol* (Marburg, 1939), pp. 231-234.

[6] J. Elema, "Gottfried Kellers Novelle 'Regine'," *Neophilologus*, XXXIII (1949), 94-103.

[7] Max Hochdorf, *Zum geistigen Bilde Gottfried Kellers* (Zürich, 1919), p. 12.

[8] Edgar Neis, *Romantik und Realismus in Gottfried Kellers Prosawerken* (Berlin, 1930), pp. 88-89.

[9] Herbert Reichert, *Basic Concepts in the Philosophy of Gottfried Keller* (Chapel Hill, 1949), pp. 71-75.

[10] F. J. Stopp, "'Sein' and 'Schein' in Keller's 'Das Sinngedicht'," *German Life and Letters*, N.S. XVI (1962-63), 277-290. Subsequent references are given in the text.

[11] Neither Karl Reichert (See note 12) nor Wolfgang Preisendanz (See note 19) allude to Stopp. Ernst May contends that Stopp's article "fördert... die Forschung wenig, indem er sich zusammenhanglos über vieles und meist Bekanntes, kaum aber über *Sein und Schein* äußert." (See note 22, p. 6.)

[12] Karl Reichert, "Die Entstehung der Sieben Legenden von Gottfried Keller," *Euphorion*, LVII (1963), 97-131.

[13] Karl Reichert, "Gottfried Kellers 'Sinngedicht' — Entstehung und Struktur," *Germanisch-Romanische Monatsschrift*, XLV (1964), 77-101.

[14] *Ibid.*, 77.

[15] *Ibid.*, 91.

[16] *Ibid.*, 77-78.

[17] *Ibid.*, 84.

[18] *Ibid.*, 96.

[19] Wolfgang Preisendanz, "Gottfried Kellers 'Sinngedicht'," *Zeitschrift für deutsche Philologie*, LXXXII (1963), 129-151. Subsequent references are given in the text.

[20] Louis Wiesmann, *Gottfried Keller* (Frauenfeld and Stuttgart, 1967), pp. 194-210. Subsequent references are given in the text.

[21] Henrich Brockhaus, *Kellers 'Sinngedicht' im Spiegel seiner Binnenerzählungen* (University of Washington Dissertation, 1968). DA, XXIX (1968), p. 258-A. It came to our attention after completion of the present article, that Bouvier had published Brockhaus' study (Bonn, 1969).

[22] Ernst May, *Gottfried Kellers 'Sinngedicht'* (Bern and Munich, 1969), p. 149. Subsequent references are given in the text.

[23] Gottfried Keller, *Das Sinngedicht. Sämtliche Werke*, XI, ed. Jonas Fränkel (Bern, 1934), p. 1. All further references to *Das Sinngedicht* will be to this edition.

[24] Preisendanz, *op. cit.*, 136.
[25] May, *op. cit.*, pp. 15-16.
[26] Wiesmann, *op. cit.*, p. 201.
[27] All references in the text to *Der grüne Heinrich* will be to the following edition: Gottfried Keller, *Sämtliche Werke*, III-VI [2nd version], XVI-XIX [1st version], ed. Jonas Fränkel (Erlenbach-Zürich, 1926).
[28] Ermatinger, *Kellers Leben*, p. 593.
[29] *Ibid.*, p. 594.

Inner and Outer Landscape in Eduard von Keyserling's *Dumala*

E. ALLEN MCCORMICK

Towards the end of Eduard von Keyserling's *Dumala* a domestic crisis is effectively avoided by means of one of those tidy bits of philosophizing we encounter so frequently in the writings of this unjustly neglected impressionist:

> Du und ich, wir leben nah beieinander. Was wissen wir voneinander? Was können wir füreinander tun? Wie die Pakete im Güterwagen, so stehen die Menschen nebeneinander. Ein jeder gut verpackt und versiegelt, mit einer Adresse. Was drin ist, weiß keines von dem andern. Man reist eine Strecke zusammen, das ist alles, was wir wissen.[1]

Thus does Pastor Erwin Werner, who is speaking to his indignant and jealous wife, seal off any avenue of communication. The quarrel dissolves in tenderness, and the pastor keeps intact and unshared the sense of bitterness and loss at the flight of the woman he secretly loves. He accpts his wife's offer of a strong grog, for "das ist wenigstens noch etwas, das einer für den anderen tun kann!" His realization that a futile and forbidden dream is over passes almost imperceptibly, and thus undramatically, into resignation, affording one more instance of that quest for the Great Experience which the figures in von Keyserling's world of Baltic estates and decaying elegance share with almost monotonous consistency.

The errant baroness returns in time for her husband's funeral, exchanges a few words with the pastor, and declares that she will remain at Dumala:

> Die Einsamkeit hat mich wieder eingefangen. So ist es mir immer gegangen. Ich habe mich gegen sie zuweilen auflehnen wollen, aber sie fängt mich immer wieder ein. (127)

The *Novelle* ends as Pastor Werner passes Dumala on his way home from a visit to the cemetery. He waves a greeting to the "stille schwarze Gestalt," is greeted in return, and drives on:

Seltsam! dachte Werner, da glaubt man, man sei mit einem andern schmerzhaft fest verbunden, sei ihm ganz nah, und dann geht ein jeder seinen Weg und weiß nicht, was in dem andern vorgegangen ist. Höchstens grüßt einer den anderen aus seiner Einsamkeit heraus! (128)

It is evident that the theme of loneliness is central to this work, as it is prominent altogether in the limited range of themes, characters, and situations one finds in the scant dozen stories by von Keyserling. Perhaps equally apparent is the fact that von Keyserling's lyrical tone, his "Stimmungskunst," represents an outstanding example of what is somewhat uneasily called the impressionistic technique. What remains puzzling, however, is the largely unexplored space between theme and technique, that is to say the failure in the modest body of criticism of von Keyserling's fiction to demonstrate how and to what degree imagery and technique mirror, and indeed support, the themes and character portrayals of the stories. It should prove worthwhile to explore the possibilities of uniting the major instances of form and content by an analysis of one of von Keyserling's most representative works.

The contours of this lyrical *Novelle* follow in the main von Keyserling's three-part plot sequence of suppressed "problem," great experience (pain or passion, or both at once), and defeat with ensuing resignation. Many of the works show a marked preference for the trivial everyday situation as opening scene: Günter von Tarniff in his bathtub (*Beate und Mareile*),[2] the young narrator in *Schwüle Tage* on his way to the family's country estate, as is Karl Erdmann in *Am Südhang*, and Pastor Werner enjoying an evening of music at home. It is this static quality which allows the character to muse or grumble or in some way betray his problem, which is invariably himself.

From the outset, then, feelings take the place of action. Pastor Werner's fine baritone fills the parsonage, brings tears to his wife's eyes, a look of piety to the old housekeeper, even a long howl from the neighbor's dog. The pastor himself is filled with "Kraft und süßem Gefühl" and gradually loses himself in the illusion of experiencing something great,

einen Schmerz, eine Leidenschaft, und dann war es nur ein Leid, etwas, das ein anderer erlebt hat... (5)

The splendid but small ecstasy gives way to tired melancholy; the domestic scene resumes with a brief discussion of Baroness Karola Werland of Dumala, with whom the pastor is accused of being in love ("etwas—nicht?"), and concludes with husband and wife retreating into their own thoughts. Lene had been happy for a brief moment, but "das Traurige war über sie gekommen, dem sie nicht nachdenken wollte." (8) And Werner is able to recapture something of his earlier mood by thinking of tomorrow's sermon, the temptation in the wilderness: "das Wilde des Kampfes der beiden Wunderkräfte in der Wüste regte ihn auf." (8) The peaceful parsonage is offensive to Werner at this moment, for "wenn einer sich beständig mit Wunderdingen abgeben muß... wo soll da der Friede herkommen?" (9) A passing image of Karola brings a sense of pain and a surge of anger at his nerves and useless tenderness.

Richard Brinkmann, in his analysis of *Beate und Mareile*, has given the name "Objektivierung des Subjektiven" to the narrative technique von Keyserling employs here as well as in most of his stories.[3] Benno von Wiese, in his interpretation of *Am Südhang*, prefers to speak of "Subjektivierung des Objektiven," explaining that the reality of any particular situation in von Keyserling's fiction is presented exclusively from the perspective of a single character.[4] The problem is admittedly rather complex and has obvious relevance to the entire issue of point of view in the *Novellen*, but one is nevertheless justified in objecting to a quarrel about priorities like these on grounds that both subjective and objective aspects experience interpenetration and undergo a fusion which, as Brinkmann himself admits, results in an "indifferente Einheit von Gehalt und Gestalt."[5] Irony, some of it self-irony in the characters themselves, does, as von Wiese stresses, serve to maintain a degree of aesthetic distance and even to "objectify" the subjective, but what strikes us as far more significant is the manner in which both reality and man's experience of it assert themselves in such a way as to reduce narrative perspective to a secondary role.

This is especially true of *Dumala*, at any rate, and the entire question of subjective-objective becomes submerged in the larger one of the relationship between elements present both in men's minds and in the world outside, i.e., between *Dumala's* emotional and 'natural' landscapes. These elements are controlled by chains of images centered primarily in contrasting color groups and in patterns of light and sound. An examination of structure and the role of these two sets of images in it should make clear just how the "indifferente Einheit" is brought about.

Von Keyserling's narrative method is best described by the word 'scenic', which gives the Novellen what von Wiese (in referring to *Am Südhang*) calls "etwas Springendes."[6] Plot unfolds in a series of short scenes, usually brief time-segments which are linked by plot progression but which nonetheless convey the impression of a series of quasi-independent mood pictures. The improvisational, momentary nature of these scenes is visual in its impact, a fact seemingly at odds with the traditional view of von Keyserling as "Seelenforscher." Objective 'events' are few, but the 'things' in this *Novelle* are omnipresent.

Dumala is composed of 21 such scenes, their points of separation being indicated by wide spacing; chapter or other divisions are lacking. Only four scenes fail to refer directly to landscape, and no less than 13 contain multiple references to the world of snow, mist, and light that surrounds the people of Dumala. The length of the scenes varies from 15 lines (the closing scene) to slightly more than 11 pages, with an average length of but five pages or less.

We may return to the scene quoted at the beginning. The packages are von Keyserling's equation for man's utter isolation, but more important, they suggest the kind of ambivalence that other images and objects throughout the *Novelle* reveal in their function as mirrors of the human heart. The opening scene between the pastor and his wife brings two opposing forces together and holds them in mutual imprisonment, for while Pastor Werner attempts to escape the "Gemütlichkeit" of the parsonage, his near-sighted, round-faced little wife is tempted to dispense grades to life, according to its comfort factor: "So ist's hübsch," "So ist's gemütlich!" In a gesture to be repeated several times in the story (by other characters as well), Werner stands at the window staring out into the landscape. The view before him is nature's analogy to the tensions that give *Dumala* its movement:

> Oben am Himmel war Aufregung unter den Wolken, zerfetzt und gebläht wie Segel schoben sie sich aneinander vorüber. Der Mond mußte irgendwo sein, aber er wurde verdeckt, nur ein schwaches, müdes Dämmerlicht lag über der Ebene... Der Wind trieb kleine Schneewirbel wie weiße Rauchwölkchen über die Ebene. Winzige Lichtpunkte waren die Fenster des Schlosses Dumala. (9)

Like the neatly wrapped parcels, these tiny points of light are images of life that seeks to maintain and assert itself against the vastness threatening to engulf it. In this initial scene Werner is able to find among the bright points those indicating the windows of Dumala. Like a moth drawn to the light, his mind conjures up the room in which Baroness Karola is sitting. But when he seeks in spirit to escape the "warme Stube" of the parsonage with its oppressive "Gemütlichkeit," into the "düstere Zimmer" of the manor, he is in fact exchanging one set of mental chains for another. Except for its lack of "Vornehmheit" and, presumably, its lower cost, the massive parsonage furniture, upholstered in black and red, is not unlike Dumala's, about which we are told that it is large and heavy and that, when the winter twilight lies upon it, it has the air of something forlorn and vanished. Another manor room has small pieces of furniture with gilded feet, and the pastor notes how they gleam in their dark corners. Karola is dressed in blue, and her lips are unnaturally red (Lene's "legitime Sinnlichkeit" is called pink!); Baron Werland's "dead" legs are wrapped in a red blanket and his face is pale as wax, affording a striking contrast with his eyes — "[Die Augen] legten sehr dunkle Flecken in diese Blässe." (17)

One might easily multiply the occurrences of colors and light intensities as they are used to convey character, emotions and states of mind throughout the *Novelle*. More to our point, however, is the antagonism and tension von Keyserling is at pains to convey both within and between the characters, and for this purpose he usually employs larger color and light categories, within which such nuances are relatively consistent but by and large less significant.

Recalling the pastor's "schwarze Gestalt" and the same phrase as applied to Karola at the end of the story, i.e., after his renunciation of love and her acceptance of solitude, we may observe that black is oppression, resignation, entrapment, concealment. Opposed to this manifested darkness of the human soul is the free, open, and apparently limitless expanse of light, seen most clearly in the vast snowscape of Dumala's world. The 'action' of the story, its symbolic movement, is from darkness to light and back again.

We may return briefly to the rooms of Dumala, both in the pastor's yearning eyes as he stares into the night and as he later continues his periodic visits there. Virtually all that is light and bright has been muted: the "grün verhangene Lampe" lends a tired sickroom light to the scene, the secretary Pichwit's bright brown eyes are heavily ringed with blue shadow, and Karola's eyes are described as "schmal... unruhig schillernd." Human figures are thus linked to the furnishings: points of suppressed life, they seem to wait for some element of brightness to awaken them and free them to live. And like the furniture, they are betrayed by the light that strikes them and causes them to glow; for example, Karola's hand, stroking her husband's useless legs, is "ganz unflimmert von scharfen, bunten Lichtern." (23) In these surroundings "Gemütlichkeit" proves to be not cozy contentment but at best the illusion of satisfaction. Karola reveals her affinity to the pastor, for she too is waiting—perhaps unconsciously—to break out. Her vision of hope is "eine lange, lange Allee. Warum sollen wir uns da plötzlich eine schwarze Mauer denken? ... Ich will hinabsehen, weit—weit—, bis da, wo ich vor Helligkeit der Ferne nichts mehr unterscheide." (20)

The dark interiors that convey a double sense of domesticity and imprisonment are placed in direct opposition to the sunlit landscape. Sandwiched between the parsonage scene and the evening visit to Dumala is the Sunday morning church service. The sacristy is filled with snowlight, the trees outside the window are covered with glistening drops of water, and there is a "helles Blitzen und Klingen" all around the church. Two leitmotifs are introduced in this scene, the path or beam of light and the sound of sleighbells. Werner is cheered by the light-filled church, for

> wenn die breiten, gelben Lichtbänder durch die hohen Fenster in den Raum fluteten, dann bekam seine Predigt auch anders helle Farben, als wenn die Kirche voll grauer Dämmerung war... (11-12)

And the bells introduce the sounds of life: at first the sleighs of the arriving congregation, among them the "Schellen von Dumala" for which the pastor anxiously waits, and in later scenes the arrival of adventure that gives hope of "rescue."

The first of these leitmotifs, the shaft of light, suggests a bridge or passageway between light and darkness, an avenue of escape from the prison of domestication. The stream of light through the church window and Karola's vision of a long tree-lined avenue leading into sheer brightness recur in varied form in the succeeding episode, which describes the pastor's night ride to the *Moorkrug* and his mad gallop over the rotten bridge with two members of his congregation. For Werner the bridge over the black waters far below is the source of "Rausch"—not the kind afforded by the tranquil but hated coziness of the parsonage but its very opposite, the sense of expectation, of the "Nieerlebte" and the expectation of breaking out. The light imagery reinforces the meaning:

> Durch die Wolken schien auf Augenblicke der Mond, ein Licht, das kam und ging, als liefe jemand mit einer Kerze eine lange Fensterreihe entlang... etwas Mondlicht fiel in die Tiefe. (30-31)

This invasion of light is most often linked to the sensuous and erotic. Werner's sermon in the light-invaded church deals with Christ's temptation; Karola's yearning for the "Helligkeit" at the end of the road is her response to the dark, confining life she leads at Dumala, and her desire to be able to distinguish nothing in all that light is readily seen as a rejection of traditional, aristocratic obligations. The scene following Werner's ride over the bridge is, like the earlier church scene, bathed in light. Werner and Karola meet by chance in late afternoon at the forest edge, the baroness' arrival having been announced by the "Schellengeklingel":

> Vor ihnen lag die Ebene, ganz übergossen von zentifolienfarbenem Licht. Die Sonne war im Untergehen... Sie schaute in die Sonne. Ihre Augen wurden wieder ganz schmal, *leuchtende Striche* zwischen den schwarzen Wimpern... Sie lachten sich an, öffneten den Mund, als könnten sie das Licht trinken. (35-36; italics mine)

When the dusk spreads over the plain Karola complains, "Alles weg," and feels she must apologize for her "Rausch": "Wie so'n bißchen Licht einen aufregt... ich bin müde." (36) But the pastor is reluctant to end the meeting; the sun has set but there is now a "glashelle Mondnacht"; moreover, since there is still no light in the parsonage he is reluctant to break the spell of the "Nachglanz" of sunset and the "Nachglanz" of the laughing bells. The notion of reflected sound and light, with its implication of the lack of immediacy and authenticity is thus effectively captured in the substantives.

These chance meetings and the regular "pastoral" visits to Dumala become less frequent when Baron Rast begins his affair with Karola. Werner's assumption of his rival's role is accompanied by a blanket of white fog that covers the landscape:

> Überall das weiße, kalte Fließen, das alles verhängte, in dem er [Werner] allein war, ganz allein. Alles andere war ausgelöscht, selbst die Töne erstarben. (49)

Rast, too, equates the fog with melancholy, lamenting the loss of open sunlit space where these bored, frustrated creatures can escape their dark interiors:

> Da muß man zusammenkriechen. Herr Pastor, an solchen Tagen müssen die Seelen in Ihrer Hand weich wie Wachs sein, wenn Sie ihnen von Licht sprechen. Na, und Licht kommt doch in der Religion vor. (50)

Indirectly, and probably unconsciously, Werner associates the fog with his rival. On returning home he hears its constant, busy whispering, "eine heimliche, traurige Geschichte, die die Nacht sich erzählte" (56), and he discovers a strange new feeling, his hatred for Rast. This scene, in which the word "Nebel" dominates throughout, again takes up the motif of bells. Their association with life, i.e., with escape and happiness, now becomes more clearly connected to the erotic:

> Weit draußen kam ein Ton durch den Nebel, kaum hörbar. Aber Karola lauschte. Ihre Hand hörte auf, über die rote Decke zu streichen, und ein leichtes Rot stieg in ihre Wangen. (50)

Later scenes are invariably interrupted by the "Schellengeklingel" which brings an air of festivity to Dumala ("Die Lichter wurden angezündet"), and even where Rast himself does not appear the bells betray his presence: "Durch den Wald kam Schellengeklingel, es entfernte sich, wurde schwächer." (60)

A brief scene between Karola and the pastor, approximately midway in the story, offers a variation of their earlier encounter in bright sunlight at the edge of the forest. There is the same effect on the pastor of richly golden light—"nur das helle, stille Leben dieses Lichtes wollte er in sich hineintrinken" (59), but Karola, in whose words one reads a confession of her love affair, is reminded of magic lantern slides. Life passes so quickly that its individual scenes take on an unreal quality (one recognizes the similarity to the pointillistic technique in impressionistic painting, in which the individual points of color must first merge to assume contour and meaning), and its participants share in this unreality. Karola points to their shadows on the snow and asks if they have changed—a reminder of their other encounter, when Werner described her shadow as "fast leichtsinnig" (38). Despite Werner's denial, the reader is struck by the appropiateness of the dark fleeting shapes on a white background, shapes without permanence or solidity.

The image is repeated a short time later, when Werner learns of Rast's nocturnal trysts with Karola. In order to see for himself, he posts himself at the rotting bridge one night and sees a dark shadow glide over the "weißer Strich," the snow-covered bridge. And when he follows the sleigh tracks to Dumala he sees "einen schwachen Lichtstreif" falling from a tower window. Overcome with jealousy, the pastor watches night after night as the "black vision" passes over the strip of whiteness above the black waters. After his discovery light gradually assumes a new meaning for him:

Licht, nicht das zeigt und aufdeckt, nein, Licht das verhüllt, das wie ein leuchtender Schleier sich über das graue Leben breitet (86)

and thus marks, even before the story's climax, his defeat and return to the darkness so admirably represented by his clerical garb. On an evening when the falling snow lays "eine bleiche Helligkeit in die Nacht" Werner removes some loose planks from the bridge but at the last moment warns Rast not to cross. Their ensuing conversation brings a confession from the pastor, but in this "sogenannte Kultur"—words spoken earlier with bitterness and scorn by Werner—nothing happens:

Draußen hing schon ein blaßgelbes Lichtband am östlichen Horizont. Über dem frischgefallenen Schnee kam der Tag sehr weiß und rein herauf. (99)

After Karola and Rast run away together, the pastor continues to spend his evenings at Dumala, waiting with the ailing Werland for Karola's return. She comes back for her husband's funeral and for the solitude that is captured in the image of the dark figure waving her greeting to the black-clad pastor who passes by in the distance.

If we re-examine the emotions of Dumala's characters and seek their analogies in the numerous images of light, darkness, color and sound, it becomes apparent that the latter constitute a strikingly consistent lexical mirror of the former. In the use of light and darkness particularly one is able to reconstrust on a symbolic level the entire action of the story. Eyes, we have observed, betray the character's interior and their respective roles in the Great Experience. The pathetic figure of Pichwit, Werland's secretary who is passionately in love with Karola, is noticeable for round, bright brown eyes ringed with blue shadow: the suffering boy whose infatuation is of the kind that lends pathos and little else to his "Knabengesicht"; in the pretty, round pink face of Lene are blue eyes which are appropiately described as "kurzsichtig"; Werland's eyes are dark spots that interrupt the paleness of his face and, indeed, represent (along with his "Haltung") the only thing still truly alive in this ailing aristocrat.

In sharp contrast to these ineffectual figures are Karola, Werner, and Rast. Karola's narrow grey eyes are described variously as "schillernd," "sehr blanke Striche," "leuchtende Striche," and on one occasion (by Werner's jealous wife) as "schmale Schlangenaugen." Rast's eyes are large and velvet brown, "mit dem feuchten, trägen Blick" which, so Lene senses, are "ruhig und frech... als streiften diese Augen langsam die Kleider von ihr ab." (44) Werner's eyes, finally, are described but once; at the end of their second walk together Karola is struck by the pastor's strange eyes: "Ach, es ist wohl die Abendsonne; wenn die sich in den Augen spiegelt, dann werden die Augen ganz wild." (61) The description, we are willing to believe, is not inaccurate, and there is certainly some point to observing the pastor's eyes but once, as they reflect the light from without. The other striking use of 'wild', we recall, was the subject of Werner's sermon.

It is perhaps unnecessary to be more explicit in relating von Keyserling's descriptions of eyes to the roles assigned their owners. Rast's predatory, boudoir eyes reveal most of what the man stands for in *Dumala*, and Pastor Werner is at bottom little more than a spectator, a feeling but passive participant, as it were, who in a double sense represents the inner drama of the *Novelle's* characters: his eyes mirror the emotional situation in the same way as the narrative itself, despite its third-person point of view, appears to be largely the result of Werner's limited field of vision.

What Pastor Werner sees is therefore essentially what the reader sees, and it is in this context that we must judge the role of light and darkness in the story. Dressed in his black talar (especially in the light-drenched church scene, where he is quite literally the focal point), Werner gives vent to the violence within him—by thrusting the problem onto Christ; on his walks—to escape the hated "Gemütlichkeit"—he takes the "finsterer Waldweg":

> Es war, als tobte und rief eine große Kraft über ihm sich aus—für ihn, tobte und rief hinaus, was in ihm hinaus wollte. (25)

Only in refracted form can the inner flame break out and spend itself. Those who protest openly, von Keyserling suggests, are not merely candidates for defeat and the kind of solitude Werner means with his packages; everyone in this Baltic society—and by implication those beyond—lives and dies in the same isolation. The protesters are rather human beings of a special sort, for in their sensuality, passion, and their insistence on reaching out for the light they become worthy of the Great Experience. To a pessimist like von Keyserling the results are no longer strictly relevant. The path of light in its many forms is hence the way *not* taken, the illusory offer of happiness which violates Dumala's formal existence.

Thus while Lene makes small scenes, Pichwit waits and weeps, and Werland simply waits, Rast the gambler and Werner the man of huge suppressed passions contend for Karola. The symbols in *Dumala* make clear how and why Rast succeeds and the pastor fails (within the special meaning of success and failure in Eduard von Keyserling's fiction). Werner attempts to sing and preach his way to inner liberation. But because what is inside is eroticism, unambiguous desire for the baroness, he cannot possibly reconcile his inner dissatisfaction with his role as pastor and husband. Both Karola and Rast recognize this. Karola mocks Werner's visits while enjoying his company: "'Gewiß hat Ihre Frau auf Sie gewartet,' sie lächelte dabei ihr leichtspöttisches

Lächeln." (24) And Rast, during the conversation in which Werner tries to warn him against compromising the baroness, mocks the pastor by questioning his motives: "Und Freund, mein Gott, Gefühle komplizieren die Sachen nur. Aber Pastor—, Pastor ist klar" (79).

But the "clarity" of pastor—and for that matter of husband, wife, neighbor, and secretary as well—is obviously a dubious one, for in each case the inner landscape, as we have called it, or Rast's "complication by feelings," is at variance with the rigidified form of these lives. Further reduction of clarity is achieved through the use of double values, not only in the figures themselves (pastor-husband as wooer) but in their emotional vocabulary. Thus *Rausch* is of two kinds, the domestic coziness that signifies flight by means of withdrawal, and the feeling of infinitude, of endless expansion or wandering which we perceive in Werner's sermon ("andächtige Ekstase") and Karola's "lange Allee." These latter, too, are clearly forms of escape, not from *Weltschmerz* but from *ennui*.

The appropiateness of the latter term reinforces our conviction that *Dumala* should be regarded as an outstanding example of literary impressionism. The conflict between man's inner life and his formal existence, which we have seen mirrored in Dumala's landscape, is at once carried out and resolved in terms of complete surrender, of which one expression is *ennui*. For what is important in this *Novelle* is not plot or action or in any real sense "Begebenheit," but simply states of mind and "Stimmungen" as they are reflected in their characters' commitment to a moment or a brief scene.

While it may be said that the external world of Dumala as setting is realistically drawn and therefore has a certain validity of its own, its true value becomes apparent only insofar as the major characters react to it. Fragmentation of form and the story's consistent use of small units accurately represent the momentary impingement of nature on, or its coinciding with, the characters. These impressions, we have seen, are almost exclusively visual and hold a more or less firm position between camera-like impartiality and a personalized distortion of the seen into a subjective view of nature. Only once in the *Novelle* does a character (Werner) see nature as a dreamscape; otherwise it has its own reality. To call this intermediate position between "objective" vision and subjective reaction impressionistic is not to extend the meaning of an already elusive literary term but rather to stress that the distinction between subject and object, which impressionism tends to break down (Brinkmann's "Subjektivierung des Objektiven"), vanishes without the one becoming subservient to the other. We call this kind of fusion a lexical mirroring in which nature functions as an undistorting parallel to man's interior.

The "Ebene," that great expanse of plain which holds Dumala, may be seen as the canvas on which a series of momentary constellations—we have counted 21 such scenes or units—occur, each in a sense disconnected and non-recurring but in their totality representative of both visual and thematic homogeneity. The spots and paths of light on this canvas are, to be sure, seen in contexts suggesting symbolic equivalents of the characters' subjective vision, but in effect no such evaluation takes place. The "schmaler weißer Strich über dem Abgrund" is, from a strictly visual point of view, no more than that. It happens to be a bridge as well, but Pastor Werner refuses to translate and hence give symbolic import to "Strich" as bridge and "Abgrund" as abyss. Visual appearance does not give way to permanent fact, and it is precisely this insistence on the phenomena of nature as non-evaluated visual impressions that makes *Dumala* a model of literary impressionism. Theme and technique, we may conclude, meet and join in exemplary impressionistic manner where inner and outer landscape share alike in the monotonous cycle of light and darkness in *Dumala*.

NOTES

[1] *Dumala*, p. 110. All references, hereafter placed in parentheses directly after the text, are to vol. I of *Eduard von Keyserling. Baltische Romane*, ed. Ernst Heilborn (Berlin: S. Fischer, 1933). This edition offers the same text as Heilborn's four-volume edition *Gesammelte Erzählungen* (Berlin, 1922).

[2] This *Novelle*, and especially its opening scene, is treated extensively by Richard Brinkmann, "Eduard von Keyserling: 'Beate und Mareile': Die Objektivierung des Subjektiven," *Wirklichkeit und Illusion* (Tübingen: Max Niemeyer Verlag, 1957), pp. 216-290.

[3] Brinkmann, pp. 231 ff.

[4] Benno von Wiese, "Eduard von Keyserling: Am Südhang," *Die deutsche Novelle von Goethe bis Kafka*, II (Düsseldorf: August Bagel Verlag, 1962), pp. 280-298. See esp. pp. 287-88.

[5] Brinkmann, p. 289.

[6] von Wiese, p. 283.

Keyserling's *Landpartie*

WAYNE WONDERLEY

In the dark year of 1918 a novella of striking coloration appeared in Germany.[1] In that year of stress the Wilhelmine era drew its last official breath, and the author of *Landpartie*, Eduard von Keyserling, also died.[2]

Born 1855 on the estate Tels-Paddern in Courland, Eduard Heinrich Nikolaus Count von Keyserling was nurtured in accordance with a traditional, aristocratic culture. Spending some time in Vienna in contact with the socialist movement, administering the paternal estates for a period, absorbing the treasures of several Italian centers of art, notably Naples, he then removed to Munich with two sisters to lead a relatively retiring, yet culturally influential life as art critic, author, and *bon vivant* of the literary coterie on the Isar. Blindness struck him in 1908.[3]

Keyserling's word art as reflected primarily in some sixteen stories and novellas (he also wrote two naturalistic novels and four predominantly lyrical dramas) is unobtrusive yet poignant, low-keyed yet penetrating, restrained yet memorable. Excelling in delineation of delicate psychic moods, his narratives are nevertheless quietly dynamic. The themes are limited to the few he was confident of playing well. With undertones of vibrant passion, the atmosphere he depicts is frequently laced with overtones of *fin-de-siècle* ennui.

Even if the author's name were not indicated, it would be difficult not to recognize Keyserling's sensitive hand in little-known *Landpartie*, for his literary modus operandi is characteristic und unmistakable. Structure and style of a Keyserlingian narration are integrally incorporated in the author's technique. Indeed, in reading any story by Keyserling one frequently experiences a feeling of *déjà vu*.

Landpartie is no exception. Here the painter uses familiar, short brush strokes synesthetically orchestrated with the composer's lambent, chamber music moods. Supporting factors concentrate kinetically with linguistic and artistic succinctness upon seeing, hearing, feeling, and smelling individually or in combination. Impressionistic, sustaining elements appear as brief and rapid suggestion of form, color, or mood, and momentary indication of immediate aspects without dwelling upon detail. Not so much things in themselves, but rather their sensuous impressions are significant. Esthetic and psychologic components are conjured up. Other backup devices include dynamism with action verb, adjective, and adverb often featuring color symbolism, vibrant pause, and characterizing leitmotif. Physiognomy, voice, hand, and clothing are stressed. Word pairs are often associated by a connecting *und*, and there are favorite words or phrases. Repetition is varied with retardation, succinct summary with indirect discourse or verbal qualifiers. Tropes are used sparingly, but are consistent and effective. There is substantial irony, bittersweet resignation, and minimal humor. A sense of the stage is suggested by dramatic entrance, exit composition, and tableau, also by anticipation, suspense, contrast, and comparison.

As often with Anton Chekhov, Hermann Bahr, or Jens Peter Jacobsen, plot is subordinated to mood. We do not expect externalized action from an atmosphere of still life. *Landpartie* is an encomium to personal freedom and, at the same time, an apotheosis of love. An outwardly enchanting but inwardly troubled prima donna is guest at an aristocratic excursion in the country. She is confronted by the importunities of male admirers and the erotic distress of an adolescent boy. By rejecting the nobles and comforting the lad she assuages her wounded ego. Yet her problems remain unsolved. A lonely *bourgeoise* and *artiste*, she can not, and probably would not, belong to this smug egocentric, aristocratic milieu.

The stark brevity of the title *Landpartie* may suggest the impressionistic distillation for which Keyserling strives. Standing as it does without even an article, it is difficult to imagine a more astringently effective formulation. If the title prepares the reader for artistic economy, the initial paragraph lends supporting evidence. Without introductory exposition, we jump with one sentence into the scene *en plein air*:[4]

> Da stand Oswald von Ramm auf der Freitreppe seines Landhauses, in seinen zitronengelben Staubmantel gehüllt, die Kapuze über den Kopf gezogen, und betrachtete nachdenklich die Equipage, die vor dem Hause hielt, den altmodischen, schweren Landauer, die dicken, schläfrigen Pferde und Gregor, den alten Kutscher, der in seiner verblichenen Livree ziemlich krumm auf dem Kutscherbock saß. (261)

With "da" serving as an emphatic demonstrative, our attention is focused upon potential kinetics. The feeling that perhaps something is about to happen is, by contrast, heightened by the passive verbal and adjectival forms on which the passage is structured.

To highlight contrast between owner and owned, the opening optical sentence features adjectives and adverbs. While Oswald von Ramm's duster is, strikingly, lemon-yellow, that which he regards is an old-fashioned, ponderous landau drawn by fat, sleepy horses, and Gregor, the old coachman in his faded livery. Examination of other Keyserlingian opening statements shows striking similarities in techniques of structure and atmosphere.

The dominant, opening mood of descriptive inertia is enlivened by a voice whose utterance however supplements facts stated in the lead paragraph. Von Ramm's fifteen-year old son, Kurt, comments to his father that what they are looking at is not exactly elegant. In replacing the carriage as the object of his father's examination, the tall, thin teener evokes a sharp reaction. Oswald reprimands his son for the type of clothing which he is wearing. A slight pause, animated by shoulder shrugging, precedes Kurt's reply. The conversational pause, which retards, supports, or substitutes for direct discourse, is frequently employed by Keyserling. Characteristically the pause is never inert, but rather is enlivened by a brief physical action as movement of a hand, or legs, a raising of eyebrows, lip pursing, blushing, or blanching. Kurt's response includes an excuse from his mother. As if on stage, the mention of the mother also serves to introduce her, for she now appears, accompanied by her father, old Baron Lundberg.

In describing Frau Malwina von Ramm, Keyserling continues to stress the visual, and now the physiognomic. She is not out of breath, but rather, qualified, a *little* out of breath; her round, pretty face is hot, and she looks out of sorts. Although this pause contains a brief, relatively static description, it is also kinetic in that Frau von Ramm and Baron Lundberg are strolling up to father and son. Again the passage is introduced and directed by an initial "da."

Taking the conversational initiative, Malwina throws down an initial conversational gauntlet to which Baron Oswald does not give an immediate verbal response. The pause is occupied by his smiling genially and contemplating his wife. She is a Renoir study in a white straw hat with bright yellow and red roses, and a duster of moth-colored silk over a pale lavender muslin dress. To mollify his wife, whom he senses to be in a challenging mood, Oswald remarks that she is very beautiful today. This evokes first a blushing, then a coy retort. What do you mean, beautiful—after all, one *does* have to wear something. Oswald responds assuagingly and suggests that the party enter the landau. As Malwina is stepping into the carriage, she complains that Gregor's livery looks dreadful. Oswald answers initially by shrugging his shoulders. He then comments to the effect that he cannot buy the coachman a livery merely because it pleases Princess Adelheid to arrange a garden party every five years. Malwina elects not to reply.

A pause filled with the remainder of the family's climbing into the landau ends the first tableau. (To facilitate analysis, *Landpartie* is divided in this study into nine scenes). What does the opening scene bring us? Several actors, some of whom are important, are introduced and somewhat characterized by what they wear, how they appear, and what they say. We are concerned with an aristocratic family about to leave its chateau for a country outing. It is summer, and dry and languid. Nerves seem to be on edge.

Scene two flashes more vivid coloration, introduces the landscape in some detail, and acquaints us further with important participants. Now that all are seated in the carriage and Kurt has climbed up beside Gregor, the fat horses, lazy and reluctant, begin to pull. The hot June day is ending:

> ... die schrägen Sonnenstrahlen ließen einen fliederfarbenen Schimmer über die Saatfelder hinzittern, die Luft war voll eines glitzernden Staubes und auf den großen Klettenblättern, den Glockenblumen und Schafgarben des Wegrains lag dieser Staub wie ein dichter, blonder Schleier. Auf den Weiden, an denen sie vorüberfuhren, lagen die Hüterkinder mitten unter ihren Schafen platt auf dem Bauch, der lange, sonnige Tag hatte sie kraftlos und gedankenlos gemacht. Malwina sehr hübsch mit ihren siebenunddreißig Jahren, aber schon ein wenig stark geworden, lehnte sich seufzend in die Wagenecke zurück und unterdrückte ein Gähnen. "Ach Gott", sagte sie, "daß die gute Prinzessin Adelheid sich auch nichts Besseres ausdenken konnte, als heute eine Landpartie zu machen." (262-263)

A mood of languor permeates the passage, which is essentially a descriptive pause laced with dynamics. Where at the outset the horses are characterized as fat and sleepy, they are now, in pulling, again called fat. Furthermore, as applied to the horses, the adjective sleepy is replaced with lazy and reinforced by reluctant. As the landau begins to move it is almost as if it were standing still and the landscape were being unrolled. Sibilants suggest the whispering sounds of the declining day. "Zitronengelb" (261) and "fliederfarben" are typical impressionistic color combinations. Slanting sun rays cause a lilac gleam to quiver over the fields of grain. Here is a subject worthy of a Monet. Would he not be tempted to capture the ever changing aspects of this iridescent, evanescent vista, even as with the famous hayfield? The polychromatic landscape is vibrant, also suggestive of treatment by a Lovis Corinth, a Max Liebermann, or a Max Slevogt. Even the air is full of glittering particles of dust.[5] Yet some dust, a thick, blond veil, is covering the flora lining the road. The group passes by shepherd children lying flat on their stomachs under their sheep, for the long sunny day has made them languid and listless. Without transition we return to the landau where we are informed that Malwina is thirty-seven, and, again, that she is pretty. Repeated and consistent association of a characteristic with an individual may create a leitmotif, for which Keyserling, like Homer, Chopin, and Wagner, evinces partiality. Compounding the movement of the landau, of which we are hardly aware, Malwina creates subdued dynamisms by sighing and suppressing a yawn. Simultaneously she leans back into the corner of the carriage, which is also a representative Keyserlingian gesture for a person in this situation. The long pause culminates in her remark about Princess Adelheid as hostess for the picnic.

The comment calls forth a reply from old Baron Lundberg preceded by a pause during which he makes a kind of quiet giggle to himself. The giggling has an exact verbal parallel to the giggling of the old Excellency in *Harmonie*. The pause is further dynamized physiognomically: The old baron's little face becomes quite red and his beard appears, by contrast, white as rimy moss.

The remainder of the tableau offers snatches of gossip concerning the hostess, her companions, and friends; further development of Malwina's character and those of her father and husband; additional delineation of natural scenery along the route of the carriage; and anticipatory introductions to party guests, primarily through Malwina's lorgnette. The impressionistic roundup is a summarizing device frequently used by Keyserling. Malwina's summary of the guests, with symptomatic comments, ends the scene. There is the usual amount of qualifiers like "ein wenig" or "ordentlich behaglich."

Again, the dialog is almost laconic, and is sandwiched in among pauses made vivid by mild dynamics. Thus, bored, Malwina raises her pretty eyebrows, again leans back into the corner of the carriage, or sighs. The old baron giggles and contributes a few pithy remarks reminiscent of an epigram by Oscar Wilde.

We learn that Princess Adelheid is giving this *fête champêtre* because she is curious to have a good look at the guest of her friend, Olga Landen. The guest is the famous opera singer, Ria Riviera, who practically makes men swoon. Also accompanying the princess from her old chateau will be chlorotic Countess Reichenau and the boring chamberlain.

Malwina remains belligerent toward her husband, permitting him no statement without challenge. She belittles his former, presumed infatuation for Ria, asserts she is above being jealous, and complains of her humdrum life. Resigned, Oswald shrugs his shoulders a little, as previously.

The woodland stretch has ended, and the carriage is approaching a new picture: meadowland in bloom crossed by a brook in which "grellgrün" trees are swaying gently. Here more color and action dispel Kurt's melancholy mood. Along the brook lustrous figures are bustling about. This then, is the party. Kurt sees ladies in bright dresses, gentlemen in summer suits and panama hats. Two lackeys wearing green and golden livery are setting up folding chairs and spreading rugs. Taking her glass, Malwina reconnoiters eagerly from the carriage, then reports her intelligence résumé. The princess has her rose hat, that means she can't bring herself to admitting she's old. Naturally the Reichenau woman is always in green—a color least becoming to her. There are the Landens and, yes, that must be the songstress, wearing all white topped with a yellow shepherdess' hat, just as if she were on stage. And is she pale! Naturally she's powdered. Moving onto the meadow, the landau halts, the passengers alight.

Scene three begins with introductions. As Malwina extends her hand to Ria with exaggerated friendliness she peers inquisitively into her face. Quickly observing the salient points she summarizes to herself: Ah, yes, the regular features of Ria's pale face suggesting aroused tension include a mouth that is too red and somewhat grayish eyes underlined by a small, black line evoking distress. Malwina adds her conclusion to the summary: painted! With his formal bow Oswald includes the mental aside which Keyserling's male characters display when introduced to such an impressive representative of *grand monde*: Well, she's really big time!

Although the author chooses economically to skip over the platitudes of introductory chit-chat with Princess Adelheid, nevertheless he has the princess fill the pause, as it were, with a continual, patient smile of greeting. For Keyserling the face is always significant. *Vultus index animi est.* The long pale face of the princess with its strong features is reminiscent of another picture. It reminds us, says Keyserling, of an eighteenth-century print of a princely visage regarding us loftily in full-bottomed wig. Except that Princess Adelheid's face gives an impression of empty peace which makes it a little lugubrious. There must be qualifiers in Keyserling's descriptions.

Now the princess speaks, inviting her guests to be gay, for after all, isn't this such a beautiful evening? Please, be completely free and easy, and you, gentlemen, may smoke. People are sitting on the cushions and rugs while servants pass sandwiches and strawberry "Bowle." Yet somehow, the stiffness remains.

The ladies sip their glasses and look to Ria, as if expecting her to provide the evening's entertainment. The stage is set. How will the next scene come off?

In scene four Keyserling displays his technique of dealing briefly and simultaneously with individual members so that the group remains a viable entity. Representative adjectives, vivid conversational phrases, and lively verbs are undergirded with restrained dynamics. To activate the stylized *Konversation* Princess Adelheid quite properly serves the initial conversational shuttlecock. Is it not true, Fräulein Riviera, stage life is very interesting, I imagine it so captivating. Not in a mood to respond, as is expected of her, by batting the conversational gambit back with a new twist, Ria merely confirms. At this point the conversation appears to run the risk of dying of irony or ennui. The vapid tone is emphasized by the predominance of pedestrian words. Frau von Landen's assertiveness saves the game as she sails in with yes, interesting, but unhealthful for the nerves! But the princess, ignoring the remark, continues valiantly with a laudatory comment on Ria's interpretation of Wagner. Now it is von Landen's turn, and we are reminded that he is fat and is wearing a white summer suit. Happy and hot ("rot") he positions himself in front of Ria with a sandwich in his hand. Von Landen recalls the first time he was presented to Ria. That was after a Wagnerian performance which had hardly left her strength to speak at the "souper." Concluding, he attempts a *bon mot* by asserting that he loves operas which leave the ladies strength for a "souper." In the ensuing pause he laughs, but no one joins him.

A Keyserlingian trait repeatedly makes the association performance-female artist-*souper*.

Ria's reticence seems to disappoint the ladies and they begin to chat quietly about their own concerns. Keyserling shows a penchant for contrasts, particularly those incorporating an unexpected, ironic switch. Such a change is involved when suddenly we are diverted from Wagnerian opera to the canning of unripened gooseberries. Kurt and fourteen-year old Erika Landen engage in a quiet quarrel. Countess Reichenau bites her pallid lower lip — which is a dynamic gesture favored by the author to fill a pause with an indication of annoyance—while staring at Ria rigidly with her bright blue eyes as if lost in an exciting novel. Again we are told that Countess Reichenau is wearing a green hat and is very pale. The mood of disenchantment grows.

A summarizing statement reaffirms the atmosphere: the day dying over the broad plain, the music of the evening gnats, all this imparts a kind of disappointing triteness to the party. Now we return to Erika and Kurt to find that they are silent, but making faces as if to cry.

But talk is lively around Ria. Lying on the grass at her feet are Baron Oswald and the handsome chamberlain whose bronze beard billows on his cheeks. Old Baron Lundberg moves his chair closer to Ria in order to recall singing beauties of his day. The chamberlain reminisces with a grating voice. Then Oswald tells of Venice. Speaking softly and using a strangely sentimental voice he remembers a sulphurously yellow sky over the *Gran canale*. Faces and voices are important for Keyserling. Thus, Malwina eyes Ria's admirers hatefully, how unpleasantly saccharin men's faces smirk whenever they are talking to such an enchantress! Following Malwina's glance, Frau von Landen whispers agreement, closing scene five with a pause which continues into the subsequent tableau.

With a minimum of discourse, scene six is further concerned with impressionistic color and mood.[6] Ria's depression, nature generally, and the effect of the setting sun on her and the others constitute this picture:

> Ria war einsilbig; sie schaute auf die Ebene hinaus, auf das leise Nicken der Halme, auf das sanfte und freie Atmen der Weite in dem roten Lichte. In der rosa Luft hingen Lerchen, und all das erschütterte und quälte sie, es war so ungewohnt groß und friedlich, und sie fühlte darin die komplizierte Enge ihres Lebens wie etwas schmerzhaft Bedrückendes. Dazu diese Herren mit ihren Erinnerungen. Es war, als würden lang verschlossen gestandene Restaurationskabinetts geöffnet, in denen es dumpfig nach Plüsch, nach abgestandenen Parfüms und Zigarettendampf riecht. (268)

Several points may be mentioned. Larks suspended in pink air suggest a pastel color slide illustrating the impressionistic school of painting. It is habitual for Keyserling to designate a main character as "einsilbig" when that person is taciturn within a group or party because of depression, disgust, or peevishness.

A summary is frequently concluded with "all das." The proclivity for word pairs joined by "und" is striking. The figure of the restaurant is intensified by olfactory elements. Finally, this expositional pause is dominated by linguistic dynamisms.

It has become unbearable for Ria to serve in the purity of the natural setting as a stimulus for recollections of gay or sentimental moments of men. Somehow, the tension must be broken. Relief comes first for the ladies in the chromatic effects of the setting sun:

Die Sonne ging hinter dem Waldsaum unter, eine farbige Erregung zitterte über das stille Land, der Bach wurde ganz rot, und die blühende Wiese lag da wie rotes Gold. In der Gesellschaft schwiegen plötzlich alle, hoben die Gesichter, lächelten mit halbgeöffneten Lippen, als wollten sie das farbige Leuchten in sich hineintrinken. (268)[7]

Again, such dabs of color remind us of the immediate, fleeting glimpses sought by the impressionist painters with their pointillist techniques and three-dimensional depth and nuance.

To spare Kurt and Erika the off-color, raucous witticisms of fat von Landen, his diplomatic wife sends the pair off for a walk. The evening red has stirred the others too. Leaving Ria to the men, Frau von Landen takes Malwina for a stroll. Olga and Countess Reichenau join them. "Die armen Männer sollen sich einmal ausleben" remarks Frau von Landen. To which Malwina gives a hostile laugh. It is not uncommon for the understanding woman in Keyserling's tales to excuse male deportment with a phrase like "Du Armer" or "Ach, die armen Männer."

The promenade continues the pause. No one speaks, yet there is activity everywhere. The motion of walking along the brook is augmented by dynamic nature. The odor of the reeds is stronger, fish jump, evening lights grow pale on the water. The fusing of colors in the diaphanous twilight spreads a kind of infinite softness and tenderness over the plain. The land is waxing sentimental. A fitting, impressionistically hazy ensemble for the alfresco salon in which seeing, hearing, smelling, and feeling are called upon synesthetically to convey the combined effects of the short, deft strokes of the painter's chiaroscuro brush.

Continuing the pause, the seventh scene depicts the chamberlain seemingly blending into this atmosphere also. Caught up in feeling, he removes his panama and wipes his brow, which is, incidentally, a bit too high. When we recall that he has been described previously as boring, the sentimental effusion which he now pours forth is not without irony. Ah yes, "mein gnädiges Fräulein," this lonely life in the country makes us oversensitive. Your presence—ah—your air of *grand monde*, and the memories—memories, why it's like seeing a camellia blooming here on our old meadow. Irritated, Ria refuses the bait. Now it's Baron Oswald's turn. Keyserling brings him into focus again, as is his wont with such a reintroduction by the phrase "Dann begann er [Oswald] zu sprechen." We recall that the manner of speaking is important. Consonant with the surroundings, Oswald's voice is now soft and lyrical. To express his feelings he sums up. Yes, memories are strange. Everything here reminds me of Venice—our brook, our light, our air—everything's Venetian today. Do you remember, *mein Fräulein*...? Another pause.

Ria stops short. Facial features and voice reveal her emotions. Irked more than usual, her eyes are piercing. A little frown shows between her eyebrows with their carefully applied makeup and her voice trembles a denial. Turning about she grasps her train and begins to run. Obviously Ria needs a physical escape. Her action signals too a dissolution of the group of male admirers, contrasts sitting with running, and heralds, soon, the end of the party.

Of course Ria's action must evoke comments from the ladies. Our prima donna is displaying a new effect they say. Ria runs until she catches up with Kurt who, bored, is sauntering along the brook. He at least is one male without remembrances. She puts her arm across his shoulders. Speaking a little breathlessly, she says let's run—you know, I'll bet you catch crayfish in the brook. When I was a little girl I did that too. You step into the brook, the water gives you a lukewarm tickle, the crayfish are quite cool when you touch them and when you drop them into your basket they whisper so.

Thus, Freudian, aqueous overtones are suggested. With an almost painful smile Kurt turns deep red. The touch of a woman's arms on his shoulders, the soft tinkle of her braclets, the powerful aroma of her orchid perfume, all of that bewilders him no end.

Still another pause enables the party to reassemble about Princess Adelheid, who proposes that they wait for the moon. Natures provides a multisensory conclusion to scene seven:

Es dunkelte bereits stark. Die Juninacht brach an mit ihrer wunderlichen Dämmerung, in der wir das Land wie durch graue Glasscheiben sehen, der Bach begann zu dampfen, von der Wiese kam ein feuchtes Wehen und brachte das starke, süße Duften der blühenden Gräser und des blühenden Klees mit. In den Saatfeldern huben die Wachteln zu schnarren an, und ringsum im Grase ließen Feldgrillen sich vernehmen, aber zögernd und abgebrochen, als wollten sie ihre Geigen stimmen. (270)

It is rare for Keyserling to permit even the suggestion of a comment by the author.

Initially scene eight reinforces the cessation of conversation. But then old Baron Lundberg, as before, works his chair a little closer to Ria in order to resume his musing about beautiful singers long dead. Keyserling regularly exploits this penchant of the aged. His conversational homerun touches, in indirect discourse, a few bases which, as usual, serve to keep the participants actively vivid. Thus, the princess tells Frau von Landen "ein wenig klagend" something ironically trivial. The others lapse into silence but make an effort to listen within themselves to the sweet tension inherent in the June evening. Some sigh. All have a feeling of missing something, perhaps an excitement moving through the twilight which ignores them as if some divine festival were being celebrated to which they are not invited. The erotic symbolism takes a concrete form as Ria feels a hand caressing her foot. Dismayed, she withdraws her foot, surmising that the teaser has to be the chamberlain. Ria feels so strange, she would like to cry, the summer evening affects her so powerfully, she too would be a part of this nature—mighty, whispering, and secure—whose every member—safe, happy, and peaceful—sings out its song of love. Yes, she yearns to belong, yet feels so greatly excluded with the restless torment and unclarity of her own life.

It is high time for the obvious request, which the princess couches in politely oblique terms. I suppose, Fräulein Riviera, that singing outside in the evening is not good for your voice? Before replying Ria thinks, yes, singing, that could release me! And so the singer begins:

Anfangs flatterten die Töne wie mühsam und unsicher in die Dunkelheit hinein, als fürchteten sie sich vor der Weite, in die sie hinaus sollten, unendlich einsam und schmerzlich klangen sie, dann aber erstarkten sie, wurden sicher und voll. Es tat Ria unendlich wohl, die Qual ihrer Seele, all das Dumpfe und Schwüle, all das Wunde und Gebrochene, ihre Begehrlichkeit und ihre Hoffnung in die Nacht hinauszurufen, in die Töne hineinzulegen und sie als Boten ihrer Sehnsucht durch die kühle, duftende Ferne hinauszusenden, damit sie sich im Nebel, in dem Wehen rein badeten und Kinder der Sommernacht würden. Ganz fern auf der Wiese erwachte eine Stimme, dort sang oder rief jemand. Es war einer jener langgezogenen, weichen Töne, wie sie auf dem Lande durch die Nacht irren, und diese fremde Stimme, die der ihren begegnete, sich ihr anschloß, diese Gefährtin der Dämmerung, sie tröstete Ria, es war, als nähme sie die Einsamkeit von ihr, die eben noch so bitter sie bedrückt. Dann plötzlich ging der Mond auf, riesengroß und rot stand er fast gewaltsam über dem bleichen Lande. Die Sängerin schwieg. (271-272)

It is not unusual for a Keyserlingian character under pressure to seek relief in music. One thinks of Gertrud in *Abendliche Häuser*. Again we find an authorial intrusion which seems a little gauche as set against the potent lyricism of the passage. The occurrence of *und* pairs is noteworthy. The dramatic climax of the aria complemented by the sudden appearance of the red moon provide the scene with an impressive finale. The climactic appear-

146

ance of a red moon at an outdoor party also has a counterpart in *Abendliche Häuser.*

For a while all remain very quiet. Then the introductory silence of the ninth scene is punctured by a Keyserlingian contrast. Countess Reichenau calls:

"Der Prinzessin ist schlecht geworden." Da fuhr alles auf. Ein wirres Durcheinander entstand, nach dem Wagen wurde gerufen, die Frauen riefen nach ihren Männern, eilig, ängstlich, als müßten sie sie vor etwas schützen. Malwina nahm Oswalds Arm: "Nein, solch ein Singen mag ich nicht", sagte sie, "man fühlt sich ja dabei wie—wie—nackt." (272)

The hasty rhythm of the passage underlines the turmoil.

By contrast again Ria would prefer to be alone for a moment. To further this wish she walks out onto the meadow toward the moon. Behind her she hears Malwina's excited voice calling Kurt. And then Ria comes upon Kurt lying crying beside an alder shrub. Kneeling beside him she asks what he is doing. Nothing, he replies, with an angry look. Ria persists. But you're crying—why—because of my singing? A strange excitement flashes over his pale face. Well—I don't know—what was it that you were singing? Countess Reichenau said you were singing love and Mama said people shouldn't sing like that. The boy continues passionately. Do you know that they're all against you, everyone of them? You should hear the way they talk about you. But me—I'm on your side.

Pausing, the singer gives her tired, distressed smile. Well, I don't care then, if you're on my side. The study ends with a final dynamism as Ria kisses the boy's tear-filled eyes.

NOTES

[1] This study was presented in condensed form 10 October 1969 at the Mountain Interstate Foreign Language Conference meeting in Asheville, North Carolina.

[2] Although *Landpartie* was not published until 1918 (in *Neue deutsche Erzähler*, Julius Sandmeier, ed. [Berlin: Furche-Verlag], pp. 259-273), its content and style suggest that it was written shortly after 1900. All references are to this edition.

[3] For more detailed accounts of Keyserling's background and work see my introduction to *Harmonie* (New York: The Odyssey Press, 1964), and the afterwords in modern reissues of Keyserlingian narratives by Baron Otto von Taube, ed., *Schwüle Tage und andere Erzählungen* (New York: Manesse Verlag, 1954) and Richard Brinkmann, ed., *Am Südhang* (Stuttgart: Reclam, 1963). Ernst Heilborn's introduction, "Eduard Graf Keyserling. Sein Wesen und sein Werk," in vol. I of the *Gesammelte Erzählungen* (Berlin: S. Fischer Verlag, 1922), remains one of the best. This four-volume collection does not include *Landpartie*.

[4] A brief but pertinent discussion of narrative openings, among other elements, during the period of impressionism is presented by Wolfdietrich Rasch, "Eine Beobachtung zur Form der Erzählung um 1900. Das Problem des Anfangs erzählender Dichtung," in *Stil- und Formprobleme in der Literatur. Vorträge des VII. Kongresses der Internationalen Vereinigung für moderne Sprachen und Literaturen in Heidelberg*, Paul Böckmann, ed. (Heidelberg: Carl Winter Universitätsverlag, 1959), pp. 448-453.

5 "Man sprach von dem silbrigen Nebel über Keyserlings Werk, aber das ist nicht ein Nebel, der verschleiert, sondern einer, in dem das Licht vibriert. Schwüle Tage, und die Sonne spielt über den bleichen schimmernden Blättern, und die weiße Schleppe der Dame streicht seidig über den glitzernden Kies. Der Lichteindruck entscheidet. Keyserling ist Pleinairist." — Ernst Heilborn, p. 25 (see note three, above).

6 Fritz Löffler, in his dissertation, *Das epische Schaffen Eduard von Keyserlings* (Munich, 1928), p. 6, says, "Das stärkste epische Talent des malerischen Impressionismus [Keyserling], das die leuchtendsten Farben in Worte einzufangen verstand, war ein Erblindender und Blinder."

7 "Aus nervös empfundenen und impressionistisch vermittelten Landschaftsregungen ersteht Atmosphäre um die Menschen. Das ist es, und in dieser silbrigen, zitternden Luft, durch die hindurch man die Geschehnisse sieht, werden Menschen, ihre Wünsche, Empfindungen und Schicksale eins mit der Landschaft, die sie empfängt." — Ernst Heilborn, p. 15 (see note three, above).

79 Personen:
Character Relationships in Schnitzler's
Der Junge Medardus

RICHARD H. ALLEN

Writing of the première of Arthur Schnitzler's *Der junge Medardus* at the Burgtheater on November 24, 1910, the theater critic Ludwig Klinenberger remarks: "Der Theaterzettel verzeichnet 79 Personen. Alles, was Beine hat, muß im Burgtheater mittun, und selbst diese personalgesegnete Bühne kann sich nur helfen, indem sie von dem nämlichen Darsteller zwei voneinander zeitlich getrennte Rollen darstellen läßt."[1] The play, written to commemorate the battle of Aspern in 1809, is not only the author's most "heavily populated" drama, but is also his longest, with five acts and a prologue (*Vorspiel*). The work has received relatively little scholarly attention; those critics who have dealt with it have frequently questioned its essential unity. The purpose of this study is to approach the drama from the viewpoint of character and character relationships. This will involve first an identification of the principal characters and their interconnections in preliminary form, then a more detailed discussion of both principal and secondary character interrationships, and finally a pointing out of some connections between these and the many "milieu-characters" that appear on the stage. I believe that such an approach to the drama will suggest a considerably higher degree of internal unity in the work than has been hitherto assumed.

In viewing the drama as a whole we can discover several spheres of action that are interconnected in the person of Medardus. First and foremost there is the history of the title-figure, whose fate it is to die for what he *would do*, but does not succeed in doing: destroying the tyrant Napoleon. Indeed, if one were to read only the first scene of the prologue and the final scene of the play, it might appear that Medardus' intention has remained fixed and unswerving throughout. His oath to the Austrian emperor was accompanied by "einen besondern Schwur... im Andenken an unsern Vater, den ich zu rächen habe." (39)[2] And at the end of the play, as he sits in prison, his fate depends only on whether he will give up this same private vow. He does not and reaffirms it publicly to Rapp, Napoleon's general: "Und so schwör' ich denn, wenn jemals die Möglichkeit sich mir böte, ich würde Napoleon töten. Vater und Oheim verlor ich durch ihn...." (213) But between the beginning and the end of the play there is a "vast domain" of events and characters which both buffet Medardus' intentions to the breaking point and tend to make of him at times a background figure.

There is the Valois intrigue and its frustration, there is the Eschenbacher tragedy, there is the "environment" of Vienna in 1809, and finally there is the Medardus-Helene love affair which seems to overshadow the Medardus-Napoleon relationship. Moreover, Medardus' presence on stage tends to become less frequent and more incidental during the course of the play (excepting the final scenes). This "tendency toward recession" most clearly begins in III, i, where Medardus appears as the dazed lover of Helene; his uncle's execution in IV, ii, briefly rouses him ("Es ist der Mühe wert zu leben, Mutter!" 177), but Helene's subsequent proposal that he work for the Valois party against the French tyrant only serves to return him to his ineffective and confused state (IV, iii). If Schnitzler had intended Medardus to be the dominant figure in the play, then those critics are quite correct who propose a radical cutting of the Eschenbacher events, a reduction of the Valois material, and a general freeing of Medardus from his Viennese environment. Not so, however, if Medardus does not in fact emerge as the sole principal and central figure.

Hofmannsthal suggests that Helene together with Medardus constitute the protagonists of the play ("Träger" and "Trägerin"), and that the love tragedy depicted is strong enough to allow Schnitzler to dispense with the historical events of 1809;[3] the irony here, of course, is that the play was written to commemorate just these events! Minor calls Helene a modern Judith, strong-willed, and goes on to say: "Sie ist zweifellos die interessanteste Gestalt in dem ganzen Stück: herzlos und doch immer verliebt, kalt im Empfinden und heiß in der Leidenschaft und dabei von eiserner Willenskraft... eine Figur wie die Adelheid in Götz."[4] If Helene is a (frustrated) Judith at the end, she is a Lady Macbeth in the middle, for whom her father's dream of a return to the French throne is all-important. Perhaps the key to her character is Minor's term *Willenskraft*, which enables her simultaneously to fall in love with the lowly Medardus and yet to remain undeterred in her resolution to restore the house of Valois (a resolution first seen in her decision to marry the Marquis for the sake of an heir). In III, ii, she persuades the distraught Medardus to leave the Valois premises peacefully, only to later recall him for a rendezvous on her own wedding night (III, iv).

In a letter to Schnitzler Brandes writes "sehr fein ist die schwache Andeutung einer geistigen Verwandtschaft zwischen Helene und Napoleon,"[5] and Hofmannsthal speaks of the "höchst geistreich verwendeten, occulten Nachbarschaft der dämonischen Napoléon-Figur."[6] Kapp calls the portrayal of Napoleon, a character who is only named, but who does not appear on the stage, a masterpiece of indirect characterization: "In dem richtigen Gefühl, daß der Anblick des Gewaltigen keine gleichstarke Wirkung erzielen würde, vermeidet es der Dichter, den Kaiser selbst auf die Bühne zu stellen, wir ahnen nur seine übermenschliche Größe."[7] Specht goes one step further and calls the French emperor the real protagonist, "der bewegende Motor des Dramas," who remains invisible and yet of whom we are conscious every minute of the play: "Ich weiß kein Napoleonstück, in dem man ihn so überlebensgroß und beherrschend spürt wie in dieser Historie, in der er unsichtbar bleibt."[8] It is evident from Schnitzler's original choice of historical material, the story of the would-be assassin Friedrich Staps, that the play was initially conceived of as the chronicle of an assassination attempt in the spirit of *in tyrannos*. Without Napoleon there could have been no Staps-Medardus figure. On the other hand, without Helene in the play—an equally monumental figure and counterbalance to Napoleon (Judith-Holofernes)—there could have been no external reason for Medardus' vacillation and the portrayal of him as a kind of modern Hamlet.

Thus there emerges the configuration of a "triangle" of principal characters: Medardus, Helene, and Napoleon. Viewed historically, Specht is right; Napoleon must be placed at the apex, with his life doubly threatened by the Viennese populace (Medardus) and by the French émigrés (Helene). But viewed dramatically, i.e., as the author has written the play, the events are seen from the vantage point of the populace (excepting the Valois scenes) in the person of Medardus; the latter is "doubly threatened" by the house of Valois (first by François, the seducer of his sister, then by Helene) and by Napoleon. Seen as a heroic tragedy, then, the strong-willed Helene is positioned against her would-be defamer (Medardus), on the one hand, and the sole obstacle to her overweening ambition, Napoleon, on the other.

Hofmannsthal's comments suggest that Eschenbacher might be construed as the protagonist of a tragedy within a tragedy. He writes: "Es wäre zu erwägen, ob man nicht viel gewänne, wenn man mit roher Hand die Eschenbacher-Tragödie ganz wegschnitte. Gewiß, sie gibt einiges schwer entbehrliches (contrastmäßig); aber sie kostet unendlich viel Zeit, Nerven, Aufnahmskraft."[9] Coupling this with Minor's characterization of Eschenbacher as both "ein politischer Raisonneur" and "das eigentliche Sprachrohr des Dichters,"[10] then we have the rather unique situation of a raisonneur who meets a tragic fate. Hofmannsthal's term *contrastmäßig* suggests poising the saddler's quiet heroism against Medardus' somewhat declamatory mediocrity (Medardus as the modern anti-hero). Indeed, there is no little justification for seeing the "Viennese protagonist" of the play not in Medardus alone, but in the complex Medardus-Eschenbacher (*Held-Antiheld*). (In a similar and analogous fashion, we can view the *Herzog* and Helene together as the bearers of the Valois thrust.) Such a conception would make the Eschenbacher story quite integral to the whole.

Considering now the interrelationships of the principal characters in more detail, we have already noted Brandes' linking of Napoleon and Helene; we have also associated Medardus and Helene as would-be assassins of the French emperor. Ratislav writes: "Medardus und Helene richten ihren Dolch gegen Napoleon, aber keiner trifft ihn, in unerschütterlicher Größe steht er am

151

Schlusse da."[11] Further connections among the trio can be cited. In II, i, Medardus rises from his (near-) deathbed to present his thanks to Helene (this involves first scaling a garden wall); yet he is still possessed of enough vitality to be able to spend a night of love with her. Eschenbacher later comments on this youthful energy: "So ein junger Mensch hat eine wunderbare Lebenskraft in sich... begräbt... seine Schwester, erledigt... eine ritterliche Angelegenheit und hat... noch Laune übrig für ein zärtlich Abenteuer." (106-107) In a similar fashion Assalagny admires Napoleon's unusual vitality (the French emperor has just sent a wedding gift to Helene und invited the nuptial pair to Schönbrunn): "Wenn man denkt, daß Bonaparte zwischen zwei Schlachten zu solchen Späßen Zeit und Laune findet... so möchte man ihn beinah bewundern." (140) In the same scene Rapp comments on Helene's voice and eyes ("welche bewundernswerte Macht"; 139). It is Nerina who later associates her mistress' power and vitality with that of Napoleon: "Und denken Sie, Doktor Assalagny, da merkte ich, daß in ihren Augen ganz derselbe drohende, starre Glanz war wie in denen des Kaisers. *Als wenn sie Geschwister wären.*" (186; italics added) The two are indeed related in a "sibling" fashion as standing in mutual dramatic opposition to Medardus. On the other hand, it is Medardus' initial Napoleon-like vitality (that Helene mistakes for strength of will), which attracts her to the youth so far below her station. In an almost Hebbelian sense the two powerful individuals, Helene and Napoleon, seem destined to collide; the highest irony is, of course, that Medardus, now confused and misdirected, should be the one to prevent this collision course through his impulsive stabbing of Helene.

Another character, the *Herzog* of Valois, suggests certain parallels to Medardus. Seeing himself as the "chosen one" ("ich als Erkorner meines Volkes"; 194), the *Herzog* here recalls Medardus, who believes himself to be—and is believed by those near to him to be—Austria's savior; in his own words his hand was "ausersehn" to assassinate Napoleon (202). Moreover, just as the *Herzog* is characterized already in the prologue as "ein armer, doppelt blinder Narr" by Anna Berger (33), so is Medardus repeatedly called "Narr," "Tor," "Wirrkopf," and "toll" during the course of the play. Just as the *Herzog* is made a fool of (*genarrt*) by Assalagny's false reports, so is Medardus betrayed (*genarrt*) by Helene ("Ich bin der Betrogene, der Genarrte, Etzelt." 125). And just as the *Herzog*'s hopes for a restoration of the house of Valois to the French throne are dashed first by his son's suicide, then by Helene's murder, so too Medardus fails in his "noble destiny" (*hohe Sendung*). Etzelt's epitath, which summarizes this failure, could equally well be applied to the *Herzog*: "Gott wollte ihn zum Helden schaffen, der Lauf der Dinge machte einen Narren aus ihm." (215) Neither the *Herzog* nor Medardus is willing to come to terms with his respective environment (*das Unabänderliche*). In spite of their difference in age both characters are essentially romantic visionaries, whose high undertakings are pinioned by the reality of events ("der Lauf der Dinge"), a reality which finds its dramatic personification in Napoleon for the *Herzog* and in Napoleon-Helene for Medardus. Several minor characters likewise hold to impossible plans. Medardus' sister Agathe and Helene's brother François flee from the world into the Danube when they perceive that they shall not be able to wed. Helene says of her brother that he was "nicht für diese Welt geschaffen" (73); like Medardus he forgot his "high destiny" because of a woman. Anna Berger also persists in an impossible love for Medardus; her subsequent death while serving as a war nurse has overtones of a mortally broken heart. The recounted story of Georg Käsmann, who shoots himself because his lot fell out to remain at home serves as the most extreme example of a character's refusal to adapt himself to *das Unabänderliche*.

But these characters, "nicht für diese Welt geschaffen," have a number of counterparts in self-effacing, realistic types. Principal of these is *Meister* Eschenbacher, who, as has been suggested, probably speaks for the author. He is realistic, practical, and sceptical; Specht calls him "ein Feind der großen Worte."[12] He is an enemy of the pseudo-heroic and questions whether any dying is rational as long as there remains a task to be done: "Das Sterben ist keine Kunst. Am Ende trifft's jeder. Wer's aber ohne Not tut, ist kein Held ... ist ein Narr, Etzelt!" (151-152). (It could be questioned whether Medardus dies for any other reason than for the sake of affecting a heroic stance.) Eschenbacher accepts his own death heroically in the best sense; to his "spiritual heir" (Etzelt) he wills the task of punishing the villainous Wachshuber. The younger Etzelt as second raisonneur is the calm voice of reason throughout the play. Although—like Theobald in Hebbel's *Agnes Bernauer* —he is in love with Agathe, he accepts the news of her alleged engagement stoically. Like Eschenbacher he is properly modest ("Man macht sich nützlich, wie man kann." 118); he remains a loyal friend to Medardus up to the end.

Medardus' mother, *Frau* Franziska Klähr, can be regarded in certain respects as the feminine counterpart to her brother, Eschenbacher (it is interesting to note that both have *helle Augen*). Like her brother she too is critical of her seemingly decadent fellow citizens: Napoleon "könnte sein Haupt ruhig in den Schoß von jedem Wiener Bürger legen." (180) But unlike the realistic Eschenbacher she tends to be more optimistic about the future: "Ich bin guten Muts für Medardus und für Agathe... und für unser Land. Ja, mir ist wahrlich, als wären die Tage der Vergeltung nahe." (48) Like Helene, however, she is strong-willed and seeks to dominate Medardus. Specht finds her to be "eine ergreifendere Gestalt" than most of the pompous heroines of the classical theater,[13] and Derré concludes that she is quite unique among Schnitzler's characters: "Cette étonnante figure n'offre guère de ressemblance avec les habituelles créations de Schnitzler. Simple et forte, elle semble appartenir à un autre âge, celui des légendes antiques ou des contes populaires, et l'on est d'abord tenté de la ranger au côté des mères de

Sparte ou des courageuses épouses de Weinsberg." The same critic further points out that *Frau* Klähr's main dramatic function is to remind her son of his grand destiny.[14] One might venture to say that as a character she not only instills but serves as the "extra-Medardus" objectification of the Viennese hatred for Napoleon (note her words in IV, iii: "Das Urteil über ihn ist längst gesprochen. Wer die Sendung in sich fühlt—darf es vollführen." 181), just as Helene objectifies the same émigré loathing. But the latter character is alo an independent agent in her own right.

Further on the Valois side *Doktor* Assalagny constitutes the émigré raisonneur, an analogue to Eschenbacher. He perceives the futility of the *Herzog*'s plans and speaks of the *Rollen* that the Valois hangers-on have to play. Like his Viennese counterpart he is also a kind of a philosopher: "Man könnte einer Krone entgegengeträumt, ja, man könnte sie errungen haben—und an einem späten Tag entdecken, daß der reichste Augenblick von allen einer war, da man in einem Frühlingsgarten nach Schmetterlingen haschte." (154) Caillard, according to Rennault, could have prevented François' suicide by attending on him better; thus he has not played his "Etzelt-rôle" well (Caillard is also the first to desert the *Herzog* for Napoleon).

Erzherzog Karl, like Napoleon, does not appear on the stage, but his spiritual presence is felt by the Viennese. Föderl finds it to be a terrible thing that Karl should not arrive in time to rescue Vienna from the French; Bargetti explains that the only miracle that could turn the course of the battle would be the Austrian archduke's arrival. For want of such a leader, one might say, the Viennese are forced to seek out one from their own ranks; but their tyrant-killer and savior, Medardus Klähr, disappoints them just as much as their archduke, who does not arrive.

Turning now to the milieu-characters, the citizens of Vienna, whose dramatic rôles are secondary to incidental, one is struck by the author's ability to breathe life into almost all of them. Specht calls it "eine fast Balzacsche Kraft der fruchtbaren Menschenformung, weniger robust, manchmal anämischer, aber von gleicher unwiderruflicher Glaubhaftigkeit und von denkwürdigerer Geistigkeit dazu."[15] Even such a minor character as *Arzt* Büdinger comes vividly alive early in the play as he tells of his domestic misfortunes. Granted the credibility of these minor characters, the question is whether they have any real function in the play, or whether, as Minor maintains, they merely serve a disconnected historical background: "Wir haben also keine dramatische Historie, sondern ein Schnitzlerisches Drama und die Geschichte nebeneinander; zu einem Ganzen haben sich Drama und Geschichte nicht verbunden."[16] Nevertheless, there are a number of character connections between *Drama* and *Geschichte*, which can only be suggested here in rather general categories.

Early in the prologue *Frau* Klähr tells her brother of the widespread enthusiasm in Vienna; later Caillard remarks that the citizens of Vienna "sind so guter Dinge, als wenn es sich um die Vorbereitungen zu einem

Fest handelte." (78) In its extreme form this same enthusiasm leads the student Bernberg to say that he would be even willing to serve the French ("Wo ist mein Vaterland? Dort, wo sie meine Gaben und meine Kräfte nützen können!" 57); or it is seen in the injunction of the *Uralter Herr:* "Schlagts ihn tot!... Was hat er denn angestellt?" (206). (We have already noted Käsmann's suicide, another case of "excessive patriotism.") More typically, this is the patriotism of the Collin songs of the prologue: "Und wer nun Wort und Schwur nicht hält, Der bleibt ein feiger Wicht." (51) The heroic death of Bargetti on the ramparts, the summary execution of Peter Tell for disciplining an obtrusive French officer, and the quiet heroism of Eschenbacher mentioned above—all of these serve as models to be followed by the aspiring young patriot. Whereas this context of patriotism serves to give credibility to Medardus' own intense belief that he shall perform great deeds, the deaths of his compatriots foreshadow and prefigure his own decision to die at Napoleon's hands.

If patriotism, feigned or real, is one side of the Viennese character depicted in the play, the other side is "spectatorship," i.e., the pleasure of being bystander to some impressive event or sight. Anna Berger fondly reminisces about the pretty French uniforms that she saw during the earlier occupation, but it is her father, Johann Nepomuk Berger, who epitomizes the "Ich hab' zug'schaut"-propensity of so many of the characters. As Agathe says, "Es ist eine gute Zeit für ihn! Neuigkeiten Stunde für Stunde." (30) Even the death of his daughter (which serves him rather as an object for declamation than it does inspire grief) gives his curiosity new justification: "Und ich sag' halt: wenn man schon weiterlebt nach so einem Malheur, da gibt's nur eins: Schaun, daß man auf andre Gedanken kommt." (197-198) For the citizens of Vienna this delight in being spectator finds its culmination in the rampart scene of the third act and in the *Schönbrunn* garden scene of the fifth. On both occasions the citizens turn out *en masse,* among which are the *eleganter Herr* and the *elegante Frau,* these coming in the spirit of visitors to a theater. On the first occasion the granddaughter of the *Uralter Herr* is the innocent victim of French shrapnel; she is survived by the old man who has seen more of life than anyone and suggests a kind of eternal spectator. On the second occasion Helene is the less-innocent victim of Medardus, who has been inflamed by false reports about her; before catching sight of Helene Medardus himself had been but one of the spectators waiting to catch a glimpse of Napoleon, and then, perhaps, finally to act out his resolution. Ultimately and tragically the Viennese along with Medardus are condemned to be no more than "spectators to the conquerer."

A third aspect of the Viennese character depicted is the transmutation it undergoes because of the war and subsequent occupation. Plank is the only one of the student recruits to have experienced war first-hand; as such he is able to diagnose his compatriots' unbounded enthusiasm for the first battle: "Und wißt ihr, was euer Geschrei und eure Lustigkeit und eure Begeisterung im Grunde bedeutet? Verschlagene Angst, nichts weiter, Höllenangst." (53) *Herr* and *Frau* Kreuzhartinger, who flee to Vienna from the neighboring Petersdorf, seek the temporary security of the city that the Viennese take for granted. Gretel is killed on the ramparts and an old citizen grows weary and becomes indifferent to the outcome of the war: "Mir is gleich. Zwei Söhne hab' ich g'habt, der eine ist in Regenburg gefallen, den zweiten haben s' in Aspern zum Krüppel g'schossen. Mir is gleich." (196) But Medardus is not indifferent to the deaths of those around him; the ignominious death of his father causes him to swear a vow of death to the emperor, Agathe's suicide leads him to swear to disgrace Helene publicly, the death of Eschenbacher induces him to reiterate his vow against the emperor. For Medardus the casulties of war are the most personal and immediate of any of those depicted in the play: father, sister, uncle. In the horrors of the times his goals vacillate, fluctuate, and become diffused.

Significantly, Schnitzler chose to have the "Bastei Szene" (i.e., III, i) preprinted in the *Neue Freie Presse* in 1910 as the public's first exposure to the play.[17] Of all the scenes in the drama it is both the most macrocosmic and the least Medardus-centered. Yet in the patriotism and enthusiasm, the love for the spectacular, and the horrors and effects of war portrayed here, we see the real Viennese protagonist, who transcends the *Bürgersohn*, Medardus Klähr, to become "der junge Medardus," the embodiment of the Viennese people with all of their human strengths and weaknesses. Torn between hatred and love, he ultimately succumbs to the inevitable and dies for the sake of his high intention. He has been overcome by Helene and Napoleon, yet in a strange, roundabout way he has "overcome" them.

NOTES

[1] Ludwig Klinenberger, "Von den Wiener Theatern 1910/11," *Bühne und Welt*, XIII, 1 (1910), 259.

[2] Citations from the play in my text are by page to: Arthur Schnitzler, *Die Dramatischen Werke*, Bd. II (Frankfurt a. M.: S. Fischer, 1962).

[3] *Hugo von Hofmannsthal — Arthur Schnitzler Briefwechsel*, ed. Therese Nickl and Heinrich Schnitzler (Frankfurt a. M., 1964), p. 247.

[4] J. Minor, "Schnitzlers 'Der junge Medardus'," *Österreichische Rundschau*, XXV, (1910), 393-394.

[5] *Georg Brandes und Arthur Schnitzler: Ein Briefwechsel*, ed. Kurt Bergel (Bern, 1956), p. 98.

[6] *Hofmannsthal — Schnitzler Briefwechsel*, p. 247.

[7] Julius Kapp, *Arthur Schnitzler* (Leipzig, 1912), p. 134.

[8] Richard Specht, *Arthur Schnitzler: Der Dichter und sein Werk, Eine Studie* (Berlin, 1922), pp. 304-305.

[9] *Hofmannsthal — Schnitzler Briefwechsel*, p. 247.

[10] Minor, 392.

[11] Josef Karl Ratislav, *Arthur Schnitzler: Eine Studie* (Hamburg, 1911), p. 40.

[12] Specht, p. 307.   [13] Specht, p. 307.

[14] Françoise Derré, *L'oeuvre d'Arthur Schnitzler: Imagerie viennoise et problèmes humains* (Paris, 1966), p. 311.

[15] Specht, p. 304.   [16] Minor, 391.

[17] *Neue Freie Presse*, Nr. 16378 (27. März 1910), 32-39.

Time in the Lyric

HERMAN SALINGER

Well may the reader of poetry, as he sits with his back to the lamp, the light streaming over his shoulder, remark to himself, in the Marvellian mode:

> But at my back I always hear
> Time's wingèd chariot hurrying near...

Poetry, along with but also over and beyond all forms of language, is rhythmic in essence, is of the very stuff and matter of Time. It takes place within the dimension, the fluidum of Time, as Lessing made clear in his *Laokoon* over two hundred years ago (1766), pointing out for his contemporaries and for posterity (now, in a film age, inclined perhaps to doubt his simplifications) "die Grenzen der Mahlerey und Poesie," as his subtitle announced.

The Oxford Book of German Verse opens with a 6-line anonymous love lyric of the 12th Century: "Du bist mein, ich bin dein." In the original mediaeval German:

> Dû bist mîn, ich bin dîn:
> des solt dû gewis sîn.
> du bist beslozzen
> in mînem herzen:
> verlorn ist daz slüzzelîn:
> dû muost immer drinne sîn.[1]

This poem, known to millions of Germans and German students over the decades and centuries, has a "foreverness" about its simple theme of love that needs no comment.

The late Professor William Frederic Giese of the University of Wisconsin began his anthology of *French Lyrics in English Verse* with an *aubade* from the 12th Century Provençal whose refrain he renders:

> Ah God! That dawn should come so soon![2]

The Oxford Book of English Verse starts off with the 13th Century "Cuckoo Song":

Sumer is icumen in...[3]

Everywhere the same time-consciousness, whether it be the German poet describing a present state of love that shall ideally continue forever, the Provençal poet fighting time's passage because it brings parting, or the hearty realistic English singer welcoming the summer.

This is hardly to be wondered at in a civilization whose basic Book opens with a phrase that at once answers the question "when?"—namely: "In the Beginning." Reference books tell us that the Hebrew title of the Book of Genesis is taken from that opening phrase so that the book itself is called in Hebrew "In the Beginning."

Time-consciousness is therefore not—as so often asserted—confined to the mediaeval and modern man. Nor is it strictly Judaeo-Christian. An Egyptian hymn from the Second Millenium B.C. begins each of its five short stanzas with the line:

Today death stands before me.[4]

Time-consciousness belongs neither to one civilization nor to one century but to the poets of all civilizations and all centuries. Nevertheless, there are variations and refinements of this time sense, varying directly with the sensitivity of the poet, with his intelligence and the degree of his self-consciousness. It does not surprise us in Shakespeare's Sonnets to find him confessing (long before C. K. Scott Moncrieff appropriated the words for his English translation of Marcel Proust) to a conscious pursuit of *temps perdu*:

When to the sessions of sweet silent thought
I summon up remembrance of things past...[5]

Whether in the ballad, with its past tense ["Marie Hamilton's to the kirk gane"][6] or the historical present ["The king sits in Dunfermline town"][7] or in the lyric (with its "emotion recollected in tranquillity"), Time is the poet's god whose only true prophet is the verb.

Rather than catalogue various kinds of time (basically only past, present and future plus variations and complications, such as using the present as a point of vantage for looking at a future, which then suddenly lifts us out of our present selves toward itself)[8]—let us look instead at various poets. Their way of handling time will be found to be at least very highly characteristic of their art and of themselves individually; it will show them for what they basically are. For instance, Lamartine. In "Le Lac" (1817) he bemoans the passage of time, the loss brought by one year, reminding the reader-hearer that his lady, one year before, had "poured her voice upon the silent night" and had admonished Time:

158

"O temps, suspends ton vol!"

Now the poet, revisiting the glimpses, asks:

Ne pourrons-nous jamais sur l'océan des âges
Jeter l'ancre un seul jour?

but he is asking this of a time which is shoreless and in constant state of flux:

".... le temps n'a point de rive;
Il coule, et nous passons!"[9]

The romantic task of this tripartite poem (1: the poet's return to the lake where he last saw his belovèd; 2: the flashback to her speech of a year ago; 3: the admonition to the future to say: "They have loved!" ["Ils ont aimé."]) —all of this cannot be accomplished in less than thirteen quatrains or fifty-two lines. So that Time takes time. This is not a hit-and-run poem, yet probably brief enough to "get in under the wire" of Edgar Allen Poe's dictum, enunciated in "The Poetic Principle" some years later, to the effect that "that degree of excitement which would entitle a poem to be so called at all cannot be sustained throughout a composition of any great length... [since] all excitements are, through a psychal necessity, transient."[10]

Shelley's "Lament," on the other hand, sings:

O World! O Life! O Time
on whose last steps I climb,
trembling at that where I had stood before;
when will return the glory of your prime?
No more—Oh never more!

accomplishing the same romantic purpose in that one stanza of five lines as does Lamartine's more extended time treatment. Shelley, to be sure, drives his point home with another five-line stanza, restating that

Out of the day and night
A joy has taken flight.[11]

This brief ten-line poem qualifies, I think, as of the hit-and-run type of lyric. It must have delighted Poe.

Shakespeare expresses a similar feeling of lamentation within (and over) time by using two spatial adverbs to indicate that he stands, emotionally speaking, on the continental divide of the eternal present:

My grief lies onward and my joy behind.[12]

The desire for time to stand still reaches an odd kind of fulfillment in the "Ode on a Grecian Urn" by the abolition of time through the substitution of something plastic and space-occupying: what William Walsh has called "the vase's character of arrested and timeless perfection."[13] Keats has achieved, by his choice of subject—or is it object?—, an absence of time and, with this, "unheard music"—"ditties of no tone." He has transformed Shelley's "never more" into evermore:

> And, little town, thy streets for evermore
> Will silent be...[14]

This is something the *Marschallin* of Hugo von Hofmannsthal's *Rosenkavalier* would have liked to achieve: the arresting of time, but when she wanted to bring it about, she mechanically had all the clocks stopped: which does not seem to be the answer. She explains her feelings to her lover, so much younger than herself, this way:

> Die Zeit im Grund, Quinquin,
> Die Zeit, die ändert doch nichts an den Sachen.
> Die Zeit, die ist ein sonderbar Ding.
> Wenn man so hinlebt, ist sie rein gar nichts.
> Aber dann auf einmal, da spürt man nichts als sie.
> Sie ist um uns herum, sie ist auch in uns drinnen.
> In den Gesichtern rieselt sie,
> im Spiegel da rieselt sie,
> in meinen Schläfen fließt sie.
> Und zwischen mir und dir
> da fließt sie wieder, lautlos, wie eine Sanduhr.
> Oh, Quinquin! Manchmal hör' ich sie fließen—
> unaufhaltsam.
> Manchmal steh' ich auf mitten in der Nacht
> und laß die Uhren alle, alle stehn.
> Allein man muß sich auch vor ihr nicht fürchten.
> Auch sie ist ein Geschöpf des Vaters, der
> uns alle erschaffen hat.[15]

This is symbolism's answer—or one of her answers—from early in our century (1911). Stopping the clocks is acting out a symbolic gesture, a ritual.

> Sag' mir, wer einst die Uhren erfund,
> Die Zeitabteilung, Minute und Stund'?

Heinrich Heine exclaims in a poem published sixty-seven years earlier (in 1844): a kind of anachreontic little poem with an existentialist tinge, answering his own question with the proffered explanation:

Das war ein frierend trauriger Mann.
Er saß in der Winternacht und sann
Und zählte der Mäuschen heimliches Quicken
Und des Holzwurms ebenmäßiges Picken.¹⁶

The inventor of kisses, however, was glowing and happy. We draw the inference that kisses are—à la Catullus—the only true measure of living time. Heine is one of the most time-conscious writers of whom it can be said that he was a forerunner of the modern period; his historical sense is highly developed and highly articulate.

The same can be said for the dramatist Friedrich Hebbel whose place as a lyricist is perhaps underestimated still. Two poems come to mind: "Nachtgefühl" (1836) and "Sommerbild" (probably June of 1844)¹⁷ In the earlier poem he stands in present time undressing for bed; in such rapid succession that the effect is almost one of simultaneity, he thinks back to his childhood when his mother used to undress him to put him into his cradle and (the poet really says "or") he thinks ahead to the end of his life when the neighbors will undress him to prepare him for the grave:

> Wenn ich mich abends entkleide,
> Gemachsam, Stück für Stück,
> So tragen die müden Gedanken
> Mich vorwärts oder zurück.

> Ich denke der alten Tage,
> Da zog die Mutter mich aus;
> Sie legte mich still in die Wiege,
> Die Winde brausten ums Haus.

> Ich denke der letzten Stunde,
> Da werden's die Nachbarn tun;
> Sie senken mich still in die Erde,
> Dann werd' ich lange ruhn.

He sleeps and dreams but he does not know which dream: that of the mother and the cradle or the neighbors and the grave. Past and future are blended and blurred in a new way in the present: new because this is not the conscious level of the present but a timeless level in the deeper dream stratum:

> Schließt nun der Schlaf mein Auge,
> Wie träum' ich so oftmals das:
> Es wäre eins von beidem,
> Nur wüßt' ich selber nicht, was.

In the other poem, equally naturalistic, one might say, by virtue of the carefulness of the poet's observation but less harsh because given a more romantic presentation (and we use the adjective "romantic" in the very sense of the blending of time with beauty, producing that Chopinesque awareness of the perishability of beauty) Hebbel reproduces what one might call the atmospheric perspective of time:

Ich sah des Sommers letzte Rose stehn,
    Sie war, als ob sie bluten könne, rot;
Da sprach ich schaudernd im Vorübergehn:
    So weit im Leben, ist zu nah am Tod!

Es regte sich kein Hauch am heißen Tag,
    Nur leise strich ein weißer Schmetterling;
Doch, ob auch kaum die Luft ein Flügelschlag
    Bewegte, sie empfand es und verging.[18]

Could we not call this a purely psychological use of time, as contrasted with Lamartine's use of it as actual time: as a commodity which the poet uses up? If not psychological, then certainly symbolistic; it seems to point ahead to Hofmannsthal and even to the delicate sense of expectancy evoked by Paul Valéry's jugglery of time in the latter half of the exquisite poem "Les Pas":

Si, de tes levres avancées,
Tu prépares pour l'apaiser,
A l'habitant de mes pensées
La nourriture d'un baiser,

Ne hâte pas cet acte tendre,
Douceur d'être et de n'être pas,
Car j'ai vécu de vous attendre,
Et mon coeur n'était que vos pas.[19]

Here the heartbeat accompanies the steps; both measure time's approach in an unbearable suspension.

Time and space can, even "pre-Proustianly," closely relate to one another. How closely they are related can be illustrated by one of Eduard Mörike's best known lyrics: "Denk es, o Seele!"

Ein Tännlein grünet wo,
Wer weiß, im Walde,
Ein Rosenstrauch, wer sagt,
In welchem Garten?
Sie sind erlesen schon,
Denk es, o Seele,

162

Auf deinem Grab zu wurzeln
Und zu wachsen.

Zwei schwarze Rößlein weiden
Auf der Wiese,
Sie kehren heim zur Stadt
In muntern Sprüngen.
Sie werden schrittweis gehn
Mit deiner Leiche;
Vielleicht, vielleicht noch eh'
An ihren Hufen
Das Eisen los wird,
Das ich blitzen sehe!

Time, in the first stanza, is implied by space. The place of the fir-tree, the place of the rosebush are unknown, consequently remote—or felt to be so. As Wolfgang F. Taraba has pointed out,[20] the space scene becomes specific in the second stanza and, with it, the time, so that the fact of death and the future become potentially imminent.

Time, in its destructive effects, is negated by the father of the Symbolist movement in poetry, Charles Baudelaire,—on whom time ordinarily bears down with the merciless weight of ennui—in a poem such as "Une Charogne," where the putrified corpse of the present warns us that this is the future fate of all beauty; yet there is a future beyond the future, the poet telling his belovèd that, although she shall surely come to this, nevertheless she must speak thus "to this dire putrescence":

Alors, ô ma beauté! dites à la vermine
    Qui vous mangera de baisers,
Que j'ai gardé la forme et l'essence divine
    De mes amours décomposés![21]

The mind itself is here a kind of timeless Grecian urn.

So also Mallarmé, as the follower of Baudelaire, seemingly ignores time (time and time again!) to paint a scene like that in "À la nue accablante tu": a mysterious event which takes place nowhere but in the imagination and at no given time. It is the "sepulchral shipwreck" of an idea, of a human vision or hope.[22]

Contemporaneously, on the other hand, a romantic naturalist like Thomas Hardy is wondering at the repetitiousness of time and its mechanical involvement in the ineluctable cause-and-effect chain:[23]

Why do I go on doing these things?
Why not cease?

Is it that you are yet in this world of welterings
And unease,
And that, while so, mechanic repetitions please?

Hardy can get even more complicated in his time sense. In his poem "Afterwards"[24] he looks forward to a time when he will be taken out of the present. Will others then be reminded of his likes and dislikes and look backward? In this way, Hardy creates a kind of "future perfect" feeling and use of the time factor. Or he, too, annihilates it as one annihilates an enemy viâ a process of pure negation, reminiscent of Baudelaire's thwarting of Time's putrefaction of beauty, only here the negation is less religious, more philosophical—a term Hardy would have eschewed:[25]

So, Time,
Royal, sublime;
Heretofore held to be
Master and enemy,
Thief of my Love's adornings,
Despoiling her to scornings:—

The sound philosopher
Now sets him to aver
You are nought
But a thought
Without reality.[26]

The time sense is perhaps most acute and most pronounced in the case of the famous lyric trio Stefan George, Hugo von Hofmannsthal and Rainer Maria Rilke and countless examples come to mind. The problem can still bear a good deal of special investigation. To pick some of these examples at random, George's "Komm in den totgesagten park und schau" is autumnal in mood, almost static in motion: we enter, we look, the wind is tepid, the late roses are wilting but not quite wilted, we pick some, we kiss them and weave the wreath. Action is kept to a minimum because we are nearing (we sense this) the end of a portion of time, so that movement is slowed almost to a standstill. (Hebbel foreshadowed this delicate sensibility, I think, in the mood of "Sommerbild" and "Herbstbild" around the middle of his century.)

Hofmannsthal's "Terzinen über Vergänglichkeit" (whether we mentally translate as "transitoriness" or "mutability," the immediacy of the German word suffers a loss) express a timeless connection in the dimension or continuum of time between the poet's self and his ancestors, also between his earlier self of childhood and his selfhood in the here and now.

An early poem of Rainer Maria Rilke's speaks to these last points of relationship:[27]

Wenn die Uhren so nah
wie im eigenen Herzen schlagen,
und die Dinge mit zagen
Stimmen sich fragen:
Bist du da?—:

dann bin ich nicht der, der am Morgen erwacht,
einen Namen schenkt mir die Nacht,
den keiner, den ich am Tage sprach,
ohne tiefes Fürchten erführe—

Jede Türe
in mir gibt nach...

Und da weiß ich, daß nichts vergeht,
keine Geste und kein Gebet
(dazu sind die Dinge zu schwer),
meine ganze Kindheit steht
immer um mich her.
Niemals bin ich allein.
Viele, die vor mir lebten
und fort von mir strebten,
webten,
webten
an meinem Sein.

Und setz ich mich zu dir her
und sage dir leise: Ich litt—
hörst du?

     Wer weiß wer
     murmelt es mit.

This striking of the clocks in the poet's "own [i.e., very] heart" is possibly what the critics,—for example Professor Hugo Friedrich—mean by "inner time"[28]: a variable time, different at night from what it was in the morning or, so to speak, of variable density. It brings childhood back and reasserts its continuative nature, making us sense a connection with mysterious other presences who relive their lives within ours.

One of the most striking—and strikingly modern—of all the treatments of the time problem in recent lyric poetry occurs in Rudolf Hagelstange's *Ballade vom verschütteten Leben* (1953). There is an extensive lyric-reflective passage in the Seventh Canto, comprising almost the entire canto, which depicts two distinct types of time: measured and finite and earthly, on the one hand, and, on the other, the immeasurable subterranean time which very closely counterfeits eternity for the men buried in the rubbled bunker. This creates a basic symbolic difference which bears out Hagelstange's total intent in his 70-page epic of modern World War II and post-war man. What we call time up above ("Yesterday... Today... on the such-and-such") appears as something very different below:[29]

> Zeit—was ist hier oben die Zeit?
> "Gestern," sagst du und "Heute", "Am Soundsovielten"...
> "Zeit"—wie Zündhölzer rasch verbrennend,
> sauber geordnet, gezählt: ein jeder
> hat seine Zündholzschachtel.
> Tagesschicht, Nachtschicht, Sonntagsschicht,
> Sonderschicht, Opferschicht—
> Schicht um Schicht wird sie abgetragen,
> Stunde um Stunde verbrannt, die "Zeit"...

This, we learn, is the time that possesses us. The time we would like to have, this time "hides itself, squats in deserted rooms, sleeps in libraries." Metaphorically,

> Ein greises Fräulein
> spult sie im Altersheim auf. Ein Mönch hat
> ganze Ballen gestapelt; ein Zuchthaus
> ein Jahrtausend auf Vorrat.

Turning then to the other type of "time": that of the entombed men in the underground bunker, leading their buried life:

> Tick-Tack sagte auch unten die Zeit. Eintönig
> wiederholte die letzte Uhr ihre Lüge...
> Längst war der Faden gerissen,
> von dem sie, wie Theseus,
> Rückkehr erhofften und Rettung aus dem
> Labyrinthe der Nacht. Eine Weile
> liefen die Rädchen noch fort; dann stockte
> unwiderruflich das Werk, und schweigend
> trat aus dem Schweigen die ZEIT.

Then, finally, the contrast between the two time-types. First, "above: the trunk reaching toward its own crown,..."

> Oben
> strebte der Stamm in die Krone.
> Bittere Früchte, die Heilkraft selber,

166

streute sie aus... Zeit schien den meisten:
Warten auf bessere Tage, auf sicheres Schema.
Zeit war: Vergessen wollen und recht behalten.
Zeit war: Strafe, neue Verirrung, war Flüchten
aus der ZEIT in die Zeit...

Contrasting with this, the underground time, indeed the underground *of*
Time itself:

Hier unten
war sie Wunde, die brannte,
täglich strömendes Blut, nicht stillbar.
Jeder Herzschlag ein müder Hammer
auf die alten Gesetzestafeln. ZEIT war
da-sein und wissen
um die schneidende Fessel und wissen,
daß sie nur tiefer schnitte; war Fallen,
endlos,
in die Schwerkraft des Schicksals.

Surely, in some ways, we have come a long way from such a poem as Hermann Hesse's "Bei der Nachricht vom Tod eines Freundes," written in a
gentler time, perhaps, or was Hesse in 1930 just as fatalistic as Hagelstange in
the mid-1940's? Hesse wrote of the impermanence of "alles Vergängliche,"
quite in contrast to Hofmannsthal's feeling, by the way, in his tercets which
had so effectively, so beautifully evoked that rare sentiment of permanence
in the midst of transitoriness. According to Hesse:[30]

Schnell welkt das Vergängliche.
Schnell stieben die verdorrten Jahre davon.
Spöttisch blicken die scheinbar ewigen Sterne.

In uns innen der Geist allein
Mag unbewegt schauen das Spiel,
Ohne Spott, ohne Schmerz.
Ihm sind "vergängliche" und "ewig"
Gleich viel, gleich wenig...

Aber das Herz
Wehrt sich, glüht auf in Liebe,
Und ergibt sich, welkende Blume,
Dem unendlichen Todesruf,
Dem unendlichen Liebesruf.

For the poet, always, is looking for the redemptive. Hagelstange, too, at the end of his "Ballad of the Buried Life" foresees "light calling the unborn, the lost" in order that a future generation may beget "at last one single child of light."

Yet is this always true? Does this hold for all modern poets? Or are we entering a different stage: a stage of the destructive? Even in the much more romantic Hesse poem (not to speak of later poets) we feel a sovereign indifference to both transitoriness and eternity, since they seem coexistent and seem to be embodied in one act: the *Liebestod*.

Destruction? Dissolution? Yes, these too have a place in poetry, especially in the poetry of our age, the post-Auden phase of the Age of Anxiety, nowhere better expressed than in the work of the American Thomas Merton and the Welshman Dylan Thomas. Merton's "Senescente Mundo" expresses a sense of worldly doom counterbalanced, appropriately, by Christ's superior power of recreation:

> *Senescente mundo*, when the hot globe
> Shrivels and cracks...
>
> Toward that fiery day we run like crabs
> With our bad-tempered armor on...
>
> Yet in the middle of this murderous season
> Great Christ, my fingers touch Thy wheat
> And hold Thee hidden in the compass of Thy paper sun...

and the poem draws toward its conclusion in a combination of destruction, dissolution and, again, redemption, for the poet concludes:

> And though the world, at last, has swallowed her own
> > solemn laughter
> And has condemned herself to hell:

[and now the redemptive note, *fortissime*:]

> His Truth is greater than disaster.[31]

Dylan Thomas acutely sensed Time (and did our lyric tradition ever give birth to a more rhythmic poet?) but nowhere perhaps more personally than in his now famous "Do not go gentle into that good night" with its haunting repetitions of the refrain:

> Rage, rage against the dying of the light.[32]

The "wild men who caught and sang the sun in flight" are, of course, the poets and creators who—(like Proust, the great poetic novelist of our century)—fought the enemy: Time, Death, Oblivion. Proust fought him with the weapon of the Memory (particularly the involuntary memory), seeing Memory as our only Mediator and Advocate in redeeming Time Lost. Dylan Thomas saw only personal defiance, whether the dying light of Time be his father's or, by obvious implication, his own.

One becomes perhaps less sure of one's ground as we proceed into present-day poetry; the poet, already sophisticated and ironical, already caring little whether he is understood and much by *whom* he is understood, becomes pointedly ironic on the point of time. Hans Magnus Enzensberger's extended poem "gewimmer und firmament" is a case in point.[33] These are two concepts, perhaps the equivalents of time and eternity, perhaps parallels to Hagelstange's finite time (*Zeit*) in the upper air and endless-seeming Time (ZEIT) in the bunker underground. Or, as Enzensberger puts it, "das gewimmer hat viele namen," one of which might be, I venture to say, "the human condition." On the other hand, "let us observe that which does not observe us," namely "das firmament":

> das keinen namen hat, das sich nicht firmament nennt,
> das firmament, den zahllosen himmel,
> aus dem die zahlen entspringen, ihn,
> kein ding, keine seele, ihn,
> der weder zeit hat noch keine zeit,
> der zeit zeitigt...
> der die sterne ersinnt...
> ich lobe den himmel...
> das gewimmer ist auf der erde.

Even thus excerpted, the lines convey a sense of Time-beyond-Time, *aside* from time, for which one needs to coin a new term—such as: atemporal time (*tempus atemporale*).

Small wonder then that we find another contemporary poet, Karl Krolow, in a poem of the late 1950's, ready to abandon time (and, along with it, communication with his fellow man) and ready to exile himself, islanded outside of time. All this in a poem significantly entitled "Robinson," to indicate that state of *naufrage d'esprit* and that self-imposed exile and insularity:

> Ich habe zu rechnen aufgehört,
> Wenn ich auch noch Finger habe,
> Die ich nacheinander ins salzige Wasser
> Tauchen kann.
>
> Insekten und Tabakblätter
> Kennen die Zeit nicht,
> Die ich früher vergeudete.

In the last part of this tripartite poem, Krolow comes out more clearly. He exiles himself from time because he (i.e., that phase of him which he calls by the name of the shipwrecked man) no longer exists within Time; rather does Time exist inside him, to be listened to and felt:

> Diese Gewohnheit, irgendwo sehr lange
> Auf einem Stuhl zu sitzen
> Und zu horchen, ob es
> In einem regnet
> Oder in der Leber
> Der Skorpion sich noch rührt!

Even the means of keeping track of time (as with the fingers in the salty water) have proved useless, have (like the clock underground in Hagelstange's *Ballade vom verschütteten Leben*) proved worn-out and inadequate:

> Gezählt sind alle Blitze,
> Alle Streichhölzer, die übrig blieben.

Finally, communication becomes useless, wearisome and is abandoned:

> Bis man es leid ist,
> Und den letzten Wimpel
> Im Meer versenkt.[34]

Time is (we must have satisfied ourselves of it by this time) a primary, almost an exclusive interest of poets. For the lyric, existing within the dimension of time and there leading its true existence, time is the lyric essence. The evolution of the poetic use of time in the last century and a half, from the appearance of Lamartine's *Méditations Poétiques* in 1820 to Rilke and through our post-World War II contemporaries to the very present, would seem to have pointed away from its externalization as a force inimical to man, becoming for a while a mediator between man and his past (an inescapable yet not necessarily hostile medium in which he exists much as he does in space) and ultimately to round the circle in our own day and become again externalized and, more than ever, remote: remote as the outer reaches of expanding space, yet simultaneously internal and indigenous in the individual's human condition. Time has become identical with space and has been explored along with space; it is interchangeable with space and possesses the same variable densities. Professor Hugo Friedrich speaks of time as receiving "an abnormal function as a kind of fourth dimension of space, uniting temporally separated [events] into one moment."[35] He cites Eliot and Valéry as examples; one cannot help recalling those great beginning lines of *Four Quartets* (from *Burnt Norton*) which echo in the inner ear:

Time present and time past
Are both perhaps present in time future,
And time future contained in time past.
If all time is eternally present
All time is unredeemable.[36]

Less serious, perhaps, but unique nonetheless, the incomparable Christian Morgenstern provides a vignette to our study; it is a little verse entitled "Unter Zeiten":[37]

Das Perfekt und das Imperfekt
tranken Sekt.
Sie stießen aufs Futurum an
(was man wohl gelten lassen kann).

Plusquamper und Exaktfutur
blinzten nur.

NOTES

1 *Das Oxforder Buch Deutscher Dichtung vom 12ten bis zum 20sten Jahrhundert*, ed. H. G. Fiedler (Oxford, 1911), p. 1.

2 W. F. Giese, *French Lyrics in English Verse* (Madison, 1946), p. 3. On p. 385 a note indicates the source in Karl Bartsch, *Chrestomathie Provençale* (Elberfeld, 1880), Col. 101. The first line of this "alba" is: "En un vergier sotz folha [fuella] d'albespi" while the refrain runs: "oi deus, oi deus, de l'alba! tan tost ve."

3 Arthur Quiller-Couch, ed., *The Oxford Book of English Verse 1250-1900* (Oxford, 1922), p. 1.

4 *Lyrik des Ostens*, ed. Wilhelm Gundert u. Walter Schubring (München, 1957), p. 9.

5 Shakespeare: *Sonnet xxx*.

6 Line 1 of "The Queen's Marie," repeated in two following stanzas. Cf. *The Oxford Book of English Verse* (Oxford, 1922), p. 432.

7 Opening lines of the famous ballad "Sir Patrick Spens." Cf. *ibid.*, p. 403.

8 I have in mind such a poem as Rilke's "Spaziergang" ("Schon ist mein Blick am Hügel, ...") Cf. *Späte Gedichte* (Leipzig, 1935), p. 123, both original and my translation also in my *Twentieth-Century German Verse* (Princeton, 1952; Freeport, 1968), pp. 21, 34-35.

9 In any edition of his works [e.g., *Oeuvres choisies de Lamartine* (Paris, Bibliothèque Hachette, n.d.), pp. 41-2] and in various anthologies [e.g., Albert Schinz, *Nineteenth Century French Readings* (New York, 1934) Vol. I, pp. 133-5].

10 Edmund Clarence Stedman and George Edward Woodberry, ed., *The Works of Edgar Allan Poe*, Vol. VI: *Literary Criticism*, I (New York, 1914), p. 3.

11 Written 1821. Cf. *The Complete Poetical Works of Percy Bysshe Shelley* (Cambridge Edition; Boston and New York, 1901), p. 410.

12 Shakespeare, *Sonnet l*, i.e., 50.

13 Cf. his essay "John Keats" in *From Blake to Byron*, ed. by Boris Ford (Pelican Books; Baltimore, 1957), p. 233.

14 In all standard editions; e.g., Richard Harter Fogle, ed., *John Keats: Selected Poetry and Letters* (New York, 1951), pp. 247-8.

15 Hugo von Hofmannsthal, *Der Rosenkavalier* (Berlin, 1910-11), p. 49. It is to be suspected that Goethean echoes play their part here. Cf. *Wilhelm Meisters Wanderjahre*, Book III,

Chapter 11: "Der größte Respekt wirdt allen eingeprägt für die Zeit, als für die höchste Gabe Gottes und der Natur und die aufmerksamste Begleiterin des Daseins." (*Goethes Sämtliche Werke*, Jubiläums-Ausgabe [Stuttgart/Berlin, n.d.], XX, p. 161.) Cf. also Wolfgang Pehnt, *Zeiterlebnis und Zeitdeutung in Goethes Lyrik* (Tübingen, 1957).

¹⁶ Occurs in *Neue Gedichte* (1844), *Neuer Frühling*, 25. Cf. Ernst Elster, ed., *Heines Werke* (Leipzig, 1924), I, p. 282, or in the Insel edition (Leipzig, 1911 *et seq.*), vol. II, p. 19.

¹⁷ Cf. *Hebbels Werke*, ed. Theodor Poppe (Leipzig: Bong n.d.), I, pp. 87, 89.

¹⁸ Cf. Hebbel's diary entry (*Zweites Tagebuch*, 2648): "Eine Rose, so reif, daß ein Schmetterling, der seine Flügel regt, sie entblättert," for the probable genesis of the poem and my reason for dating it as of June 1844. *Op. cit.*, IX, p. 450.

¹⁹ Paul Valéry, *Poésies* (Paris, 1930), p. 128.

²⁰ In an article in Benno von Wiese, *Die deutsche Lyrik* (Düsseldorf, 1956), vol. II, pp. 91-97. The text of the poem appears in all editions of Mörike, also in the *Oxford Book of German Verse*.

²¹ Cf. *Oeuvres complètes de Ch. Baudelaire* (Paris: Alphonse Lemerre, n.d. [1917?]): *Les Fleurs du Mal*, pp. 142-4.

²² Text and translation in *Stéphane Mallarmé. Poems* [translated by Roger Fry with commentaries by Charles Mauron] (New York, 1951) pp. 122-4 [commentary, pp. 280-1]; however, the best exegesis is probably that of Emilie Noulet. Cf. her *L'Ouevre poétique de Stéphane Mallarmé* (Paris, 1940).

²³ "Why Do I?" Cf. Thomas Hardy, *Human Shows Far Fantasies* (London, 1925), p. 279.

²⁴ Thomas Hardy, *Collected Poems* (London, 1925), p. 521.

²⁵ That is, judging by the final sentence of his "Introductory Note" to the last volume of verse Hardy prepared for the press during his lifetime, issued after his death: "I also repeat what I have often stated on such occasions, that no harmonious philosophy is attempted in these pages — or in any bygone pages of mine, for that matter. T.H." [*Winter Words* (New York, 1928), p. vi.]

²⁶ *Human Shows Far Fantasies* (cf. n. 23), p. 120.

²⁷ *Die Frühen Gedichte* (Leipzig, 1920), pp. 101-2. Text and translation also in my *Twentieth-Century German Verse* (Princeton, 1952), pp. 24, 25.

²⁸ Hugo Friedrich, *Die Struktur der modernen Lyrik* (Hamburg, 1956), pp. 17, 40.

²⁹ Rudolf Hagelstange, *Ballade vom verschütteten Leben* (Leipzig, 1953), pp. 43-45, 47-8. (Also available as Insel-Bücherei Nr. 687; original text and my translation, with exegetic introduction by Charles W. Hoffmann, as *Ballad of the Buried Life*, Chapel Hill, n.d. [1962]).

³⁰ *Die Gedichte von Hermann Hesse* (Zürich, 1942), p. 364.

³¹ Thomas Merton, *The Tears of the Blind Lions* (New York, 1949), pp. 31-2.

³² *The Collected Poems of Dylan Thomas* (New York, 1957), p. 128.

³³ Hans Magnus Enzensberger, *landessprache* (Frankfurt a/M., 1960), pp. 87-101; more especially, pp. 97-8. I feel that I am indebted (for some of my insights into Enzensberger's work) to a forthcoming article by Professor Helmut Gutmann of Vassar College, though he is not responsible if I have hit beside the mark! Cf. H. Gutmann, "Die Utopie der reinen Negation: Zur Lyrik H. M. Enzensbergers," *The German Quarterly*, XLIII (1970), 435-52.

³⁴ Cf. Karl Krolow, *Ausgewählte Gedichte* (Frankfurt a/M., 1962), pp. 71-2; also *Fremde Körper*, (1959) pp. 69-71; my translation in Karl Krolow, *Poems Against Death* (Washington D.C., 1969), pp. 38-40.

³⁵ *Op. cit.*, pp. 149-150.

³⁶ T. S. Eliot, *Four Quartets* (New York, 1943), p. 3.

³⁷ Christian Morgenstern, *Alle Galgenlieder* (Berlin, 1932), p. 65. See also the "*Anmerkungen*" by Morgenstern's fictitious Dr. Jeremias Müller, specifically to lines 5 and 6 of this very poem. Concerning the passivity of the two last-mentioned tenses, Morgenstern has Dr. Müller comment: 'Fin de siècle,' (Cf. *Christian Morgenstern über die Galgenlieder* [Berlin, 1921], p. 54.)

As a kind of postscript, it should be noted that the rôle of Time in the poetry of William

Wordsworth — and his rôle in the discovery and poetic development of the time sense for his own and subsequent modern poetry — could well form a separate study of some length. The subject has, however, already been more than adumbrated by two investigators: Wylie Sypher and E. D. Hirsch, Jr. In his *Rococo to Cubism in Art and Literature* (New York, 1960), Professor Sypher (esp. pp. 67-68, 89-91, 94-100) illuminates the importance of certain Wordsworth poems (notably passages in "The Prelude" and especially "Lines Written Above Tintern Abbey") and ultimately points a fairly consistent line of development from the Abbé Jacques Delille through Lamartine, Wordsworth and Baudelaire down to Marcel Proust. E. D. Hirsch, Jr., in *Wordsworth and Schelling: A Typological Study* (New Haven, 1960) contributes (*passim* but esp. Chapter 5) substantively to the topic of Wordsworth and Time.

Relativity in Physics and in Fiction

MARTIN DYCK

There are some striking analogies between physics and fiction. In a basic sense, both physics and fiction are fiction. Yet in another basic sense, both fiction and physics are physics. In what sense is physics fiction? Well, what else is it? Truth? A physicist would object to such a classification. Reality? Past the midtwentieth century we are no longer so naive as to assume that there is such a thing as definable reality. More accurately: there is no *one* definable truth or reality. And since there is more than one conception of truth and reality, to any *one* observer all but his own concept of truth and reality must be fictitious. And since we cannot be so subjective as to accept the truth and reality of one individual, or one group, or one society, or one branch of knowledge, or one age as truth and reality binding on all and always binding (though we do not deny any individual, or group, or age the bliss of pursuing his or its own fictions) we are forced to conclude that all concepts of truth and reality are fictitious. Perhaps physics should be described as physical reality, or a set of theories of physical reality, or of the physical universe. Each of these propositions holds true. And each is circular. And each is incomplete. Each leaves out myriads of qualities and iridescences that impinge, physically, on the human senses and imagination. If a physicist should object by saying that what his systems and theories leave out is due to his science not having caught up with all phenomena he would further confirm hitherto established physics as fictitious because new insights will lead to a modified fiction and a clearer realization of the fictitiousness of current physics. If he should object by surmising that man will *never* entirely grasp nature's mysteries he would in so surmising proclaim that man's physics must *always* remain fiction. And his hunches about the unexplored might be classified as unpublished fiction—unless, of course, he is a cosmologist. But to be a cosmologist is to be a poet. Man cannot exist in the void. He needs a solid footing in the universe. And what could be more solid than fiction?

Perhaps we can bypass fiction in defining physics as a skeleton of the universe together with its forces and functions, independent of human perception. That bypass is blocked too. There is no perception other than human for us humans: no matter how far an instrument of physics may be removed from the simple five senses that instrument's readings must filter through some of these senses. And those readings must be organized and interpreted by the human mind. And since such interpretations and organizations have been continually evolving through the centuries, an elementary mathematical-historical induction will show that present-day physics also must change and in the process of changing continually confirm its fictitious nature. Physics is a fiction of the human imagination. It is powerful fiction. But it is not more powerful than fiction. Poetical fiction can wield more power with less hardware.

But in what sense is fiction physics? What distinguishes fiction (poetical fiction, that is) from any other web of words (mostly discursive or descriptive) is that a writer of fiction creates or evokes, say, in a novel, a universe that coheres and functions sensually, physically, among other cohesive functions, of course, whatever the degree of remove of that sensual, physical modality from the "real" experience of pinching a cheek or kicking a ball. We sensually experience, both in and after the act of reading a novel, its ingredients and its whole—we see and touch and feel and smell the characters, the cities, the events, the atmosphere, the drifts of meaning, and the streams of action. In a sense, the sensual impression of the universe of a novel is not "real," and yet we know that the better the piece of fiction the "more real" it is in every sense than "reality." Many a maid we have known fades from our memory: yet Natascha's sensual presence in the imagination is indelible. We cannot deny, of course, the fact that to many readers fiction is not "real." To satisfy such readers we might classify literary fiction as pseudo-physical, or quasi-physical, or "meta"-physical. Yet a moment's reflection makes us aware that fiction is pseudo or quasi or meta in relation to "physical reality," or, more precisely, in relation to "physical" "reality," or, to please the most fastidious definer, in relation do "'physical' 'reality,'" in the same manner, though perhaps in a different degree, as physics, the science, is an image quasi or meta or pseudo, of "'physical' 'reality.'"

What physics and fiction, each in its dual capacity as physics-and-fiction, have further in common, is space and time, or, more specifically, space-time. What are space and time? Space and time are, as it were, fictitious lines, or, if you prefer, painless physical lines, running through each of the realms of physics and fiction. Every novel has its own peculiar space-time. Each of these space-times may be regarded as a metamorphosis, be it a smoothing, or a ruffling, or some other stylization, of some aspect of the space-time of physics; and we recall that the space-time of physics also is, or has become, both historically and conceptually, a metamorphosis, be it a smoothing, or a ruffling, or some other form of stylization, of the space-time of "'physical' 'reality.'" Space and time are among the most powerful and most persistent and most indispensable fictions of the human mind.

175

With these affinities of space-time between physical or "physical" and fictitious or "fictitious" reality or "reality" in mind we might review some general aspects of relativity theory, general and special, with special attention to any possible affinities with fiction. There is no such thing as absolute time. There is no such thing as absolute space. Each observer—and each event—possesses its own space-time. "Common Sense" and Galileo and Newton could reconcile the observations of the same event by several observers by taking into account their respective location, time, and mode of movement at each point-time of observation, and with the solid referential support of absolute time and absolute space. All three have been, and are, roughly right but delicately wrong. Relativity theory, among other things, assigns each observer his own special time and space and refines the pre-relativistic equations transforming the observations of one observer of an event to those of another observer of that event by introducing a new factor: the speed of light. Each observer is now imprisoned in a sort of barbed-wire mesh of his own space-time; a mesh that distorts his vision, in his own peculiar way, of anything outside and thwarts his efforts to reach anything outside *unless* he appeals to something that may be called the new Deity Absolute: the speed of light, which is hauntingly independent of any system of observation.

Several more observations seem in order before proceeding to a consideration of space-time in literature. We should, I think, abandon any notion of a novelist consciously applying relativity theory in or to his works. Many modern writers, we are, of course, aware, were versed, some of them deeply, in some branch of science, notably medicine. Among twentieth-century German writers in this category may be mentioned Gottfried Benn, Alfred Döblin, Robert Musil, Hermann Broch. Surely most of them had a good grasp of relativity theory in its general manifestations, a theory so popular and so glamorous at the time when these writers were students. Yet I doubt if any one of them even *considered* applying the theory to his poetry or fiction. And even if scholarship should one day "prove" that some writer actually did "apply" the theory in his works: we know by now that more often than not a writer's working intentions are like the scaffolding of a building that must be discarded to see and enter the building itself. It does not follow from these remarks that affinities between physics and fiction do not exist in the works of some modern authors. In any age, dominant theories and tendencies, be they mythological in the age of myth, or theological in the Middle Ages, or physical in our own era—have a way of penetrating other branches of knowledge, be it ever so tenuously, be they ever so incognate. Naturalism and romanticism exemplify such interrelations for literature and its incognately cognate sister disciplines.

In the twentieth century the marked preoccupation with space and time in literature and criticism[1] is in some ways, and in some degree, related to the preoccupation with space and time in relativity theory. And if not related in any of the narrower senses of relatedness one may wish to impose, we must still accept as fact the coincidence of serious attention to space and time in both realms. Recognition of this fact of coincidence is important, but strictly speaking, not prerequisite to our arguments. What is almost unexplored in literary criticism, however, though there is growing awareness of it, surprisingly unexplored in view of the preoccupation with each of them, is that peculiar fusion of space and time in a literary work, most conspicuously in the larger prose works, that lends many elements and several levels of meaning and structure a certain characteristic modality and identity. We recall here the obvious fact that the linking of space and time is infinitely older than relativity theory; indeed, no philosophical surgeon succeeded in *really* separating the twins. And the older they get the more they tend to coalesce. I think many a novel possesses such a pervasive space-time informing many elements and levels within the novel. In examining *War and Peace* in his *Aspects of the Novel*, E. M. Forster[2] comes intriguingly close to seeing space and time welded, in the novel, into one homogeneous whole when he points out that one of the reasons that the novel is not depressing is "probably because it has extended over space as well as time." But then he pulls the two apart again, wrongly, I think, by concluding that "space is the lord of *War and Peace*, not time." With all due allowances for the different modalities of space and time in literary space-time (as distinct from a certain formulaic homogeneity of the four dimensions in physics) and for a certain commonly encountered reciprocity between space and time, I ask: Is not the lord of *War and Peace* an intimately linked space-time in which the temporal and spatial strands, both of vast dimension (though vast in different ways and degrees), intertwine, mirror, inform and reinforce each other? The space-time in *War and Peace* flows, so it seems to me, evenly, inexorably, breaking and building, wounding and healing. At times one of the dimensions is, or both in their union are, gathered up for a while, for a stretch, for a stretch-while, and then smoothed out again.

We now shift our perspective to an entirely different space-time, that of the *Magic Mountain* of Thomas Mann. In this novel too space and time are tightly interwoven. But whereas for *War and Peace* we might choose the vast Russian plains together with an "Asiatic" concept of time as a metaphor to represent the space-time, the "magic mountain" itself yields the best image of the space-time of the novel it designates. The whole novel may be regarded as a stream of metaphoric, symbolic, narrational energies flowing down from the metaphoric mountain's peak. At the beginning of the novel space-time sets in tightly on the peak, as it were, only to descend, as it were, gradually, in widening circles of slowing time and stretching space: of stretching-slowing space-time. The space-time of the *Magic Mountain* is affine to that of an individual abandoning himself to the forces and successive states of languor, torpor, and stagnancy, or, in the mode of our central metaphor, to that of an individual sliding down the mountain while somewhere below, in the

Tolstoyan plains, Life and History flow by, on a scale more extensive, more even, and more objective. More specifically, Hans Castorp's stay in the TB sanatorium begins near the peak of the metaphoric space-time mountain. Space and time, as we noted, set in densely. Castorp relishes time, on his arrival, minute by minute, space inch by inch; space-time, inch-minute by inch-minute. No wonder he is so terribly exhausted on the first day, a day packed with "days" of fresh excitement. Space-time continues, during the next few days, tightly and briskly, door-slam by door-slam, table by table. Indeed, so tight is space that it presses neighbor against neighbor through walls so thin, o sin, so thin! And the walls—and the dolls—grow thinner and thinner, TB dinner after TB dinner, TV sinner after TV sinner. And the space—and the pace—sink lower—and wax slower. And then day by day, week by week, walk by walk, month by month, chapter by chapter, year by year, Chauchat by Chauchat... Castorp's space-time is stretching-slowing to the lax and leisurely space-time of Madame Chauchat who emits an aura of vast laxity and lax vastness, an aura somehow reminiscent of Tolstoyan space-time. Castorp comes perilously close, on his way down the metaphoric mountain, to losing all sense of space and time, all directed movement, both in the outward and inward snow, and hence his very existence. Yet his innermost desire remains, metaphorically speaking, and speaking meta-physically, to transcend through descent, in a sort of snowy-glowy, chilly-thrilly, wildly wicked Cha-Cha-Chat avec Madame Chauchat! And when he finally reaches the bottom of the metaphoric mountain we lose sight of him in space-time vast and vague—we know not quite where—we know not quite when—except that it is somewhere at some time of Europe-on-the-Brink-of-World-War-One: where he fades out like a romantic song.

The last ring of space-time in the *Magic Mountain* blends into that of German Romanticism about the turn of the eighteenth and nineteenth centuries. In some of its most distinctive forms German Romantic space-time is almost *unendlich*, spanning time from a receding beginning to a progressive end, from the mythological past into the eschatological future, and in space, flowing like a river, backward and forward, into the past-and-future, toward a realm somewhere between Rome and Jerusalem and India. Upon that metaphoric river move vessels with treasures of romantic import toward a point-and-moment that is *ewig* and *unendlich* and *wunderbar*. *Et spiritus Novali ferebatur et dixit:* "Fiat Romanttzzia!" *Et dixit Sophia:* "Facta est Romantt-zzia!"

Each of the three examples shows man in a peculiar space-time with a peculiar rhythm of movement and mode of existence: one walking back and forth in a vast plain, another sliding down a mountain, and the third traveling in some romantic vehicle toward some southeasterly Never-Nowhere. Each seems incapable of transforming, if the need or occasion arose, to the space-time of the other two in the sense of a quasi-Galilean transformation. Perhaps something analogous to the speed of light can reconcile the three viewings of the human condition, in a manner quasi-Lorentzian.

Thus we have seen aspects of relativity novel to novel. Relativity may also be discerned within a single novel. But such relativity (in the restricted senses we are exploring) is rare. Writers are seldom capable of creating, within one novel, two points of view so independent as to be irreconcilable by a suitable quasi-Galilean transformation. The more antithetical they are, the more related the points of view of two characters, or some other twosome, tend to be: inversely related. That is why violently opposed characters can interact more often. Settembrini and Naphta are so neatly and in so many ways opposed to one another that they can have a lot of interaction. Their points of view turn on the same pivot, only in opposite directions. There is some independence in their modes of existence. In the verbal duels they hit, in the real duel they miss, one another. Naphta kills himself instead of Settembrini. He would not have reached him by shooting him. Settembrini deliberately misses Naphta. He would not have reached him by shooting him. The duel is a show of reconciliation, of transformation only. It shows that transformation and reconciliation are impossible in a quasi-Galilean sense. In the existential confrontation, then, of Naphta and Settembrini we can almost speak of relativity.

In his *Speculations about Jacob* Uwe Johnson fails, I think, though he obviously exerts himself to do so, to achieve two truly unrelated perspectives, East and West German. Robbe-Grillet, in *Le Voyeur*, has brilliantly succeeded in breaking apart his space-time into islands, each crisp and clear in itself, but the whole strangely incoherent and intangible. Yet the islands do cohere. What links those cleverly isolated space-time islands are bridges of irrelation —stronger than any bridges of correlation he might have built. The reader intuitively knows that underlying the fragmented space-time clusters is a whole elusive but present. There is only one observer in the novel, the author, and hence no relativity.

I can think of only one example of two truly independent observers within one work of literature. That work is Goethe's *Faust*, a work transcending genre distinctions—it may be viewed as a poem, or as drama, or as a novel— and hence with a range of relevancy as narrow as the novel and as broad as literature at large. The observers in *Faust* are Faust and Mephistopheles and, in a restricted sense, the Lord. Let us examine the way Faust and Mephistopheles move—physically and metaphorically—as a clue to their ways of feeling and seeing and talking and doing and being.

Faust's ideal mode of movement is rectilinear. He feels he must move on a straight line toward some aim. The mode of movement of Mephistopheles is antirectilinear. He has no purpose but to thwart purpose. Whereas Faust is distressed, in the first scene of the poem proper, at being caught in a mire of *Herauf, Herab und Quer und Krumm*, in motion without meaning, Mephistopheles is uncomfortable on a straight track. He loves to twist a straight line. He loves to twist. The geodesics of his gestures and thoughts and paths are weird and wicked, crooked and cringing, sinuous and tortuous. We recall and retrace the obliquely circular path upon which he approached rectilinear Faust in the scene "Vor dem Tor": "Bemerkst du, wie in weitem Schneckenkreise / Er um uns her und immer näher jagt?" We can pursue Mephistopheles' methodical diffusion of Faust's incorrigibly linear motion scene after scene: in "Auerbachs Keller" his diffusive efforts are not directed toward Faust, and yet they are, indirectly directed, as part of Mephistopheles' oblique approach: "Falsch Gebild und Wort / Verändern Sinn und Ort!/ Seid hier und dort!"; in the "Hexenküche" the "allerlei wunderliche Bewegungen durcheinander" are analogous to, in the sphere of meaning, the "Hexeneinmaleins": a ritual celebrating antilinear, anti-Faustian arithmetic, with the basic operations, in the words of Lewis Carroll, of addition, distraction, uglification, and derision: with all these trends culminating in the "Walpurgisnacht" where rectilinear Faust is made to follow the zigzag of the will-o'-the-wisp:

> Aber sag' mir, ob wir stehen,
> Oder ob wir weitergehen?
> Alles, alles scheint zu drehen,
> Fels und Bäume, die Gesichter
> Schneiden, und die irren Lichter,
> Die sich mehren, die sich blähen.

The physics of Mephistopheles is crooked. Are we surprised, then, to discover in his metaphysics and metaphorics nothing but a straight extension of his crooked physics? He views his own mode of movement and existence as that common to all men. Man is a long-legged grasshopper: "wie eine der langbeinigen Zikaden, / die immer fliegt und fliegend springt / und gleich im Gras ihr altes Liedchen singt." Whereas Faust hopes to ascend and transcend on a straight line to ultimate purpose, Mephistopheles sees man in general and Faust in particular pursue an absurdly oscillating zigzag in which each zig is taken back by a zag. Such motion is self-annihilating. Mephistopheles is a nihilist. Mephistopheles hates and combats life, all life. Yet somehow he is closer to life than Faust. We cannot help interpreting Mephistopheles' "crooked" movement and Faust's rectilinear movement in the sense in which Novalis associated "krumme Linie" with life and the straight line with "die Regel."[3]

In the moment of purposeful action Faust travels, or thinks he travels, a straight path. But looking back he sees a zigzag not unlike that defined by Mephistopheles as man's eternal course. The career of Faust is a sequence of ups and downs. Three observers discern in those ups and downs three different paths. In the perspective of Goethe's Lord each up moves Faust a little higher so that the series of ups will lead him ultimately to redemption and transcendence. In the perspective of Mephistopheles the ups and downs form the meaningless movement of the grasshopper that can never really rise above the grass. In his own perspective, Faust's ups are a rectilinear ascent to heights of ecstasy, his downs a rectilinear descent to the lower depths of despair, and in retro-intro-spective moments he too can see the banal zigzag of the path he has traveled. Each of the three observers dwells in his own space-time, with his own geometry of vision, and hence his own image of Faust's rhythm of movement and existence. Here is relativity.

Another type of relativity in Goethe's *Faust* permutes the two magic mountains in the poem, the one in the First "Walpurgisnacht" and the one in the "Third Walpurgisnacht" as we shall designate, in a special sense, Faust's final ascension and transfiguration. The lord of one mountain is Mephistopheles; the lord of the other, the Lord. One may be called Mount Venus; the other, Mount Virgin. Faust climbs both. He is rising on the sin escalator to the peak of Mount Venus (though heroically resisting the trend by concentrating on the deeper meaning of it all) and he is rising on the soul elevator to the summit of Mount Virgin. Mount Venus and Mount Virgin, soul elevator and sin escalator are so similar—the "ewiger Wonnebrand" and "glühendes Liebeband" of *Pater ecstaticus* could be burning on either mountain—that at times it is hard to tell which is which, if it is easy to see which is witch. Thus we have witnessed one event on one mountain through the eyes of two observers, Faust in two different space-times, or, conversely, two observation points of Faust's upward striving.

Goethe had to cope with a third relativity problem in the poem. He had to intermerge the space-time of Helen's Ancient Greece with that of Faust's Modern Germany. To arrange for the meeting of Faust and Helen he had Wagner, a sort of mechanicophilosophical engineer, invent, with the information theory of Mephistopheles, a space-time machine: Homunculus. A quasi-Galilean transformation would not have worked. Helen could not function in Mediaeval or Renaissance or Eighteenth-Century Germany; Faust would have fumbled meeting Helen in *Ancient* Greece. Goethe brilliantly achieves a point-moment in space-time for the meeting by moving Faust, the untiring wanderer over the face of the earth, toward Helen primarily in space, and by moving Helen, whose image endures through time but would evaporate in the wrong space, primarily in time toward Faust. And then, for a moment the rhythm of their words and souls and bodies is one.

A fourth case of relativity in Goethe's poem revolves about Faust's death. A scholarly *Streit um Faust II*[4] has failed to establish who loses and who wins, legitimately, Faust or Mephistopheles. It had to fail if the search was—as indeed it was—for an absolute answer. Surely Goethe saw the dilemma and left it in a state of relativity. Both win and both lose. Each wins in his own space-time and loses in that of the other. But the Lord and Goethe are biased in Faust's favor. In the era of Goethe, the ending could not have been one of symmetric relativity between Faust and Mephistopheles—though the poem frequently achieves such symmetry. At the end of the poem the symmetry had to be skewed upward and Faustwise.

Next we shall try to define relativity for two readers of the same novel. For this purpose, the space-times of the readers must be separated by a gulf of irrelation. We choose a certain type of early Soviet reader and a certain type of Western reader, the latter perhaps from the existentially piercing years following World War II. To what extent each reader objectively represents his society or times is irrelevant to our discussion. It suffices for our argumentation to know that some such readers, still to be introduced, existed. Each of the readers is a prisoner of his own very special poetico-politico-historical space-time. The Western reader, steeped in Kafka and Rilke and cognate authors, views himself as part of a system descending metaphorically and metaphysically. He can no longer identify himself, in his innermost longings, with the ancient metaphorical and metaphysical forces of transcendence through ascendance that have held sway over the poetical imagination from earliest times through the Middle Ages into the nineteenth century. Beginning in German Romanticism and steadily growing during the nineteenth century ran a contrary trend, subterranean in earlier times, that of transcending through descending. This trend reached a climax, to choose some examples from the German sphere, in the works of Thomas Mann, Benn, Trakl, Rilke, and others. In the words of Rilke: "Wir alle fallen, diese Hand da fällt."[5] For our Western reader the whole universe is gently wafting downward, metaphorically, metaphysically, politically, historically: he has a vague sensation of "Spätzeitlichkeit," an illusory feeling of *The Decline of the West*,[6] and a more real awareness of the decline of the Austrian Empire where so many metaphorically downward drifting writers and fictitious figures had their habitat. But since the Western reader dwells in the same universe that produced, say, the *Magic Mountain*, he is descending at the same rate as the metaphoric energies in the novel. Thus his descent becomes suspended, as it were.

The Soviet reader (and we recall that we mean a special case of an earlier Soviet reader) imagines himself to exist (or has been taught so) poetically, politically, historically, metaphorically, metaphysically, in an ascending universe popping up, up, up into poetico-politico-physical space with positive-posited postulates. A space-time feeling of this kind has its historical background: the relative lateness of Russia's emergence as a major power. It has its poetical dimension: the human condition, real or fictitious, is seen as rising (having not yet exhausted, as the West has through centuries, the magic ritual of transcending through ascending), with poets writing in the temper of Schiller (which is absolutely impossible in the sphere of our Western reader), too early in the day of time to slide down, in the dusk of "Spätzeitlichkeit," a magic mountain of mellow civilization. The Soviet reader reminds us of Faust. He reminds us of Schiller. His motto is: Look up! Build up! Climb up! But what is he climbing? A Marxian Magic Mountain.

Now we ask both readers to read Thomas Mann's *Magic Mountain*. The Soviet reader in his ascending space-time finds, on reading the novel, the events and values of Mann's descending space-time doubly downward directed. "Decadent!" he cries. And he sincerely means it—in a sort of figurative literalness, and vice versa. The Western reader, on the other hand, descending at a rate similar to that in the novel, is aware that the downward movement is projected upon a previous "classical" upward still firmly implanted as a set of clichés in the minds of the middle class readership whom the novel addresses; he is aware that the negative is projected upon a previous positive, evil upon good, and so forth. He is aware of a symmetry and balance between the present downward and the previous upward. "Paradox!" is his observation. Thus each reader is informed by a kind of PPP factor. The Soviet: Progress to Proletarian Paradise. The Western: Politzer, Parable, Paradox.[7]

And conversely, the Western reader inspecting a certain type of Soviet novel can no longer yield to the upward pull of enthusiasm and idealism, that seem to him at his stage of the human and artistic game naive and primitive at best, artificial and obsolescent at worst. He comments: "Idealistic Popcorn." But the Soviet reader, rising on the same illusory escalator on which the Soviet novel is rising, finds himself in rosy-cozy rapport with what he is reading. He naturally concludes: "Realism." Yet the observations of the Western and the Soviet reader can be reconciled by defining and translating their modes of movement and existence. There is more relativity in the example. In relativity theory the clock of a receding system is slower, that of an approaching system faster. In the two space-times defined the Western reader of Soviet literature finds the Soviet clock slower, and, apparently paradoxically, the Soviet reader finds the Western clock slower. The Soviet reader thinks his clock is faster because he imagines himself higher up on his ladder, and hence on *the* ladder, of progress. To him the Western novel, and reader, is static, regressive, "reactionary," incapable of renewal. Yet the Western reader finds the Soviet clock slower, set by obsolescent late nineteenth-century positivism and ticking away the sort of classical metaphorics and metaphysics that even the major Soviet poets of the earlier twentieth century had outgrown.

If now we consider two approaching space-time systems, say, East Germany and Russia, each will find the clock of the other faster in some ways. The East German reader may see "social realism" more advanced in Soviet fiction. And a Russian reader may detect in East German fiction more advanced aspects of Western civilization. In relativity theory, furthermore, the measuring rod of a receding system is shorter, that of an approaching system longer. If the rods are thought of as measuring values it is easy to see how the mutually receding Western and Soviet systems regard one another's values as shrinking; whereas East Germany and Russia, as magnifying. The relativistic juxtaposition of Western versus Soviet reader of the *Magic Mountain* can be expanded by including Red China: Chinese-Western relativity would appear then as an intensified variant of Soviet-Western in most details; and Chinese-Soviet relativity, as a mild variant of Soviet-Western, with Russia in the role of the West.

Indeed, many of the most important problems of literary criticism may be viewed as problems in relativity. Every author, every work, every era, every reader is confined to his own space-time; any two instances give rise to a formulation of relativity: reader to reader or work to work, as we have seen, or novel to translation, one translation to another, narrator to narration, one point of view to another, and so forth. That trend of modern literary criticism which views each work as its own unique independent universe (we need not recite here the various labels for the trend) and dissociates it from all absolutes is analogous to some crucial aspects of relativity theory.

Relativity theory is pertinent to that view of contemporary man which recognizes him as an unsheltered and disinherited creature.[8] As such he has become an isolated observer of events, part of a lonely crowd of such observers, each enclosed in his own curved space-time, in the warping of his own imagination. No quasi-Galilean transformation between the observers is possible, or else it is vacuous and futile. Relativity theory may console him in the manner reminiscent of the existentialist: be proud to be a resident of your own space-time, with your own clock showing your own time and not merely a zone relative to some standard time, a possessor of your own measuring rod commensurate to your own needs and not to some absolute yardstick preserved in some museum. Listen to your own heart-beat and not to some distant drummer whose rhythm is not tuned to yours. Have the courage to travel your own geodesic and to unfold by the geometry of your own space-time. But apparently such isolation is contrary to human nature. Man is like a chemical element dangling with valences seeking union with other elements, or like a relativity observer yearning to reconcile his observations with those of other observers since he no longer has a shelter of absolutes.

The modern novel abounds in such observers. K. in *The Trial* thinks himself in the field of gravitation of an elusive court and an inscrutable law, two intangible absolutes. Yet has he not obstructed himself with the geometry of his own space-time? Is he not conducting his own trial? Does he not simply refuse to acquit himself? Does he not annihilate himself in order to reach other observers?

Our last example shall be a work of fiction that has not yet been published as formal fiction though it is being written every day. It is a story more real than physics and stranger than fiction. It is the tale of a city. And it is a tale of two cities. It is a story about one city in one place at one time. And it is a story about two cities farther apart than the London and Paris of Dickens. Through the single city runs a fictitious wall built and to be broken by the laws of physics; a wall separating the city into two distinct space-times moving apart, one toward Leningrad, the other toward New York City. Each has its own map. Each considers its own map as relatively absolute and the map of the other as absolutely relative. O Berlin Absolute, are you gone forever? Who shall solve your relativity problem? Once upon a time there walked within your walls a man who had thought a great deal about such problems. He might have solved yours if only you could have kept him. His name was Einstein.

NOTES

[1] It suffices here merely to mention such critics as Emil Staiger, Hans Meyerhoff, Georges Poulet, Gaston Bachelard.

[2] New York: Harcourt, Brace & World, 1954, p. 39 [first published in 1927].

[3] Novalis, *Schriften*, ed. P. Kluckhohn & R. Samuel (Leipzig: Bibliographisches Institut, n.d. [1929]), III, p. 151.

[4] Title of the study by Ada M. Klett (Jena, 1939).

[5] See Bernhard Blume's analysis of this aspect in *Modern Language Notes*, LX (1945), 295-302.

[6] Title of the well-known work by Oswald Spengler, first published in Munich in 1918-1922.

[7] Heinz Politzer, *Franz Kafka: Parable and Paradox* (Ithaca: Cornell University Press, 1962).

[8] See Erich Heller, *The Disinherited Mind* (Cambridge: Bowes & Bowes, 1952).

Rilke and Heidenstam:
Public Thanks and Hidden Trails

GEORGE C. SCHOOLFIELD

In an article, "Charles XII Rides in Worpswede," the present writer advanced the theory that a reading of Verner von Heidenstam's *Karolinerna* had been at least a partial inspiration of Rilke's poem, "Karl der Zwölfte von Schweden reitet in der Ukraine"; textual evidence was offered which indicated a direct influence from Heidenstam's stories about the warrior-king upon Rilke's picture of "ein junger König aus Norden."[1] Newspaper and epistolary material, come upon recently, gives proof that Rilke not only had read *The Charles Men* before writing his poem, but that he was acquainted with other works of Heidenstam as well.

Early in 1909, Fredrik Böök, docent in literary history at Lund, Oscar Levertin's successor as book critic of *Svenska Dagbladet*, and, despite his tender years (he was only 26), already a leading force in Sweden's cultural life, undertook to prepare a birthday page in the paper for his particular literary idol, Verner von Heidenstam,[2] who had played a considerable role in *Svenska Dagbladet's* foundation, and the shaping of its editorial policy. The Swedish Vergil, who had hoped to awaken his people to a new sense of their historical mission, would turn 50 on July 6, 1909, and the event deserved proper celebration. Indeed, even the liberal *Dagens Nyheter*, looking askance at Heidenstam and his admirers, found itself compelled to note the birthday festivities at Naddö, the scald's home near Vadstena on Lake Vättern, but did its duty with sour brevity: "Verner von Heidenstam is turning fifty today, and in connection with this event he will be the object of a paying of homage so extensive that surely very few Swedish prophets and poets ["siare och skalder"] have had the chance to experience anything like it. A large number of deputations and private parties from all the nooks and crannies of the land have steered their course to Naddö, his fair poet's dwelling beside Lake Vättern, and the congratulations which, with the aid of post and telegraph, find their way thither, will of a certainty be difficult to count."[3]

In all likelihood, the prophet and poet of Naddö did not delve into the hostile *Dagens Nyheter* on his great day; instead, one likes to hope, he picked up *Svenska Dagbladet* and turned to the ovation Fredrik Böök had prepared. There were twenty-nine congratulators in all: literary scholars (Vilhelm

Andersen, Gunnar Castrén, Valdemar Vedel, Evert Wrangel), creative writers (Gustav Fröding, Per Hallström, Selma Lagerlöf, Sigfrid Siwertz, Anders Österling), artists (Carl Larsson, Carl Milles, Georg Pauli, Alf Wallander), philosophers (Harald Høffding, Vitalis Norström), churchmen (Nathan Söderblom), explorers (Sven Hedin), Finland-Swedish essayists (Werner Söderhjelm), publishers (Heidenstam's own: Karl Otto Bonnier), editors (Anna Maria Roos and Torgny Segerstedt, the latter of whom, directing Gothenburg's *Handels- och Sjöfartstidning* thirty-odd years later, would institute an anti-German policy which must have made Heidenstam turn in his fresh grave), bank directors (Ernest Thiel), philologists (Fredrik Wulff), historians (Carl Hallendorff, Fredrik Troels-Lund), bird-lovers (Paul Rosenius), and the unclassifiable Ellen Key.[4] The non-Scandinavian realm was represented by two quite disparate figures: Professor P. E. Pavolini of Florence, Heidenstam's Italian translator, who wrote his words of congratulation in Swedish, and the "distinguished German poet" ("den utmärkte tyske skalden"), Rainer Maria Rilke, who made his bow in his native tongue.

Through the offices of *Svenska Dagbladet*, Böök, in May, 1909, had asked Rilke to contribute to the birthday-page;[5] his name, evidently, had been suggested by Ellen Key, who also was able to provide his current Parisian address. Rilke was in Provençe when the inquiry arrived, but answered it immediately upon his return to Paris. He directed his affirmative reply, of June 1, 1909, not to Böök's newspaper but to Böök himself, and, as a further sign of the pleasure he took in the plan, he added a paragraph in which he apologized for the shortness his contribution of necessity would have: "Es wird mir in dieser Zeit leider nicht möglich sein, mich über die Eindrücke, die ich dem Werke Verner von Heidenstams verdanke, eingehend auszusprechen; gleichwohl entspricht es sehr meinem Bedürfnis[,] mich der Ehrung, die Sie ihn [sic] vorbereiten[,] herzlich anzuschließen, und ich bitte Sie, mir wenigstens den Raum zu sichern, den ein kurzer Fest-Gruß beansprucht." Docent Böök was in luck, whether he knew it or not; just as Rilke did not like to have his poems appear in anthologies, so he resisted efforts to lure him into expressing himself on public questions or public figures. Exceptions proving the rule are: the enthusiastic essay on the Gothenburg "Samskola" in *Die Zukunft* (January 1, 1905), his contributions to the volume *Religionsunterricht: Achtzig Gutachten* (1906) and to *Die Lösung der Judenfrage* (1907), the letter to Hugo Heller which Hermann Bahr was allowed to reprint in *Die Bücher zum wirklichen Leben* (1908), the Heidenstam-appreciation for *Svenska Dagbladet* (July 6, 1909), and the greeting to Ellen Key on her sixtieth birthday, in the Swedish magazine *Idun* (December 5, 1909). In later years, Rilke avoided such performances more sternly still, giving Richard Dehmel cause to sneer at him ("Rilke hat sich gedrückt") when he refused, understandably enough, to participate in a post-Armistice "Warnruf" to the triumphant Allies.[6] It is perhaps noteworthy, for the rest, that all the public statements just listed—save the one on the Jewish question

—have some Scandinavian connection: the statement on religious instruction holds up the "Samskola" as a model, the letter to Heller culminates in a tribute to J. P. Jacobsen, and ends with Ibsen. Furthermore, the statements on Heidenstam and Ellen Key appeared in organs not likely to come to the attention of the German public. Did utterances on Swedish institutions and Scandinavian authors (two of the three of them made in "inaccessible" publications) seem less binding than possible proclamations made on German affairs and in the German press? Rilke's last public statement on a German-language author was the review of Richard von Schaukal's *Ausgewählte Gedichte*, made at Schaukal's request and appearing in *Die Zukunft* (April 1, 1905).[7]

On June 28, 1909, Rilke sent his contribution for *Svenska Dagbladet* off to Lund, where Böök lived; it was accompanied by a brief but friendly note in which Rilke once more told of his happiness at the opportunity afforded him. "Ich wiederhole meine Versicherung, daß ich Ihnen für den Anlaß sehr dankbar bin, der mir diese aufrichtige Aussprache meiner Bewunderung gestattet." Since Rilke's birthday-greeting to Heidenstam is not easily accessible,[8] it would be well to reprint it here, in the totality of its "Bewunderung":

Damals, vor Jahren, bei einem Aufenthalt im gastfreundlichsten Schweden, habe ich Gedichte von Verner von Heidenstam sagen und singen hören. Es war ihnen, erinnere ich mich, eigen, sich von Zeile zu Zeile zu verdichten; aber wenn man sie im halben Helldunkel des Zimmers fast schon zu sehen und zu fassen meinte, so verflüchtigten sie sich und man athmete sie ein mit der dunklen Luft.

Später, als ich die Geschichte seiner Ahnin las, der heiligen Frau aus königlichem Stamme, da kam ich auch in diesem Buch zu einer Stelle, wo alles sich darin Gestaltete sich forthob, in Schwingungen überging, verschwebte.

Ich weiß nicht, ob diese Erscheinung der Kunst Verner von Heidenstams wesentlich ist; denn über dasjenige seiner Bücher, das mir am nächsten steht, kann ich mir gar keine Rechenschaft geben.

Diese 'Karoliner' entdeckte ich mir, als ich ganz jung war. Ich weiß nicht, wie oft ich sie gelesen habe. Es entmuthigte mich nicht, in ihnen ein Gelingen zu finden, zu dem mein Können noch in keinem Verhältnis stand. Dieses hinreißende Buch rückte das Leben irgendwie näher heran an meine Bewältigung. Es erzeugte in mir eine Lust und eine Entschlossenheit, einmal Menschen zu schreiben, wenn ich die Wirklichkeit erlernt haben würde auf dem weiten Weg über die Dinge. Ich begriff, was es hieß, einer Gestalt mächtig sein [sic]; daß es sich darum handelte, sie nicht ängstlich festzuhalten, sondern sie immer wieder neu zu ergreifen oder doch, wo sie unfaßbar war, ihre Form auszusparen mit Anderem, Faßbaren [sic].

Der Takt und die Kühnheit, womit hier ein Lebendiges bewältigt war, überzeugten mich ein für alle Mal. Die Anordnungen entfernter großer Aufgaben spiegelten sich in meiner Seele.

Und nun, im Zurücksehn, wird es mir klar, daß dieses Buch zu den bedeutendsten Gegenständen gehört, an denen meine Bewunderung und mein Willen sich gebildet hat.

Rainer Maria Rilke

Paris, im Juni 1909.

The eulogy requires some comment. It is interesting to learn that Rilke had some familiarity with the lyrics of Heidenstam. The room whose chiaroscuro formed the background for the "speaking and singing" of Heidenstam's poetry was located in the second of Rilke's residences "im gastfreundlichsten Schweden"—"Furuborg," the home of James and Lizzie Gibson at Jonsered, a small industrial community near Gothenburg, where the poet stayed from late September until early December, 1904. During 1905-06, Rilke carried on a brief correspondence, of which more will be said later on, with Heidenstam himself; in a letter to Heidenstam of February 22, 1905, he recalled the readings he would afterwards mention in the article for *Svenska Dagbladet*: "in dem Augenblicke, da ich Ihren Namen schreibe, kommt so Vieles über mich: Erinnerungen an Stunden, die über Ihren Büchern seltsam und verglühend vergangen sind, Klang und Nachklang kurzer, wunderbar schwerer Gedichte, die ich vor Monaten in Jonsered bei Freunden Ellen Keys' habe sagen hören (eines Abends besonders, da das Kaminfeuer den Raum formte,—ausdehnte und zu sich zusammenzog)—und Dankbarkeit für so Vieles, was aus Ihren Worten und Versen kam und was zu nennen ich nicht vermag."[9] Ellen Key had also received a contemporaneous report on these literary evenings from Lizzie Gibson, a report which says, among other things, that Rilke understood some spoken Swedish: "En kväll läste J[immie] Almkvist—läste mycket, mycket långsamt och översatte det R. M. icke förstod—men det behöfdes icke mycket."[10] It could be assumed that James Gibson followed a technique with Heidenstam's verse similar to that he used with Almqvist: first reading in the original and then a verbal translation.

What poems of Heidenstam were presented to Rilke? Reidar Ekner[11] suggests that the Gibsons read the early poetry of *Ensamhetens tankar*; these short, difficult, and very personal lyrics would answer to the description given in the letter to Heidenstam ("kurzer, wunderbar schwerer Gedichte.") Two more arguments might be advanced in support of Ekner's suggestion. Because of their brevity, the "Thoughts of Loneliness" would lend themselves particularly well to the kind of linguistic treatment they received for the sake of the Austrian guest. And, more important, a detail from the contribution to *Svenska Dagbladet* can be put to work here: Rilke says that the poems were spoken *and sung*. (The Gibsons were a musical family, and singing was extremely common in their circle: on November 13, after Rilke had given the triumphant reading of the *Samskola* essay and some of his poems at Furuborg, the guests trooped off to the railroad station singing Viktor Rydberg's *Atenarnas sång*.[12]) Vilhelm Stenhammar, later to be associated with Heidenstam as the setter-to-music of the patriotic poem-cycle, *Ett folk*,[13] had composed settings for *Ensamhetens tankar* in the 1890's. It is possible, of course, that other Heidenstam poems were "read and sung" to Rilke during the Furuborg evenings. The Gibsons no doubt knew the song-collection, *Svensk lyrik*, made to the texts of other contemporary poets (especially Karlfeldt) by Vilhelm Peterson-Berger; Heidenstam was represented here with "Gullebarns vaggsånger" and "Höstsång," the second of which might have seemed particularly appropriate for the autumn days at Furuborg. Also, one wonders if Rilke's hosts could have failed to give the Austrian at least a taste of the "Tiveden" cycle which opens the *Dikter* of 1895. Earlier, at Borgeby in Skåne, Rilke had been captivated by the chateau's apple-orchard and the bright-green beech woods of Sweden's most southerly province, so much like those of Denmark; now, he was bewitched by the wilder fir-forests of middle Sweden,[14] and would surely have been interested to learn how Heidenstam described them in the ingressus of his cycle:

> Hör furornas dova sorgemusik,
> med förstämda trummor och tubor i moll,
> en blåkullahymn med suckar och skrik
> i ödemarken diktad av troll![15]

But here one enters the realm of guess-work.[16]

The eulogy's mention of the poems poses, then, more problems than it solves; the same may be said for the revelation that Rilke had read Heidenstam's novel, *Heliga Birgittas pilgrimsfärd* (1901). Sometime after returning from his Swedish trip, it may be assumed, Rilke went through the story of "der heiligen Frau aus königlichem Stamm."[17] Did he do so because of his passion for "Frauenbücher," even though in this case (as in Fru Marie Grubbe's) the story of the fascinating woman from the past was written by a man? Or because, at work on *Malte*, he had the feeling that Birgitta might find a place in the gallery of remarkable Scandinavian women—Leonora Christina Ulfeldt, Hilleborg Krafse, Christine Munk, Anne Sophie Reventlow, Julie Reventlow—which he was assembling for his novel? Or because Birgitta, with her *Revelations*, might have been included among those mystically inclined and literarily gifted "lovers" whose works Malte knew: Mechtild, Therese of Avila, Rose of Lima? Rilke was certainly not above using novels as sources of information about historical figures whom he found intriguing: witness his hint to Count Birger Mörner about the help which the Count's bad historical novel, *Dess höga plaisir*, had afforded him as he formed his picture of Anne Sophie Reventlow.[18]

190

If the opening sections of the eulogy in *Svenska Dagbladet* give rise to minor literary-historical problems, however, its long conclusion solves a more important one: the question of when Rilke became acquainted with Heidenstam's novel about Charles XII. Rilke indicates that he had known the book for a long time; he discovered it "als ich ganz jung war." Therese Krüger's translation, *Karl XII. und seine Krieger* (which consisted only of the first part of Heidenstam's text) had appeared at the publishing house of Albert Langen (Bjørnsterne Bjørnson's son-in-law) in 1898, thus when Rilke was 23; he wrote his poem on Charles XII between October 2 and October 21, 1900. The remainder of the paragraph on *Karolinerna* in *Svenska Dagbladet* bespeaks an overpowering enthusiasm, of the sort from which poetic inspiration might readily spring—as a matter of fact, the stimulus is directly described: "Es erregte in mir eine Lust und eine Entschlossenheit, einmal Menschen zu schreiben." Next, the eulogy appears to contain a criticism of the work which the reading of *Karl XII. und seine Krieger* had produced: in Heidenstam's book, young Rilke had found "ein Gelingen... zu dem mein Können noch in keinem Verhältnis stand." To Rilke, looking backward, "Karl der Zwölfte von Schweden reitet in der Ukraine," in its lack of plasticity and its peculiar over-emphasis on the monarch's peculiar virginity, may well have seemed to fall short of what Heidenstam had achieved—and of what the Rilke of 1909, the poet of the carefully modeled *Neue Gedichte*, was presently achieving.[19] Then the birthday-greetings of 1909 close with thanks rendered for the gift, as it were, of one of the best-known of the poems in *Buch der Bilder*; Rilke had already offered the same thanks, and confessed the same literary connection, in that letter to Heidenstam of February, 1905, where he had talked of the hours, "die seltsam und verglühend über Ihren Büchern vergangen sind." In *Svenska Dagbladet*, however, the nature of "those many things... which I cannot name," and which deserve gratitude, is made much clearer.

The Gibsons had doubtless begun to talk about *Karolinerna* during those evenings in their home; they knew that Rilke had written a poem on the same topic, and it would be amusing to learn whether or not Rilke owned up to his close prior acquaintance with Heidenstam's masterpiece. On October 19, 1904, from Furuborg, Rilke wrote a letter to Ellen Key which was something less than ingenuous in its references to *Karolinerna*. "Aber doch zu einer Frage und Bitte: ich fühle mich verpflichtet nun auch an Juncker's Verlag etwas ernstlicher zu denken und ihm zu guten Sachen zu verhelfen. Wegen 'Kvinden skabt af Manden'[20] habe ich ihm geschrieben. Nun habe ich in der letzten Zeit überall so Wunderbares von Heidenstam's 'Caroliner' gehört; und da ich mir eine deutsche Übersetzung verschaffen will, erfahre ich, daß es keine giebt. Ist das nicht erstaunlich! — Würden Sie, liebe Ellen Key, nicht einmal (gelegentlich) bei Heidenstam anfragen, ob er schon jemanden zu einer Übertragung ins Deutsche autorisiert hat und ob, zusagenden Falls, die Übersetzung schon einem Verlage zugesprochen ist? — Wenn noch keine deutsche Ausgabe vorbereitet wird, wer, glauben Sie, könnte dieses merk-würdige Buch übersetzen? Giebt es jemanden? Ich denke es müßte für den Juncker'schen Verlag ein großer Fortschritt sein, die 'Caroliner' zu erwerben."[21] As a part of Rilke's loose connection with the publishing firm of Axel Juncker, it was his task to suggest new material; he had recently attempted, for example, to interest Juncker in issuing a translation of Kierkegaard's letters to Regine Olsen, the Danish edition of which Rilke had acquired while at Borgeby.[22] Now, reminded of Heidenstam by the Gibsons, it occurred to him that a full edition of *Karolinerna* would sell on the German market; Therese Krüger's rendering, over which he had pored before writing "Karl der Zwölfte von Schweden reitet in der Ukraine," consisted only of the first part. However, wishing to cover his tracks about the inspiration of "Karl der Zwölfte," he misled Ellen Key as he asked her for information, pretending that he had only just heard of *Karolinerna*. (He was obviously less sensitive on the subject of inspiration five years later on, at the time of the contribution to *Svenska Dagbladet*, when he was an established, even a famous poet.) Rilke knew that Ellen Key, a good friend of Heidenstam, could get the information needed; he also knew that Ellen Key, because of the wide distribution of her books in Germany, must be familiar with the available translators. Still, he could not make himself tell her the awful truth about his past with Heidenstam.

The next step in the negotiations is not easily discernible. Heidenstam is not mentioned again in the correspondence between Rilke and Ellen Key; however, one guesses that Ellen Key put the query to Heidenstam, learned of Therese Krüger's partial translation (of which Rilke was already aware), and reported her findings to her Austrian friend. She may have added, too, that she was an acquaintance of Miss Krüger—her *Missbrukad kvinnokraft* had been translated into German by the Danish woman—and may even have suggested that Rilke go to see her when next in Denmark. Probably she adduced the names of two other possible translators as well, for on November 20 Rilke reported to her: "Therese Krüger hat mir *sehr* lieb geschrieben. Ich werde in Charlottenlund (zwischen Hellerup und Klampenborg) wohnen können, wenn ich nun (es wird nur für 8-10 Tage sein) durch Kopenhagen komme. Das ist mir sehr lieb. Dann hat Mizi Franzos selbst sehr freundlich geschrieben. Ein Brief von Emmi Hirschberg aus Florenz kam…"[23] (Mimi Franzos, under the pseudonym "Francis Maro," was the official translator into German of Ellen Key's works, Emmi Hirschberg was a member of the circle of Key-enthusiasts which Grete Schurgast had assembled at her Pension Ludwig in Berlin.)[24] From the little evidence at hand, it seems unlikely that Rilke made a very determined effort to find Therese Krüger during his final passage through Denmark (December 2-9, 1904); in consideration of the story he had fabricated for Ellen Key, he no doubt decided that it would be just as comfortable not to find her. At Lou Andreas-Salomé's suggestion he had made a serious effort to locate the polylingual Miss Krüger (who had translated Lou's *Friedrich Nietzsche* into Danish) while in Copenhagen in September (RMR-LAS, *Briefwechsel*, Zürich-Wiesbaden, 1952, p. 190: October 17, 1904); but the Therese Krüger he found was merely an elderly teacher of languages. And in December he reported cryptically to Lou: "Therese Krüger ist bei dem Uralten auf Damgaar[d], — wenn es geht werde ich sie auf der Durchreise in Fredericia sehen" (RMR-LAS, *Briefwechsel*, pp. 198-199: December 4, 1904).[25] There was time for Rilke to interrupt his journey to Germany at Fredericia junction (the estate of Damgaard was not far away), but probably he did not: it would have been embarrassing to continue the pretence, in Miss Krüger's presence, that he had never heard of her partial translation of *Karolinerna* before Ellen Key told him about it.

Immediately upon arriving in Oberneuland from Scandinavia, Rilke wrote to Axel Juncker, requesting a copy of *Das Buch der Bilder* to send to Sweden as a Christmas gift (December 17, 1904); on February 15 he asked for three more.[26] The first copy of the book, which Juncker had published in 1902, went to the Gibsons; one of the trio from February was sent to Heidenstam, an appropriate gift, since it contained "Karl der Zwölfte von Schweden reitet in der Ukraine." Encouraged by Ellen Key, Heidenstam had written to Rilke about the possibility of a new German edition of *Karolinerna*;[27] Rilke replied with his letter of February 22, 1905, accompanying it with *Das Buch der Bilder*: "Von meinen Büchern sind mir die meisten älteren sehr fern; nur das Buch Gedichte, welches ich nun in Ihre Hände lege, steht mir noch ganz nahe, obwohl es schon seit fast drei Jahren erschienen ist. Sollte es Ihnen sympathisch sein, so werde ich glücklich sein, Ihnen später das eine oder andere meiner Bücher zu senden; besonders aber soll keines von den zukünftigen Ihnen fehlen: denn ich bin sehr stolz auf Ihre Teilnahme an mir..." As she had many other prominent Scandinavians, so Ellen Key had showered Heidenstam with pro-Rilke propaganda; and Heidenstam had indicated his interest in Rilke's works in his letter.

Apart from the introductory revelations about Rilke's regard for Heidenstam's poetry and the closing statements he makes about the gift of his own, the letter of February 22 also contains a discussion of the real business at hand, the possible publication of a new *Karolinerna* in German. Not knowing whether or not Ellen Key has told Heidenstam of his "recent discovery" of the novel, and yet wanting to give Heidenstam the impression that he has long been familiar with his *magnum opus*, Rilke slides past the problem with a flattering ambiguity: "ich habe dieses Buch (das mir in allen Tagen gleich nahe ist) auch jetzt wiedergelesen." Then he sabotages Ellen Key's suggestion that Therese Krüger might be entrusted with the task of preparing a complete translation. He does not attack Therese Krüger's work directly; one suspects that he feels she has done a bad job, but, not knowing Swedish, he is hardly in a position to say so. Instead, he puts the main blame for the failure of the first German version on its publisher, Albert Langen. He has just spent several happy hours with the book, but: "ich spreche ja leider allerdings von der deutschen Ausgabe in der Übersetzung des Fräuleins Krüger; meine Überzeugung stimmt mit Ihrer Meinung völlig überein; der verhältnismäßige Mißerfolg dieser Ausgabe ist ohne Zweifel durch den Verlag verschuldet; die durch nichts begründete Umschreibung des Titels, die stillose Ausstattung erklären vieles; dann, daß man nur den ersten Teil gebracht hat. Aber es muß in der That auch eine gewisse Gleichgültigkeit des Verlages diesem Buch gegenüber bestanden haben; ich halte es (obgleich ich die Deutschen nicht liebe und die momentane Stimmung in Deutschland besonders drückend empfinde[28]) für unmöglich, daß ein Buch von der grandiosen und hinreißenden Macht der 'Karoliner' unbeachtet vorbeigegangen wäre, wenn man es in genügend viele Hände hätte gelangen lassen." Simultaneously, Rilke also torpedoes a second suggestion made by Ellen Key: that selections from the entire book might be published, instead of simply slicing the book in half, as had happened in the case of the Langen edition. (Ellen Key, it should be pointed out, occasionally had her own books tailored to fit the German reading public; in her *Människor*, for example, she replaced the Goethe essay with an exciting novelty, a portrait of the Swedish Romanticist, Almqvist.) Evidently, Rilke had at first approved Ellen Key's idea, something for which he now apologizes: "Die Idee Ellen Key's, eine verständige Auswahl herauszugeben, überzeugte mich im ersten Augenblick und ich stimmte ihr bei; seither aber habe ich so deutlich gefühlt, daß jegliche Auswahl ein Zerreißen dieses Werkes ist, das in so hohem Grade ein Ganzes ist, ein Untrennbares, ein lebendes Wesen, an dem jedes Organ und jedes Glied seine Stelle und seine Aufgabe hat. So fühle ich es jetzt, und daß ich in diesem Gefühle Ihnen näher bin, zeigt mir Ihr Brief..."

Noting the care with which Rilke dissected (and destroyed) Ellen Key's two proposals, one might almost feel that Rilke was no longer very concerned about the book's appearance under the banner of Axel Juncker. One would be right. Between the veiled objections to Therese Krüger and the less veiled (and, artistically speaking, quite justified) hesitation about a selection from the novel, Rilke had revealed that it was no longer his job to find books for Juncker to publish: "Indessen hat sich aber meine direkte Verbindung mit dem stuttgarter Verlag [i.e., Juncker], dessen Lektor ich eine Zeitlang war, sehr gelockert, so daß ich im Augenblicke keinen direkten Angriffspunkt zur Verwirklichung meines Planes habe." Rilke-scholarship has found out all too little about the poet's relationship with Juncker, who had already brought out two of his works, the 1902 edition of *Das Buch der Bilder* and *Die Letzten* and who, in 1906, would issue two more: the second enlarged edition of *Das Buch der Bilder* and *Der Cornet*.[29] It is obvious, however, from the numerous requests which Rilke made of Juncker at this time, that the relationship was by no means as dead as Rilke would have liked to have Heidenstam believe. On December 17, 1904, replying to Juncker, Rilke had mentioned receiving a letter and a check from the publisher. The letter seems to have included questions—about Rilke's willingness to give all his future books to Juncker, or about the laxity with which the poet had been functioning as a publisher's reader?—which Rilke did not particularly want to answer; he excused himself with illness, promising to return to the questions as soon as he felt better. In February, Juncker, still without the detailed reply he wanted, indicated his impatience; on February 15, Rilke sent further medical excuses,[30] and just a week later he told Heidenstam that his connections with Juncker had become very tenuous indeed.

The published correspondence between Rilke and Anton Kippenberg, the new owner of the Insel-Verlag, begins only in November, 1906, shortly after Kippenberg had taken over control of the house; however, by the early months of 1905, the Insel-Verlag had already indicated its strong interest in Rilke's latest volume of verse, *Das Stunden-Buch*: the manuscript was in the hands of the Insel's editors by May 1, 1905, and the book was published there in the autumn of the same year. (Under its earlier chief, Rudolf von Pöllnitz, the Insel had published the second edition of *Vom lieben Gott und Anderes* —now revised and called *Geschichten vom lieben Gott*—in 1904). When Rilke told Heidenstam that his ties to Juncker had been weakened, he was simply predicting what he hoped would be the case. The Insel was ready to offer good terms, and perhaps Rilke wished even then, in February, 1905, to become a permanent member of the Insel's sleek stable. Juncker, a capricious and stingy soul, could be abandoned with no regrets; on November 29, 1905, Rilke complained to Ellen Key that: "Juncker sprach davon, daß bald eine neue Auflage des B.d.B. nöthig sein wird. Die will ich sorgfältig vorbereiten und auch einen Kontrakt machen, denn von der ersten, die also doch gekauft worden ist, hab ich gar nichts gehabt."[31] A year later, Rilke quickly accepted Anton Kippenberg's offer of publishing all his future work and of acquiring the rights to everything he had brought out at other houses in the past. There then began the long and bitter struggle to pry Juncker loose from the works, especially the lucrative *Cornet*, to which he held title.

Rilke had, he knew, committed himself too deeply to Heidenstam with his vaunted "plan" for the publication of a new translation of *Karolinerna*. Juncker was the one publisher over whose choice of books he had any influence at the time,[32] but he wanted his relations to Juncker to grow cooler, not warmer. He was not enough of a business man, nor was he sufficiently interested in Heidenstam's cause, despite his protestations to the contrary, to look elsewhere for a publisher, and so he fell into an abashed silence, writing nothing to Heidenstam for more than a year. Meanwhile Heidenstam, heaping coals of fire on Rilke's head with each package, sent book after book from his extensive production to Oberneuland, whence they were forwarded to the vagabond poet; and finally, on January 12, 1906, in Rodin's villa at Meudon, Rilke summoned the courage to write a letter of thanks: "Sie haben mich durch so viele liebe Sendungen ausgezeichnet und erfreut; im tiefsten erfreut, und ich habe in einem zu rasch vergangenen Jahre nicht einmal Zeit gehabt, Ihnen zu danken." There were two external factors, apart from

Rilke's sense of having committed a dreadful crime against good manners, which made him put pen to paper, and, as a matter of fact, made the job easier. His *Stunden-Buch* had just come out, and he could repay gift with gift. But, more important, he had been freed from his obligations concerning *Karolinerna* by the announcement, among the books coming out for the Christmas trade of 1905, of a new and complete translation of the book: *Die Karoliner: Erzählungen aus der Zeit Karls XII.*, rendered into German by Gustav Bergman and published at C. J. E. Volckmann's Verlag in Rostock. "Ich höre übrigens, daß ein deutscher Verlag jetzt eine vollständige Ausgabe der 'Karoliner' gemacht hat. Damit ist ja mein großer Wunsch in Erfüllung gegangen. Ich bin sicher, daß dieses Meisterwerk jetzt auch in deutschen Händen so geschätzt und so ehrfürchtig gehalten sein wird wie die Herzen der anderen Völker es längst behandeln. Ich wünsche Ihnen neue Freude zu diesem unvergeßlichen Buch..." The letter closes with wishes for a second kind of joy, too, "Freude zu neuem Schaffen, zu neuer Arbeit, mit der Sie Ihres Volkes Reichthum und Ruhm vergrößern," and with the rather bloodless suggestion that, if Heidenstam should ever be in Paris, then Rilke would like to be informed, so that he might hasten, "Sie von Herzen zu begrüßen." As far as one knows, the Parisian meeting never took place; Heidenstam could tell from this second letter (which opened so bombastically, "Verehrter Dichter," and which was so full of vague flattery) that nothing more remained to be said between himself and his colleague on the Continent.

Yet Rilke did realize that he had been dealing with an important literary figure, and that he, somehow, had failed him: both in his implied denial of Heidenstam's influence on his "Karl der Zwölfte" in the letter to Ellen Key, and in the way he had tried to make use of Heidenstam in his business dealing with Juncker. In his relations with friends and acquaintances, Rilke demonstrated, for the most part, good will and good intentions, but he was not infrequently driven from the straight and narrow by the demon of personal advantage and personal vanity; and, in turn, he was not very proud of what he had done under the demon's whip. A bad conscience speaks in the eulogy contributed to *Svenska Dagbladet*. And yet more than a bad conscience: Rilke had been an admirer, a strong one, of *Karolinerna*, and the poems of Heidenstam, despite his having seen them darkly through the glass of James Gibson's impromptu translation, had inflamed his poetic imagination. Amidst the empty phrases of the second letter to Heidenstam, a single note of warmth and sincerity can be heard; it occurs as Rilke speaks of the poems: "... ich muß mich doch meistens an die Übersetzungen halten, besonders seit ich wieder fern von Schweden und meinen schwedischen Freunden bin, [bin ich] nicht mehr an den Klang gewöhnt, den ich so sehr liebte... Aber manchmal, besonders wo ich vor Ihren *Gedichten* stehe, springt, über alles hinweg, ein Verstehen, ein Einsehen, ein unermeßliches, helles Begreifen auf mich über, so daß ich mich doch zu denen rechnen darf, die zu Ihrem reichen Werke eine Beziehung haben. Und dessen bin ich innig froh."[33]

[1] G. C. Schoolfield, "Charles XII Rides in Worpswede," *MLQ* (September, 1955), 258-267.

[2] In the volume, *Verner von Heidenstam: fragment och aforismer, jämte studier kring Heidenstam* (Stockholm, 1959), the editor, Carl Fehrman, has included Professor Böök's amusing account of his first meeting with Heidenstam, "Mitt första möte med Heidenstam" (pp. 33-46).

[3] "Naddö i fest till Heidenstamsjubileet i dag," *Dagens Nyheter* (Stockholm, tisdagen den 6 juli 1909), No. 14071, p. 1. Translation by the author.

[4] It is worth noting that Böök did not recruit any Norwegians for his page; only Sweden, Finland's Swedish-speaking minority, and Denmark are represented. Heidenstam's patriotic stand in the crisis over the Swedish-Norwegian Union in 1905 had not been forgotten in the new nation of western Scandinavia.

[5] Rilke's two letters (of June 1 and June 28, 1909) to Fredrik Böök are in the Böök-Archive of the Lund University Library; they are quoted here with the late Professor Böök's generous permission.

[6] Richard Dehmel, *Ausgewählte Briefe* (Berlin, 1922-23), II, p. 447: letter of December 23, 1918, to Richard von Schaukal.

[7] Only the introduction to Regina Ullmann's *Von der Erde des Lebens* (1910) provides an exception. Rilke's other literary "appreciations" in subsequent years are of non-German authors, Marianna Alcoforado and the Comtesse Anne de Noailles (1907), and Maurice de Guérin (1911).

[8] *Svenska Dagbladet* (Stockholm, tisdagen den 6 juli 1909), No. 179, p. 10. The greeting should be placed in the *Sämtliche Werke*, VI (Frankfurt am Main, 1966) between the contribution to *Die Bücher zum wirklichen Leben* and the introduction to Regina Ullmann's book.

[9] Rilke's two letters to Heidenstam (of February 22, 1905 and January 12, 1906) are in the possession of the Övralidstiftelse. They have been transmitted to the present writer through the gracious aid of Professor Carl Fehrman (Lund).

[10] "One evening J[immie] read Almqvist — read very, very slowly and translated whatever Rilke did not understand — but it was not often necessary." The sentence is to be found in an undated letter from Lizzie Gibson to Ellen Key in the Royal Library, Stockholm; just before it occurs, Lizzie Gibson describes the industrious but idyllic life the couple led with the poet, telling how everyone went about his own work, meeting at mealtimes ("arbetar hvar och en för sig, träffas om måltiderna"), and how they spent "härliga och gudomliga aftnar" ("splendid and sublime evenings") reading aloud to one another — "jaktslottsaftnar," Lizzie Gibson calls them, thinking of the company assembled at the "Jaktslott" of Carl Jonas Love Almqvist's *Törnrosens bok*, and described in the "Rahmen-erzählung," *Jagtslott*, of that collection. The sentence describing Jimmie's reading of Almqvist has been quoted by Reidar Ekner in his excellent article, "Rilke, Ellen Key och Sverige," *Samlaren*, 86 (1965), 5-43 (p. 26); however, as it appears there, a small but not insignificant omission has been made: Ekner omits the second "mycket" in "mycket, mycket långsamt," "very, *very* slowly." Was Rilke's knowledge of Swedish, especially spoken Swedish, really as good as Ekner assumes it to be in his newspaper article, "När Rilke vistades i Göteborg," *Göteborgs Handels- och Sjöfartstidning* (måndag 6 september 1965), p. 3: "Med sin intuitiva språkbegåvning hade Rilke således hunnit lära sig förstå svenska." ("With his intuitive gift for languages, Rilke had thus succeeded in learning to understand Swedish.")

[11] Ekner has based his brief section on Rilke and Heidenstam in his article (see note 10 above) on Rilke's two letters to Heidenstam, without reference to the subsequent tribute to Heidenstam in SD, the letters to Böök, or — the most important aspect, after all, of the Rilke-Heidenstam complex — the relationship between Rilke's poem on Charles XII and *Karolinerna*, and the subsequent story of Rilke's interest in the novel. However, it should be remembered that Ekner's principal concern is a detailed description of Rilke's friendship with Ellen Key; his article is thus a major contribution to Rilke-scholarship, and should be carefully studied by every scholar seriously concerned with the *facts* about Rilke's life and works.

¹² The scene is described by Jimmie Gibson in a letter to Arthur Bendixson of November 14, 1904, in the Gibson family papers, Göteborgs stadsbibliotek.

¹³ See| Staffan Björck, *Heidenstam och sekelskiftets Sverige: Studier i hans nationella och sociala författarskap* (Stockholm, 1946), pp. 158-160. *Ett folk*, in Stenhammar's setting, contained one number that would become familiar to every Swede, the anthem "Sverige."

¹⁴ Paul Gibson, Jimmie's and Lizzie's youngest son, recalls that Rilke took long walks in the woods surrounding the lakes at Jonsered, the Aspensjö, on whose south side Furuborg lies, and the Ramsjö. The terrain is such that Rilke probably did as much climbing as walking — a vigorous kind of relaxation which no doubt had something to do with the excellent fettle in which he found himself as he left Sweden in December.

¹⁵ In translation: "Hear the muted funeral music of the firs,/ with drums out of tune and minor-keyed tubas,/ a Brocken-hymn with sighs and shrieks/ in the wilderness composed by trolls."

¹⁶ One might be tempted to postulate an influence of Heidenstam's poetry about the Swedish forest primeval on Rilke's poem, "Oben wo die großen Stimmen wohnen,/ in den Kronen dieser hohen Föhren…," which Rilke subjoined to his letter of October 2, 1904 (*Briefe 1904-1907*, Leipzig, 1939, pp. 51-52) to Ellen Key, following a description of a day spent wandering in the woods with James Gibson and an evening around the hearth-fire at Furuborg. (The poem's text, in the version sent Ellen Key, has been reprinted in *Sämtliche Werke*, III, p. 780; for a discussion of the poem's first version, given to James Gibson, and the circumstances surrounding its composition, see Reidar Ekner, "Rilke, Ellen Key, och Sverige," 23-24). However, it is not sure that the Heidenstam readings at Furuborg had already begun (Rilke had been there briefly early in September, and had returned, after an abortive attempt to establish Clara and himself in Copenhagen, on September 28); besides, Rilke did not need literary prompting to make him poetically aware of the new and somewhat strange milieu in which he found himself, and, particularly in his earlier "storm-poems" (for example, the "Sturmnacht" of 1898/99 and the "Sturm" — for Clara Westhoff — and "Aus einer Sturmnacht" of 1901) had showed himself to be fascinated by a related aspect of nature's power. On the other hand, it may be worth noting that one of the two storm-poems he wrote at Furuborg — where his lyric vein became active again, after a quiescent period at Borgeby, the Scanian chateau where he had spent the summer — has a reference to a figure from Heidenstam's literary world: in the "Sturm" ("Wenn die Wolken, von Stürmen geschlagen") from Furuborg, two of the strophes tell the story of Mazeppa's famous ride; Heidenstam recounts the heroic tale from the old hetman's past in the first part of *Karolinerna*. (The second storm-poem from Furuborg, "Abend in Skåne," recalls a gale which Rilke had experienced at Borgeby on August 12, but which took lyric form only under the influence of the "ganz großer Sturm" of late October which, as Rilke told Lou Andreas-Salomé in a letter of November 3, 1904, "prepared the Jonsered landscape for the winter.")

¹⁷ It had come out in German as *Die Pilgrimfahrt aer heiligen Birgitta: Erzählung*, einzige autorisierte Übersetzung von E. Stine (Dresden, 1903). Several other works of Heidenstam were available in German at the time Rilke wrote the eulogy for *Svenska Dagbladet: Classicität und Germanismus: Einige Worte über den Weltkampf* (Vienna, 1900), *Landschaften und Menschen* (Strassburg, 1901), *Sankt Göran und der Drache* (Leipzig, 1902), *Hans Alienus* (Munich, 1901), *Die Schweden und ihre Häuptlinge* (Munich, 1909), and *Der Stamm der Folkunger, I: Folke Filbyter* (Munich, 1909). In 1905-06, Heidenstam appears to have sent the Swedish originals of a number of his works to Rilke (cf. the letter of January 12, 1906), but Rilke told him that, save for the poems, he had to stick to German translations. No direct evidence exists that Rilke carefully read any of the works in German just listed; yet one of the most famous passages in his letters is surprisingly like a section in *Hans Alienus*. The hero of Heidenstam's novel-of-ideas offers his thoughts about Americans: "[The American] is a cruel parody of intellect. He cannot go past a knoll beside the road without climbing it and forcing his explanations, which in the final analysis are no explanations, on the passers-by… In golden ages man is directed most principally by his imagination and his natural desire to exist. Isn't it the apple's goal to become the freshest and most

perfect of apples, and not to become the knowledge of what an apple was?" (*Samlede verk*, IV, p. 152).

Rilke writes to Witold Hulewicz on November 13, 1925: "Noch für unsere Großeltern war ein 'Haus,' ein 'Brunnen,' ein ihnen vertrauter Turm, ja ihr eigenes Kleid, ihr Mantel: unendlich mehr, unendlich vertraulicher; fast jedes Ding ein Gefäß, in dem sie Menschliches vorfanden und Menschliches hinzusparten. Nun drängen, von Amerika her, leere gleichgültige Dinge herüber, Schein-Dinge, Lebens-Attrappen... Ein Haus, im amerikanischen Verstande, ein amerikanischer Apfel, oder eine dortige Rebe, hat nichts gemeinsam mit dem Haus, der Frucht, der Traube, in die Hoffnung und Nachdenklichkeit unserer Vorväter eingegangen war" (*Briefe 1921-26*, Leipzig, 1940, pp. 374-375). Can Heidenstam have planted the seed of the 'American apple' in Rilke's memory, from which, transformed, refined, and its source long ago forgotten, it emerged some twenty years later?

[18] Cf. Rilke's letter of September 5, 1915, Mörne Archive, Örebro Stadsbibliotek: for years he has asked whether there were still more works by the author of *Allerhöchst Plaisir*; he — Rilke — has long been "immer unter der Nachwirkung jenes kleinen, bezaubernden Buches," which tells the story of Anne Sophie in detail.

[19] It is worth noting that Rilke, in his description of what he had learned, as an artist, from the reading of *Karolinerna*, takes up the theme of "aussparen," of attempting to delineate an evasive main figure by filling in its surroundings "mit Anderem, Faßbaren." The theme is used in his epicedium for Luise von Schwerin (*Sämtliche Werke*, II, pp. 9-10, written in 1906):

> Aber denen, die dich nicht erfahren,
> kann ich, hülflos, nichts versprechen als:
> dich aus allen Dingen auszusparen...

and in the passage about Ingeborg Brahe in *Malte:* "Damals zuerst fiel es mir auf, daß man von einer Frau nichts sagen könne; ich merkte, wenn sie von ihr erzählten, wie sie sie aussparten, wie sie die anderen nannten und beschrieben, die Umgebungen, die Örtlichkeiten, die Gegenstände, bis an eine bestimmte Stelle heran, wo das alles aufhörte..." (*Sämtliche Werke*, VI, pp. 785-786).

[20] Fru Hulda Garborg's *Kvinden skabt af Manden* (Christiania, 1904) was an answer to Otto Weininger's *Geschlecht und Charakter*. (Fru Garborg was the wife of Arne Garborg, the Norwegian landsmål novelist.)

[21] The passage is omitted from the two printed versions of the letter (*Briefe 1902-1906*, pp. 223-224, and *Briefe 1904-1907*, pp. 55-56). The original manuscript is in the Ellen Key Archive, Royal Library, Stockholm.

[22] In this case, Rilke was successful; *Søren Kierkegaards Verhältnis zur 'ihr'*, translated by Raphael Meyer, came out at Juncker's Verlag in Stuttgart in 1905.

[23] Unpublished letter in the Ellen Key Archive.

[24] See Ellen Michelsen, *Brev från Ellen Key: 1907-1925* (Stockholm, 1952), pp. 20-21, for a brief description of the group. In the letter of November 6, 1906 to Ellen Key (in a paragraph omitted from the printed version of the letter: *Briefe 1906-1907*, pp. 92-95), Rilke tells how he became acquainted with the Schurgast circle.

[25] Even the omniscient Ernst Pfeiffer cannot say who "der Uralte" was; he suggests, in his note on the letter (p. 552), that he may have belonged to the circle of Therese Krüger at Damgaard. Therese Krüger herself, one of those shadowy transmissive figures, like Laura Marholm and Julius Hoffory, between Scandinavia and Germany (figures all deserving closer attention from scholarship), was the friend of numerous notables of the age. She played a not inconsiderable role in the "Nietzsche-feud" of 1889-1890 between Georg Brandes and Ola Hansson (see Brandes's letter of January 4, 1890, and Therese Krüger's undated letter, both to Laura Marholm, in the Ola Hansson Archive, Lund University Library); later on, she corresponded both with Ellen Key and Lou Andreas-Salomé (see Ellen Key's letters of November 20 and December 12, 1908, as well as

Therese Krüger's letter dated Damgaard, September 13, 1905 [?], all to Lou Andreas-Salomé, in the Andreas-Salomé Archive, Göttingen).

[26] Letters to Axel Juncker in the Houghton Library, Harvard University.

[27] Presumably this is the letter which Rilke mentions to the Gibsons in the postscript of his letter of January 19, 1905: "Eben kam ein langer Brief von Heidenstam. Ich athme tief, sooft ich eine schwedische Marke sehe" (Gibson Family Archive, Göteborgs stadsbibliotek).

[28] One would guess that Rilke refers here to the wave of jingoism which swept over Germany (can one speak of a single "wave" of jingoism in the nation of Wilhelm II?) during the Tangier crisis.

[29] Portions of the correspondence from Rilke to Axel Juncker are located in the Royal Library, Copenhagen, and the Houghton Library, Harvard; the main body, however, is on deposit in the Deutsche Literatur-Archiv of the Schiller National-Museum, Marbach. When the present writer, visiting Marbach in 1966, asked to see the Juncker letters, he was told that they were "gesperrt," since a printed version of them was being prepared. Recently, an informative resumé of their contents has appeared: Renate Scharffenberg, "Rilke und sein Verleger Axel Juncker," *Imprimatur*, 5 (1967), pp. 67-80.

[30] Letter to Axel Juncker in the Houghton Library, Harvard University.

[31] A short passage from this letter has been published in *Briefe 1902-1906*, p. 277.

[32] In later years, and especially during the war, Rilke exerted a considerable influence over the choice of books for publication by the Insel-Verlag.

[33] Rilke kept himself *au courant* about German translations of Heidenstam's lyrics. He formed an opinion ("teilweise gut") of the translation which Friedrich Stieve published in 1910 (cf. Rainer Maria Rilke-Katharina Kippenberg, *Briefwechsel*, Wiesbaden, 1955, p. 70: November 8, 1913); and, in 1916, recommended Stieve to Birger Mörner, the Swedish historical novelist and travel writer, as a possible translator of the verse in Mörner's novel, *Bråvallahus*, citing the Heidenstam translations as examples of Stieve's ability (letter of October 28, 1916, in the Mörner Archive, Örebro).

Two Examples of Twentieth-Century Art: Giorgio di Chirico and Franz Kafka

PHILLIP H. RHEIN

The paintings of Giorgio di Chirico and the writings of Franz Kafka are two isolated examples of the complex and often puzzling techniques employed by many twentieth-century artists. Unfortunately, the critical commentary on their work is frequently even more difficult to understand than the works themselves. Many of their critics become enmeshed in the artists' seemingly individual, intellectualized emotions, derive little or no meaning from them, and completely lose the relationship between Chirico's and Kafka's art and ordinary human experience. The same critics often see nothing beyond what they imagine to be an intricate network of subjective symbols, invented as meaningless playthings of a word and a paint juggler.

But it is not symbols at all—let alone experiences transposed into symbols and networks thereof—that these artists, or any artists, generally work with or initially try to create. This only seems so from the outside. Art is far more like playing a game whose rules are yet to be worked out as one goes along. The artist or writer or composer has done one thing and is trying to do another within his medium, stretching its possibilities to the utmost and at the same time producing something that has a form, a depth, a movement or whatever, that satisfies him enough to call it finished. The game may end by producing new or employing old symbols, but it does not begin that way. Certainly all art possesses that quality which transfers the mathematical, physical, and chemical formulae of line, mass, and color into something different from pure science. The lines in a painting are not merely the shortest distance between two points, mass is not the same mass with which physics is concerned, and color on a canvas is not the same stuff that comes in tubes. Even the behavior patterns that the word-artist employs to reveal a fictional character to us are not the same behavior patterns that the psychologist studies.

Yet these statements do not deny a relationship between art and the "real" world. What they do do is clarify the difference between experience, mathematics, science, and art. Or in other words, they highlight the fact that an art object presents something other than what is or is not possible in real life. It presents what is felt and imagined as possible to the artist, regardless of

201

whether or not we think it possible in life. If we continue to insist upon a tangible relationship between our experience of the world and the artists' presentation of the world, we impose an unnecessary obstacle onto a clear understanding of art. The "real" world may be photographed and case studies may be found in doctors' files—but art, other than for rare instances to the contrary, must be distinct from both.

Art elements are of course reminiscent of our world, and their inter-relations are also reminiscent of the fundamental ways in which the original elements common to both art and life are related; however, the painting, the poem, the musical composition, together with their elements, do not exist before they appear. The creator of these things cannot preview them, or plan them in advance, in the way that the photographer may study the objects of his composition before he actually photographs them. The elements of art arise in the act of executing them, and their creator meets with them as they emerge. Thus the feelings and images of the art object are no longer quite the same as those which served in real life, for they no longer only refer to the day-to-day world, but they now also refer to the artists' subjectively felt and imagined world.[1] For example, the sunflower of Van Gogh looks like the flowers of Arles, but the flower on the canvas does not exist; it cannot be found in reality. Part of that reality had to be negated so that Van Gogh could discover the unity and the completeness he desired.

All painters, unless their aim is to reproduce the impression of the painted object photographically, all sculptors and so on, understand this creative process and know immediately when other artists have been cheap or when they have been cheap themselves. Dali knows that he has mastered a certain technique of Lasur to perfection and used it *ad infinitum* so that one can talk about it; for he does it coldbloodedly and repetitiously, which is the very opposite of an artist's search for something still better. This search for some kind of perfection applies to Titian and Rembrandt, to Breughel or Beethoven, to lesser lights like Menzel and Leibl, and is absent only from the commercial illustrator, who has not the time to do himself justice and must, once a technique is mastered, turn out a glib product to satisfy the customer.

Literature is different in many ways, but a true artist will avoid found objects, as it were; and just as a painter will not put a strand of hair or horseshoe into a picture except when he is interested in textures, neither does the writer stick a fingernail in his book when he describes a hand. And for the same reason he will not use expressions that have been used by others and may be easy for communication, but not real enough to satisfy his need for perfection.

The art object then reflects the world as the artist perceives it. The elements are the same in the "real" world as they are in the artist's perception of that world, but they are selected and combined in such a way that their relationship may not be easily recognized. And in the same way that the real world provided the frame of reference to the artist's imagined world, there also exists a moment in time when the relationship between the artist and the becoming art object is unified. This close association between the artist and the art object exists only for the amount of time it takes to complete the painting, the composition, the poem. Once completed, the art object attains an existence of its own, totally independent of its creator. The *Mona Lisa*, for example, exists independently of Leonardo and has so existed since the moment he decided that the painting was finished. To alter her would be to create something other than what we have come to identify as the *Mona Lisa*.

But it is the moment of creativity—before the final moment of completion, when the artist and the art object are still united as one—that can aid our understanding of art. If we grant that the artist reflects his experience of the world in his created object, then it follows that his impressions and experiences of the real world are essential to an understanding of his projected imagined world. It is through this concept that we can progress a degree toward the understanding of the created object. And if the argument is extended to one of its logical conclusions, two intuitively comparable art objects should then be factually comparable if one can reasonably establish that these two objects are the creative projection of a commonly experienced "real" world into the artists' possible world.

The paintings of Giorgio di Chirico and the writings of Franz Kafka serve as an excellent illustration of this point. Upon first glance, these men apparently have little in common other than their being of the same generation.[2] Chirico is a surrealist painter of Italian parentage who was born in Greece, travelled in Italy and finally settled and painted in Paris. Kafka is of Jewish parentage, lived in Prague and wrote in German. However, beneath these differences of nationality, religion, and media that exist between the two men, there lies an intimate association of artistic stimuli, purpose, and technique; and by analyzing these we are led to a better understanding of not only Chirico and Kafka but also of one creative method of modern art.

Their biographies provide an interesting starting point for comparison. Although the father-son conflict is sufficiently handled in most psychological studies to satiate our desires, an examination of Chirico's and Kafka's artistic portrayal of this almost universal problem can provide one key to the understanding of their art; for the men project their personal experiences of the universal into the products of their talent.[3] Two polar heredities met in and sought conquest of both Chirico and Kafka. Their fathers were practical, realistic, self-confident, and strong-willed business men, while their mothers were impractical, dreamy, shy, and sensitive women. Neither Chirico nor Kafka ever attained the synthesis of his father's dynamic bourgeois existence and his mother's aesthetic world of dreams. Both men were taunted by their fathers' robustness, by their fathers' enforcement of a right founded on person and not on reason, and by their own personal inability openly to challenge their fathers' strength. Chirico's and Kafka's preoccupation with the father-son relationship permeates their artistic creations. In Chirico's answer to the surrealist's request for him to describe the dream which impressed him the most, he clearly expresses his feelings toward his father:

> I struggle in vain with the man whose eyes are suspicious and very gentle. Each time that I grasp him, he frees himself by quietly spreading his arms, which have an unbelievable strength, an incalculable power. They are like irresistible levers, like allpowerful machines, like those gigantic cranes which raise from the swarming shipyards whole quarters of floating fortresses with turrets as heavy as antediluvian mammals. I struggle vainly with the man of suspicious and very gentle glance. From each grasp, however frenzied it be, he frees himself easily, laughing and barely raising his arms... It is my father who thus appears to me in my dream, and yet when I look at him, he is not at all as he was when I saw him alive, in the time of my childhood. Nevertheless, it is he. There is something *far off* in the whole expression of his face, something which perhaps existed when I saw him alive and which now, after more than twenty years, strikes me with full force when I see him again in a dream.[4]

To find a parallel expression in Kafka's writing, we need only to turn to his *The Letter to My Father*. Although this particular quotation makes no mention of the dream, the haunting, hesitant, and nightmarish quality of the dream is apparent:

> You had worked yourself up to such a position by your own strength, that you had unlimited confidence in your own opinion... From your armchair you ruled the world. Your opinion was right, everybody else's was mad, eccentric meshuggah, not normal. At the same time your self-confidence was so great that there was no need for you to be consistent, and yet you were always right. You often even happened to have no opinion whatever on a subject, in which case any possible opinion on the subject must, without exception, be wrong. You could swear at the Czechs, for example, and then at the Germans, and then at the Jews, not for any particular reason but for every reason, and in the end there was nobody left but yourself. For me you developed the bewildering effect that all tyrants have whose might is founded not on reason, but on their own person... Courage, decision, confidence, pleasure in this or that could not hold out to the end, if you were opposed to it, or even if your opposition were only presumed—and presumed it might well be... In your presence—you are an excellent orator, the moment it is a question of anything that concerns you—I began to stammer and stutter, even that was too much for you, so finally I shut up, at first probably out of pigheadedness, later because I could neither think nor speak in front of you. And as it was you who really brought me up, it affected my whole life in all its aspects.[5]

The understanding of the tormented father-son relationship so clearly developed in the above quotations is essential to the interpretation of many of Chirico's and Kafka's works. One of Chirico's most powerful paintings *The Child's Brain*, 1914 (Soby, plate 30) gives visible form to the father's authority over the family. The strong, mustached figure dominates the canvas. His closed eyes appear to shield one from an otherwise shattering force which would repulse him. Kafka's helplessness and hopelessness in the face of his father's strength is most poignantly expressed in the two short stories, *The Judgment* (1913) and *The Metamorphosis* (1913). In both of these stories the father's debasement of the son causes disaster and sudden collapse.

The feeling of rejection and of excommunication begins with Chirico's and Kafka's personal father-son relationship and is expanded by both artists into their view of the world. In order to emphasize man's inner conflicts, the figures and the events that fill the worlds of Chirico's paintings and Kafka's writings are foreign to what we conventionally refer to as reality; yet these same compositions and actions are surrounded by material things with which each of us is familiar. Chirico's eerie mannequins are placed in a recognizable although somewhat fantastic world. Kafka's characters, be they metamorphosed or mechanized, live and act in material surroundings not unlike our own. This background of reality, in which the characters and events are depicted, compels the viewer or reader to concentrate upon the characters themselves. We are forced to grant that these seemingly absurd automatons in the artists' minds, at least, must have some relationship to the real world in which they function. It is but one step further to acknowledge these figures and events as representatives of some fundamental reality. Each artist takes only those features of everyday existence which are necessary to identify his characters as human. The artists' interest is not in the character analysis of a particular individual, but rather in the particular individual (distorted though he may be) as representative of the afflictions of mankind in general. Artistic distortion is used as a means of emphasis. Chirico and Kafka both turn to a world which is rational and yet unnatural—to a world in which unnatural beings and unnatural events are worked out in a very rational way.

Chirico employs an unexpected combination of color, form, and perspective which makes the real appear unreal, the unreal real. He uses geometrical constructions and physical laws in a completely detached, illogical manner: shadows can fall anywhere regardless of the laws dictated by the source of light. He questions all conventional ideas of associations. Perspective lines have no terminating point; shadows which have no apparent source jut across the canvas. Chirico himself has written:

Sometimes the horizon is defined by a wall behind which rises the noise of a disappearing train. The whole nostalgia of the infinite is revealed to us behind the geometrical precision of the square. We experience the most unforgettable movements when certain aspects of the world, whose existence we completely ignore, suddenly confront us with the revelation of mysteries lying all the time within our reach and which we cannot see because we are too short-sighted, and cannot feel because our senses are inadequately developed. Their dead voices speak to us from near-by, but they sound like voices from another planet.

We must not forget that a picture must always be the reflection of a profound sensation, that profound signifies strange, and strange signifies not-known or perhaps entirely unknown. A work of art, if it is to be immortal, must go far beyond the limits of man. Good sense and logic have no place in it. That is the way in which a painting can approximate to a dream-like or child-like state of mind.[6]

Chirico's paintings exhibit a strange combination of eerie figures and fantastic settings. He sought to rid art of every known subject, idea, thought, and symbol. He attempted to withdraw art from human fetters, and to illuminate things under a new aspect as though they were being illuminated for the first time. He combines diverse elements in such a way that they immediately alter our preconceived ideas of what painting must contain. Yet, each element is combined with the others to find its place in the composition. Logic has no place in the inspiration, but it is the strong controlling factor in the completed composition. Chirico transports us to a world of his own conception: a world which brings confusion to the mind of the viewer. This world is peopled by machine-like men. Chirico's automatons share a basic similarity one to the other; yet there is no indication that these figures communicate or are capable of communication. One figure is juxtaposed to another, but there is little physical contact between them. They rarely touch; and if they do, it is a frantic grasping similar to that experienced by Frieda and K. in Kafka's *The Castle* (1921). There is animal contact without human communication. The viewer feels that communication must exist, but the way to this communication is blocked by some invisible force. Chirico powerfully portrays the absence of communication which exists between indistinguishable men.

Kafka redefines the meaning of life in a way not dissimilar to the technique used by Chirico. His writings exemplify Chirico's desire for the "dreamlike or childlike state of mind." Logic as we ordinarily speak of it has no meaning to Kafka. His is a world beyond the limits of man's work-a-day experience but not beyond man's understanding. It is not a fairytale world of dreams, but a world of dreams in which so much of reality is retained that the reader is forced into recognition. Gregor in *The Metamorphosis* is metamorphosed into a gigantic vermin. This obviously illogical metamorphosis is treated in terms of the clearest, most concise logic, and the logical treatment of the illogical is true for all of Kafka's writings. Once the original situation is accepted, the dénouement follows in the most logical manner. Kafka, like Chirico, makes us change our preconceived ideas of what art must contain, but this art is not arbitrarily conceived. Each element is combined with the others to find its place in the composition.

Kafka's characters are alone, rejected by other men. They seek communication, and at times valiantly struggle to attain it; but their intentions and actions are always misunderstood. There exists no communion with their fellowmen. Their vain efforts are cast aside, and their trial becomes identified with themselves. The living, human qualities no longer breathe, and Kafka seems to be saying that the love, the warmth, and the beauty of life can neither be felt nor experienced by man excommunicated from man.

The world as revealed by Chirico and Kafka is a product of their personal, inner experience; and yet the persistent preoccupation with details by both painter and author overcomes any tendency we may have to feel transported out of reality. We are forced to be concerned with the living, the human, the real; and this emphasis upon detail is most significant when we are aware of the economy of expression in all the works of these artists. Nowhere are we bogged down under a torrent of needless visual or verbal description. In fact, the reality depicted by Chirico and Kafka is so intense that at times the viewer or reader is spellbound by the stark nakedness with which he is faced. The real world as it is commonly understood is retained by both artists as an environmental backdrop to unreal or strange characters who are misfits in an otherwise fluid situation; and the audience of either Chirico or Kafka is constantly tossed between the extremes of reality and unreality which are on the point of meeting but never meet.

I shall choose two visual images from Kafka's writing in order to illustrate the striking similarity in conception between Chirico and him. Kafka paints Chirico cities in words. The city of *The Castle* is described by Kafka in the following paragraph:

> ... so he [K.] resumed his walk, but the way proved long. For the street he was in, the main street of the village, did not lead up to the Castle hill, it only made towards it and then, as if deliberately, turned aside, and though it did not lead away from the Castle it got no nearer to it either. At every turn K. expected the road to double back to the Castle, and only because of this expectation did he go on; he was flatly unwilling, tired as he was, to leave the street, and he was also amazed at the length of the village, which seemed to have no end, again and again the same little houses, and frost-bound window-panes and snow and the entire absence of human beings—but at last he tore himself away from the obsession of the street and escaped into a small side-lane, where the snow was still deeper and the exertion of lifting one's feet clear was fatiguing; he broke into a sweat, suddenly came to a stop, and could not go on.[7]

Both Chirico's and Kafka's cities have vacant, haunting streets. The girl with the hoop in Chirico's *Melancholy and Mystery of a Street* (1914; Soby, plate 28) is placed in a street exactly like the street of *The Castle*. The girl frantically runs to nowhere; the street is a never-ending highway which leads beyond the open wagon, past the shadowed building into the bright sunlight. But the brightness is overcast by the shadow of an unidentified figure, and we feel that the child shall never reach her destination. Like the road in the village, this road also leads to nowhere. The eye and the mind are forced to begin again.

There is an equally amazing similarity between the artistic portrayal of the people who seek recognition behind the cold facades of the empty streets. Chirico's figures are machine-like. Only certain features are emphasized. The viewer is struck by apparent coldness. This bold delineation invites our imagination, and soon we no longer see mere outlines but are able to perceive a composite whole—a picture of man stripped of his lush, sensual qualities. The seduction of physical beauty is removed, and we are faced with the powerful workings of the inner being. The basic similarity of beings in Chirico's paintings (one to the other) brings us back to Kafka. Kafka in agreement with Chirico emphasizes only certain features of his characters. We could sketch Frieda in the style of Chirico. Kafka introduces her to us:

> The beer was drawn off by a *young girl* called Frieda. An unobtrusive *little girl* with *fair hair*, *sad eyes* and *hollow cheeks*, but with a *striking look of conscious superiority*...

> ... the *low-cut cream-coloured blouse* which sat oddly on her *poor thin body*... Her *hands* were certainly *small* and *delicate*, but they could quite as well have been called *weak* and *characterless*....[8]

Kafka nowhere gives a detailed description of Frieda. The description we have is scattered over several pages. The reader has a verbal picture of a personality enclosed in a thin body with expressive eyes and delicate hands. The details italicized above are sharp, architectural but in no way complete.

The comparison of the artists does not terminate with the above examples. The colors are intense in Chirico's and Kafka's descriptions. Chirico uses vivid shades; Kafka chooses the starkness of glaring white. There is no use of soft, delicate shades. The definite architectural composition in Chirico's painting is comparable to the clear, concise, architectural structure of the Kafka quotation. The parallels are striking: bold color—vivid language; linear compositon—definite statements; the enigma—the unfathomable. We are carried to the never-ending, visually by Chirico, verbally by Kafka.

Both artists, through their understanding of the world around them, employed the objects of that world—our world—in such a way that we are trapped by our superficial familiarity with these objects and are forced to free ourselves by looking upon the familiar in a new and strange way. There is no doubt that Chirico's and Kafka's understanding of the world was in part shaped by their common experience of that world, by their relationships within their families and societies; but the fact that they chose similar techniques to convey that experience attests not so much to the intellectual and artistic atmosphere of the time in which they created as it does to the artistic method employed by these two men to stretch the possibilities of their media in order to produce something that had a form, a depth, and a movement all its own. Their reaction to the world and their handling of experience, like that of all serious artists, was nothing that can be caught in a formula, unless we say that the formula is a search for some kind of perfection. Everything else is beside the point.

NOTES

[1] Chirico wrote in 1919: "A work of art must narrate something that does not appear within its outline. The objects and figures represented in it must likewise poetically tell you of something that is far away from them and also of what their shapes materially hide from us." *Artists on Art*, ed. Robert Goldwater and Marco Treves (New York, 1945), p. 440.

[2] It is possible that Chirico and Kafka were aware of each other's ideas on art and literature. They were both acquainted with Alfred Kubin, the painter and writer, although there is no evidence that Kubin discussed the theories of either of the artists with the other.

[3] In a report of interviews conducted for a BBC television series of six British artists (Edith Sitwell, poet; Victor Gollancz, publisher; Henry Moore, sculptor; Albert Finney, actor; Cecil Beaton, photographer, designer; Evelyn Waugh, novelist), each of these people speaks of his relationship to his parents (primarily the father) and his need for parental approval. "Six English Self-portraits," ed. Hugh Burnett, *Harpers Magazine* (April 1965), 56-63.

[4] James Thrall Soby, *The Early Chirico* (New York, 1941), p. 5.

[5] Max Brod, *Franz Kafka, a Biography* (New York, 1941), pp. 22-23.

[6] Jacques Lassaigne, "Evocation of the World Invisible," *History of Modern Painting from Picasso to Surrealism* (Geneva, 1950), pp. 104-105.

[7] Franz Kafka, *The Castle* (New York, 1948), pp. 14-15.

[8] *The Castle*, pp. 47-50. Italics mine.

Hermann Hesse as an Editor

JOSEPH MILECK

As an author, Hermann Hesse added considerably to literature. As an essayist and reviewer, he wrote a great deal about it. And as an editor, he did much for it. His place in world literature is firmly established.[1] His literary essays are familiar to most of his many serious readers.[2] His older following has not forgotten the reviewer who for decades was featured in may of the leading newspapers and literary periodicals of Germany, Switzerland and Austria.[3] But only a few long-time devotees, collectors of Hesseana and bibliographers, remember the editor. The scope of Hesse's editorial activity has never been assessed, and in fact could not have been assessed before the *Hesse-Nachlaß* in the Schiller-Nationalmuseum in Marbach a.N. became accessible in February 1965.[*]

I. PUBLISHED BOOKS

Hesse's editorial work spanned a period of twenty-five years. It began with the periodical *März* in 1907, was extended to books in 1910, interrupted by the war in 1915, resumed in 1918 and terminated in 1932. Of the fifty-eight books edited by Hesse, only eleven belong to the period 1910-15, forty-six were published from 1918 to 1926, and the last item, a small collection of Goethe's poems, appeared in 1932. Some of these publications are devoted to single writers, more are anthologies, and most are in the form of series. With their literary samplings of prose and poetry from roughly the latter part of the eighteenth to the outset of the twentieth century, the major portion of these books presents a thin coverage of Modern German Literature with a decided Romantic and Alemannic coloration. Familiar Romantics and kindred spirits—Novalis, Eichendorff, Arnim, Brentano, Jean Paul, Hölderlin, Mörike and Storm—join company with a wide array of lesser and more obscure Swabian and Swiss authors—Emanuel von Bodman, Ludwig Aurbacher, Ludwig Finckh, Johann Peter Hebel, Hermann Kurz, Wilhelm Schussen, Emil Strauß and Christian Wagner; Gustav Gamper, Paul Ilg, Felix Moeschlin, Jakob Schaffner and Robert Walser. But Hesse's editorial

[*] I am deeply indebted to Dr. Bernhard Zeller, Director of the Schiller-Nationalmuseum, for permitting me to examine Hesse's still uncatalogued editorial plans of 1924-25, and for permission to publish Hesse's outline of Nov. 6, 1924.

interests were not limited to German Literature or for that matter to literature in general. Foreign literatures in German translation are represented by such as Tolstoi, Gorkij, Korolenko, Hamsun and H. G. Wells, and by anthologies of old Oriental, Italian and French tales. Three publications are given to selections from the *Gesta Romanorum* and Heisterbach's *Dialogus miraculorum*, the latter, both translated and edited by Hesse. One book consists of a collection of famous murder trials, another concentrates on amusing anecdotes, and for yet another, Hesse gathered a series of early nineteenth-century reports on magnetism, clairvoyance and ghosts. The literary material edited by Hesse underlines his basic literary inclinations, these last mentioned diverse texts reveal some of his sundry stray interests.

The introductory or concluding remarks which Hesse generally added to the books he edited, vary considerably in their length and consequence. His accompanying comments for the series publications, with the exception of the *Merkwürdige Geschichten und Menschen* (1925-27), are characteristically but a page or less in length and of little import. His separate publications, on the other hand, were usually graced by essays three to seven pages long and are of correspondingly greater significance. These are the critical appraisal and the warm acclaim of a scholar-writer intent upon informing and advocating. When dealing with a single author, Hesse, almost invariably characterized both the man and the artist, commented upon his reception in Germany over the years, and added interesting asides about his own introduction to and later relationship with the writer in question. General interests or persistent concerns diverted him upon occasion from this pattern. The introduction for Salomon Geßner's *Dichtungen* (1922) and the concluding remarks for *Hölderlin* (1925) and *Novalis* (1925) are particularly noteworthy in this regard. The seventeen page Geßner essay is just as much an excellent study of European culture of the eighteenth century as it is of Geßner. And the Hölderlin and Novalis studies, psychography more than biography, are significant extensions of Hesse's lifelong interest in the psychology of the artist.

Hesse became an editor of books for the same personal and cultural reasons he had become a reviewer. Editing, like reviewing, was a convenient and interesting way to supplement his income while rendering a service to the literary world. It is quite obvious from remarks repeated in his introductions that Hesse considered himself to be a guiding intermediary, a literary propagandist in the best sense of the expression. *Titan* (1913) was to help re-awaken popular interest in Jean Paul. Eichendorff's *Gedichte und Novellen* (1913) and *Hölderlin* (1925) were to contribute to a renewed interest in these authors. *Lieder deutscher Dichter* (1914) were intended to bolster a generally lagging interest in poetry. *Novalis* (1925) was to help popularize a figure never widely read or adequately understood. *Dreißig Gedichte* (1932) were to familiarize German youth with Goethe. Christian Wagner's *Gedichte* (1913), *Alemannenbuch* (1919) and *Die junge Schweiz* [1919] were efforts to introduce a wider reading public to little known contemporary Alemannic writers. The *Gesta Romanorum* [1914] and *Geschichten aus dem Mittelalter* (1925) were meant to foster a wider interest in Latin tales of the Middle Ages, and with such as *Geschichten aus Japan* [1922], *Novellino* [1922] and *Sesam* (1925) Hesse hoped to acquaint more readers with old tales from other lands and cultures.

While Hesse's reviewing and editing were financially motivated and service directed, the extent of this secondary involvement was strictly determined by his psychic state and creative mood. From the very outset these activities were diversional filler-committments consigned primarily to the restless or more often troubled lulls between major works. It was between *Unterm Rad* (finished Dec. 1903) and *Gertrud* (begun 1906-07) that Hesse became a regular contributor of reviews to four major publications[4] and a co-founder of the periodical *März*. It was during the troubled lull between *Gertrud* (finished early 1909) and *Roßhalde* (begun July 1912) that he stepped up his reviewing sharply and began his editing of books. And it was in the successive very restive lulls between *Roßhalde* (finished spring 1913) and *Demian* (begun Sept. 1917), *Demian* (finished Oct. 1917) and *Klein und Wagner* (begun May 1919), the discontinuation of *Siddhartha* in early 1920 and its resumption in mid 1921, and between the ending of *Siddhartha* (May 1922) and the beginning of *Steppenwolf* (late 1924) that Hesse's editorial work became his principle diversion.

1 *Der Lindenbaum*. Deutsche Volkslieder. Berlin: S. Fischer, 1910, 267 pp.
Revised 1924, 194 pp.
Selections made by Hesse, M. Lang, and E. Strauß.

2 *Eduard Mörike*. Mit Bildnis. Leipzig: Hesse & Becker, 1911, 87 pp. Hesses Volksbücherei No. 598. Deutsche Lyriker, H. 8.
Vorwort, pp. 3-13.

3 Eichendorff, Josef von, *Gedichte und Novellen*. Berlin: Deutsche Bibliothek, 1913, X, 196 pp. (Deutsche Bibliothek, Bd. 59).
Vorwort, pp. V-VII.

a *Aus dem Leben eines Taugenichts und anderes*. Berlin: Deutsche Bibliothek, 1934, 307 pp. (Deutsche Bibliothek, Bd. 59a).
Text and Vorwort (pp. 7-9) same as preceding item.

b *Gedichte und Novellen*. Ausgewählt und eingeleitet von Hermann Hesse. Zürich: Scientia A.G., 1944, 320 pp.
[Vorwort], pp. 7-12, is slightly altered.

c *Novellen und Gedichte*. Ausgewählt und eingeleitet von Hermann Hesse. Zürich: Buchgemeinschaft Ex libris, 1955, 320 pp.
[Vorwort] (pp. 7-12) same as b.

d *Novellen und Gedichte*. Ausgewählt und eingeleitet von Hermann Hesse. München: Droemer, 1955, 320 pp.
[Vorwort] (pp. 7-12) same as b.

e "Ein Dichter der Romantik: Josef Freiherr von Eichendorff," *Ex Libris* (Zürich), 7, No. 3 (1952), 4-5. The revised Vorwort of b.

1 Geleitwort. Typescript (2nd version) in the Hesse-Nachlaß, Marbach a.N.

4 Jean Paul, *Titan*. Leipzig: Insel-Verlag [1913]. 2 Vols.: 397 pp., 406 pp.
Ed. and abridged by Hesse.
Nachwort, Vol. 2, pp. 403-406.

5 Wagner, Christian, *Gedichte*. München: Georg Müller, 1913, 110 pp.
Vorwort, pp. 5-8.

6 *Das Meisterbuch*. Berlin: Deutsche Bibliothek [1913], XII, 351 pp.
Vorwort, pp. V-VII.

7 *Der Zauberbrunnen*. Die Lieder der deutschen Romantik. Weimar: Kiepenheuer, 1913,
216 pp. Liebhaber Bibliothek, Bd. 10.
Geleitwort, pp. 3-6.

8 *Des Knaben Wunderhorn*. Alte deutsche Lieder gesammelt von L. A. von Arnim und
Clemens Brentano. Berlin: Deutsche Bibliothek [1913], XXX, 236 pp.
Nachwort, pp. 233-236.

9 *Morgenländische Erzählungen* (Palmblätter). Nach der von J. S. Herder und A. J. Liebeskind
besorgten Ausgabe neu herausgegeben. Leipzig: Insel-Verlag, 1913, XVI, 334 pp.
Nachwort, pp. 330-331.
2nd ed. Wiesbaden, 1957, 303 pp.

10 *Gesta Romanorum*. Das älteste Märchen- und Legendenbuch des Christlichen Mittelalters. Nach der Übersetzung von J. G. Th. Graesse. Leipzig: Insel-Verlag [1914], 323 pp.
Einführung, pp. 5-8.
4.-7. Tsd. 1920, 286 pp.; 8.-10. Tsd. 1924, 289 pp.

11 *Lieder deutscher Dichter*. Eine Auswahl der klassischen deutschen Lyrik von Paul Gerhardt
bis Fr. Hebbel. München: A. Langen [1914], 248 pp.
Vorwort, pp. 5-11.

a "Vorrede zu einer lyrischen Anthologie," *Wissen und Leben*, 7 (1914), 472-476.
1 Vorwort. Typescript in the Hesse-Nachlaß, Marbach a.N.

12 *Für Freunde guter Bücher*. Ein weihnachtlicher Berater unter Mitarbeit von Hermann
Hesse. Herausgegeben von K. A. Lang. München-Pasing: K. A. Lang u. Co., 1915,
38 pp.
Einleitung und Berichte (by Hesse), pp. 1-20.
a Weihnachten 1916, 32 pp. With book reviews by Hesse.
b Weihachten 1917, 24 pp. Without contributions by Hesse.

13 Claudius, Matthias, *Der Wandsbecker Bote*. Eine Auswahl aus den Werken. Leipzig:
Insel-Verlag [1915], 73 pp. Insel-Bücherei, No. 186.
Nachwort, p. 73.
Same Nachwort in the many subsequent editions (e.g., 143.-152. Tsd., 1958, p. 94).
1 Nachwort. Typescript in the Hesse-Nachlaß, Marbach a.N.

14 *Bücherei für deutsche Kriegsgefangene*. Herausgegeben von H. Hesse, Richard Woltereck.
Bern: Verlag der Bücherzentrale für deutsche Kriegsgefangene. Vols. 1-22, 1918-1919:

1 Hesse, Hermann, *Alte Geschichten*: Der Zwerg, Ein Wandertag, 55 pp.

2 Keller, Gottfried, *Don Correa*, 64 pp.
Vorwort, p. 5 (without signature).

3 *Für Stille Stunden*. Aus der neueren deutschen Lyrik, 48 pp.
(with three poems by Hesse).

4 Bartsch, Rud. Hans, *Der Steirische Weinfuhrmann*. Drei Erzählungen, 48 pp.

5 *Dichtergedanken* (Herder, Goethe, Jean Paul, Novalis, Stifter), 63 pp.
Geleitwort, pp. 7-9.

6 Strauß, Emil, *Der Laufen — Musik* (aus *Freund Hein*), 47 pp.
Geleitwort without signature, p. 5.

7 *Zeitvertreib*. Eine Sammlung von Anekdoten und Witzen, 76 pp.

8 *Kleinstadtgeschichten* (H. Kurz, H. Chr. Andersen, Fr. Huch, E. v. Bodman, L. Thoma, and Hesse's "Die Verlobung"), 118 pp.

9 Schäfer, Wilhelm, *Anekdoten und Sagen*, 63 pp.
Geleitwort, p. 7.

10 Fürst, Artur: Alexander Moszkowski, *Das kleine Buch der Wunder*, 103 pp.
Vorwort, p. 5.

11 *Vierblatt* (Tolstoi, Dauthendey, Paquet, H. Mann), 60 pp.

12 *Ein badisches Buch* (Gedichte und Prosa), 130 pp.
Bemerkung der Herausgeber, p. 130.

13 Hesse, Hermann, *Zwei Märchen:* Augustus, Iris, 52 pp.

14 *Die junge Schweiz* (J. Schaffner, F. Moeschlin, A. Steffen, R. Walser, P. Ilg, G. Gamper), 101 pp.
Geleitwort, pp. 7-8.

15 Bonus, Artur, *Isländerbuch*, Zwei Geschichten aus dem Isländerbuch, 107 pp.
Vorwort without signature, p. 5.

16 Storm, Theodor, *Immensee, Schimmelreiter, Gedichte*, 181 pp.

17 *Strömungen*. Sieben Erzählungen neuer Dichter (A. Madelung, W. Korolenko, K. Hamsun, M. Gorkij, R. Michel, A. Holitscher, O. Alscher), 88 pp.
Geleitwort, pp. 7-8.

18 *Schüler und Studenten*. Drei Erzählungen (Stifter, A. Zweig, Paquet), 55 pp.

19 *Aus dem Mittelalter*, 64 pp.
Geleitwort without signature, p. 7.

20 Mann, Thomas, *Zwei Novellen: Das Eisenbahnunglück, Tonio Kröger*, 88 pp.

21 *Seltsame Geschichten* (J. Schaffner, Th. Mann, Lynkeus, K. Hamsun, G. Meyrink, H. G. Wells), 92 pp.

22 *Lustige Geschichten* (J. P. Hebel, L. Aurbacher, F. Gerstäcker, P. Rosegger, L. Thoma, L. Finckh, W. Schussen), 70 pp.

15 *Heimatbücher für deutsche Kriegsgefangene*. Herausgegeben von der deutschen Kriegsgefangenenfürsorge. Bern: Verlag der Bücherzentrale für deutsche Kriegsgefangene (ed. by H. Hesse and R. Woltereck):

1 *Badisches Buch* [1918], 130 pp.
"Bemerkung der Herausgeber," p. 130.
This is also Vol. 12 of preceding *Bücherei für deutsche Kriegsgefangene*.

2 *Ein Rheinisches Buch*, 1918, 144 pp.
"Zum Inhalt dieses Buches," pp. 143-144 (probably by Hesse).

3 *Ein Pommern Buch*, 1918, 77 pp.
"Zum Inhalt dieses Buches," p. 77 (probably by Hesse).

4 *Aus der meerumschlungenen Heimat*, 1918, 332 pp.

5 *Bayernbuch*, 1919, 103 pp.

6 *Ein Sachsenbuch*, 1919, 127 pp.
"Zum Inhalt dieses Buches," p. 127 (probably by Hesse).

7 *Ein Schwabenbuch*, 1919, 105 pp. Compiled by Hesse and Walter Stich.
Nachwort, p. 105 (probably by Hesse).

16 *Alemannenbuch*. Bern: Verlag Seldwyla, 1919, 117 pp.
"Alemannisches Bekenntnis," pp. 7-9.
"Das Alemannenbuch freilich hat einen großen Fehler: es fehlt darin der beste Alemanne, Emil Strauß.... [Er] zog ... seine Mitarbeit plötzlich schroff wieder zurück — es war der endgültige Bruch einer alten Freundschaft." (an unpublished letter sent to Hans Popp, Nov. 9, 1934, in Wayne-Hesse-Collection, Wayne State University, Detroit).
Typescript letter by Hesse [1919] sent to various authors explaining his project and requesting contributions for it in the Hesse-Nachlaß, Marbach a.N.

17 *Ein Luzerner Junker vor hundert Jahren*. Aus den Lebenserinnerungen von Xaver Schnyder von Wartensee. Bern: Verlag Seldwyla, 1920, 205 pp.
Nachwort, pp. 202-205.

18 Geßner, Salomon, *Dichtungen*. Leipzig: Haessel, 1922, 92 pp. Die Schweiz im deutschen Geistesleben, Bd. 2.
Einleitung, pp. 5-21.

a "Salomon Geßner," *Die schöne Literatur*, 23 (1922), 161, 164.
Shortened version of Einleitung.

19 *Merkwürdige Geschichten*. Bern: Verlag Seldwyla:

Vol. 1 *Die wunderbare Gesellschaft in der Neujahrsnacht*. Erzählungen von Jean Paul [1922], 157 pp.
Nachwort, pp. 155-157.

Vol. 2 *Novellino*. Novellen und Schwänke der ältesten italienischen Erzähler [1922], 203 pp.
By Franco Sacchetti, Giovanni Fiorentino, Niccolo Machiavelli, Masuccio *et al.*
Trans. by A. von Keller.
Nachwort, p. 203.

Vol. 3 *Geschichten aus Japan* [1922], 183 pp.
Tales taken from A. B. Mitford, *Tales of Old Japan*; translated into German by I. G. Kohl.
Nachwort, pp. 182-183.

Vol. 4 *Aus Arnims Wintergarten* [1922], 182 pp.
Nachwort, pp. 181-182.

Vol. 5 *Mordprozesse* [1922], 192 pp.
Taken from a French collection by Pitaval and from Paul Joh. Anselm Feuerbach's *Merkwürdige Kriminalrechtsfälle*.
Nachwort, p. 179.

Vol. 6 *Zwei altfranzösische Sagen*. Erzählt von A. von Keller [1924], 206 pp.
Nachwort, pp. 205-206.

20 *Geschichten aus dem Mittelalter*. Konstanz: K. Höhn, 1925, 189 pp.
Einführung, pp. 8-11.
Tales from *Dialogus miraculorum* by Caesarius von Heisterbach, trans. by Hesse.

21 *Merkwürdige Geschichten und Menschen*. Berlin: S. Fischer:

1 *Die Geschichte von Romeo und Julie*. Nach den italienischen Novellenerzählern Luigi da Porto und Matteo Bandello, 1925, 122 pp.
Nachwort, pp. 121-122.

2 *Hölderlin.* Dokumente seines Lebens, 1925, 231 pp.
Nachwort, pp. 229-231.
Selections made by Hesse and Karl Isenberg.
Nachwort is a revision of "Über Hölderlin," *Betrachtungen* (1928), pp. 203-208.
1 Nachwort. Typescript in the Hesse-Nachlaß, Marbach a.N.

3 *Novalis.* Dokumente seines Lebens und Sterbens, 1925, 164 pp.
Nachwort, pp. 160-164.
Selections made by Hesse and Karl Isenberg.
Nachwort is same as "Nachwort zu *Novalis*," *Betrachtungen* (1928), pp. 208-211.

4 *Sesam.* Orientalische Erzählungen, 1925, 159 pp.
Taken from *Tuti-Nameh*, translations by Georg Rosen, and from *Palmblätter*, translations by A. J. Liebeskind.
Nachwort, p. 159.

5 *Blätter aus Prevorst.* Eine Auswahl von Berichten über Magnetismus, Hellsehen, Geistererscheinungen, *etc.*, aus dem Kreise J. Kerners und seiner Freunde, 1926, 190 pp.
Nachwort, pp. 189-190.

6 *Schubart.* Dokumente seines Lebens, 1926, 187 pp.
Nachwort, pp. 182-187.
Ed. by Hesse and Karl Isenberg.
Nachwort is same as "Nachwort zu Schubart," *Betrachtungen* (1928), pp. 235-241.
1 Nachwort. Typescript in the Hesse-Nachlaß, Marbach a.N.

7 *Die Geschwister Brentano in Dokumenten ihres Lebens*, 1927, 182 pp.
Ed. by and Nachwort by H. Levon-Derwein.

22 *Märchen und Legenden aus der Gesta Romanorum.* Leipzig: Insel-Verlag [1926], 71 pp.
Insel-Bücherei, No. 388.
Nachwort, pp. 69-70, differs slightly from the Einführung for the *Gesta Romanorum.*
Leipzig: Insel-Verlag, 1914, pp. 5-8 (item 10).
Ed. of 1956 (Leipzig) has the same Nachwort, pp. 72-73.

23 Goethe, Joh. Wolfgang von, *Dreißig Gedichte*. Zürich: Lesezirkel Hottingen, 1932, 65 pp. Festgabe zum 100. Todestag, 22. März 1932.
Einleitung, pp. 3-8.

a "Über Goethes Gedichte," *Dank an Goethe* (1946), pp. 21-27.
1 Geleitwort zu Goethes Gedichte (1931). Autograph in Bodmer-Hesse-Collection (in the possession of H. C. and Peter Bodmer, Zürich, Switzerland).

II. UNFINISHED PLANS FOR PUBLICATION

When Ruth Wenger left him only three or four months after their marriage in January 1924, Hesse went into deep depression, the suicidal depression which was eventually to find its therapeutic expression in *Steppenwolf*. Immediately he sought relief in intensified editorial activity. Together with Richard Woltereck, he had edited *Bücherei für deutsche Kriegsgefangene* (1918-19) and *Heimatbücher für deutsche Kriegsgefangene* (1918-19). He had been the sole editor of *Merkwürdige Geschichten* (1922-24). His editorial work was now to be extended to his favorite period, 1750-1850. In a letter of Nov. 6, 1924, Hesse broached the matter to the *Deutsche Verlags-Anstalt* of Stuttgart, outlining his plan as follows:

Es handelt sich, kurz gesagt, um eine große Bücherreihe, welche etwa "Die deutschen Erzähler" oder besser "Deutsche Prosa" heißen würde und welche, in einzeln käuflichen, aber uniform ausgestatteten Bänden das schlechthin Klassische, Beste der großen Zeit der deutschen Prosa, etwa von 1750 bis 1850, bringen würde... Das Ganze würde etwas ähnliches darstellen, wie es für die Zeit vor 40 Jahren etwa Kürschners Nationalbibliothek war, nur daß es sich lediglich um Prosa, vorwiegend erzählende, handelt, und daß der zeitliche Rahmen durch die Daten der Blütezeit unsrer deutschen Prosadichtung festgelegt ist. Daß wir heute diese Zeit erkennen und als längst fest abgeschlossen empfinden, daraus ergibt sich der neue Standpunkt, von dem aus die Sammlung geleitet würde. Sie bedeutet, wie ich sie plane, eine Sammlung des klassischen deutschen Vätergutes an Prosa, im Sinn einer Zusammenfassung und mahnenden Aufzeichnung der einstigen großen Tradition.

Hesse's nephew, Carlo Isenberg (1901-45), was to be his assistant, and their work could begin at once. The reaction of the *Verlags-Anstalt* was favorable and Hesse's plan evolved as follows:

A Das klassische Jahrhundert deutschen Geistes 1750-1850.
Einführungsworte (Basel im Frühling 1925), 1 p. typescript.

I Kreis um den jungen Goethe (2 vols.). Geleitwort, 1 p. typescript.
These volumes were to include: Jung-Stilling, Joh. Merck, Lavater, Herder, Wagner, Maler Müller, Fr. Stolberg, Lenz, Klinger.

II Schlegel (Fr.). Sagen (1 vol.).

III Aus deutschen Selbstbiographien. Auswahl aus einem Jahrhundert deutscher Selbstbiographie. Herausgegeben von Hermann Hesse (a number of volumes).
Geleitwort des Herausgebers, 1 p. typescript.
These volumes were to include: F. Ch. Oettinger, Fr. Freiherr von der Trenck, Schubart, G. Hippel, Joh. C. Lavater, G. A. Bürger, J. G. Seume, Karl H. von Lang, E. M. Arndt, Immermann, Karl Hase.

IV Deutsche Kultur (1 vol.).

This, Hesse's first series of intended publications was sent for approval to the *Deutsche Verlags-Anstalt* in April 1925. In discussion, the project waxed grander and the 1st series was soon replaced by a more extensive 2nd series.

B Deutscher Geist 1750 bis 1850.
"Sinn u. Plan der Reihe..." [1925], 2 p. typescript.
Einführungsworte [1925], 1 p. typescript.

I Der Geist von Weimar (1-2 vols.). To include: Wieland, Herder, Goethe, Schiller.

II Geist der Romantik (3 vols.).
[Vorwort], 5 p. typescript.
Gedanken zum Geleitwort d. Romantik, 1 p. typescript.
To include: A. W. Schlegel, Fr. Schlegel, Schleiermacher, Novalis, Ritter, Schelling, Steffens, Gundelfinger, Holtei, Novalis, C. Schlegel, Schelling, Wackenroder, Tieck, Runge, C. D. Friedrich, C. G. Carus, Solger, Rahel, Kleist, Ad. Müller,

Jean Paul, Hölderlin, Gunderode, Brentano, Bettina von Brentano, A. von Armin, Brüder Grimm, Görres, Bischof Sailer, Eichendorff, Uhland, Chamisso, Hoffmann, F. Schubert, Schumann, Mesmer, G. H. Schubert, Passavant, Baader, Kanne, Kerner, Daumer, Fechner.

III Deutsche Bildnisse (1 vol.).
Nachwort des Herausgebers, 1 p. typescript.
To include: Dürer, Klopstock, Lenz, Freiherr von Stein, Hölderlin, Uhland, Tieck, Blücher, Jean Paul, Pastor Roller in Lausa, Chamisso.

IV Der Kreis um den jungen Goethe (1 vol.).

V Romantische Reisen (1 vol.).

VI Aus deutschen Selbstbiographien (1 vol.).

VII Vergessene Meister der Prosa. Ausgewählt von Hermann Hesse (2 vols.).
Nachwort, 1 p. typescript.
To include: Chr. L. Liscow, J. Möser, Joh. G. Zimmermann, S. Geßner, H. P. Sturz, M. A. Thümmel, C. F. D. Schubart, J. G. Jacobi, J. H. Merck, J. J. Engel, H. Pestalozzi, W. Heinse, G. A. Bürger, Maler Müller, Die Brüder Stolberg, Lenz, Klinger, G. Förster, K. Ph. Moritz, A. W. Schlegel, H. Steffens, J. Fr. Fries, Th. Hippel, J. W. F. Solger, Just. Kerner.
Nachweis der Texte, 3 p. autograph.

VIII Friedrich Schlegel. Romantische Sagen des Mittelalters (1 vol.).
Geleitwort des Herausgebers, 2 p. typescript.

This is the series of 1925 outlined in the contract drawn up by the *Deutsche Verlags-Anstalt*. If successful, the series was to be extended beyond these volumes. And indeed, Hesse already had in mind a long list of additional works.

C 1 Aufsätze und Briefe von deutschen Gelehrten (1 vol.).
To include: Winckelmann, Niebuhr, Humboldt, Vischer, Görres, Fallmerayer, A. W. Schlegel, Schelling, Hegel, Creuzer, Schleiermacher, Viktor Hehn, Schopenhauer, Fechner.

2 Der Wandsbecker Bote, der rheinländische Hausfreund und das Volksbüchlein (1 vol.).
To include: Claudius, Hebel, Aurbacher.

3 Der Zug nach Italien.

4 Deutsche Reiseschilderungen um 1800.
To include: Thümmel, H. Förster, Seume.

5 Nachromantische Erzähler (1 vol.).
To include: Hauff, Droste, Büchner, Grillparzer, H. Kurz.

6 Orientreisen im 17. Jahrhundert.
Nachwort des Herausgebers, 1 p. typescript.
Table of contents, 2 p. typescript.
To include: Johann von der Behr, Walter Schultzen, Laurentium Slisansky.

7 Romantische Erzählungen (1-2 vols).
To include: Fouqué, Arndt, Kerner, Chamisso.

8 Spuk- und Hexengeschichten aus dem Rheinischen Antiquarius.
Nachwort, 1 p. typescript.
Table of contents and instructions for typesetter, 4 p. typescript.

9 Zwei baltische Dichter (1 vol.).
  To include: Hippel, Bogumil Goltz.

D These anthologies were to be supplemented by a series of publications devoted to single
  authors. A few volumes were readied for print and many more remained in the planning
  stage.

  1 Achim von Arnim's Erzählungen. Ausgewählt von Hermann Hesse.
    Nachwort des Herausgebers, 1 p. typescript.

  2 Clemens Brentano als Erzähler. Herausgegeben von Hermann Hesse.
    Nachwort des Herausgebers, 1 p. typescript.

  3 Friedrich Hebbel's Prosa. Herausgegeben von H. Hesse.
    Nachwort, 4 p. autograph.

  4 Heinrich Stillings Jugend. Von Johann Heinrich Jung.
    Herausgegeben von Hesse.
    Nachwort des Herausgebers, 3 p. typescript.

  5 Justinus Kerner's Prosa-Dichtungen.
    Nachwort des Herausgebers, 2 p. typescript.

  6 Eduard Mörike. Erzählungen. Auswahl von Hermann Hesse.
    Nachwort des Herausgebers, 1 p. typescript.

  7 Adalbert Stifter. Ausgewählte Dichtungen (2 vols.).
    Nachwort des Herausgebers, 2 p. typescript.

  8 Ludwig Tieck. Märchen und Novellen. Ausgewählt von Hermann Hesse.
    Nachwort des Herausgebers, 2 p. typescript.

  For those volumes which remained in their planning stage, Hesse left a 1 p. typescript
  outlining his intentions.
  Authors included: Bräker, Eichendorff, Goethe, Gotthelf, Heine, Hoffmann, Hölderlin,
  Immermann, Jean Paul, Kleist, Lessing, Lichtenberg, Moritz, Münchhausen, Musäus,
  Novalis, Schiller, Wieland.

This grand plan of 1924-25 was never realized, and largely because of a number of painful misunderstandings between Hesse, his old publisher, S. Fischer, and his prospective new publisher, the *Deutsche Verlags-Anstalt*. When the *Verlags-Anstalt* learned that Hesse was to continue as editor for Fischer's *Merkwürdige Geschichten und Menschen*, the series taken over from the *Verlag Seldwyla*, it balked. Fischer was unwilling to give up his series, and the *Verlags-Anstalt* would only publish *the* Hesse-series and not just another series of books edited by Hesse. Both hurt and angry, Hesse obligingly offered to accept a termination of his contract with the *Verlags-Anstalt*. The offer was accepted on May 26, 1925. Not a single volume of the entire series was ever to be published.[5]

III. NEWSPAPERS AND PERIODICALS

Hesse helped to found and to edit a number of newspapers and periodicals for the same reasons he took to editing books. It meant added income, helped to allay the restlessness or the agony of the lulls in his creativity and was again a public service—not the primary cultural commitment of his books, but a more socio-political oriented service. In 1907, *März*, a positive counterpart to *Simplicissimus*, began its crusade against the despotism of Wilhelm II, the militarism of the Empire and against Prussia's *Junkertum*. Hesse served as co-editor until marital problems and the growing demands of his art induced him to resign toward the end of 1912.

It was in conjunction with his volunteer work for the *Fürsorge für deutsche Kriegsgefangene* in Bern that Hesse helped in early 1916 to found the *Sonntagsbote für die Kriegsgefangenen* and its supplement, the *Deutsche Internierten-Zeitung*. These slim publications, which Hesse also helped edit from July 1916 until Dec. 1917, were neither intent upon news nor concerned with social changes or political matters. Their scattering of poems and short stories was primarily to remind the prisoners of war that they were not forgotten and to afford them some diversion, and thereby to lend them strength to endure their lot.

In October 1919, vigorously programmatic *Vivos Voco* heralded a new Germany and a better world, and to help prepare the way for this better tomorrow, began to champion the cause of the needy, to focus attention upon children and particularly their education, to denounce anti-Semitism and to acclaim pacifism and internationalism. Though co-founder and co-editor of both *März* and *Vivos Voco*, and though in complete agreement with the criticism of one and the aspirations of the other, Hesse chose in each instance to confine his activities to the literary sections.[6] Before the war he was not yet ready to become embroiled in the social and political problems of the day, and by late 1919 he was convinced that further direct appeals to the German people by a Hermann Hesse could serve little purpose. His admonitions and exhortations of 1917-19[7] had fallen on deaf ears. He had taken generals and politicians to task for their militarism and narrow-minded nationalism, had berated artists and intellectuals for their fair-weather humanitarianism, and had made a fervent appeal for more civilized human relationships. His essays were termed *Humanitätsduselei* and he a *Vaterlandsfeind*.[8] His name became anathema. Nothing was left for him to do now but to support the cause silently and to hope. When by the end of 1921, resurgent nationalism and spreading Communism began to dispel this hope, Hesse terminated his editorial association with Vivos Voco. This marked the end of his career as an editor of newspapers and periodicals.

1 *März*. Halbmonatsschrift für deutsche Kultur (ab 5. Jg., Wochenschrift). München: Albert Langen.

1, i (1907) — 3, i (1909). Herausgeber: Ludwig Thoma, Hermann Hesse, Albert Langen, Kurt Aram.

3, ii (1909) — 3, iv (1909). Herausgeber: Ludwig Thoma, Hermann Hesse, Kurt Aram, Robert Hessen.

4, i (1910). Herausgeber: Ludwig Thoma, Hermann Hesse, Kurt Aram.

4, ii (1910) — 6, iv (1912). Herausgeber: Ludwig Thoma, Hermann Hesse.

2 *Aus der Heimat.* Sonntagsblätter für die deutschen Kriegsgefangenen und Internierten. Eds. Otto Schultheß, Hermann Hesse, and Rudolf von Tavel (Bern: Francke). Only 1 issue appeared, Oct. 1915, 16 pp.
Founded by Richard Woltereck with the assistance of H. Hesse and O. Schultheß. Changed somewhat, this became the 1st issue of *Der Sonntagsbote für die deutschen Kriegsgefangenen* (Bern: Francke), 1916, 16 pp.

3 *Der Sonntagsbote für die deutschen Kriegsgefangenen.* Herausgegeben von der Schweizerischen Hilfsstelle für Kriegsgefangene Pro captivis, in Bern. Ed. Rudolf von Tavel (Bern: Francke).
Founded by R. Woltereck with the assistance of H. Hesse and O. Schultheß, 1916.
Although not listed as such, Hesse also served as co-editor, 1916-17 (see "Zur Einführung." *Deutsche Internierten-Zeitung* [Bern: Francke], No. 1, July 1, 1916, p. 1).

4 *Deutsche Internierten-Zeitung* (Sonderausgabe des Sonntagsboten für die deutschen Kriegsgefangenen). Herausgegeben von der Deutschen Kriegsgefangenen-Fürsorge Bern in Gemeinschaft mit der Schweizer Hilfsstelle Pro Captivis, in Bern. Eds. Richard Woltereck and Hermann Hesse (Bern: Francke).
Hesse was co-editor from July 1, 1916 to Dec. 2, 1917 (Nos. 1-62).

5 *Vivos Voco.*

1 (Oct. 1919-Nov. 1920). Eine deutsche Monatsschrift. Herausgegeben von Hermann Hesse und Richard Woltereck (Leipzig: Seemann & Co).

2 (March 1921-Dec. 1921). Zeitschrift für neues Deutschtum. Herausgeber: Franz Car Endres, Hermann Hesse, Richard Woltereck (Leipzig: Vivos Voco Verlag).

★ ★
★

Hesse became involved in editorial activities for three main reasons: financial, diversional and cultural-socio-political. Each of these considerations was present in varying degrees in most of his various editorial ventures. These editorial ventures reflect some of his many diverse and often diametrically opposed inclinations and interests: his leaning toward the regional and his espousal of the cosmopolitan, his penchant for the past and his attachment to the present, and his respect for the classical and love of the romantic. Hesse's editing of periodicals ended with *Vivos Voco* and in disillusionment, in 1921. His editing of books, to all intents and purposes, terminated in anger and frustration with the collapse of his grand plans of 1924-25. *Dreißig Gedichte* (1932), Hesse's contribution to the centennial of Goethe's death, marked a renewed interest in editing. Had the times been more auspicious, it is very likely that other books would have followed. But such was not the case. With the advent of National-Socialism, Hesse quickly became a *persona non grata.* By the mid-Thirties he was a widely acknowledged Jew-lover and traitor to the German cause.[9] German publishing houses ceased abruptly to have any use for Hesse the editor, and Hesse, in turn, stunned and outraged by his lot in Germany, quickly lost all interest in any further editing. He continued almost until his death and for his usual reasons to contribute reviews regularly and primarily to Swiss newspapers, and to write short introductory or concluding remarks for books edited by others and again primarily published in Switzerland, but he never again returned to editing, a diversion which had once almost become more than just a pastime.

NOTES

1 Translations into forty languages attest to this international acclaim.
2 Many of these essays appear in: *Gesammelte Schriften* (Frankfurt a.M.: Suhrkamp, 1957), Vol. 7.
3 *E.g.: Berliner Tageblatt* (1915-35), *Die Propyläen* (Beilage zur *Münchener Ztg.*; 1904-34), *Vossische Ztg.* (Berlin; 1915-35), *National-Ztg.* (Basel; 1920-56), *Neue Zürcher Ztg.* (1904-62), *Neue Freie Presse* (Wien; 1928-33), *Die Zeit* (Wien; 1904-15), *März* (München; 1907-17), *Die Neue Rundschau* (Berlin; 1909-36), *Vivos Voco* (Leipzig; 1919-24), *Schweizerland* (Chur; 1915-21).
4 *Die Neue Rundschau, Neue Zürcher Ztg., Die Propyläen* and *Die Zeit* (Wien).
5 For more information related to this exercise in futility, see Hesse's unpublished correspondence of 1924-26 with the *Deutsche Verlags-Anstalt*, with S. Fischer, and with Carlo Isenberg (Hesse-Nachlaß, Schiller-Nationalmuseum in Marbach a.N.).
6 For *März*, Hesse contributed reviews regularly from 1907 until 1917; for *Vivos Voco*, from 1919 until 1924. In *März*, he featured such writers as Altenberg, Bang, Bartsch, Björnson, Dauthendey, A. France, Br. Frank, Hamsun, J. V. Jensen, K. Kraus, Lagerlöf, Maeterlinck, Th. Mann, Mauthner, Meyrink, Owlglas, J. Schaffner, Schussen, Shaw, Strindberg, Thoma, Verhaeren and Voigt-Diederichs; in *Vivos Voco*, such writers and critics as Bertram, Curtius, Flake, Gropius, Herzog, Heuß, Klabund, Mereschkowski, Pannwitz, Schreyer, Spranger, and Tillich.
7 See *Krieg und Frieden* (Zürich, Fretz & Wasmuth, 1946).
8 See "Weltgeschichte" (Nov. 1918), *Gesammelte Schriften*, Vol. 7, pp. 121-126.
9 See *Die Neue Literatur* (Leipzig), 36 (1935), 685-687; 37 (1936), 57-58, 239-242.
10 From 1910 to 1962, Hesse wrote accompanying remarks for some forty books, catalogues and periodicals.

Compassion and Absurdity:
Brecht and Marx on the Truly Human Community

There is a passage in the *Economic and Philosophic Manuscripts of 1844* which clearly reveals both the secular humanism as well as the existentialist thinking inherent in Marx's conception of the final cause of the Communist Kingdom of Man, i.e., of positive Communism.[1] For what Marx emphasizes in this passage is that the ultimate goal of society, the aesthetic and free man restored to his humanity because his relations to his fellow humans are expressed on the level of being rather than of having, rests on the realization of "the theory which proclaims man to be the highest essence of man":[2]

> Assume *man* to be *man* and his relationship to the world to be a human one: then you can exchange love only for love, trust for trust, etc. If you want to enjoy art, you must be an artistically-cultivated person; if you wish to exercise influence over other people, you must be a person with a stimulating and encouraging effect on other people. Every one of your relations to man and to nature must be a *specific expression*, corresponding to the object of your will, of your *real individual* life. If you love without evoking love in return—that is, if your loving as loving does not produce reciprocal love; if through a *living* expression of yourself as a loving person you do not make yourself a loved person, then your love is impotent—a misfortune.[3]

The assumption underlying the establishment of the truly human community from which man is at present alienated, this "real community of man" representing "life itself, physical and intellectual life, human morality, human activity, human enjoyment,"[4] has been succinctly summarized by Siegfried Landshut: "Das Verhalten des Menschen zum Menschen und zu sich selbst soll durch nichts anderes bestimmt sein als durch seinen Charakter als Mensch."[5] This assumption is at one and the same time ethical in that it calls for the respect of the individual on the basis of his humanity,[6] metaphysical in that it implies the equating of man's true essence with the notion of aseity, and existential insofar as it demands for man an unrestricted freedom of individual development. Only a Communist ordering of society, Marx contends, will create the conditions necessary for the fulfillment of this assumption in the real world: "Only in community with others has each individual the means of cultivating his gifts in all directions, only in the community, therefore, is personal freedom possible."[7] This community, an association of free individuals, is, in the words of Herbert Marcuse, "a society wherein the material process of production no longer determines the entire pattern of human life. Marx's idea of a rational society implies an order in which it is not the universality of labor, but the universal satisfaction of all individual potentialities that constitutes the principle of social organization. He contemplates a society that gives to each not according to his work but his needs. Mankind becomes free only when the material perpetuation of life is a function of the abilities and *happiness* of associated individuals."[8]

Underlying positive Communism is a redemptive idea, as Robert Tucker has emphasized ("the thread that holds the entire system together"[9]). Marx's primary concern was the total regeneration of man, of every man without exception. His goal demands a universal application, or, to use his own phraseology, signifies the establishment of the "brotherhood of man" once the "nobility of man"[10] is accorded recognition. This idea, which is central to the proper understanding of Communism in its ethical, metaphysical, and existential aspects, is at the basis of Paul Tillich's definition of Marxism as "a resistance movement against the destruction of love in social reality."[11] In its most general form the type of love Marx wanted to see restored in the human community was the love of neighbor. He felt the existence of such a love to be completely incompatible with, and hence, essentially the direct negation of the "ethical" principle on which capitalist society is based.[12] Erich Fromm, in full agreement with Marx on this point of his philosophy, explains this incompatibility as follows: "Wenn der Mensch fähig sein soll zu lieben, muß seine Entfaltung das höchste Ziel der Gesellschaft sein... Nur in einer Gesellschaft, in der, wie Marx gesagt hat, die volle menschliche Entfaltung des Einzelnen die Bedingung der Entfaltung aller ist, kann auch die Liebe zu einer gesellschaftlich relevanten Haltung werden."[13] Fromm is able to agree with Marx because his own conception of the meaning of love of neighbor rests on the latter's teaching concerning man's true nature. Fromm's exposition of this conception reads almost like a commentary on the often-quoted but usually misunderstood lines at the end of Brecht's "An die Nachgeborenen," which equate the advent of Communism with a time when "der Mensch dem Menschen ein Helfer ist":[14]

Die Liebe, die allen Arten der Liebe zugrunde liegt, ist die Nächstenliebe. Damit meine ich das Gefühl der Verantwortlichkeit, der Fürsorge, des Respektes, und des Wissens gegenüber allen anderen menschlichen Wesen; charakteristisch für sie ist das Fehlen der Ausschließlichkeit. Wenn ich die Fähigkeit des Liebens entwickelt habe, kann ich nicht umhin, meinen Nächsten zu lieben. In der Nächstenliebe liegt das Erlebnis der Vereinigung mit allen Menschen, das Erlebnis der menschlichen Solidarität und der menschlichen Einheit. Die Nächstenliebe beruht auf dem Wissen, daß wir alle eins sind. Die Unterschiede in Talent, Intelligenz und Wissen sind unwichtig im Vergleich zu der Identität des menschlichen Kerns, der allen Menschen gemeinsam ist... Die Nächstenliebe ist Liebe zwischen Gleichen, aber selbst als Gleiche sind wir in Wirklichkeit nicht immer "gleich", denn da wir Menschen sind, brauchen wir Hilfe—heute ich, morgen du. Dieses Verlangen nach Hilfe bedeutet nicht, daß der eine hilflos, der andere stark ist. Hilflosigkeit ist ein vorübergehender Zustand: die Fähigkeit auf eigenen Füßen zu stehen und zu gehen, ist dagegen der übliche und dauerhafte Zustand.[15]

An integral part of both Fromm's and Marx's definition of love of neighbor is the freedom which proclaims all men to be equal in the real world on the basis of their shared humanity. Fromm describes this relation between equals in terms of a mutual respect, a concept replete with Marxist ideas on human nature and the human community, and directly antithetical to the social order of the commodity-man:

Respekt ist weder Angst noch Furcht; entsprechend der Wurzel dieses Wortes (respicere—ansehen) bedeutet Respekt die Fähigkeit, einen Menschen so zu sehen, wie er ist, und seine einmalige Individualität zu erkennen. Respekt bedeutet das Streben, daß der andere wachsen und sich entfalten kann. Dem Respekt fehlt daher jede Tendenz der Ausbeutung... Es ist klar, daß Respekt nur möglich ist, wenn ich *selbst* meine Unabhängigkeit erreicht habe, wenn ich ohne fremde Hilfe stehen und gehen kann, also ohne einen anderen beherrschen und ausnutzen zu wollen. Respekt gibt es nur auf der Grundlage der Freiheit...[16]

If now we turn to Brecht to see how well he understood and expressed Marx's ideas on the existential basis of the truly human community, one point must be borne in mind. Neither man made any formidable effort to describe the better world to come after the destruction of the capitalist system, i.e., after the triumph of negative Communism. The overriding preoccupation of both was with the status quo, with what Brecht described as the "barbarous antiquity" of the present,[17] which they knew, and so wanted all men to know, as monstrous and therefore inhuman, as irrational, and therefore absurd. Their belief in the ultimate rationality of man convinced them that, once society was organized along rational lines, man would find his own way, a way filled with limitless possibilities of development.[18] Hence, any depictions on Brecht's part which treat the post-capitalistic world are usually glimpses gleaned from the world as it exists here and now. It has been frequently pointed out that Brecht never wrote a work dealing directly with the positive side of Communism. Those who would soften his commitment to Marxism take solace from this fact. The simple truth is, however, that he was but following the example of his mentor. Marx himself has never been taken to task by his followers on that account. On the contrary, he has been praised by them for his refusal to construct utopian dream-castles. The disciple certainly was not "greater" than the master. Brecht's validity (and, perhaps, even greatness) as a literary interpreter of Marx lay in his ability to transfer to his own world, that of the creative artist, both the kernel teachings of positive Communism and the restraint employed by Marx in explicating them. Thus, the starting point of Marx's teachings on the community of equal, free, and aesthetic individuals, is expressed as follows:

> But one of the most vital principles of communism, a principle which distinguishes it from all reactionary socialism, is its empiric view, based on a knowledge of man, that differences of brain, of intellectual capacity, do not imply any difference whatsoever in the nature of the stomach and of physical needs; therefore the false tenet, based upon existing circumstances, "to each according to his capacity," must be changed, in as far as it relates to enjoyment in its narrower sense, into the tenet, "to each according to his need," in other words, a different form of activity, of labor, confers no privileges in respect of possession and enjoyment.[19]

It becomes thoroughly poetized by Brecht in the following poem:

> O Sprengen des Gartens, das Grün zu ermutigen!
> Wässern der durstigen Bäume! Gib mehr als genug. Und
> Vergiß nicht das Strauchwerk, auch
> Das beerenlose nicht, das ermattete
> Geizige! Und übersieh mir nicht
> Zwischen den Blumen das Unkraut, das auch
> Durst hat. Noch gieße nur
> Den frischen Rasen oder den versengten nur:
> Auch den nackten Boden erfrische du.[20]

The "vital principle" is retained—it is the point of the poem—but the cold, philosophical compassion of Marx is transmuted into the warm, aesthetic compassion proper to the vehicle of the poet. In fact, in this instance, Brecht goes beyond the sentiment of the quotation from Marx. He hints at the Marxist notion of the aesthetic man,[21] described elsewhere by him as the man who lives "für das Extra."[22]

In the Brechtian world, which is still a place dominated by Marx's monster, capital, and peopled by the reified victims of exploitation and class warfare, examples of a human relationship based on mutual respect and the recognition of the absolute equality and existential freedom of all men occur within the framework of the status quo. And because they do, Brecht depicts them simply as temporary suspensions of class differences. The most obvious instances are to be found in *Das Verhör des Lukullus* and *Herr Puntila und sein Knecht Matti*. The original version of the former actually ends with a friendly discussion between the Roman general and his peasant-judge. During the final scene[23] class differences are completely forgotten, as both men meet on the level of their common humanity to exchange ideas on a type of cherry tree which the general once introduced into Italy and the peasant judge later planted. This confrontation between the accused and his accuser, spiritually united for the moment as a result of their common contribution to the furtherance of mankind's true interests, the pursuit of peace and plenty, seems to cast genuine doubt on the outcome of the trial. This impression is strengthened by the fact that unlike his other plays of seemingly doubtful issue, *Mutter Courage* and *Der gute Mensch von Sezuan*, Brecht later saw fit to revise the ending of this play in a positive vein with the unequivocal condemnation of Lucullus.[24]

In the ninth scene of *Puntila*[25] we are confronted with a similar situation. Again the world of having gives way to the world of being, this time on two levels, one chimerical and falsely idealistic, the other temporary but authentic. In this scene the intoxicated Puntila attempts to overcome the "natural" differences of class by having his daughter become engaged to Matti, the chauffeur. Because he is drunk, Puntila sees in Matti a fellow human being worthy of his respect, and those opposed to the engagement on quite realistic grounds, the minister, the judge, and the lawyer, he regards as subhumans. Yet, as Matti quite effectively demonstrates, in the real world from which Puntila has temporarily fled, the attempt to dispel class differences by wishful thinking is bound to fail. At the same time that Matti is carrying out his demonstration, Brecht furnishes us with an authentic example of a confrontation between persons of different classes who for the moment participate naturally but subconsciously in their common humanity. This time the symbolic catalyst is not a cherry tree, but something equally prosaic, mushrooms. In his scorn for class differences and with egalitarian gusto Puntila forced some of his guests to sit down at the dining-room table with his servants. The minister's wife, a class-conscious snob, was seated next to Laina, the cook. In an embarrassed attempt to make conversation she asked the cook: "Haben Sie schon Pilze eingelegt dieses Jahr?"[26] From that moment both women become oblivious to the furious altercation over class differences around them; and when the scene ends on a note of utter discord, Laina and the minister's wife leave the room like old friends, still engrossed in their discussion over the best way to preserve mushrooms—affording the spectator a minute glimpse of the world that is not yet, that world to come which must still be portrayed within the limits of the present reality.

The confrontation of Lucullus and the peasant, of the minister's wife and the cook, are clearly exemplifications of the Marxist doctrine of the universal love of neighbor based on the existential equality of all human beings, or, as Marx termed it, on "the nobility of man."[27] One can find this assertion confirmed in a poem that affords us an insight into the philosophy underlying Brecht's favorite concept of "friendliness." Its basis is identical with Marx's views on man's authentic essence. To the work in question, a translation of one of Waley's Chinese poems, Brecht significantly gave the title, "Die Freunde."

> Wenn du in einer Kutsche gefahren kämst
> Und ich trüge eines Bauern Rock
> Und wir träfen uns eines Tages so auf der Straße
> Würdest du aussteigen und dich verbeugen.[28]
> Und wenn du Wasser verkauftest
> Und ich käme spazieren geritten auf einem Pferd
> Und wir träfen uns eines Tages so auf der Straße
> Würde ich absteigen vor dir.[29]

The most direct dramatic expression of positive Communism, of the essential connection between the notion of the nobility and brotherhood of man on the one hand and Marx's doctrine of aesthetic man on the other, occurs at the end of one of Brecht's last original plays. For this reason *Schweyk im Zweiten Weltkrieg* may well be the most optimistic play Brecht ever wrote— in a very relative sense, of course, since his version of the Marxist dream-poem of humanity is set off against the background of an all too hostile real world. The playwright introduces his vision of the future Marxist society through the words of Baloun, a character who is the direct counterpart of Anna-Anna,[30] Galileo, and "Papa." The human aspirations of these three dramatic figures were symbolically depicted in terms of their culinary interests. Schweyk's friend is at one with them when he asserts man's right to live aesthetically, "für das Extra," via a rhetorical question: "Ich eß halt sehr gern. Gesegns Gott… Kann das eine Sünde sein?"[31] Baloun fondly recalls a brief but happy time, when men were able to *enjoy* their fill without depriving their fellow man: the precondition for a reality defined by a universal love of neighbor based on respect for man as man. In direct opposition to the heavenly wedding feast of the Gospels, from which many are excluded,[32] the celebration that Baloun describes indicates that redemption is truly catholic and attests to the ultimate solidarity of the human race on the sole basis of a shared humanity:

> In Pudonitz, wie meine Schwester geheiratet hat, haben sies wieder mit der Menge gemacht, 30 Leute, beim Pudonitzer Wirt, Burschen und Weiber und auch die Alten, haben nicht nachgegeben, Suppe, Kalbfleisch, Schweinernes, Hühner, zwei Kälber, und zwei fette Schweine,

vom Kopf bis zum Schwanz, dazu Knödl und Kraut in Fässern und erst
Bier, dann Schnaps. Ich weiß nurmehr, mein Teller wird nicht leer,
und nach jedem Happn ein Kübl Bier oder ein Wasserglas Schnaps
hinterdrein. Einmal war eine Stille, wie in der Kirchen, wie sie das
Schweinerne gebracht ham. Es sind alles gute Menschen gewesn, wie sie
so beinander gesessn sind und sich vollgegessn ham, ich hätt für jeden die
Hand ins Feuer gelegt. Und es waren allerhand Typen darunter, ein
Richter beim Landgericht in Pilsen, im Privatleben ein Bluthund für
die Diebe und Arbeiter. Essen macht unschädlich.[33]

Brecht's depiction of the aesthetic society corresponds to and could have
been directly inspired by Marx's, who also resorted to the image of communal
eating when attempting to give some intimation of what the new society
would be like. Like Brecht's image, Marx's anticipatory symbol was drawn
from the real world about us, the world of having:

When communist *workmen* associate with one another, theory, propaganda, etc., is their first end. But at the same time, as a result of this
association, they acquire a new need—the need for society—and what
appears as a means becomes an end. You can observe this practical
process in its most splendid results whenever you see French socialist
workers together. Such things as smoking, drinking, eating, etc., are
no longer means of contact or means that bring together. Company,
association, and conversation, which again has society as its end, are
enough for them; the brotherhood of man is no mere phrase with them,
but a fact of life, and the nobility of man shines upon us from their
workhardened bodies.[34]

If, in the last analysis, Marx's ethos is inseparable from a compassion for the
helpless and the underdogs of history, it should not surprise us that Brecht
chooses the idea of the guest to depict the elemental ethical basis for citizen-
ship in the Marxist Kingdom of Man. For, as Fromm has emphasized,[35]
respect for the stranger lies at the core of the concept of love of neighbor.
In fact, it has been a Christian existentialist philosopher who has had recourse
to the same image in order to protest against a society dominated by the idea
of having and thus forced to regard man for what he has, rather than for
what he is. Hence, Gabriel Marcel is brought to lament "the disappearance
of the sense of hospitality today, at least in the countries which have been
submerged by technical progress." He defines this sense of hospitality as
"above all the sort of piety which is shown in the East to the unknown
guest—simply because he is a guest, because he has entrusted himself to a
man and his dwelling." His protest is not unlike Brecht's when he concludes:
"But these are the very bonds between man and man that are tending to
disappear in a world where individuals, reduced to their abstract elements,

are more and more merely juxtaposed, and where the only hierarchies that remain are founded either on money or on educational qualifications whose human significance is practically nil."[36] Brecht's "Lied vom 'Kelch'," which complements Baloun's account of the Pudonitzer wedding feast, defines positive Communism as a universal community in which every member has attained the status of a guest. As no other poem of Brecht's, it drives home the point that the highest essence for man is man himself. The pious blasphemy implicit in the poem is not accidental—for Marxism is not only a social revolt against the capitalist order in the name of justice; it is in a very real sense a metaphysical revolt against the order of grace in the name of human suffering. It would be difficult to find anywhere else among Brecht's writings a more accurate and more compassionate expression of the final cause of Communism:

> Komm und setz dich, lieber Gast
> Setz dich uns zu Tische
> Daß du Supp und Krautfleisch hast
> Oder Moldaufische.
>
> Brauchst ein bissel was im Topf
> Mußt ein Dach habn überm Kopf
> Das bist du als Mensch uns wert
> Sei geduldet und geehrt
> Für nur 80 Heller.
>
> Referenzen brauchst du nicht
> Ehre bringt nur Schaden
> Hast eine Nase im Gesicht
> Und wirst schon geladen.
>
> Sollst ein bissel freundlich sein
> Witz und Auftrumpf brauchst du kein
> Iß dein Käs und trink dein Bier
> Und du bist willkommen hier
> Und die 80 Heller.
>
> Einmal schaun wir früh hinaus
> Obs gut werde
> Und da wurd ein gastlich Haus
> Aus der Menschenerde.
>
> Jeder wird als Mensch gesehn
> Keinen wird man übergehn
> Ham ein Dach gegn Schnee und Wind
> Weil wir arg verfrorn sind.
> Auch mit 80 Heller![37]

This most Marxist of Brechtian poems, superficially optimistic, is implicitly a very sad poem. For in a profound sense it is also expressive of the atheistic existentialist protest against the implacability of destiny which underlies Marxism as a metaphysics. Deep down both philosophies are fired by the conviction that the controlling demiurge of this world has done far more harm to man than he could ever do to it. The passionate wish of the most consequential of all of Camus' absurdists, the emperor Caligula, to make the impossible possible, to have the sun set in the east, to reduce the sum of human suffering, and all because men die and are not happy, and the rhetorical questions of Dmitri Karamazoff, whose heart, consumed with a frenzy of pity, could not understand why babies cry, why people are poor, and why the steppe is barren—these existential protests against the lot of man, abandoned and cheated by his gods, are basically no different from the protest implicitly contained in Brecht's answer to the question: "Was aber gilt als Gipfel des Glücks den sterblichen Menschen?" His answer was, "Wenn man nur wenig gelitten und viel sich im Leben gefreut hat."[38] The fundamental difference between the Marxist and the existentialist, in their common protest against destiny, manifests itself only on the subjective level. Both refuse to submit to the wretchedness of the human condition, but the latter's refusal is expressed through defiance, whereas the Marxist goes beyond scorn. He is convinced that man's miserable condition can be abolished. If that conviction is a false one—and there are many who believe it is a false conviction stemming from a false metaphysics—then in the final analysis the Marxist *Weltanschauung* becomes on the objective level as tragic as the existentialist.[39] Like atheistic existentialism, it becomes merely a quixotic refusal to submit to an unchanging, arbitrary, and cruel destiny, a futile protest against the fact that the poor will always be with us. What remains is a compassionate concern for man, because he can expect no solace from the nonexistent gods of theology and the hostile gods of the social hierarchy. Small wonder then that the "Lied vom 'Kelch',", which is a product of Brecht's Marxist humanism, is so much like his "Weihnachtslegende" of 1923. Written three years before his conversion to Marxism, the poem is but the reverse side of the Marxist dream-poem of humanity. It expresses that which the later poem tries so hard to abolish and at the same time that which gives the "Lied vom 'Kelch'" its reason for being. For "Weihnachtslegende" enunciates, in the same prayer form, the compassion which is born of atheism and which sees man as abandoned by his gods, alienated, and metaphysically isolated. It also asserts the solidarity of human suffering which on the objective level will never emerge as the solidarity of human happiness—call it Communism or what you will. If in the "Lied vom 'Kelch'" God is deliberately excluded from the inn of human happiness, He is reluctantly excluded from the Christmas celebration of alienated man — but He is excluded. Both poems are identical in their inherent blasphemy. But because it is an act of piety to man, such impiousness is closer to the divine than the disin-

231

terested blasphemy of those who, in the name of their perverted concept of God, remain without compassion in the face of human suffering. God does not spew from his mouth the hot and the cold, only the lukewarm. Without being aware of it, Brecht was never closer to the ethos of Marx as a universal compassion than in his Christmas poem of 1923, written at the height of his absurdist phase. Reading this poem and comparing it with its Marxist counterpart, "Das Lied vom 'Kelch'," one should bear in mind the observation that the Marxist Brecht's Grusche made in *Der Kaukasische Kreidekreis* at a time when she felt desperately lonely and helpless: "Vor dem Wind mußt du dich nie fürchten, der ist auch nur ein armer Hund... und der Schnee, Michel, ist nicht der Schlimmste."[40] The same boundless compassion which embraces man is extended to all nature, animate and inanimate. Like goodness, compassion is diffusive, the compassion of the existentialist and Marxist Brecht:

Am heiligen Abend heut
Sitzen wir, die armen Leut
In einer kalten Stube drin
Der Wind geht draußen und geht herin.
Komm, lieber Herr Jesus, zu uns, sieh an:
Weil wir dich wahrhaft nötig han.

. . . .

Komm, Schnee, zu uns herein, kein Wort:
Du hast im Himmel auch kein Ort.

. . . .

Komm, Tier, zu uns herein nur schnell:
Ihr habt heut auch keine warme Stell.

Wir tun ins Feuer die Röck hinein
Dann wird's uns allen wärmer sein
Dann glüht uns das Gebälke schier
Erst in der Früh erfrieren wir.
Komm, lieber Wind, sei unser Gast:
Weil du auch keine Heimat hast.[41]

NOTES

[1] Positive Communism is simply the form society will take after the triumph of negative Communism, i.e., the negation or destruction of capitalism. The latter was defined by Brecht as "die Vernichtung derer, die Güte unmöglich machen" in the notes appended to *Die Mutter*, at the end of a long passage which is a vehement defense of Communism as *the* doctrine of universal salvation (*Versuche* [Berlin and Frankfurt, 1949-1959], Heft 5-8, 240).

[2] "Contribution to the Critique of Hegel's Philosophy of Right" in K. Marx and F. Engels, *On Religion* (Moscow, 1957), p. 58.

[3] *Economic and Philosophic Manuscripts of 1844* (Moscow, 1961), p. 140 — hereafter cited as *Manuscripts*.

⁴ K. Marx, *Selected Essays*, tr. H. J. Stenning (New York, 1926), p. 130.

⁵ "Einleitung" in K. Marx, *Die Frühschriften* (Stuttgart, 1953), p. xl.

⁶ Fundamentally, the ultimate ethical goal of Marxism is no different from that envisioned by G. E. Lessing: "... sie wird kommen, sie wird gewiß kommen, die Zeit der Vollendung, da der Mensch ... das Gute tun wird, weil es das Gute ist, nicht weil willkürliche Belohnungen darauf gesetzt sind ..." ("Die Erziehung des Menschengeschlechts" in *Lessing* [Leipzig, 1952], III, 482) or from the type of ethics which Walter Kaufmann considers far superior to Christian "Lohnmoral" (*Critique of Religion and Philosophy* [New York: Doubleday Anchor, 1961], pp. 228 ff.). Ethically, there is a striking similarity between Lessing's conception of the better world to come at the end of "Erziehung" and those formulated by Maxim Gorki (*Mother* [Bombay: Jaico, 1948], pp. 134-135) and V. I. Lenin (*State and Revolution* [New York, 1932], pp. 68, 73-74).

⁷ K. Marx and F. Engels, *The German Ideology*, Parts I and III, ed. R. Pascal (New York, 1947), p. 74.

⁸ *Reason and Revolution: Hegel and the Rise of Social Theory* (Boston: Beacon, 1960), p. 293 (emphasis added). Cf. Marcuse's contention that Marxism is permeated with "the idea, of the free and universal realization of individual happiness" (p. 294) and Brecht's definition of Communism as "happiness" (*Brecht/Dessau: Lieder und Gesänge* [Berlin, 1957], p. 20).

⁹ *Philosophy and Myth in Karl Marx* (Cambridge, 1961), p. 24.

¹⁰ *Manuscripts*, pp. 124 and 125.

¹¹ *Protestantische Vision* (Stuttgart, 1952), p. 6. Cited and trans. by Erich Fromm, *Marx's Concept of Man* (New York, 1961), p. 59.

¹² In capitalist society, Marx wrote in the *Manuscripts* (p. 129), every individual "only exists for the other person, as the other exists for him, in so far as each becomes a means for the other." Each becomes for the other that which he can be in relation to money. Thus every man becomes "the *self-conscious and self-acting commodity* ... the commodity-*man*" (p. 85); human relationships degenerate into "material relations between persons and social relations between things" (*Capital* [New York: The Modern Library, n.d.], p. 84). In his poetic version of the *Manifesto* Brecht put it this way: "Duldend kein anderes Band zwischen Menschen als nacktes Intresse / und die gefühllose Barzahlung... / Persönliche Würde verramscht [die Bourgeoisie] / Grob in den Tauschwert" (*Brecht: Ein Lesebuch für unsere Zeit*, ed. Walther Victor [Weimar, 1958], p. 95).

¹³ *Die Kunst des Liebens* (Frankfurt: Ullstein, 1959), p. 170. The passage is missing from the English edition (*The Art of Loving* [New York: Harper Colophon, 1962]).

¹⁴ *Gedichte* (Frankfurt, 1960-1965), IV, 145.

¹⁵ *Die Kunst des Liebens*, pp. 70-72.

¹⁶ *Ibid.*, pp. 48-49. Cf. the observation of the Marxist moral philosopher Howard Selsam in this regard: "The real problem is to create such conditions as will make all men really 'neighbors'. It will not be necessary then to *command* love, for love will follow from the very relationships of men" (*Socialism and Ethics* [New York, 1943], p. 42).

¹⁷ In a revealing Keuner anecdote, "Das Altertum" (*Kalendergeschichten* [Hamburg: Rowohlt, 1953], pp. 133-134), probably the most succinct summary of Brecht's views on the execrable world of having, capitalism is described as the direct negation of Marx's aesthetic man (thanks to a division of labor which enslaves human potential to one occupation), and as the affirmation of man as a commodity-being.

¹⁸ Cf. the ending of *Das Badener Lehrstück vom Einverständnis* in *Versuche*, Heft 1-4, 139-140.

¹⁹ *The German Ideology*, pp. 189-190.

²⁰ *Gedichte*, VI, 8.

²¹ One aspect of positive Communism is the restoration of pleasure to man's physical and intellecutal senses. Once man is able to produce in freedom from animal or physical need, his life-activity will be marked by creative spontaneity, freedom from restraint or compulsion, and pleasure, or in the words of Tucker (*op. cit.*, p. 158): "The alienated world will give way to the aesthetic world." Man's actions will then be performed in accordance with the laws of beauty, and his senses will become humanized: "For the starving man

233

it is not the human form of food that exists, but only its abstract being as food; it could just as well be there in its crudest form, and it would be impossible to say wherein this feeding activity differs from that of *animals*" (*Manuscripts*, p. 109). The divorce of pleasure from human activity was, of course, a favorite Brechtian theme. Galileo (*Stücke* [Frankfurt, 1957-1967], VIII, 113-114) and Brecht's alter egos, Kalle and Ziffel (*Flüchtlingsgespräche* [Berlin and Frankfurt, 1961], pp. 141-142, 158-160), griped about it bitterly.

22 In *Die Tage der Kommune* (*Stücke*, X, 365) the communard, "Papa," justifies revolution on the basis of Marx's notion of aesthetic man or of the humanization of the senses: "Denn wozu lebt man? Der Curé von Sainte-Héloise hat meiner Schwester zufolge die Frage beantwortet mit: für die Vervollkommnung seiner selbst. Nun wohl: was brauchte er dazu? Er brauchte dazu Wachteln zum Frühstück... Mein Sohn, man lebt für das Extra. Es muß her, und wenn man Kanonen dazu benötigt. Denn wofür leistet man etwas? Dafür, daß man sich etwas leistet. Prosit!"

23 *Stücke*, VII, 258-262.

24 See *Stücke*, VII, 267, for an explanation of the changes.

25 *Stücke*, IX, 112-142.

26 *Ibid.*, p. 124.

27 *Manuscripts*, p. 125.

28 In *Der Kaukasische Kreidekreis* Brecht effectively made use of this Chinese method of showing respect for the person of another. When Azdak, the judge, confronts the bandit Irakli, the Robin Hood of Grusinia, he rises from his judgment seat and bows. Irakli returns the compliment in the same way (*Stücke*, X, 268). That most charming of love scenes which depicts Grusche's engagement to Simon, the soldier, ends as follows: "Er verbeugt sich tief vor ihr. Sie verbeugt sich ebenso tief vor ihm" (p. 164). Grusche's one wish is that her adopted son will grow up into the kind of man before whom "wird sich verbeugen / Der ehrlichste Mann" (p. 205).

29 *Versuche*, Heft 10, 139 (Arthur Waley's translation is to be found in his *A Hundred and Seventy Chinese Poems* [London, 1918], p. 37). Brecht's interest in Chinese poetry and philosophy seems to have been determined almost entirely by his Marxist convictions. His deep admiration for the philosopher Mo Tzu (Reinhold Grimm, *Brecht und die Weltliteratur* [1961], pp. 22-25) may very well have been due to the fact that the latter's doctrine of universal love resembles Marx's (cf. Arthur Waley, *Three Ways of Love in Ancient China* [New York: Doubleday Anchor, 1956], pp. 129-130; H. G. Creel, *Chinese Thought from Confucius to Mao Tse-Tung* [New York: Mentor, 1960], p. 53; and Clarence Burton Day, *The Philosophers of China* [New York, 1962], pp. 63-64).

30 The heroine of the ballet *Die sieben Todsünden der Kleinbürger* (Frankfurt, 1959), written by Brecht in 1933.

31 *Stücke*, X, 119.

32 *Matt.* 22:1-14. The parable ends with the ominous words of exclusion: "For many are called but few are chosen."

33 *Stücke*, X, 120-121. This picture of the ethical basis of positive Communism in terms of a sensuous activity which transforms man's animal functions — in this case the consumption of food — into truly human activity, was repeated by Brecht somewhat more succinctly as follows, in answering the question, "Was wär, deines Bedünkens, das Köstlichste unter der Sonne?": "Das: Wenn Fröhlichkeit rings in der Stadt die Gemüter erfüllet. / Und dann schmausen die Gäste im Saal und lauschen dem Sänger / Bank an Bank, in Reihn, und rundum über den Tischen / Türmen sich Brot und Fleisch und der Mundschenk schöpft aus dem Mischkrug / Keinem fehlenden Wein und bringt ihn und füllet die Becher: / Das ist köstlich, ist mir bei weitem das Schönste auf Erden ("Der Wettkampf des Homer und Hesiod" in *Versuche*, Heft 11, 126).

34 *Manuscripts*, pp. 124-125.

35 *Die Kunst des Liebens*, p. 72.

36 *Men against Humanity*, tr. G. S. Fraser (London, 1952), p. 192.

37 *Stücke*, X, 121-122.

38 "Der Wettkampf des Homer und Hesiod" in *op. cit.*, p. 127.

[39] For those who are unable to believe in positive Communism, Marx's *Capital* becomes an existentialist work, whose hero, as Landshut (*op. cit.*, p. liv) has pointed out, is a monstrous personification of capital. And Brecht's poetization of Marx's *magnum opus, Der Dreigroschenroman,* also becomes a picture of relentless human exploitation, a description of misery eternalized by a set of inhuman relationships which both oppressors and oppressed accept as natural, and a depiction of institutionalized absurdity presented in a calm, matter-of-fact, pseudo-scientific style. But for the fact that Communism lurks in the shadows as a *deus ex machina,* both works would be representations of an abiding tragic situation. The same could be said of most of Brecht's other Marxist works. In this connection Günther Anders' observation that Kafka had only one literary forebear, namely Marx, is interesting (*Franz Kafka,* tr. A. Steer and A. K. Thorlby [New York, 1960], p. 13).

[40] *Stücke,* X, 204.

[41] *Gedichte,* II, 105-106.

The Artist-Intellectual,
in or versus Society? A Dilemma

RANDOLPH J. KLAWITER

The following reflections on three of the most outstanding German novels of the twentieth century, viz. Robert Musil's *Der Mann ohne Eigenschaften*, Hermann Hesse's *Das Glasperlenspiel*, and Thomas Mann's *Dr. Faustus*, are offered with full cognizance of the fact that these particular works of fiction are an all but inexhaustible source of literary, sociological and psychological themes and complexities, concerning each of which an extensive monograph might be written (the selective bibliography alone at the end of this essay indicates what scholarship has already been devoted to some of these aspects). The present study then makes no claim to greath depth of insight or to comprehensiveness of treatment. It attempts rather merely to isolate one element that underlies and thus unites in spirit these three works, namely the attitude of each writer *vis-à-vis* the position of the artist-intellectual in society, and to delineate within the context of the plot of each story the various solutions to this problem proffered, albeit tentatively, by the authors themselves.

I

Sed quia tepidus es,
et nec frigidus,
nec calidus, incipiam
te evomere ex ore meo.
(Rev. 3, 16)

Robert Musil's unfinished novel, *Der Mann ohne Eigenschaften*, portrays in epic fashion the mind of the German intellectual and the state of German society in the years immediately prior to the First World War. Although the plot as "plot" is intricate and complex, it functions almost solely as a vehicle by means of which the various characters are brought into contact with one another and through which the philosophic inquiries of the author are given some semblance of coherent form. The central foci of the novel are its main protagonist, Ulrich, the motivating catalyst of the "Parallel-aktion" and the convicted sex murderer Moosbruger.

236

Emperor Wilhelm II of Germany is to celebrate on a grand public scale the 13th anniversary of his coronation (1918). Not to be outdone by their brothers to the North, the Austrians conceive of an equally elaborate celebration in honor of the 70th anniversary of the coronation of Franz Josef, their "Emperor of Peace." The formation and interaction of the members of the planning committee function as the nucleus of the story since in one way or another each character of the novel reacts for or against the committee and its grandiose dreams: Count Leinsdorf, a representative of the enlightened, but still paternalistic Austrian nobility; Hermine Tuzzi, the wife of the Minister of Foreign Affairs, referred to as Diotima, a frustrated composite of intellectual pretention, artistic sensibility, social awareness (viewed through the myopic prism of class snobbery) and animal passion, constrained only by the ephemeral bonds of acceptable social decorum; Paul Arnheim, a Prussian representative of the 20th century Renaissance Man, who strives to equalize within himself the rival claims of intellectual pursuits and commercial success; General Stumm von Bordwehr, the embodied spirit of the ever present but appropriately incompetent military complex; the Jewish family of Leo Fichel, caught in the cross-current of self-identity versus assimilation; Ulrich, the artist-intellectual, who would portray his society through the perspective of symbolic relief but who, in the final analysis, becomes so enmeshed in the intricate vortices of intrapersonal detail that he is rendered hopelessly "denatured," a man without dominant personal characteristics of his own, thus functioning solely as a mirror for those about him.

Considered individually the several characters appear as little more than reflections of stereotyped human beings; viewed *in toto*, however, the interwoven complexities of the various types present a sharply delineated portrayal of Austro-German thought and society at the turn of the century. In Count Leinsdorf, Musil depicts the social decay of the Austrian nobility which, through years of non-involvement, has been reduced to the level of the "privileged effete." Vaguely aware of the needs and rights of the working class, Leinsdorf nonetheless operates on the principle that true nobility should be "felt not heard," and thus, although he personally would bestow rewards for services rendered, his idealism has estranged him from the slowly emerging mass culture. General Stumm von Bordwehr is a searing depiction of the military establishment, a frame of mind that finds its stability within the rigid confines of "classification" and regimentation, an attitude buttressed by an unswerving conviction of class consciousness. As an individual the General is a likeable personality, for he is in reality little more than a caricature of the person he believes himself to be, but as a representative of the military he reflects a caste that has lost all contact with the society that supports it and, having become so enamored of its own importance, it can no longer master its own profession. An institution, however, that has become a mere travesty of its former self is tragic, not amusingly ludicrous. In the person of Paul Arnheim, Musil voices a condemnation of the emotionless, stereotyped Prussian mentality so wholly orientated toward commercial prowess that any admixture of intellectual or artistic proclivities results only in affectation. Though driven to the "Parallelaktion" by a desire to fulfill his intellectual pursuits, Arnheim can involve himself only on a pedantic, metaphysical level, for his basic materialistic motives dominate his every concern, from his expensive hotel rooms and extensive wardrobe to his passion for the acquisition of the Galatian oil fields. Like many another "denizen of the tea party set," Diotima strives to display intellectual gifts that far surpass those with which nature has endowed her. The utter pretentiousness of her character is illustrated not so much by the adoption of a pseudonym redolent of the dialogues of Socrates as it is by the sardonic humor that forms the background to her attempts to explain to Ulrich her metaphysical principles of the unity of love and sex, namely her seizures due to menstrual cramps. By nature, Diotima can be likened to a great "earth-mother of the social elite" who attracts pseudo-intellectuals, as fire must draw moths, but any relationship between her and her devoted coterie is doomed from the outset to frustration. It is in the person of Ulrich, however, that Musil has most poignantly portrayed his criticism of society. Like Musil himself, Ulrich is a dispassionate character in matters of the mind or affairs of sex. Although he can gratify his endless streams of lovers, he himself experiences no emotion through his various encounters and even his father's death leaves him unmoved. His cynicism has destroyed any individual qualities within him and thus he can accurately mirror the qualities of those about him—through his eyes contours of society are brought into focus: Diotima's shallowness, Arnheim's duplicity, General Stumm's foolish incompetence, the basic selfishness of Nietzsche's super race as embodied in the sexual tension between his friend Walter and Walter's animal wife Clarissa, the natural goodness and love in the servants Soliman and Rachel as opposed to the "socially proper" relationships of their masters and mistresses, the ludicrous posture of pre-war anti-Semitism as embodied in Sepp who inveighs against the abstraction "Jewishness" and yet marries a Jewess.

In speaking of the pre-mechanized Austria Musil refers to it as Kakania (cf. *kaiserlich-königlich*), a type of unnatural reality which has remained ensnared in its established values and ideals, a society in which the intellectually oriented "Parallelaktion" could never really materialize; for while the few vainly strive to simulate activity, the majority remains blissfully inert, lulled into antipathy by the soothing strains of Strauß and the savor of the current "Heuriger." The most striking symbol of the decadent lethargy that has settled upon Kakania is the alluringly attractive personality of Moosbruger. In daring to actualize in his person the fascination of sex and physical force, Moosbruger has not only posed an all but insoluble judicial problem—officially his actions have placed him beyond the pale of the sane citizen, thus his incarceration in an insane asylum—but he has awakened in society as a whole those very drives which "good people" have endeavored to suppress and thus he represents those very passions the Kakanian society has not dared to attain (cf. the various visitors to the asylum, some drawn by mere curiosity, others, i.e., Clarissa, who have come to defend him, haunted by the specter of a man who might somehow unite the intellect of the Nietzschean Ulrich and the demonic passion of Moosbruger).

Indirectly the whole novel forms a treatise on the problem of the artist versus society. Since Kakania has become a parody of life there is a distinct dividing line between thought and action wherein the actions of the stereotyped characters are predictable but curiously undefined. Unlike the Victorian novel, *Der Mann ohne Eigenschaften* is pervaded by a spectrum of muted figures, neither black nor white, and thus the artist as creative agent is an all but contradictory impossibility. The very atmosphere of the society in which Ulrich finds himself is such that he could never come to grips with a single being or situation that might challenge his artist's soul. Stripped of the principle of creative activity, the artist can function only as the cynical reflection of decadence enthroned as a way of life. To create, the artist must withdraw from the arena of action and ponder its effects upon him—for Ulrich or Kakania such an escape is impossible since everything from birth to death is regulated on the social level, adjusted and classified within the confines of bureaucratic efficiency. Withdrawal and, therefore, depth are denied the artist in such a two dimensional environment and with their loss all hope for true art is but self-deception.

In a sense, the main theme of Musil's unfinished epic is the pressing urgency of social questions forced upon a wholly decadent and thus indifferent society. Every aspect of society is treated, every philosophy of life is touched upon but no solution is ever forthcoming, not because the author himself necessarily had no ideas of his own nor because the novel itself remained incomplete. The answer lies rather in the nature of society itself which defies a total literary vivisection and analysis, especially a society which seems to be dying from within of a disease that is neither recognized as such nor one that would be combated were it so recognized. Although the artist in Musil's view is doomed to failure, he himself has not failed and his particular novel has become a classic, portraying a sensitive and perceptive vision of a decaying society for which the cataclysm of war was a salutary, cleansing purgative.

II

Amen dico vobis:
Quamdiu fecistis uni ex his
fratribus meis minimis,
mihi fecistis.
(Matt. 25, 40)

Das Glasperlenspiel by Hermann Hesse tells the story of a man who conquers the seemingly inevitable and whose fate at long last grants him the chance to perform that task to which he is naturally predisposed, namely to serve. It is fundamentally a portrayal of the place of the intellectual in society, cast in relief through the actions of the main protagonist, Joseph Knecht. Underlying the entire novel is the unstated question: what purpose is intellectual acquisition to serve? Is it not possible that knowledge can become an end in itself rather than a means, thus breeding narrowmindedness instead of an active world-consciousness and a true humanitarianism? Possible? Yes—one need but contemplate the society of Castalia and the quasi religious aura which enshrines its every order and function to realize to what a degree the intellectual life can become an object of veneration in itself, beyond the confines of which the inhabitants of such a society never venture. Since it is the psyche of man that dominates all, the physical characteristics of Knecht are never mentioned and, like the society as a whole, he too gradually loses his human equilibrium in a pursuit of purely spiritual phenomena, a quest that clearly demonstrates that this "new dispensation" has become as degenerate as the old order which it sought to replace.

The chief protagonists of the novel represent the various possible solutions to the unstated dilemma of the intellectual in or rather versus society. Tegularius seeks in Castalia a refuge from life, a retreat that can be attained and safeguarded only through machine-like solving of research problems. The entire scope of his preoccupation is delimited within the term "technique"—all else is a *terra incognita* for him and in his effete bias he neither can nor wills to cope with life as a whole. In the person of the Music Master, Hesse would illustrate that such a restrictive position need not necessarily destroy an individual provided he is prepared to shift the main emphasis from the "self" to "others", whereby technique becomes the means or the vehicle that unites the one and the many. The Music Master, however, is in a sense as provincial as Tegularius for his love of mankind is defined wholly in terms of abstract concepts, each concrete individual viewed solely as but a notational unit within the symphonic whole of mankind. Like the classical devotees of the Enlightenment, the Music Master has risen above pure knowledge to the more sublime heights of culture but he too fails to grasp the inherent dichotomy in the living, operative entity called man; like Tegularius, he too views the worth of man only in the abstract, thus formal technique is sacrificed in favor of ideal concepts, and contact with the concrete reality of life is not even once considered. Isolation of the intellectual is possible, but in isolation the mind as well as the person of man is moribund.

In the person of Father Jacobus Hesse envisioned an initial approach toward personal involvement, a tentative rapprochement between man and the goals toward which he aspires via the agency of religion. Just as Christianity preserved and in its own way promoted the culture of Western Europe during the Middle Ages, so too does Father Jacobus protect and promote the exploration and betterment of the *condition humaine*. For him, however, as for monasticism before him, a gulf exists between those to be saved and those who are to act as surrogate saviors—the isolated life of the intellectual within the confines of Castalia is a barrier between mind and matter as impenetrable as the mortared walls of any medieval monastery. The priest can perceive the dilemma, he realizes the problem involved and what is at stake, but he too fails to act because of his basic orientation, his inability to combine the creativity of a scholar with an active involvement in the reality of life.

If isolation and retreat are not the answers, what can be said for a complete and wholehearted involvement in the world? Hesse's response to this query is embodied in the figure Plinio Designori, a man of the world whose appearance in Castalia is jarring, an unwelcome anomaly. Unable to renounce the world he has left and thus unable to adopt the attitudes of his new environment, Designori is a person at war within himself, a man whose goals have lost their foundation, casting him adrift in a vacuum somewhere between mind and matter. Leaving Castalia, however, poses no solution for him for he can no longer readapt himself to his former modes of life and thought and thus he vainly struggles to establish a new equilibrium in his vacillations from one extreme to another. Even a position of neutrality, symbolized by his new home and his endeavors for his son, Tito, prove fleeting and illusory. Once encountered, the life of the intellect cannot be renounced with impunity for only the strong, the man who is able to evaluate and love both positions, can fuse the two terms into a new reality. Plinio is not such a person and as a broken man he too retreats, away from and not into the world of the soul.

For Hesse, Joseph Knecht symbolizes the true intellectual, a man whose primary motivating force is his desire to realize in his life a viable equilibrium between the two poles of human activity. He is attracted to the intellectual sphere and the cultures of the past and thus he can befriend Tegularius and the Music Master; he can also appreciate the connecting bonds between the academic and the secular and thus he honors Father Jacobus. In Plinio's position, however, he can likewise espy a certain element of truth but he is forced to refute Plinio's stance as he is to reject those of his other friends for basically the same reason, they are all alike one-sided and thus unbalanced. Truth as something vibrantly alive and humanly cogent lies not at either extreme but somewhere in the middle. Man is neither disembodied spirit nor spiritless beast, he is a composite of both and as such truth for him entails the conjunction of mind and matter. When Knecht renounces his position as *Magister Ludi* to enter life beyond the borders of Castalia, he publishes a circular letter stating his reasons for doing so, a letter that decries the stultifying blindness of the purely academic attitude but at the same time praises Castalia as the protector of the spirit. The true intellectual is indeed the guardian of the *Weltgeist* at any given moment of time and thus he cannot prostitute his calling by serving merely as the mouthpiece of one particular political bias. Detachment is necessary if he is to function as the conscience of the era—detachment but not complete isolation for the mind can guide and inspire only that which it has experienced. To withdraw from society into an idealized world of concepts is to condemn oneself to the level of a mere librarian of the repositories of past glories; to renounce the spirit for political agitation is equally disastrous for then one substitutes expediency for truth and demagoguery for philosophic discernment. A union of the two extremes is necessary, but is it possible to achieve it? Knecht abandons Castalia and seeks to establish such a union between mind and matter but in his attempt he fails; he is destroyed by that very nature that he formerly renounced, not because he was wrong in his attempt but rather because he was unprepared to meet and overcome the exigencies of the task at hand. The spirit was willing indeed but the flesh was weak. Joseph does not die, therefore, as a punishment for attempting the difficult but rather because he had dared to enter history and was willing to accept the consequences of human existence, to actualize in his person the solemn warning of Father Jacobus that to deal with history means to abandon oneself to chaos and yet retain a belief in ordination and meaning. His death is thus not tragic in the sense that, like Oedipus, he had delved too relentlessly into the secret of fate, but tragic only insofar as all deaths are tragic—the *dénouement* in the inescapable drama of the human condition. In a sense it is reminiscent of the words once employed to describe the Bead Game: "Es bedeutete eine erlesene, symbolhafte Form des Suchens nach dem Vollkommenen, eine sublime Alchimie, ein Sichannähern an den über allen Bildern und Vielheiten in sich einigen Geist, also an Gott."[1] The pure intellectual cannot hope to survive in the physical world for he is not equipped to counter its demands with sufficient force and thus Knecht must die. His death, however, was a willed form of martyrdom, in a sense a self-offering in the hope of reconciling apparently eternally warring camps. In Tito, a son of the world tutored by Knecht, Hesse would seem to envision a slowly evolving union of the two extremes, a merging of the two diverse impulses that can be accomplished not by revolution but only through the successive stages of an evolutionary process.

Although a sense of pessimistic gloom seems to pervade the novel in spite of the power of its message—it was after all written during the zenith of the Nazi orgy in Europe—Hesse's "philosophy of synthesis" is still not wholly eclipsed even here. In the final analysis, what is synthesis if not a living receptivity to all shades and gradations of stimuli, the personal reaction to which fosters and eventually matures man's quest for self-knowledge? The devotees of the metaphysical Bead Game strove to materialize in thought a *unio mystica* of the disparate arts and sciences, a rapprochement heightened and fortified by introspection. Trained thus in terms of Hegelian dialectic, what would be more logical than the eventual interjection of the consequent antithesis to their approach to reality, whereby the synthesis would no longer

---

[1] Hermann Hesse, *Das Glasperlenspiel* (Frankfurt am Main: Suhrkamp, 1954), p. 51.

remain a psychic game but rather a lived experience? Were this to occur, could the next dialectical confrontation be avoided, the *face-en-face* encounter between a spiritually informed secular life and the divine reality which admits of no multiplication of incongruent factors, a synthesis, therefore, of the One with the Many? Such an ultimate union demands, however, more than mystic contemplation, it postulates total self-abandonment, a complete submersion of the self-conscious personal ego into the limitless reaches of the infinite Ego; it demands in a word, death. Joseph, the servant, must consequently die, passing from the scene of partial activity into the realm of complete receptivity, thereby bridging the chasm between temporal historicism and its unavoidable chaos on the one hand, timeless eternity and its inherent sense of an endlessly progressive order on the other.

III

Dixit eis Jesus: Si caeci essetis,
non haberetis peccatum;
nunc vero dicitis: Quia videmus.
Peccatum vestrum manet.
(John 9, 41)

The theme of the complex relationship that ensues between the artist and society is pursued on a three-fold level in Thomas Mann's *Dr. Faustus:* the personal, the political and the transcendental. The first two levels are intricately interwoven in the person of the musician Adrian Leverkühn and his fictional biographer Zeitblom, whereas the third is embodied in the nature of music as a symbol. It is of decisive importance that the form of the novel is biographical for thus impersonal "fact" is filtered through the medium of a third-person perspective whose cogency is derived from the immediacy of a first-person report. Inasmuch as the novel is constructed in its every detail around the subjectivity of the first-person narrator, it is impossible to separate or distinguish between Zeitblom's function as a fictive biographer and as a figure in the novel. From a strictly formal point of view, the significance of Zeitblom also allows a two-fold avenue of approach, that of the biography itself and that of the genesis of this biography. Zeitblom thus serves a double purpose—he has to compose the biography of a friend and at the same time he is made to comment upon the course of his undertaking. Through the use of authorial comment the construction of periodization is assured, thus spanning the time gap between the past (Leverkühn), the present (Zeitblom) and the future (the reader). This division of time is of the greatest significance for the novel and its central theme in that it permits the period encompassed by the actual writing of the novel (the initial years of World War II) to parallel the narration of Leverkühn's tragedy, in a sense enhancing the tragedy of the individual and vicariously functioning as its subterranean fundament.

As a representative of the age stretching from Bismarck to Hitler, Leverkühn cannot be said to be identical with any one specific individual. Absorbing the historical figure of Nietzsche into himself, he also expresses the contingent and opposing movements and *Weltanschauungen* of the entire period. As has often been pointed out, however, the portraiture of this age is only conditionally accurate since it is depicted from the subjective vantage point of Mann himself, thus reflecting Mann's preoccupation with the more questionable, suspect aspects of human motivation, his predilection for the problematic relationship between society and the artist and the grave concern he felt for contemporary developments in Germany.

The subjectivity of the first-person narrator has also a further significance since it was through the immediacy of his relationship with Leverkühn that Zeitblom was confronted directly with a demonic element that serves as an intensifying factor in his (Zeitblom's) biographical narration. Thus Zeitblom as a narrator and as an existential figure in his work are identical, the two functions as inextricable in Mann as in his creation. The novel is consequently constructed from the point of view of a humanist, every detail existing in "fact" only because the narrator had experienced it as such. Reality in the novel, therefore, participates in a double aspect—on the one hand the slight distance that separates Mann from the material of his story, on the other the use of historical and/or literary events as a montage against which larger issues stand out in sharper relief (cf. the portrait of Mann's mother as Mrs. Rodde, the fate of his sister reflected in that of Clarissa, etc.). It is again the fictive first-person narrator that strikes a balance between these two aspects; although individual characteristics of real persons are discernible, the nature of the novel as a portrait of an entire age assumes that the basic problems are real but the main characters are real only to the degree that they embody these problems *per se* without reference to any particular individual. They are, therefore, not identical with any specific historical personality for as ideal figures they absorb within their fictive reality the reality of history itself.

A more essential factor of the novel is Mann's arrangement of the represented time continuum. Superficially considered it would appear that two distinct time spans are under consideration—the biographical aspect of Leverkühn's life extending from 1885 to 1930 and the actual writing of the biography between 1943 and 1945. These two periods of time are united in the person of the narrator who relates personal experiences with reference to both time divisions thus weaving into the texture of the past the personal experiences of the present. The relationship between the musical creations of Leverkühn and the tragic developments in Germany are clearly realized and become evident in this division of time. The position of the reader is also an integral element of time in the novel, the future namely, for although the work ends with the absolute hopelessness of total destruction, it poses a question to future generations, a question that is likewise a task to be undertaken and hopefully fulfilled: "Wann wird aus letzter Hoffnungslosigkeit ein Wunder, das über den Glauben geht, das Licht der Hoffnung tagen?"[1]

Thus far we have considered only Mann's attitude concerning the immediate relationship that exists between the artist and his time, in a sense the immediacy of time in the artist. It remains for us to examine, if only cursorily, Mann's conception of the artist and his art. The one dominant symbol of *Dr. Faustus* is Mann's vision of the "world without transcendency" in which a complex of motifs are operative and interactive: theology, demonology, music; the problem of music in conjunction with the Faust figure and this in turn with the psychology of the German mentality; the problem of genius and the motif of the pact with the devil; these various motifs concentrated then in the question of the basic nature of music as it is related to the German soul on the one hand and German history on the other.

The old Faust figure as transformed by Goethe into a vehicle of classical-romantic perspectives is retransformed by Mann into a vehicle of psychological analysis. The original Faust figure retains only a certain demonological, neurotic atmosphere to which Mann conjoins the atmosphere of the characteristic musicality of the German temperament, a cultural-critical motif which forms the crystallization point of the entire novel. At times music is conjured forth in the name of passion, or a morality in opposition to pure aestheticism, or an animal glorification of life; again music might represent the principles of modernity or conservatism in the form of Wagnerian total objectivity; or again music might symbolize a melancholic apolitical or almost anti-democratic bias. In any event music is the antipode of reason and progress, politics and democracy, being in essence the reflection of the spiritual excellences of the German soul, a battle cry of an emotional nationalism. And yet in the pivotal conversation between Leverkühn and the devil, it is the devil who states that, like sin and evil, music is a supremely theological factor. Like sin, therefore, music is a product of evil since it stems from the recesses of animal potency, beyond the pale and control of man's higher faculties of reason and will. But again, considered as a natural by-product of man's animal nature, the demonic potency inherent in art cannot be equated with evil for it rises to the surface not in opposition to reason or morality but as a natural expression of the force of life which sustains human existence. Thus when judged, or perhaps prejudged, solely by certain undisciplined intoxicating effects emanating from it, the demonic in music can be suspect, indeed feared as the fountainhead of uncontrolled passion, the extended effects of which are then able to encompass even the elemental nature of love, which thus also is viewed as something evil.

The ambivalence of these views forms a perplexing coloration to the whole of *Dr. Faustus* for at times music, i.e., art is seen as a divine gift by reason of man's nature, at other times it is represented as the excrescence of black magic, both of which aspects have driven the German temperament to attain either

---

[1] Thomas Mann, *Doktor Faustus*. Gesammelte Werke, VI (Frankfurt am Main: S. Fischer, 1960), p. 676.

the heights of romantic-mystical transfiguration or to sink to the perverse excesses of an alliance with Satan.

The concatenation of music, theology and the German psyche illustrates most poignantly the demonic essence of music. If one can but compromise the nature of theology, revealing it to be nothing more than a snare of the devil whereby the reason of man can seduce the soul from its unquestioning submission to the *fiat* of God (a position *in extremo* of Luther's Reformation theology), then it all but inexorably follows that a nation such as Germany, that is by nature addicted to theology and to music (an art form that proceeds most directly from the well-spring of the purely animal in man), is *ipso facto* a fallen, perverse people.

In contrast to Goethe's devil, Mann's is wholly secularized, the classical metaphysical nucleus of the struggle with evil assuming for Mann a psychological-physiological complex whereby the antagonists are no longer God and Satan but rather various aspects of contemporary reality and 20th century culture. Two particular elements of human existence are specified as the humus in which the demonic is spawned—sex and disease, united in Leverkühn in the form of venereal disease. Localizing a source of evil in a natural potency of man, Mann has not only forged a relationship between sex and evil, but he has questioned the very essence of human love of which sex is the most natural expression. The one woman Leverkühn ever loved was the very person from whom he contracted syphilis!

Music, the soul of Leverkühn's whole life, is thus seen as the very incarnation of the spirit of evil, the fruits of which are disease and isolation from one's fellowman. Art is then by nature a creative expression of both infirmity and vitality, a formal union of subterranean force with terrestrial debilitation wherein disease is the catalyst but not the cause of creativity. As in Goethe's *Faust*, so in Mann's *Dr. Faustus*, two souls inhabit the selfsame breast; for Mann these two "souls" would seem to be disease and a vital life force, a psychological extension of the classical concepts of good and evil. For both Goethe and Mann, however, the nature of genius remains in the final analysis beyond the grasp of reason, a transcendental phenomenon, be its origin demonic or divine.

Mann's ambivalent attitude toward the relevance of the artist to the rest of society informs almost all of his works from *Buddenbrooks* through *Tonio Kröger* and *The Magic Mountain* to *Dr. Faustus*. As Mann grew older, his sympathies seemed to weigh evermore heavily in favor of society, the life of activity and encounter, the sane and physically beautiful. In *Dr. Faustus* his solution might even be said to be anti-artist. Leverkühn is the very embodiment of the incompatibility of the artist either to adapt himself to his milieu or for the milieu to accept, if not necessarily understand, the artist. From his very birth Leverkühn was an isolated soul—born on a farm away from the bourgeois society of Germany, he never really escaped his fated cell. In school he remained a recluse and when he removed to the south of Germany

—the haven of physical beauty and animal passion—he chose a small secluded village for his home. His final act of escape into solitude was his regression into madness. As the man, so his art: misunderstood by his contemporaries, judged as sheer cacaphony, it is stigmatized with the most condemning term of opprobium, i.e., impractical, as unfit for society as the artist was for military service. When in a fit of final desperation and fury, born of fear and contempt alike, the artist does attempt to explain the soul of the artist to the uninitiated masses, no one understands him for no one, not even his best friend Zeitblom, can appreciate the plight of his soul. Some are blinded by uncomprehending love for him, some perceive only an external rhetoric, the rest are repulsed with disgust or disbelief. With no one to share his soul's ecstacy or agony, Leverkühn flaunts the ultimate in defiance of "sane reason," he takes refuge in insanity. By nature a breed apart from the masses of humanity, the artist is not equipped to cope with society's demands and thus he must perish. To be wholly self-sufficient he is not able, to prostitute his transcendental patrimony he is too proud and, therefore, he has no choice but to succumb. One cannot escape the feeling that Mann himself believed in his declining years that the blond and blue eyed animals of this world can obviously thrive without the sensitive, temperamental species of the Tonio Kröger breed, whereas the artist cannot survive without his counterpart no matter how he might look down upon it—the law of the survival of the fittest shall not be repealed.

IV

Quocumque enim perrexeris, pergam:
et ubi morata fueris,
et ego pariter morabor.
Populus tuus populus meus,
et Deus tuus Deus meus.
(Ruth, 1, 16)

If what has been asserted thus far is true, what conclusions can be drawn concerning the German novel of the 20th century? The most obvious response is that the novel reflects a deep concern about the rapidly changing world situation. Fiction no longer portrays a static society for the simple reason that the nature of society has become bewildering, complex and fluid. The society and mores as they existed at the turn of the century have been forever destroyed in the holocaust of two catastrophic wars and a new order has assumed their place, an order, however, that is yet unrooted and ephemeral if only because its rarified atmosphere lacks the depth of perspective that time alone can grant. In the works discussed above the primary concern of the authors was not the nature of this new order, a nature as yet undefinable for it itself has yet to establish its own end or even some tentative means thereto; their concern was rather the relationship between this new

247

dispensation and the artist-temperament struggling for survival beneath its new banners. Although differing in degree, the authors treated (as well as most contemporary writers) are essentially pessimistic in their prognosis — the artist, and by extension any individual sensitive to the dichotomy that exists between a mass materialistic civilization and the individual psyche striving to realize its own form of personal fulfillment, must eventually either acquiesce to the standards of society or perish beneath the weight of castigation or, what is even worse, complete indifference.

In *Das Glasperlenspiel* Hermann Hesse would demonstrate that the artist (i.e., the intellectual or the true humanist) cannot remain totally segregated from society and continue to remain true to his vocation. The intellectual society of Castalia had become so wholly inbred and inert through its willed self-ostracism from the rest of the world that its one specific gift to civilization, the Bead Game, had atrophied to the point of complete uselessness, its once valid and valuable contribution to the preservation of culture now devoid of relevancy. Such total self-perpetuating stultification cannot fail to repulse the true artist-intellectual, who for his own sake as well as that of his fellow man must eventually escape the bonds of complete segregation. On the other hand, total involvement is also not the answer; Designori lost all claim to intellectual achievement by his choice to reenter the secular society and Knecht, when he finally does abandon the confines of Castalia, is crushed by his new environment. Although the solution in Hesse's terms is not completely without hope nor beyond the realm of the possible, the gulf of the probable yawns seemingly endless between the inescapable reality of the "here and now" and the realm of that "consumation devoutly to be wished."

A compromise, or rather a compromised position, forms the basis of Thomas Mann's *Dr. Faustus*. Here the artist protagonist does retain a somewhat tenuous contact with society, a contact, however, that produces only friction since it is based neither on mutual understanding nor mutual consent. Physically as well as emotionally, Leverkühn remains isolated from his society. Calling his best friend by only his last name, he is incapable of a truly selfless love and his one contact with secular society in the form of his woeful *femme fatale* results in a fatal case of syphilis. Society and the artist are seemingly incompatible and at the climax of the novel the artist is driven mad in his futile attempt to explain his artistic tribulations to an audience that cannot and wills not to comprehend. To gain true perspective the artist must remain aloof from society, but to do so results in the vacuous pedantry of Castalia; not to do so, on the other hand, compromises the artist's "objectivity" thereby placing him in an untenable position. A damned if you do and damned if you don't situation, devoid of any redeeming glimmer of hope. Like Hesse, Mann is a realist *vis-à-vis* the abyss of the probable, but unlike Hesse his own temperament could foresee not even the slightest illusion of "a rosy fingered dawn" of a possibly better tomorrow.

Robert Musil's *Der Mann ohne Eigenschaften* depicts a totally social environment in which no artist could ever exist. Ulrich, the only representative (or should we not say a pseudo-representative) of the artistic world is nothing more than a soundingboard and reflecting surface mirroring the reality of the characters he encounters. He himself possesses no individual qualities, no ambition, no desire and certainly no artistic motivation. Such an insipid, shallow milieu merely saps the genius of the artist, absorbing his personality as a sponge absorbs water. With nothing against which to react and without the sobering effect of distance, the establishment of correlative relationships is impossible and without the awareness of the relationship between objectives realized and goals yet to be attained, all art and thought and culture are doomed. For Musil, as for Mann, total involvement is just as self-destructive as total self-isolation is for Hesse. Herein lies the dilemma of the modern German intellectual—both total segregation and complete involvement are impossible and yet even partial involvement is hardly tenable since it engenders more conflicting fields of interest (which eventually must also destroy art) than it creates plains of fruitful mutual intercourse.

The nature of this dilemma is so oriented toward the very personality of the artist-intellectual that the contemporary novel has had to assume a psychological form in which the characters function more and more as symbols within a manufactured environment in order that the nature of the conflict itself may be illustrated. In a manner strikingly analogous to the Mystery Plays of the late Middle Ages, ideas and ideals have once again usurped the stage of action, concepts and conflicts have tended to replace people and personalities since the concern of literature as well as that of life in general is now the survival of "individuality" and not the triumphs and defeats of a particular "individual."

From the death of Goethe to the total destruction of Germany in the wake of Nazi barbarism, slowly but inexorably the German temperament has been weaned increasingly from its spiritual heritage which postulated the value of human action only with reference to an infinite source of good. Taught by Kant that the infinite was beyond the reason of man, by Schopenhauer that the will to act is the cause of pain, by a misunderstood Nietzsche (via a Bismarck, a Wagner and ultimately an Adolf Hitler) that individual might purifies itself, rendering it by right superior to the yet impure masses of humanity, and then ultimately schooled in the horrors of existential fear and the all too proximate "abomination of desolation" by the catastrophic devastation of two world wars, the German soul has found itself hopelessly adrift between the chaotic activity of a nationalistic Scylla and the abysmal despair of a personal Charybdis. To submit to either order is a perversion of the haunting ghosts of a long inherited tradition, but to remain entirely detached from either is impossible. Such a dilemma is indeed overwhelming, inspiring despair. Born into a society that has been building in oppression for 150 years, forthright resistance is fatal and yet a torturous coexistence is equally dangerous to the stability of the character of the true intellectual. In sheer desperation, therefore, the German artist has progressed beyond any thought of direct action; he sees what society has developed into and he can only lament and cry the woe of the Prophets of the Old Testament. Because no positive action seems feasible, his problem has become an internal one, a trial of personal conscience. A fight for what is impossible, a return to the old order, is as useless as it is impossible and thus the German intellectual wages a more significant and equally destructive war (if it is lost) within himself to justify his own existence.

BIBLIOGRAPHY

For a far more extensive and penetrating analysis of the ideas and themes that I have but cursorily discussed or merely alluded to in the foregoing essay I direct the reader to the following studies:

A. Robert Musil: 1) Elizabeth Albertsen, *Ratio und Mystik im Werk Robert Musils*. München: Nymphenburg, 1968; 2) Sibylle Bauer and Ingrid Drevermann, *Studien zu Robert Musil*. Köln–Graz: Böhlau, 1966; 3) Wilhelm Bausinger, *Studien zu einer historisch-kritischen Ausgabe von Robert Musils Roman "Der Mann ohne Eigenschaften."* 1st ed. Reinbek bei Hamburg: Rowohlt Verlag, 1964; 4) Werner Hoffmeister, *Studien zur erlebten Rede bei Thomas Mann und Robert Musil*. The Hague: Mouton, 1965; 5) Ernst Kaiser and Eithne Wilkins, *Robert Musil: Eine Einführung in das Werk*. Stuttgart: Kohlhammer, 1962; 6) Robert Musil, *Utopie Kakanien: Ein Querschnitt durch den Roman "Der Mann ohne Eigenschaften."* Eingeleitet und ausgewählt von Hans Heinz Hahnl. Graz: Stiasny Verlag, 1962.
B. Hermann Hesse: 1) Werner Dürr, *Hermann Hesse: Vom Wesen der Musik in der Dichtung*. Stuttgart: Silberburg-Verlag, 1957; 2) Joseph Mileck, *Hermann Hesse's "Glasperlenspiel."* Berkeley, Calif.: The University of California Press, 1952; 3) Käte Nadler, *Hermann Hesse: Naturliebe, Menschenliebe, Gottesliebe*. Leipzig: Koehler und Amalang, 1957; 4) Ernst Rose, *Faith from the Abyss. Hermann Hesse's Way from Romanticism to Modernity*. New York: New York University Press, 1965.
C. Thomas Mann: 1) Gunilla Bergsten, *Thomas Manns Doktor Faustus. Untersuchungen zu den Quellen und zur Struktur des Romans*. Stockholm: Svenska bokförlaget, 1963; 2) Erich Heller, *The Ironic German. A Study of Thomas Mann*. Boston: Little, Brown, 1958; 3) Margrit Henning, *Die Ich-Form und ihre Funktion in Thomas Manns Doktor Faustus und in der deutschen Literatur der Gegenwart*. Tübingen: Niemeyer, 1966; 4) Hans Egon Holthusen, *Die Welt ohne Transzendenz. Eine Studie zu Thomas Manns Doktor Faustus und seinen Nebenschriften*. 2nd ed. Hamburg: H. Ellermann, 1954; 5) Thomas Mann, *Die Entstehung des Doktor Fausuts. Roman eines Romans*. Amsterdam: Bermann-Fischer, 1949; 6) Jürgen Scharfschwerdt, *Thomas Mann und der deutsche Bildungsroman. Eine Untersuchung zu den Problemen einer literarischen Tradition*. Stuttgart-Berlin-Köln-Mainz: Kohlhammer, 1967; 7) Kurt Sontheimer. *Thomas Mann und die Deutschen*. München: Nymphenburger Verlagshandlung, 1961.

UNIVERSITY OF NORTH CAROLINA
STUDIES IN THE GERMANIC LANGUAGES
AND LITERATURES

Initiated by RICHARD JENTE (1949-1952), *established by* F. E. COENEN (1952-1968)

Publication Committee

SIEGFRIED MEWS, EDITOR

For other volumes in this series see page ii.

Send orders to: (U.S. and Canada) The University of North Carolina Press, P. O. Box 510, Chapel Hill, N. C. 27514
(All other countries) Feffer and Simons, Inc., 31 Union Square, New York, N.Y. 10003.
Reprints may be ordered from: AMS Press, Inc.,
56 East 13th Street, New York, N.Y. 10003